BETWEEN DELEUZE AND FOUCAULT

EDITED BY NICOLAE MORAR, THOMAS NAIL AND DANIEL W. SMITH

EDINBURGH
University Press

Edinburgh University Press is one of the leading university presses in
the UK. We publish academic books and journals in our selected subject
areas across the humanities and social sciences, combining cutting-edge
scholarship with high editorial and production values to produce academic
works of lasting importance. For more information visit our website:
edinburghuniversitypress.com

Edinburgh University Press Ltd
The Tun – Holyrood Road, 12(2f) Jackson's Entry, Edinburgh EH8 8PJ

Typeset in 10.5/13 Adobe Garamond by
IDSUK (DataConnection) Ltd, and
printed and bound in Great Britain by
CPI Group (UK) Ltd, Croydon CR0 4YY

A CIP record for this book is available from the British Library

ISBN 978 1 4744 1507 1 (hardback)
ISBN 978 1 4744 1509 5 (webready PDF)
ISBN 978 1 4744 1508 8 (paperback)
ISBN 978 1 4744 1510 1 (epub)

Contents

Acknowledgments   vii

Introduction: Between Deleuze and Foucault   1
Nicolae Morar, Thomas Nail and Daniel W. Smith

PART I ENCOUNTERS

1. Deleuze and Foucault: A Philosophical Friendship   11
   François Dosse

2. Theatrum Philosophicum   38
   Michel Foucault

3. Michel Foucault's Main Concepts   59
   Gilles Deleuze

4. When and How I Read Foucault   72
   Antonio Negri, translated by Kristopher Klotz

PART II METHOD AND CRITIQUE

5. Critical Problematization in Foucault and Deleuze:
   The Force of Critique without Judgment   87
   Colin Koopman

6. Foucault's Deleuzian Methodology of the Late 1970s   120
   John Protevi

7. Deleuze's *Foucault*: A Metaphysical Fiction   128
   Frédéric Gros, translated by Samantha Bankston

PART III CONVERGENCE AND DIVERGENCE

8. Speaking Out For Others: Philosophy's Activity in Deleuze
   and Foucault (and Heidegger)   139
   Leonard Lawlor and Janae Sholtz

9. Deleuze and Foucault: Political Activism, History and Actuality   160
   Paul Patton

10. Becoming and History: Deleuze's Reading of Foucault   174
    Anne Sauvagnargues, translated by Alex Feldman

11. Foucault and the "Image Of Thought": Archaeology, Genealogy,
    and the Impetus of Transcendental Empiricism   200
    Kevin Thompson

12. The Regularities of the Statement: Deleuze on Foucault's
    Archaeology of Knowledge   212
    Mary Beth Mader

PART IV DESIRE, POWER AND RESISTANCE

13. Desire and Pleasure   223
    Gilles Deleuze, translated by Daniel W. Smith

14. Against the Incompatibility Thesis: A *rather* Different Reading
    of the Desire-Pleasure Problem   232
    Nicolae Morar and Marjorie Gracieuse

15. Biopower and Control   247
    Thomas Nail

16. Two Concepts of Resistance: Foucault and Deleuze   264
    Daniel W. Smith

APPENDIX

17. Meeting Deleuze   285
    Paul Rabinow

18. Foucault and Prison   288
    Gilles Deleuze and Paul Rabinow

Notes on Contributors   294
Index   299

Acknowledgments

François Dosse, "Deleuze and Foucault: A Philosophical Friendship," is a slightly revised version of Chapter 17 of François Dosse, *Gilles Deleuze and Felix Guattari: Intersecting Lives*, trans. Deborah Glassman (New York: Columbia University Press, 2011), 306–30. Reprinted with the permission of François Dosse and Columbia University Press.

Michel Foucault, "Theatrum Philosophicum," originally appeared in Michel Foucault, *Aesthetics, The Essential Works of Foucault*, Vol. 2, ed. James D. Faubion; trans. Donald F. Brouchard and Sherry Simon (New York: The New Press, 1998), 343–68. Reprinted with the permission of the publishers.

Gilles Deleuze, "Michel Foucault's Main Concepts," originally appeared in *Gilles Deleuze, Two Regimes of Madness: Texts and Interviews 1975—1995*, revised edition; ed. David Lapoujade; trans. Ames Hodges and Mike Taormina (New York and Los Angeles: Semiotext(e), 2007), 246–65. Reprinted with the permission of the publishers.

Gilles Deleuze, "Desire and Pleasure" originally appeared as "Désir et plaisir," ed. François Ewald, *Magazine Littéraire* 325 (October 1994), 57–65. The translation appeared in *Foucault and His Interlocutors*, ed. Arnold I. Davidson (Chicago: University of Chicago Press, 1997), 183–92. Reprinted with the permission of the publishers.

Antonio Negri, "When and How I've Read Foucault," translated by Kristopher Klotz, was originally published as "Quand et comment j'ai lu Foucault" in *Michel*

Foucault: Cahier de L'Herne 95, eds. P. Artières, J.-F. Bert, F. Gros and J. Revel (Paris: L'Herne, 2011). We would like to thank the author, editors and publisher for their permission to publish an English translation of the article.

Frédéric Gros, "Deleuze's Foucault: A Metaphysical Fiction," translated by Samantha Bankston, was originally published as "Le Foucault de Deleuze: Une Fiction Métaphysique" in *Philosophie* 47 (1995), 53–63. We would like to thank the author and the publisher for their permission to publish an English translation of the article.

Paul Rabinow, "Foucault and Prisons", originally appeared in *Two Regimes of Madness: Texts and Interviews 1975–1995*, revised edition; ed. David Lapoujade; trans. Ames Hodges and Mike Taormina (New York and Los Angeles: Semiotext(e), 2007), 277–86. Reprinted with the permission of the publishers.

Introduction:
Between Deleuze and Foucault[1]

NICOLAE MORAR, THOMAS NAIL
AND DANIEL W. SMITH

Gilles Deleuze and Michel Foucault are widely accepted to be central figures of post-war French philosophy. Foucault (1926–84) held a chair in the History of Systems of Thought at the prestigious Collège de France, and remains one of the most-cited authors in the humanistic disciplines. Deleuze (1925–95), who taught at the University of Paris-St Denis until his retirement in 1987, authored more than twenty-five books, and was one of the most important and influential European philosophers of the post-war period. Cultural theorists, historians, philosophers and others have devoted considerable effort to the critical examination of the work of each of these thinkers, but despite the strong biographical and philosophical connection between Foucault and Deleuze, very little has been done to explore the relationship between them. This is the first edited volume to address this critical deficit with a rigorous comparative discussion of the work of these two philosophers.

DELEUZE'S COURSE LECTURES ON FOUCAULT

In particular, this edited volume is motivated by the recent (2011) online publication of Gilles Deleuze's course lectures on Michel Foucault (1985–6) at the *Bibliothèque Nationale de France* (French National Library) in Paris. The BNF collected the available recordings of Deleuze's seminar lectures at the University of Paris VIII and converted them into digital files. Needless to say, the task was a painstaking one, but the MP3 files have now been made accessible online through the Gallica search engine at the library (gallica.bnf.fr).

When Foucault died in 1984, Deleuze was so affected by the death of his friend that he began lecturing and writing a book on him immediately. When asked why he wanted to write such a book, Deleuze was quite clear: "it marks an inner need of mine, my admiration for him, how I was moved by his death, and his unfinished work."[2] Deleuze's desire for some kind of reconciliation with Foucault seems to have been a mutual one. According to Didier Eribon, one of Foucault's most heartfelt wishes, knowing that he would not live long, was to reconcile with Deleuze.[3] After speaking at Foucault's funeral, Deleuze's book project on Foucault began as a lecture series given at the University of Paris VIII, between 1985 and 1986. But these lectures were not merely a scholarly commentary on Foucault's work. They were, in the words of Frédéric Gros, "[a] means [of] discovering the founding principles, [and] laying bare the inherent metaphysics of [Foucault's] thought."[4] "It is amazing to see," Gros admits in an interview with François Dosse, "how Deleuze, who couldn't have had any knowledge of the Collège de France lectures, was so accurate in his interpretation."[5]

From 1985 to 1986, Deleuze gave a weekly seminar on Foucault, every Tuesday, at the University of Paris VIII. The seminars were scheduled for two hours but often lasted three or even four hours, and functioned as a kind of laboratory in which Deleuze would experiment with the ideas and concepts he was in the process of developing. Some of these eventually made their way into his book on Foucault, but there are many analyses that find no parallel in his published book, *Foucault*. For this reason, some of the most innovative philosophical scholarship on Foucault can be found in these lectures.

For example, while Deleuze's published book on Foucault is approximately 40,000 words long, his transcribed lectures on Foucault are over 400,000 words long. On 8 April 1986, Deleuze gave a three-hour seminar that developed an original conception of Foucault's concept of biopower through a wide-ranging reinterpretation of the Foucauldian corpus. The seminar is a *tour de force*, and clarifies the enigmatic relationship of Deleuze's concept of "control societies" with Foucault's concept of biopower, that scholars have struggled with for years. However, in his published book on Foucault that was the result of these seminars, the analysis of this entire seminar was compressed into scarcely more than a single page that never even mentions the word "biopower."[6] It would be difficult, even for philosophically informed readers, to discern the breadth of the original analysis from the summary presented in the book. Indeed, Deleuze's published book on Foucault is simply a précis of the more detailed material presented in the seminars.

We believe that these lectures offer an incredible contribution to both Deleuze and Foucault studies and an opportunity to formally reflect (in this edited volume) on the relationship between two of the greatest thinkers of the twentieth century. In addition to this edited collection we applied for and received two grants in 2011 to form a team to undertake a transcription of Deleuze's seminar on Foucault. The transcriptions were completed by Annabelle Dufourcq in 2013 and are now available on the Paris VIII website. In conjunction with the transcription project, we organized an international conference entitled "Between Deleuze and Foucault" in

November 2012, and again in November 2015. We are now currently working on an English translation of our transcriptions. It is our hope that Deleuze's lectures and this edited volume will prompt a critical revaluation of the philosophical connection between Foucault and Deleuze.

BETWEEN DELEUZE AND FOUCAULT

The relationship between Foucault and Deleuze, however, is as strong as it is disparate: it is perhaps best described as a parallelism. As Deleuze says, "I never worked with Foucault. But I do think there are a lot of parallels between our work (with Guattari) and his, although they are, as it were, held at a distance because of our widely differing methods and even our objectives."[7] While the two were drawn together through their novel readings of Nietzsche, their commitment to a non-teleological theory of history, their activism in contemporary politics (with prisons, '68, Palestine, etc.), their return to the stoics, and a theory of the event, Deleuze and Foucault were often decisively divided in their methods and motivations.

For example, what is the difference between Deleuze's concept of desire and Foucault's concept of pleasure? Why were the two authors so opposed to the other's choice in terminology? Is the difference semantic or is there a really an important philosophical difference between them? If both the concepts of desire and pleasure are meant to be radical departures from the psychoanalytic notion of desire as lack, why does Deleuze choose to stick with the psychoanalytic word "desire" and Foucault with the more amorphous term "pleasure"? This divergence is clearly manifest in a letter Deleuze wrote to Foucault: "I cannot give any positive value to pleasure, because pleasure seems to me to interrupt the immanent process of desire. . . . From my point of view, this is precisely how desire is brought under the law of lack and in line with the norm of pleasure."[8] This divide is also noticeable from Foucault's side. In an interview recently translated by Daniel W. Smith and Nicolae Morar, Foucault emphasizes this very problem.

> I believe the problem of "pleasure-desire" is currently an important problem. I would even say that it is *the* problem that has to be debated in this re-evaluation – this rejuvenation, in any case – of the instruments, objectives, and axes of the struggle . . . Deleuze and Guattari obviously use the notion in a completely different way. But the problem I have is that I'm not sure if, through this very word, despite its different meaning, we don't run the risk, despite Deleuze and Guattari's intention, of allowing some of the medico-psychological presuppositions [*prises*] that were built into desire, in its traditional sense, to be reintroduced. And so it seems to me that, by using the word pleasure, which in the end means nothing, which is still, it seems to me, rather empty of content and unsullied by possible uses – don't we have here . . . a means of avoiding the entire psychological and medical armature that was built into the traditional notion of desire?[9]

Deleuze similarly expressed concern over the concepts of truth and subjectivity. As Jacques Donzelot recalled, "Deleuze often spoke to me about that, saying: 'Jacques, what do you think, Michel is crazy, what is this old idea about truth? He's taking us back to the old idea of truth-telling! I can't believe it!" Deleuze, in a letter to Foucault, continues, "The danger is: is Michel returning to an analog of the 'constituting subject' and why does he feel the need to resuscitate the truth even if he does make it into a new concept?"[10]

Consider too Foucault and Deleuze's divergent concepts of apparatus (*dispositif*) and assemblage (*agencement*). Both concepts seem to be aiming to replace structuralist concepts of organization with the assembly of heterogeneous elements, but why have they chosen such different terms/methods to do so? Again, are these real philosophical differences that are mutually exclusive? Are they strategic choices relevant in a certain axis of struggle, or are they terminological differences disguising philosophical homologies? While there has been much written on both concepts, very few scholars have taken the time to clarify the differences and similarities between these two concepts in depth and in relation to their original French meanings.

Even, and perhaps especially, in terms of politics, Foucault and Deleuze seem so similar and yet so different. Foucault's concept of biopower (the statistical political control over life itself) and Deleuze's concept of societies of control (post-disciplinary forms of modulated and flexible control) seem to both be offering new concepts of post-institutional/ disciplinary political power. However, Foucault and Deleuze choose very different methods of analysis (genealogy vs schizoanalysis) and have different motives for doing so (to understand the emergence of liberalism vs to understand the schizophrenic breakdown of contemporary capitalism). How have these approaches shaped the alternatives that Foucault and Deleuze then propose (ethical self-transformation vs revolutionary nomadism)? Why does Foucault, in his later work, then turn to a revitalization of the concept of the subject, a term Deleuze rarely uses, except in his book on Foucault? If Foucault was against the use of the word desire because of its historical overdetermination, why now does he return to the terminology of the subject and self?

The convergences and differences between Foucault and Deleuze on these topics and others are further complicated by a third body of literature: the one they wrote about each other's work. Foucault wrote *Theatrum Philosophicum* (1970) as a review of Deleuze's *Difference and Repetition* (1968) and *Logic of Sense* (1969) where he made the oft cited claim that "perhaps, one day, this century [the twentieth] will be called 'the Deleuzian century.'"[11] The two also recorded a conversation entitled "Intellectuals and Power" (1972), later publishing it in the journal, *L'Arc*. After Foucault's death, Deleuze, of course, published his book, *Foucault* (1986) soon after. Deleuze also wrote several articles on Foucault, "Breaking Things Open, Breaking Words Open," "Life as a Work of Art," "A Portrait of Foucault," as well as a private letter to Foucault, delivered by François Ewald in 1977, titled, "Desire and Pleasure"

(1994). These writings clarify some issues while multiplying and deepening others. Above all, they express a deep admiration and complex philosophical friendship whose implications have yet to be fully explored.

A PHILOSOPHICAL FRIENDSHIP

In addition to their philosophical similarities and differences, it is also important to reflect on the nature of the friendship between Foucault and Deleuze. Together, Deleuze and Foucault launched a French revival of Nietzsche against phenomenology. In 1977, they helped co-edited Nietzsche's complete works for Gallimard;[12] they attended a major Nietzsche conferences together (1964);[13] and they were both friends of Pierre Klossowski, who dedicated his book *Nietzsche and the Vicious Circle* (1969)[14] to Deleuze and *The Baphomet* (1965)[15] to Foucault.

Both Deleuze and Foucault were political activists together in the Prison Information Group (GIP). As Judith Revel interestingly suggests in an interview with François Dosse: "Foucault took experience and practices [from the GIP] as his point of departure and conceptualized from there. Deleuze and Guattari invented war-machines then tried them out."[16] Whereas Foucault wrote *Discipline and Punish* only after the GIP, Deleuze and Guattari became interested in the decentralized non-representational structure of the GIP only after writing about these themes in *Anti-Oedipus*. In each case the GIP gave birth to a whole new relation between intellectuals and power for both Deleuze and Foucault. "A theorizing intellectual, for us," they say "is no longer a subject, a representing or representative consciousness."[17] Their involvement in the GIP, according the Deleuze's seminar on Foucault, was not at all an "academic critique of representation," but as a specifically "practical critique of representation,"[18] that supported a "non-centralized movement" that "we both" saw as an extension of the events of May 1968.[19]

But the friendship between Deleuze and Foucault is also marked by a long silence: during the last eight years of Foucault's life, Deleuze and Foucault did not speak to each other. Why? Perhaps it was because when Foucault and Deleuze both demonstrated against the deportation of the Baader–Meinhof group's attorney Klaus Croissant from France, Foucault refused to sign the petition because he wanted to more carefully define his support for Croissant?[20] Perhaps it was because Deleuze hated the *nouveaux philosophes*, whereas Foucault supported them? Perhaps it was because Deleuze supported Mitterrand's Socialist presidency, but Foucault thought it was best to criticize them, just as one would criticize any other party in power? Or perhaps it was because "Foucault didn't like *Anti-Oedipus*," as Jacques Donzelot claims.[21] Or perhaps, it was the infamous letter Deleuze wrote to Foucault criticizing his concept of pleasure in the *History of Sexuality*? Or perhaps, as Deleuze says, in a 1990 interview with James Miller, when asked directly about his and Foucault's mutual silence:

(1) There's obviously no single answer. One of us could have answered one way one day and another way the next. Not because we are fickle. But because there are many reasons in this area and no single reason is "essential." And because none of them is essential, there are always several answers at once. The only important thing is that I had long agreed with him philosophically and on specific occasions, I no longer made the same evaluations as he did on several points at once. (2) This didn't lead to any "cooling" of relations between us, or to any "explanations." We saw each other less often, as if by the force of circumstances. And from there on, it became more and more difficult to meet up again. It is strange, we didn't stop seeing each other because we didn't get along, but because we weren't seeing each other any more, a kind of incomprehension or distance between us took hold. (3) I can tell you that I constantly miss seeing him, increasingly so. So what stopped me from calling him? That's where a deeper reason comes into it. Rightly or wrongly, I believed that he wanted greater solitude, for his life, for his thinking; that he needed this solitude, keeping in touch only with the people who were close to him. I now think that I should have tried to see him again, but I think I didn't try out of respect. I am still suffering from not having seen him again, even more so because I don't think there were any external reasons.[22]

ON THE COMPOSITION OF THIS VOLUME

With the growing interest in Foucault's recently translated course lectures at the *Collège de France* (1973–84), and our recent transcription of Deleuze's course lectures on Foucault, released by the *Bibliothèque Nationale de France* (2011), the editors of this volume believe that the time is ripe to address the relationship between Foucault and Deleuze directly. We have taken the cue for our title from Paul Patton and John Protevi's 2003 book *Between Deleuze and Derrida*.[23] Like this earlier volume, our collection of essays brings together both senior and junior scholars from diverse backgrounds to clarify the implications of an ongoing important philosophical encounter that took place between two of the greatest French thinkers of the post-war period.

The volume is divided into four sections. The first section stands apart in that it contains two texts in which Foucault and Deleuze directly commented on each other's work. Foucault's essay "Theatrum Philosophicum" was published in 1970 in the influential French journal *Critique*.[24] It contains the famous comment that "perhaps one day, this century will be known as Deleuzian," but this oft-cited soundbite can conceal the depth of Foucault's engagement with two of Deleuze most important yet difficult texts: *Difference and Repetition* and *Logic of Sense*. Deleuze's piece entitled "Michel Foucault's Main Concepts" is an article that Deleuze wrote in 1984 immediately after Foucault's death, but left unpublished. Instead, Deleuze decided to devote his 1985–6 seminar to Foucault's work, which resulted in the publication of his book *Foucault* in 1986. The article, which was not published until 2003,[25] shows that the broad outlines of Deleuze's reading of Foucault were already in place, although some of the material in the article finds no parallel in the 1986 book. These two primary texts are supplemented by François Dosse's analysis of the complex friendship between Foucault and Deleuze, as well as Antonio Negri's account of the context in which he himself first read and appropriated Foucault's writings.

The middle three sections form the substance of the volume and contain articles by an array of prominent scholars organized around three fundamental themes: methodology and the notion of critique; convergences and divergences between Foucault and Deleuze; and the concepts of desire, power, and resistance. The volume concludes with an appendix containing the text of an interview that Paul Rabinow conducted with Deleuze shortly after Foucault's death, prefaced by Rabinow's own recollections of the context of the interview and an analysis of its content.

The editors would like to thank the each of the scholars who have contributed to this book for their extraordinary work as well as their unflinching support. We also owe a debt of gratitude to Samantha Bankston, Alex Feldman, and Kristopher Klotz, who translated several of the essays in the volume, superbly and at short notice. Carol MacDonald, at Edinburgh University Press, is a meticulous yet accommodating editor, and it has been a pleasure to be able to rely on her steady hand and keen eye during the production of the volume.

NOTES

1. An earlier version of this essay was published as "Introduction," *Foucault Studies*, Special Issue on Foucault and Deleuze, 17 (April 2014): 4–10.
2. Gilles Deleuze, *Negotiations, 1972–1990*, trans. Martin Joughin (New York: Columbia University Press, 1995), 94.
3. François Dosse, *Gilles Deleuze and Félix Guattari: Intersecting Lives*, trans. Deborah Glassman (New York: Columbia University Press, 2010), 328.
4. Frédéric Gros, "Le Foucault de Deleuze: une fiction métaphysique," *Philosophie* 47, (September 1995), 54.
5. Frédéric Gros, "Interview with François Dosse," in Dosse, *Gilles Deleuze & Félix Guattari*, 327.
6. Gilles Deleuze, *Foucault*, trans. Seán Hand (Minnesota: University of Minnesota Press, 1988), 84–5.
7. Gilles Deleuze, "Fendre les choses, fendre les mots" [1986], in *Pourparlers* (Paris: Minuit, 1990), 117.
8. Gilles Deleuze, "Desire and Pleasure," in *Two Regimes of Madness: texts and interviews 1975–1995*, ed. David Lapoujade, trans. Ames Hodges and Mike Taormina (Los Angeles: Semiotexte, 2006), 131.
9. Michel Foucault, "The Gay Science," trans. Nicolae Morar and Dan Smith, *Critical Inquiry* 37:3 (Spring 2011), 385–403. In his letter, Deleuze mentions an earlier encounter

with Foucault when Michel told him, "I cannot bear the word desire; even if you use it in another way," in Deleuze, "Desire and Pleasure."

10. Dosse, *Gilles Deleuze and Félix Guattari*, 318.

11. Foucault made this remark in his 1970 essay on Deleuze, "Theatrum Philosophicum," which is included in *The Essential Works of Foucault, Vol. 2, Aesthetics, Method, and Epistemology*, ed. James D. Faubion, trans. Roburt Hurley and others (London: Penguin Press, 1998), 343, translation modified.

12. Friedrich Nietzsche, *Œuvres philosophiques complètes*, ed. Gilles Deleuze, Michel Foucault et al. (Paris: Gallimard, 1977).

13. Dosse, *Gilles Deleuze and Félix Guattari*, 307.

14. Pierre Klossowski, *Nietzsche and the Vicious Circle*, trans. Daniel W. Smith (Chicago: University of Chicago Press, 1997).

15. Pierre Klossowski, *The Baphomet*, trans. Sophie Hawkes and Stephen Sartarelli (Hygiene, CO: Eridanos Press, 1988).

16. Judith Revel, "Interview with François Dosse," in Dosse, *Gilles Deleuze and Félix Guattari*, 313.

17. Dosse, *Gilles Deleuze and Félix Guattari*, 312.

18. Gilles Deleuze, *Paris VIII Foucault Seminar*, BNF audio archives, 7 January 1986.

19. Ibid.

20. This hypothesis is further developed by Paul Patton in "Activism, Philosophy, and Actuality in Deleuze and Foucault," *Deleuze Studies*, vol. 4, 2010, supplement, 84–103, especially 85.

21. Jacques Donzelot, "Interview with François Dosse," in Dosse, *Gilles Deleuze and Félix Guattari*, 315.

22. Gilles Deleuze, "Letter to James Miller (7 February 1990)," in James Miller, *Michel Foucault* (Paris: Plon, 1993), 346.

23. Paul Patton and John Protevi (eds.), *Between Deleuze and Derrida* (London and New York: Continuum, 2003).

24. Michel Foucault, "Theatrum philosophicum," in *Critique* 282 (November 1970), 885–908.

25. Gilles Deleuze, "Sur les principaux concepts de Michel Foucault," in *Deux régimes de fous: Textes et entretiens 1975–1995*, ed. David Lapoujade (Paris: Minuit, 2003), 226–46.

PART I

Encounters

CHAPTER 1

Deleuze and Foucault:
A Philosophical Friendship

FRANÇOIS DOSSE

"Perhaps one day this century will be known as Deleuzian."[1] Michel Foucault's lucid remark, made in 1969, has often been repeated. As for Deleuze, "Gilles deeply admired Michel Foucault."[2] Although they saw each other frequently and fought alongside each other for the same political causes, they never really worked together. Yet as the final tributes were being paid to Foucault at La Salpêtrière before a crowd of several hundred mourners, it was Deleuze who stood and read an excerpt from the preface to *The Use of Pleasure*. Some basic disagreements were surely motivated by a certain rivalry as to who incarnated the authority of critical thinking, at least so far as Foucault was concerned, according to Paul Veyne, a close friend of his. "I got the feeling that Foucault saw Deleuze as a rival."[3] Foucault was exasperated to see Nietzsche's works linked so closely to Deleuze's reading and teased Veyne, telling him that what he really liked in Nietzsche was "Deleuze's Nietzsche."[4]

Deleuze, however, was not jealous of Foucault, toward whom he always claimed some closeness. "I never worked with Foucault. But I do think there are a lot of parallels between our work (with Guattari) and his, although they're as it were held at a distance because of our widely differing methods and even our objectives."[5] Regarding their putative rivalry, "I'll say this: the fact that Foucault existed, with such a forceful and mysterious personality, the fact that he wrote such wonderful books, with such style, has never caused me anything but delight."[6] For Deleuze, any rivalry toward Foucault, for whom he felt only admiration, was unimaginable. "Perhaps we met too late. I respected him deeply. The atmosphere changed when he came into a room. There was something different in the air. Things changed. It was atmospheric. Something emanated from Foucault. Foucault's gestures were astonishingly sharp and elegant."[7]

Their story starts in October 1952, in Lille. Deleuze and his friend Jean-Pierre Bamberger were teaching at Amiens High School at the time and attended a lecture by Foucault, who was giving a psychology course at the University of Lille. In the early 1950s, Foucault was quite close to the French Communist Party and Deleuze was on target: "What I heard quite clearly reflected a Marxist perspective."[8] At the end of the conference, Bamberger invited them both to dinner at his place. Their first meeting was icy; it seemed unlikely that they would meet again.

They met again in 1962; it had taken ten years. At that point, Foucault was a professor at Clermont-Ferrand and was finishing his *Raymond Roussel* and *The Birth of the Clinic*. Deleuze had just published *Nietzsche*, which Foucault had liked very much. As Jules Vuillemin had been elected to the Collège de France, a position opened up at the University of Clermont-Ferrand. Foucault suggested that Deleuze might replace Vuillemin; Deleuze came to Clermont and spent the day with Foucault, whom he had not seen since the dinner in Lille. "The meeting went very well, and everybody was happy. The philosophy department approved Deleuze's appointment unanimously and Vuillemin got it approved by the faculty board in a unanimous vote."[9] The promise of collaboration between Foucault and Deleuze within the same philosophy department was stillborn, however, as the Ministry of Universities had already decided to appoint Roger Garaudy, a high-ranking French Communist Party and Politburo member. During this period, Deleuze was posted at the University of Lyon, and he and Foucault opposed Garaudy, a shared position that brought them closer to one another. "They saw each other regularly when Deleuze traveled to Paris. And without really becoming intimate, they were friendly enough for Foucault to lend his apartment to Deleuze and his wife when he was away."[10]

In the early 1960s, Foucault and Deleuze were working together for Gallimard on an edition of Nietzsche's complete works, which profoundly changed the way Nietzsche had been read in France until then.[11] Both men also participated in one of the most important occasions of the "return to Nietzsche": the 1964 conference at Royaumont. Both were close to Pierre Klossowski, who had translated *The Gay Science* in 1954; this was their first major meeting in a philosophical undertaking. Deleuze had met Klossowski through Marie-Magdeleine Davy's circle during the war. When Klossowski published *Nietzsche and the Vicious Circle* in 1969, he dedicated it to Deleuze, in homage to his *Nietzsche and Philosophy*.

Both Deleuze and Foucault worked on Klossowski individually, and each discovered a common object of inquiry inspired directly by his writings.[12]

Both philosophers saw in Klossowski's work an extension of the tradition of transgressive literature, crossing fiction with philosophy along the lines of a simulacrum. "The paradoxical *mimesis* that both actualizes and exorcizes makes the simulacrum the point where the relationship between the profane and sacred is inverted."[13] It was important to question the false identity of things and beings by breaking them open in the ways made possible by the simulacrum and the proliferation of masks. Here, the Foucauldian theme of the death of man, which had made *The Order of Things* a success and a scandal, came to the fore. "Klossowski's entire work moves toward a single goal: to assure the loss of personal identity, to dissolve itself."[14] Foucault and Deleuze thus consolidated their Nietzscheism – or anti-Hegelianism – using the simulacrum as a war-machine against thought based on identity and representation. Deleuze admired Klossowksi's last novel, *The Baphomet* (dedicated to Foucault), which provided a way out of the moral and theological dilemma between Good and Evil by showing that the two systems are not alternatives but simultaneous, constituting "a grandiose sequel to Zarathustra."[15]

Separately – Deleuze was in Lyon, and Foucault was in Sidi Bou Saïd in Tunisia – both were enthusiastic about May '68. In his seminar on Foucault, Deleuze insisted on the importance of the event for understanding the issues in Foucauldian philosophy, which are theoretical and practical. In 1986, recalling this founding event, Deleuze pointed out its international importance and its contagious energy, which was as hard to describe as to imagine in the desert of the 1980s.[16] For Deleuze, calling into question the various forms of centralization was the agent of this rupture.

During the summer of 1968, when the creation of a university at Vincennes was being considered, Foucault was designated to create the philosophy department. He quite naturally contacted Deleuze, who had to decline temporarily for reasons of ill health. Deleuze was publishing *Difference and Repetition* and *The Logic of Sense* at the time, which Foucault greeted as a philosophical revolution. He was enthused by what he described as a "bolt of lightning that will be named Deleuze: a new way of thinking is possible; thought is possible once more. It does not lie in the future, promised by the most distant of new beginnings. It is here in Deleuze's texts, springing forth, dancing before us, in our midst; genital thought, intensive thought, affirmative thought, a-categorical thought."[17] As early as 1969, Foucault had clearly understood Deleuze's philosophy as first and foremost a "philosophy of the event," as François Zourabichvili later demonstrated.[18] Foucault showed how the fundamental question posed by Deleuze is that of knowing what thinking is, situating thought within the "affirmative disjunction"[19] of the event and the phantasm. As if echoing Foucault, Deleuze concluded his seminar on 20 May 1986, with the remark, "Only one thing has ever interested Foucault: what does it mean to think?"[20]

The Prison Information Group Adventure

In the early 1970s, their philosophical proximity extended to politics when Foucault created the Prison Information Group (GIP), which Deleuze joined shortly thereafter. The GIP was born out of the dissolution in May 1970 of the GP (Proletarian Left) by Interior Minister Raymond Marcellin. The ruling party was hardening its repressive policy regarding left-wing agitation in the post-1968 period and imprisoning several of the group's militants, including Alain Geismar. In September 1970, the imprisoned militants began a twenty-five-day hunger strike to be granted political-prisoner status, but the strike failed. In January 1971, they began a new hunger strike that elicited greater public support.

Alfred Kastler, Paul Ricoeur and Pierre Vidal-Naquet requested an audience with Minister of Justice René Eleven and were promised a commission to rule on the conditions of imprisonment. Finally, after thirty-four days without food for some, "the lawyers Henri Leclerc and Georges Kiejman, in a press conference at the Saint-Bernard chapel on 8 February 1971, announced the end of the hunger strike"[21] and the creation of a special detention regimen for the prisoners. During the press conference, three well-known intellectuals, Michel Foucault, Pierre Vidal-Naquet and Jean-Marie Domenach, the director of the journal *Esprit*, announced the creation of the GIP. Initially, the group grew directly out of the Maoist current of thought to protect GP militants being prosecuted by the government and given arbitrary sentences. The former GP members had in fact created a Political Prisoners Organization that was overseen first by Serge July and then by Benny Lévy, but the GP soon became independent.

Without having any prior consultation, Daniel Defert suggested Foucault's name to organize a committee to investigate the general situation in prisons. Foucault accepted, and "at the end of December, he brought together at his home the people he thought would be able either to create or to prepare a commission of inquiry into prisons."[22] The group quickly agreed on their method of inquiry. The lawyer Christine Martineau was finishing a book on work in prisons and, with the help of the philosopher Danielle Rancière, had already designed a questionnaire to distribute to the prisoners: "Our model was Marx's workers' survey."[23] In the end, thanks to Foucault, who was disappointed by the popular inquiries led by Maoist militants after 1968,[24] the plans for a commission of inquiry turned into the GIP. The GIP was entirely decentralized (one group per prison). Very quickly, this Parisian model gained ground in the provincial prisons to which the militants had been sent. As a form of organization, it immediately appealed to Deleuze for its practical and effective resistance and because it broke with all forms of centralized bureaucratic machinery, defining itself instead as a microstructure. "The GIP developed one of the only left-wing groups that worked without being centralized. . . . Foucault knew how not to behave like the boss."[25]

Using as an excuse the mounting tension since the September 1971 Clairvaux prison riots, which had culminated in a guard and a nurse being taken hostage by two prisoners, Buffet and Bontens, the Minister of Justice, decided to try to calm the anxious prison guards and punish the prisoners collectively by refusing to let them receive their Christmas parcels that year. The decision fueled further protests in the prisons: in the winter of 1971–2, thirty-two rebellions broke out, during some of which prisoners destroyed cells and occupied rooftops. On Christmas Eve, the GIP organized a demonstration in front of the Santé Prison in Paris that both Foucault and Deleuze attended. Violent clashes broke out throughout the month of December, notably at the prison in Toul, where fifteen prisoners were wounded.

GIP intellectuals were occasionally asked to go to the provinces. In Nancy, for example, a riot had been strongly quelled and charges had been brought against six of the two hundred rioters. Deleuze, along with Daniel Defert, Hélène Cixous, Jean-Pierre Faye, Jacques Donzelot, among others, made the trip to join the protest demonstration. Foucault could not attend, having been arrested after helping an immigrant who was being beaten up in the metro. In Nancy's central town square, Jean-Pierre Faye was chatting with a journalist from *L'Est Républicain*, who was commenting on how uninteresting the demonstration was. Faye advised him to wait a few minutes longer before judging it. "As soon as I said those prophetic words, the cops rushed us."[26] Deleuze stood up on a bench to speak, was quickly cut off by the police, and said, "Since my boss isn't here, I'm going to speak in his place." As the police were charging, Deleuze was overcome by his respiratory problems and became seriously ill; he lay down on the ground and became semicomatose. Foucault's young friend Jacques Donzelot was extremely concerned and stayed with him. "When he came to, he said to me, 'Oh, are you here with me? How kind of you!'"[27]

At Paris VIII, when Donzelot defended his thesis on "Policing the Family"[28] – his thesis director was Jean-Claude Passeron – Deleuze proposed that he be part of the jury. "I suddenly got stage fright. I couldn't think of anything to say, so I just said, 'Why do I have to give a formal summary, since you've already read my work?' Deleuze stepped in, saying, 'Don't worry, I'll summarize your thesis for you.' Great!"[29] When the time came to publish the thesis, Deleuze offered to write the preface, but that caused tensions between Foucault and Deleuze. Donzelot had just defended a very Foucauldian thesis, and when he told Foucault that Deleuze was going to write the preface, he got a sharp reply. "I detest that sort of thing, I can't stand it when old men come and put their stamp on young people's work."[30] In the end, so as not to ruffle Foucault, Deleuze wrote an afterword instead of a preface.[31]

On 17 January 1972, the GIP managed to persuade Sartre and Foucault to demonstrate together at a protest against repression in prisons. A small group of public figures aimed to get inside the Ministry of Justice on Place Vendôme to hold a press conference. The cream of Parisian intelligentsia sat down in the ministry halls to listen to Foucault, who started to read the declaration made by the Melun prisoners. The police intervened half-heartedly as the demonstrators jeered and yelled "Jail Pleven!" or "Pleven's a murderer!" "The cops push harder. They get mad. Sartre resists. Foucault resists. Faye resists. Deleuze resists and can't stop laughing. But the cops end up winning and manage to throw all of us right back out onto the sidewalk."[32] Finally kicked out of the Ministry of Justice, which was now protected by a three-deep ring of armed and helmeted riot police, the press conference was held in the offices of the *Libération* press agency on rue Dussoubs.

Shortly thereafter, on 31 January 1972, Deleuze wrote a text entitled "What Our Prisoners Expect from Us" for the *Nouvel Observateur*.[33] He listed the prisoners' demands concerning the lifting of censorship, the disciplinary committee and disciplinary wards, using their labor and their conditional liberation, seeing the prisoners' statements as something completely new: not a "public confession" but a "personalized critique."[34] During the demonstrations, Foucault was especially attentive to Deleuze and worried about his health. On 16 December 1972, during confrontations with the police, Claude Mauriac was with Foucault and a small group just after a police charge. "Have you seen Deleuze? I hope he hasn't been arrested . . . That's how worried Michel Foucault was – he was very pale."[35]

Apart from the actions concerning prisons, the GIP also organized to protest acts of repression and racism. During the spring of 1971, the Jaubert affair broke. Alain Jaubert, a *Nouvel Observateur* journalist, was a witness to police violence during a demonstration by French West Indians. He was carted off in a police van and beaten up by the special service responsible for crowd control.[36] At a meeting chaired by Claude Mauriac, Foucault announced the creation of an investigative committee. A press conference was held on 21 June 1971. Denis Langlois spoke first, then Deleuze. "An initial group of questions starts with the communiqué released by the Prefecture of Police on May 30 . . . This communiqué is entirely unbelievable because it wasn't written to be believed. It has another goal – to intimidate."[37]

In the fall of 1971, a young Algerian manhandled the female concierge of his apartment building in Goutte d'Or. The concierge's husband saw it happen, retrieved his rifle, and killed the Algerian, claiming that it was an accident. The case cast the mounting racial tensions in the neighborhood into full light, and demonstrations were organized to denounce the racist murder. Foucault created a new investigative committee, whose members included Deleuze, Jean Genet, Claude Mauriac, and Jean-Claude Passeron, among others. On 27 November 1971, Sartre and Foucault led a meeting in the Goutte d'Or in the name of an "Appeal to the Workers of the Neighborhood" signed by Deleuze, Foucault, Michel Leiris, Yves Montand, Jean Genet, Sartre, and Simone Signoret.[38]

These militant actions in 1971 and 1972 gave Deleuze and Foucault an opportunity to start a dialogue about how they defined the new responsibilities of intellectuals with respect to power. It was during the 1972 interview that Deleuze used Guattari's formula: "We are all groupuscules."[39] For Deleuze, the GIP was the expression of a new type of organization that could renew the relationship between theory and practice, setting them in a more concrete, local, and partial framework. "A theorizing intellectual, for us, is no longer a subject, a representing or representative consciousness."[40] Foucault similarly argued that the universal role of intellectuals as the incarnation of the discourse of Truth was over, because societal democratization allowed every social group to express its dissatisfactions perfectly well without them. Rather, intellectuals should concentrate on the struggle against forms of power. Their job is to determine the various loci of power and to trace their genealogy.

Although the two friends grew closer during these years with respect to the political sphere, their ideas about political engagement were not exactly the same. "On one hand, Foucault took experience and practices as his point of departure and conceptualized from there. Deleuze and Guattari invented war-machines and then tried them out."[41] Thus Foucault, who spent time at Saint-Anne and was interested in psychiatry, created the GIP, then wrote *Discipline and Punish*, and worked on an analysis of power. Deleuze and Guattari, by contrast, produced concepts and machines and then tested what they produced in social reality. Guattari's ideas were inscribed within a whole series of social practices linked to Marxism, institutional psychotherapy, and a series of research groups like the CERFI (Centre d'études, de recherches, et de formation institutionnelles), which were experimental sites for the concepts he had worked out with Deleuze.

Despite his reticence with respect to Guattari and his desire to remain at a distance from his groups, Foucault did let himself be persuaded by Deleuze to be involved in several issues of the CERFI's publications. He contributed to two issues of *Recherches: The Public Works of Power* and *Three Billion Perverts* in 1973.[42] At the same time, during the 1971–2 academic year, Deleuze participated in Foucault's seminar at the Collège de France, where Foucault was analyzing the nineteenth-century case of Pierre Rivière, who, at the age of twenty, slit the throats of his mother, brother, and sister and left behind his memoirs, which were partially published in 1836.

A TIME OF DISCORD

The other period when Foucault and Deleuze were both politically engaged came in 1977, during the Klaus Croissant affair. On 11 July 1977, the Baader–Meinhof gang's attorney came from Germany to Paris seeking political asylum: in his own country he was being treated as a Baader "agent" and as the terrorists' puppet. As soon as he arrived in Paris, the German authorities requested his arrest and deportation. On 30 September, the French police arrested him. The attorney Gérard Soulier, a friend of Guattari's who was very active in the CINEL (Centre d'Initiatives pour de Nouveaux Espaces Libres), learned of the arrest while reading *Le Monde* as he was about to drop off to sleep. "That woke me up!"[43] He leapt up from the couch, got out the legal directory, and called Jean-Jacques de Felice, Tubiana, and Antoine Compte, who organized a press conference with Henri Noguères, the president of the League for Human Rights. On 26 October 1977, Minister of Justice Alan Peyrefitte declared, "France cannot become a sanctuary for terrorists." In early November, a hearing was held in the tenth chamber of the Court of Appeal in Paris to rule on the request for deportation; on 16 November 1977, as a small crowd was gathering in front of the Santé Prison along with Foucault and Deleuze, the police charged. Croissant was escorted to the German border.

By this point, the disagreements between the two friends were threatening their friendship. Both joined the demonstration against the deportation of Croissant, but Foucault refused to sign the petition, which already included the names of Deleuze and Guattari, since he thought it was too complacent with respect to the Red Army Faction terrorists and wanted to more carefully and specifically define his support to Croissant.[44] Claude Mauriac remembers calling Foucault "to ask him how he'd reacted to Guattari's phone call about the deportation request for Baader's attorney, Klaus Croissant. We'd had no prior discussion but had both refused to sign the text, agreeing on a definite *no* to deportation but refusing to take responsibility for what the text said about Germany."[45]

Years later, Foucault's American biographer, James Miller, asked Deleuze what had changed their friendship so irrevocably. On 7 February 7 1990, five years after Foucault's death, Deleuze gave a three-point response:

(1) There's obviously no single answer. One of us could have answered one way one day and another way the next. Not because we are fickle. But because there are many reasons in this area and no single reason is "essential." And because none of them is essential, there are always several answers at once. The only important thing is that I had long agreed with him philosophically and on specific occasions, I no longer made the same evaluations as he did on several points at once. (2) This didn't lead to any "cooling" of relations between us, or to any "explanations." We saw each other less often, as if by the force of circumstances. And from there on, it became more and more difficult to meet up again. It is strange, we didn't stop seeing each other because we didn't get along, but because we weren't seeing each other any more, a kind of incomprehension or distance between us took hold. (3) I can tell you that I constantly miss seeing him, increasingly so. So what stopped me from calling him? That's where a deeper reason comes into it. Rightly or wrongly, I believed that he wanted greater solitude, for his life, for his thinking; that he needed this solitude, keeping in touch only with the people who were close to him. I now think that I should have tried to see him again, but I think I didn't try out of respect. I am still suffering from not having seen him again, even more so because I don't think there were any external reasons.[46]

This letter says a lot, but is also evasive. To better understand this radical break, we have to scrutinize several points of disagreement. In the first place, in 1977, Deleuze and Foucault had diametrically opposed positions regarding the new philosophers: Foucault supported them, but they were violently challenged by Deleuze.[47] In addition to the Croissant affair, they also diverged deeply on the Israeli–Palestinian question. Edward Said spoke with James Miller about this in November 1989. He saw the Middle East conflict as one of the major causes of their disagreement: he got the information from Deleuze himself, which Deleuze did not contradict when Miller put the question to him.[48] While Deleuze wrote a long article glorifying Yasser Arafat,[49] Foucault denounced the UN resolution equating Zionism with racism,[50] and in 1978, in the middle of the Lebanese crisis, he attacked the totalitarianism of Syria and the Soviet Union but spared Israeli politics.

In 1981, when the Socialists were voted into power in France, a new political disagreement arose. Deleuze was won over and even excited by the early days of Mitterrand's presidency. He thought it best to demonstrate goodwill and allow the Socialists to carry on with their work. Foucault thought it better to criticize them, just as one would criticize any other party in power, if not more so, because now the Communists had become part of Pierre Mauroy's government. When Jacques Donzelot met Deleuze for the last time, it was "in 1981, at the Panthéon. He was following Mitterrand. I ran into him; I was walking the other way. He said to me, 'What's happening is fantastic!' and I answered, no, that Mitterrand was a cynical politician who had been successful. He was thrilled!"[51] Their divergent judgments became obvious when General Jaruzelski staged a coup d'état in Poland in 1981, crushing the dreams of the *Solidarnost* leader Lech Wałęsa. Foucault and Bourdieu drafted an appeal criticizing the weaknesses of this new Socialist government in the face of a new Stalinesque show of strength. Deleuze was asked to sign but declined; he signed a different appeal written by Jack Lang and revised by Jean-Pierre Faye denouncing the repression in Poland while at the same time praising Mitterrand's actions.

In addition to their political disagreements, Deleuze and Foucault also admitted their many philosophical differences, even if these could not account for the severance of their ties. After expressing great admiration for *Difference and Repetition* and *The Logic of Sense* when they were published, Foucault was perplexed by *Anti-Oedipus* in 1972. While he did write a preface to the 1977 American edition, in which he hailed *Anti-Oedipus* as the first ethical book to be written in a long time, according to Donzelot this was not a true reflection of Foucault's feelings about his friend's book. "Foucault didn't like *Anti-Oedipus* and told me so quite often."[52] Jacques Donzelot wrote his own enthusiastic critique for *Esprit*,[53] something that Foucault was glad not to have to do. For him, the book was "a language effect, like Céline. He [Foucault] took my paper to give it to an American journal, managing in that way to feel justified for not having written anything about it."[54]

In the first volume of his *History of Sexuality*, Foucault settled his accounts with psychoanalysis and with Lacan's theory of lack.[55] He argued against the Freudian conception of desire and strongly refuted the claim that society had become progressively repressive since the classical age. He demonstrated that, to the contrary, discourses about sex were proliferating rather than slowly diminishing. Foucault's criticism of desire and "desirers" caught Deleuze and Guattari in the crossfire. In response, Deleuze wrote Foucault a personal letter that he sent through François Ewald, describing his arguments point by point – the letter was published as "Desire and Pleasure."[56] In it, Deleuze asked if it could be possible to consider as equivalent what pertained, for him, to the "body without organs-desires" and what pertained for Foucault to "body-pleasures." He recalled how virulently Foucault had rejected the concept of desire: "the last time we saw each other, Michel said very kindly and affectionately, something like: I can't stand the word desire; even if you use it differently, I can't stop myself from thinking or feeling that desire equals lack, or that desire is said to be repressed."[57] Deleuze, along the lines of Spinoza, saw pleasures as so many obstacles along the path of the desire to be, of *conatus* (striving), self-accomplishment, or perseverance in being, that could therefore only lead to loss. Pleasure, for him, interrupted the "immanent process of desire."[58]

Wounded by the letter, Foucault did not reply. He saw it as one more reason to break off their friendship. "Shortly afterward, Foucault abruptly decided that he would see no more of Deleuze."[59] To better understand why Deleuze's skepticism so offended Foucault, we need to bear in mind that despite the obvious and immediate public success of his book, which led to a reprint of twenty-two thousand copies after an initial print run of twenty-two thousand, and despite very favorable press reviews, Foucault's circle was disconcerted by the book's central argument questioning the battle against repression. It was hard to understand, after an entire decade of doing just this, how the battle on behalf of the freedom of sexual minorities could be viewed as a deployment of biopower. There were vocal criticisms and expressed incomprehension; Baudrillard's *Forget Foucault* was the final straw, so stunning the weakened philosopher that he abandoned the entire edifice that he had planned. It was only after seven years of silence, after having thoroughly revisited its premises, that he published the second volume of his *History of Sexuality*.

The question of desire was altogether central in the split with Deleuze; after all, questioning desire had initially brought them together.[60] Deleuze and Foucault both thought that Freud and Lacan had failed to really examine desire by reducing it to lack or interdiction. "But if the two philosophers were more closely aligned on behalf of a common cause than before, their differences still remain irreconcilable."[61] In 1983, Foucault was very clear about their disagreement during a long interview with Gérard Raulet, who asked him if he agreed with the idea that there was some similarity between his thought and Deleuze's. "Would this similarity extend to the Deleuzian conception of desire?" Foucault's succinct answer was categorical: "No, that's the point."[62] In fact, they gave different answers to a common line of inquiry. Both were concerned with building a non-fascist life ethic and agreed on the absence of naturalness and the spontaneity of desire ordered into arrangements, but Deleuze and Guattari saw desire as a concatenation of arrangements within a decidedly constructivist perspective. "Deleuze's philo-sophical stroke of genius is to invent a new vitalism, to seek the conditions not of possibility but of reality between expression and construction."[63] What was also playing out in their different concepts of desire was the way that each appropri-ated Nietzsche, whom Deleuze used particularly for the way he addressed desire in *The Will to Power*; Foucault was more interested in the question of truth in *On the Genealogy of Morality*.

Deleuze's conception of desire was rooted in Nietzsche and also strongly influ-enced by Spinoza's power of being. Deleuze introduced the power of being into an ontology. In January 1986, in his seminar on Foucault, Deleuze went back to the Foucauldian conception of desire/pleasure, explaining Foucault's refusal of the con-cept of desire and attachment to the idea of the body and its pleasures as the expres-sion of a sexless sexuality with which he concluded his work *The Will to Knowledge*. According to Deleuze, the will to replace a "molar" conception with sex at its center by a "molecular" approach to multiform pleasures was inspired by Proust's defini-tion of the three levels in *Sodom and Gomorrah*: the great group of heterosexual rela-tions; a second level where same refers to same, man to man and woman to woman; and a third level that is "no longer vertical, but transversal,"[64] in which each man has a feminine aspect and each woman a masculine aspect that do not communicate with each other, whence the absolute need for four terms and molecular arrange-ments. Pulverizing the theme of guilt, Proust "even talks about local pleasures."[65]

THE TRUTH

The publication of *The Will to Knowledge* created a new disagreement between Foucault and Deleuze about the return of the theme of truth. As Jacques Donzelot recalled, "Deleuze often spoke to me about that, saying 'Jacques, what do you think, Michel is completely nuts, what's this old idea about truth? He's taking us back to that old idea, veridiction! Oh, it can't be!'"[66] In his letter to Foucault, Deleuze explicitly voiced his concern about seeing this term return in Foucault's work. "The danger is: is Michel returning to an analog of the 'constituting subject' and why does he feel the need to resuscitate the truth even if he does make it into a new concept?"[67] For Foucault, it was not a question of revisiting the traditional confrontation between true and false. Talking with Paul Veyne one night about truth in Heidegger and Wittgenstein, Foucault added "literally (because I wrote his sentence down): the question is why truth is so little true?"[68] If it is indeed a question of arousing from its slumbers an old traditional concept, it is "to make it play on a different stage, even at the risk of turning it against itself."[69]

But in his 1977 letter, Deleuze expresses his sheer surprise concerning the means for Foucault's changing views. Starting from the idea that systems of power are, like those of counter-powers, bearers of truth, Foucault made the question of truth depend on the question of power. Thus the "problem of the role of the intellectual in Michel's thought" was raised, along with "his way of reintroducing the category of truth, since, by completely renewing it and making it depend on power, he can find material in this renewal that can be turned against power. But here, I don't see how."[70] Trying to understand the Foucauldian use of the true in his 1985–6 seminar, Deleuze perceived a disjunction in Foucault's thought between the realms of seeing and of saying, the visible and the spoken. Starting from this paradoxical tension, the game of truth is played out, for speaking is not seeing. But both philosophers grant the two positions truth. Foucault ends up finding in the objective of truth the function of philosophy: "I can't see many other definitions of the word 'philosophy' besides that one."[71] By contrast, for Deleuze, the importance of an affirmation or a concept is not determined by the truth: "on the contrary, it's its importance and its novelty that determine its 'truth.'"[72]

Crossovers between Foucault and Deleuze exist on many levels: they often used the same authors and sources, but in different and often irreconcilable ways. For example, when Deleuze stopped writing portraits in the history of philosophy, he drew heavily from Stoicism for *The Logic of Sense*. Foucault also drew from Stoic arguments in his very late works. He had already allusively adopted the Stoic outlook of *The Logic of Sense* in stating that it was necessary that utterances be granted their specific "materiality," which would be something on the order of incorporeal materiality. Deleuze and Foucault also had a common enemy in Platonism and made use of the same aspects of Stoicism, such as the primacy of the event. "Foucault and Deleuze also emphasize that the Stoic art of the event seeks to insert the self into the immanence of the world and of time."[73] But they used the Stoics differently. Deleuze's was more of a philosophical history of philosophy wherein the Stoics shifted the entire way of thinking within which "philosophy gets confused with ontology."[74] Deleuze tended to look at the early Stoics, whereas Foucault favored the later Stoics of imperial Rome, the reputed moralists such as Epictetus or Marcus Aurelius.

For both of them, their relationship to the Greeks was mediated by Nietzsche; for Nietzsche, from the Greek age onward, the philosopher is he who affirms life. "The will to power in Nietzsche means the affirmation of life, and no longer judging life as the sovereign-Desire."[75] Foucault's interest in the Greeks in *The Use of Pleasure* was also derived from Nietzsche, but he put forward some very personal propositions: who could be the free man chosen to shepherd the civic community in the Greek city of antiquity? "Only he who knows how to govern himself is apt to govern others."[76] Deleuze identifies this as Foucault's central idea, which broke with his previous work: this government of self is removed from both knowledge and power to become a veritable "art of the self."[77] However, this strength of subjectification is not primary because it remains dependent on the singularity of the "Greek diagram."

Where Foucault and Deleuze used the Stoics in similar ways, they were also very different if we compare Deleuze's fundamentally affirmative and resolutely Spinozan philosophy and metaphysical approach and Foucault's fundamentally Kantian philosophy, integrating negativity occasionally to the point of skepticism. "For me, his books are great works of skepticism. That is where the truth of Foucault lies, in a modern skepticism linked to a quite mysterious form of engagement."[78] Spinoza was not unimportant to Foucault. "Daniel Defert told me that Foucault had used Spinoza, which was on his bedside when he died. He was in the process of rereading him."[79]

Just as Deleuze adhered closely to Spinoza in his idea of temporality or eternity proper to the *conatus* and eluding *chronos*, Foucault preferred just as strongly the practice of discontinuities and radical rents in the fabric of time. Here, Deleuze favored an ontology of ever-increasing power, whereas Foucault was closer to Kantian criticism. In his 1985–6 seminar, Deleuze remarked, "there is a neo-Kantianism peculiar to Foucault."[80] During what he called his "little promenade" through Kant, Deleuze paid vibrant tribute to Kant's insight, which he thought extraordinary.[81] According to Deleuze, Foucault found the Kantian gap in his manner of distinguishing between seeing and speaking, which were so different in nature that one could not be reduced to the other. If this gap could not be filled, how could knowledge exist? What Deleuze saw in this Kantian question was an analogy between Kant's situation of being caught between understanding and intuition and Foucault's grappling with the two heterogeneous dimensions of "visible" and "utterable."

Reversing their usual roles, while Deleuzian vitalism – considered dangerous – has often been contrasted with Foucault's neo-Kantianism and credited with being more respectful of established limits, Deleuze called Foucault's positions dangerous on several occasions. He explained what he meant. "Dangerous, yes, because there's violence in Foucault. An intense violence that he mastered, controlled, and turned into courage. He trembled with violence at some demonstrations. He saw what was intolerable. . . . And his style, at least up to the last books that achieved a kind of serenity, is like a lash, it's a whip twisting and relaxing."[82] Deleuze agreed with Paul Veyne that Foucault was a warrior ready to transform the history of thought into a war-machine, in a polemilogical approach fascinated by death. Deleuze, for his part, was more on the side of cunning, of ancient Greek intelligence, of the *Metis*, of laughter and a devastating sense of humor.

THE PLAY OF MIRRORS

The philosopher Judith Revel observed the game of mirrors between two philosophers, each of whom went his own way while touching on very similar themes at several moments in their exchanges, a relationship very strong but always oblique.

Both had a close relationship to history but each from a different position. The more Kantian Foucault posed the question of the conditions of possibility; Deleuze was concerned with the conditions of reality. In 1968 and 1969, Foucault was delighted to discover the foundations for a politics of difference in Deleuze's work, which echoed his quest for the figure of the other and alterity that had led to his 1961 *History of Madness*. He felt comforted in his positions; Deleuze allowed him to define a way out of structuralism that he would later disown but that he was still ardently defending in 1967. Both philosophers were fascinated by schizophrenia as a way of escaping binary structural codification. "The schizophrenic experience appeared to create a space for narratives that were also manuals for breaking down the code."[83]

In his lectures at the Collège de France in the early 1970s, Foucault developed the idea of the medicalization of society, of the psychiatrization of the social realm, and of the institutionalization of the uses of power, which needed to be countered by anti-institutional uses of knowledge. This position was not far removed from the arguments put forward by Deleuze and Guattari in *Anti-Oedipus* or from the use of institutional psychotherapy at La Borde.[84] Yet what appeared to be a common perspective was not one, in fact, because the horizon of Foucault's enquiry at the time was concentrated on the question of power, whereas Deleuze and Guattari were interested in the processes of subjectivization: group-subjects and collective subjects of enunciation. "Then Foucault turned his attention to subjectivization, which was the case in *Discipline and Punish*, and we thought that they would meet but they didn't."[85]

Judith Revel, who has studied the echoes between the thought of the two philosophers, vouches for the effects of their falling out in the late 1970s when Foucault got involved in ethical issues: "When you look at instances from 1977–1978 onward, there are no more references to each other. There's a real silence."[86] On the other hand, regarding the frequent use of spatial metaphors, Foucault and Deleuze, like most of their generation of intellectuals, were very close, which translated a sort of determination on their part to leave Hegelianism and the subjacent philosophy of history behind via spatiality and the logical patterns that it suggested: that of the plane of immanence for Deleuze and Guattari, with its strata and smooth spaces, holes and lines of flight, which enabled a cartography of phenomena. Foucault somewhat similarly defined the general history that he advocated as the possible deployment of a "space of dispersion."[87] As Deleuze emphasized, underlying Foucault's use of the terms genealogy and archaeology lies a geology, with its sheets, landslides and discordances. In fact, Deleuze defined Foucault as a "new cartographer." Of course, Deleuze and Foucault positioned themselves very differently with respect to history, as Deleuze said quite clearly in 1988: "We, Félix and I, always fancied a universal history, which he [Foucault] hated."[88]

24

TWO PHILOSOPHIES OF THE EVENT

Foucault and Deleuze both broke free from the philosophy of history in the sense of Hegelian-Marxist teleology to make way for a philosophy of the event. As far as their relation to history, historians and the archive was concerned, both were tireless in their different ways of pursuing the sudden appearance of something new, the momentary flashes that upset habits and ready-made thoughts. These moments of crystallization, which were so essential to understanding what was at stake in both social history and the history of thought, were revealed in periods of crisis and change, something that Deleuze himself said when discussing Foucault's work, beginning with its shifts and passages, which reveal moments of crisis whose traversing elucidated the tensions borne by thought between its virtual and actual states. In his attentiveness to the new, Foucault belonged to the French epistemological school of Bachelard and Canguilhem and to Nietzschean genealogy. Starting from this tradition, he advocates a discontinuist approach to time, favoring the radical breaks that he called *épistémè* for a while, although he abandoned the term after *The Order of Things*.[89]

Following Nietzsche, Foucault replaced the quest for temporal origins and causalities with a critical positivism seeking to identify discontinuities by describing their material potentialities. Second, he aimed to identify the singularity of events beyond their acknowledged finality. Finally, eventualization made it possible to make the figure of the conscious subject as well as its illusion of mastering time less important: "Effective history brings out the most unique characteristics and most acute manifestations of events."[90] Foucault contrasted the three Platonic modalities of history with his own deconstructive use of historical myths. History as recognition was replaced by the parodic use of reality, history as continuity by a destructive use of identity, and history as knowledge by a destructive use of truths. From this perspective, history as a total synthesis was seen as a trap, because, according to Foucault, "a possible task remains one of calling into question everything pertaining to time, everything that has taken shape within it, everything that resides within its mobile element, so as to make visible that rent, devoid of chronology and history from which time issues."[91]

Deleuze and Guattari's understanding of the event emphasizes the way it appears suddenly as something new, as a beginning, as its own origin. In *Dialogues*, Deleuze speaks about a "surface flash."[92] In *What Is Philosophy?* Deleuze and Guattari use Péguy's *Clio* to explain that there are two ways of thinking about the event – by recording its effectuation in history and its conditioning or by returning to it, situating oneself within it and passing through all of its components and singularities. In 1980, *A Thousand Plateaus* announced the importance of evenemential scansions, as each of the thirteen plateaus has an inaugural date: "History will never be rid of dates. It is perhaps economy or financial analysis which better demonstrate the presence of the instantaneity of these derisory acts in a total process."[93]

This way of thinking about events was not a form of presentism. On the contrary, philosophy as the creation of concepts must break with its own period. It is fundamentally untimely and inactual according to the Nietzschean conception that Foucault shared. "Act against time, therefore upon time, and hope thereby to plant the seeds of a time to come."[94] Deleuze differentiated history from becoming. The creation of something new was always inactual and constituted a becoming, which certainly needed history and situations in order not to remain completely undetermined, but they elude it at the same time. Becoming breaks out of time and is never reduced to it.

This was the case for May '68, an event that Deleuze, Guattari and Foucault all experienced intensely. For all three, viewing it only as an historical moment when France was mired in social conflict would be to overlook its essential creativity. It defied the traditional approach of understanding history and even created its crisis. Deleuze and Guattari agreed with this position, since for them, history could not explain what happens. Time creates a crisis in causality beneath which lies a law of pure chance, rendering it ontologically secondary but negating it. In *The Logic of Sense*, Deleuze challenges two approaches to the event: the essentialist Platonic perspective that subsumes the plurality of events under a single pure Event and the circumstantialist approach that reduces the event to a witnessed accident. He insists on the plurality of events as "jets of singularity"[95] and emphasizes that the event itself raises questions: "The event is problematic and problematizing in its own right."[96] In *The Fold*, Deleuze repeats Whitehead's question: "What is an event?" In his view, the event manifests itself as a vibration resounding with infinite harmonics in a vast series, like the rising of something new that is at once public and private, potential and actual, and marked by intensities.

Under these conditions, is it possible to develop a philosophy of the event and bind it within discourse? The event exceeds its discursive expression. Foucault, after *The Archaeology of Knowledge*, veered toward a genealogical program that, in *The Order of Discourse*, his inaugural lecture at the Collège de France, overvalues the discursive level. He laid out a program for calling life, crime and madness into question by examining the conditions of the validity of knowledge. It was a matter of restoring "to discourse its character as an event"[97] following relations of discontinuity: "Discourses must be treated as discontinuous practices."[98] In this respect, Foucault presented himself as a contented positivist from *The Archaeology of Knowledge* (1969) onward, concerned with investigating the enunciative foundation for itself, in its positive, actual existence.

Deleuze expresses this excess with respect to the articulation of the event by insisting on its singularity, referring to Duns Scotus and his concept of *haecceity*

26

to define its individuality. Two essential characteristics follow. First, the event is defined by the simultaneous coexistence of two heterogeneous dimensions in a time where future and past continually coincide and overlap while remaining distinct and indiscernible. Second, the event is what happened, so that its emerging dimension is not yet separated from the past, an intensity that comes and is distinguished simply from other intensities. The ideal event, as Deleuze defines it in *The Logic of Sense*, is therefore a singularity or a collection of singularities.

To think the event, Deleuze and Guattari believe that it must follow two distinct temporal modes. First, there is its coming into being within a state of affairs, in present circumstances where it partakes of a particular time frame called *Chronos*, by virtue of which it fixes things and people to some degree. But at the same time, the event cannot be reduced to its coming into effect, thus the need to envisage a second temporal dimension that Deleuze and Guattari call the time of *Aiōn*, a paradoxical eternity where something incorporeal and ineffectuable exceeds and opens onto the indefinite time of the event, a "floating line that knows only speeds and continually divides that which transpires into an already-there that is at the same time not-yet-here, a simultaneous too-late and too-early, a some-thing that is both going to happen and has just happened."[99]

For Deleuze and Guattari, this insistence on the Event refers to the sphere of action according to the teachings of Spinoza's practical philosophy but also to those of the Stoics.[100] A Stoic path that, in an *élan vital*, consists in being worthy of what happens, of supporting and valuing every glimmer that might be contained in what happens: an event, a speed, a becoming. An *Eventum tantum* can be imperceptible yet change everything:

> Making an event however small is the most delicate thing in the world: the opposite of making a drama or a story. Loving those who are like this: when they enter a room they are not persona, characters, or subjects but an atmospheric variation, a change of hue, an imperceptible molecule, a discrete population, a fog, or a cloud of droplets. Everything has really changed. Great events, too, are made in this way: battle, revolution, life and death. . . . True Entities are events.[101]

Deleuze, Reader of Foucault

Throughout his career, Deleuze paid very close attention to Foucault's publications and regularly reviewed them. Notably, he wrote two studies in 1970 and in 1975, one on *The Archaeology of Knowledge* and the other on *Discipline and Punish*.[102] And more importantly, in the 1985–6 academic year, he devoted his entire course to Foucault, publishing *Foucault* the following summer.

That he devoted himself to Foucault's writings immediately after Foucault's death showed the strength of their relationship and Deleuze's struggle to mourn someone who was more than a friend. When asked why he wrote a book on Foucault, Deleuze's answer was quite clear: "It marks an inner need of mine, my admiration for him, how I was moved by his death, and his unfinished work."[103] Deleuze's way of mourning Foucault was to elucidate the particular logic of his thought by seeking its coherence through the crises, leaps and incessant displacements that it traversed. Following Martial Guéroult's views, Deleuze agreed that each text formed an integral part of the complete works of an author and none could be examined without that context. Everything needed to be conveyed and its logic and movement reconstructed. "A thought's logic is like a wind blowing us on, a series of gusts and jolts. You think you've gotten to port, but then find yourself thrown back out onto the open sea, as Leibniz put it. That's particularly true in Foucault's case."[104] Deleuze therefore retraced Foucault's evolution in his writing, finding both a profound unity and fundamental shifts. All of Foucault's work, according to Deleuze, is articulated around the distinction between seeing and speaking. He is fundamentally dualistic on this matter, deploying two mutually irreducible dimensions: "But for him, the primacy of statements will never impede the historical irreducibility of the visible – indeed, quite the contrary."[105]

Deleuze identified important evolutions in Foucault's work. Until the publication of *The Archaeology of Knowledge* in 1969, the major question was that of knowledge. Then, with *Discipline and Punish* and *The Will to Knowledge*, Foucault started working on a new dimension – power. Deleuze wanted to understand what had led him to change from one register to another, suggesting that Foucault's problem was that of the double, and "the utterance is the double of something which is identical to it."[106] Knowledge being the integration of power relations, he therefore played from a double score, that of relations of force, composing power, and that of relations of forms, composing knowledge. Specific singularities arise therefore from an endogenous relationship between knowledge and power.

But this mirroring between knowledge and power leads to a dead end and requires a third axis to recreate a dynamics. Deleuze thought that this third axis was already present, though to a lesser degree, and that it became much more important in Foucault's later work and particularly in his last two books, with the study of modes of subjectification, mistakenly read as the return of the subject. This dimension of subjectification "was present in Foucault, but not as such, it was intermingled with knowledge and power."[107] The question was therefore one of finding out how power and knowledge attempt to take over this third axis of subjectification in order to reappropriate it. Deleuze locates the dynamic in Foucault's thought here, for "the more power tries to conquer subjectification, the more new modes of subjectification form."[108]

28

Deleuze often read the work of other philosophers through the prism of his own positions and preoccupations. Had he fathered another Deleuzian child in his *Foucault*? This seems to be the opinion of Potte-Bonneville, who sees Deleuze's text as the best introduction to Foucault, encouraging us to read and study his work further. But he also suspects it of hiding aspects of Foucault's thought. "Thus the question of history disappears completely, which is quite strange when discussing Foucault."[109]

When the Foucault specialist Frédéric Gros published a study of Deleuze's reading, he spoke of it as a "metaphysical fiction,"[110] for he did not recognize the Foucault that he knew at all, though he recalls that for Deleuze, understanding Foucault was not a question of providing a scholarly commentary of his work: "For Deleuze, understanding an author, in a way, means discovering the founding principles, laying bare the inherent metaphysics of their thought."[111] It would also mean being able to create an imaginary Foucault, to dream up a metaphysical double. Frédéric Gros does, of course, acknowledge the extraordinary coherence that Deleuze's reading of Foucault's work elucidates: "reading Foucault, Deleuze recognizes how he was marked by his reading of Bergson."[112] Since writing his review in 1995, Frédéric Gros has been able to measure the accuracy of some of the main lines of Deleuze's reading:

> Deleuze's book is a true philosophical work. Everything he says about the relationship between utterances and visibilities shows that he understood something very important, which I later heard in Foucault's last lectures at the Collège de France, that Deleuze could not have had. It was the idea that he was constructing a direct ethics by making correspondences between visible acts and *logoï*, utterances. It is amazing to see how Deleuze, who couldn't have had any knowledge of the Collège de France lectures, was so accurate in his interpretation.[113]

As Robert Maggiori wrote when Deleuze's *Foucault* came out, he does not "explain Foucault, because Foucault explains himself very well in his books, nor does he provide a commentary, of which there are already plenty. Like a miner who respects the rock that resists his pick but knows how to find the treasure in its veins, Deleuze mines Foucault's writings to extract the most productive elements of his thought."[114]

DEATH

The rumor began circulating in Paris during 1984. Foucault was very ill and nobody knew what was wrong with him, although a few people heard that he had been hospitalized. Deleuze was concerned for his friend, whom he had not seen since the late

1970s. "Two weeks before Foucault died, Deleuze called me. He was very worried and wondered if I had any news. 'Do you know what is going on? What has he got?' I didn't know anything except that he was in the hospital. Then Deleuze said, 'Maybe it's nothing. Foucault will leave the hospital and come and tell us that everything is all right.'"[115] According to Didier Eribon, one of Foucault's most heartfelt wishes, knowing that he would not live long, was to reconcile with Deleuze. They never saw each other again. The fact that Daniel Defert asked Deleuze to speak at Foucault's funeral was a sign of how much both men wanted to smooth over their differences, even beyond the separation of death.

Deleuze hated conferences but made an exception for his friend, participating in the international colloquium organized in January 1988 in homage to Foucault. His paper was entitled "What Is a *Dispositif*?"[116] In his lecture on Foucault, Deleuze referred to Foucault's death in the context of the value he gave to impersonal pronouns and his critique of linguistic personology. In *The Space of Literature*, Blanchot writes of death as an event, coming from beyond the body. "One dies. . ." Foucault reinterpreted this theme and "died according to his interpretation."[117] "Foucault was telling us something that concerned him directly,"[118] that death is not the indivisible, final limit defined by doctors and moralists. One is never done with death: "Foucault lived death like Bichat. That's how he died. He died by taking his place within the 'One dies' and in the manner of 'partial deaths.'"[119]

Beyond their differences and disputes, after the death of both men, can we reasonably speak about a "Foucault–Deleuzeanism"? It would be pointless to coin a term that might miss the singularity of both philosophers, eliminating their disagreements and producing some *faux-semblant* in the name of some ecumenical sterility. Rather, we will describe a "disjunctive synthesis" similar to the relationship between Deleuze and Guattari.

In addition to their shared philosophical heritage, they were also close in the way that they used literature, approaching it in a clinical fashion that set them apart from professional philosophers, whose work was most often limited to academic texts. In *The Logic of Sense*, Artaud's scream deconstructs Lewis Carroll's ingenious surface connections, and Deleuze finds Artaud at the very center of Foucault's inquiries. "The unthought as the double of thought, and at the very end of *The Order of Things*, Foucault reinterprets the theme of the double that he shares with Artaud, Heidegger, and Blanchot."[120] Here Foucault identifies an experience similar to Artaud's, who had reached within thought an element that could not be thought and that becomes a "vital impotence" for the writer.[121]

The theme of the double appears in one of Foucault's first books, written about Raymond Roussel, another writer.[122] On the distortion between seeing and saying, Foucault again finds his inspiration in literature. Roussel formulates the relationship to language, coupling it to the will to push words to their limits, a tendency common to both Foucault and Deleuze. "Break things open, break words open."[123] One of Roussel's writerly strategies was to construct two sentences around a tiny difference that would fundamentally change the overall meaning.[124] For both Foucault and Deleuze, literature is neither an illustration nor a curiosity. It is valuable as an experiment, an act of creation – and since, for Deleuze, philosophy consists in creating concepts, literature accompanies it in its creative work.

We can see in this relationship between Foucault and Deleuze more than shared foundations; Deleuze allowed Foucauldian thinking to develop. Deleuze's "Postscript on Control Societies," published in 1990, follows from Foucault's work.[125] Deleuze, like Foucault, felt implicated by current events and wanted to conceptualize change. Deleuze starts with the historicization proposed by Foucault, who had delineated a model of society founded on sovereignty, in which power reveals itself as the capacity to inflict death. In eighteenth- and nineteenth-century France, a disciplinary model came into being according to the schema of "the great confinement," which led to the generalization of closed universes where discipline affected every part of the social body. Numerous prisons, barracks, schools and factories were built on the model of the Panopticon. The function of power was no longer to put people to death but to discipline their bodies, make them live, maximize their utility, and let them die.

Foucault had begun to perceive the emergence of a new model, one centered on biopower and the biopolitical control of populations and that seemed slightly out of step with disciplinary concepts. Deleuze began with Foucault's intuitions and expanded them. His 1990 article identified the advent of a new type of society, "societies of control," which emerged after World War II and ended with a general crisis of all forms of confinement: "It's simply a matter of nursing them through their death throes."[126] Deleuze's analysis, which he was already developing in his seminar on Foucault, was prophetic. In this management of life in all its shapes and forms, he rightly foresaw a whole new type of management, based on control and transformation of the legal subject. This legal subject is no longer limited to the person, as it was in the age of humanism, because it implied populations other than human, cereal crops as well as herds of cattle, sheep as well as poultry, and every other living being. In the age of control societies, the legal subject becomes the living, "the living within man."[127]

Imprisonment is no longer needed, "because we know that everybody will be on the highway at a given hour. Probability calculations are much better than prisons."[128] From the 1980s on, Deleuze notes the breakdown of the entire fabric of enclosure, particularly that of factories that were affected by temporary work, by working at home, and flextime. At school, there was less discipline but far more control: "Individuals become 'dividuals,' and masses become samples, data, markets, or 'banks.'"[129] These various transformations destroy the former rigidity of the discipline to pave the way for the microchips and mobile phones that make it possible to constantly control each person, in an open space where outside and inside are no longer useful categories. "The key thing is that we are at the beginning of something new."[130] Fresh forms of subjectification and resistance to control needed new directions.

NOTES

1. Michel Foucault, "Theatrum Philosophicum" (1970), in *Dits et écrits* (Paris: Gallimard, 1994), 2:76. English translation in Michel Foucault, *Language, Counter-Memory, Practice: Selected Essays and Interviews*, ed. Donald F. Bouchard (Ithaca: Cornell University Press, 1977), 165–97.
2. Fanny Deleuze, interview with the author.
3. Paul Veyne, interview with the author.
4. Ibid.
5. Gilles Deleuze, "Fendre les choses, fendre les mots" (1986), in *Pourparlers* (Paris: Minuit, 1990), 117, translated as "Breaking Things Open, Breaking Words Open," in *Negotiations, 1972–1990*, trans. Martin Joughin (New York: Columbia University Press, 1990), 85.
6. Ibid. 117.
7. Gilles Deleuze with Claire Parnet, *L'abécédaire de Gilles Deleuze* (1988), three DVDs (Montparnasse: Arte Video, 1997).
8. Gilles Deleuze, quoted in Didier Eribon, *Michel Foucault* (Paris: Flammarion, 1989), 83.
9. Ibid. 162.
10. Ibid. 163.
11. See François Dosse, *Gilles Deleuze and Félix Guattari: Intersecting Lives*, trans. Deborah Glassman (New York: Columbia University Press, 2010), chapter 7, "Nietzsche, Bergson, Spinoza: A Trio for a Vitalist Philosophy," 129–49.
12. Michel Foucault, "La prose d'Actéon" (1964), translated as "The Prose of Acteon" in *Aesthetics, Methods, Epistemology*, ed. James D. Faubion (New York: The New Press, 1999); Gilles Deleuze, "Klossowski ou les corps-langages" (1965), translated as "Klossowski or Bodies-Language" in *The Logic of Sense*, trans. Mark Lester with Charles Stivale; ed. Constantin Boundas (New York: Columbia University Press, 1979).
13. Philippe Sabot, "Foucault, Deleuze et les simulacres," *Concepts* 8 (2004), 6.
14. Gilles Deleuze, *The Logic of Sense*, 283.
15. Ibid. 299.
16. Gilles Deleuze, Paris VIII seminar (28 January 1986), Bibliothèque nationale de France sound archives.
17. Michel Foucault, "Theatrum Philosophicum," in *Dits et écrits*, 2:98; *Language, Counter-Memory, Practice*, 165–97.
18. François Zourabichvili, *Deleuze: Une philosopie de l'événement* (Paris: PUF, 1994). English translation in François Zourabichvili, *Deleuze: A Philosophy of the Event: together with The Vocabulary of Deleuze*, trans. Kieran Aarons, ed. Gregg Lambert and Daniel W. Smith (Edinburgh: Edinburgh University Press, 2012), 33–136.

19. Michel Foucault, "Theatrum Philosophicum," in *Dits et écrits*, 2:85; *Language, Counter-Memory, Practice*, 185.

20. Gilles Deleuze, Paris VIII seminar (20 May 1986), Bibliothèque nationale de France sound archives.

21. Philippe Artières, Laurent Quéro and Michelle Zancarini-Fournel, *Le groupe d'informations sur les prisons. Archives d'une lutte 1970–72* (Paris: IMEC, 2005), 28.

22. Daniel Defert, "L'émergence d'un nouveau front: les prisons," in *Le groupe d'informations sur les prisons*, 317. Around twenty people gathered at Foucault's home for the meeting, including Daniel Defert, Casamayor, Jean-Marie Domenach, Louis Joinet, Frédéric Pottecher, Christian Revon, Jean-Jacques de Felice, Christine Martineau, Danielle Rancière and Jacques Donzelot.

23. Ibid. 318.

24. Notably by the Bruay-en-Artois affair of 1972. Near the miners' quarters in Bruay, the naked, mutilated body of a teenage girl named Brigitte Dewèvre, a miner's daughter, was found. Pascal, the judge, quickly decided to charge the solicitor Pierre Leroy. The Maoist daily *La Cause de Peuple* considered that only a bourgeois pig could have committed such a crime and a popular tribunal was formed in the name of necessary popular justice.

25. Gilles Deleuze, Paris VIII seminar (28 January 1986), Bibliothèque nationale de France sound archives.

26. Jean-Pierre Faye, interview with the author.

27. Jacques Donzelot, interview with the author.

28. Jacques Donzelot, *La police des familles* (Paris: Minuit, 1977).

29. Jacques Donzelot, interview with the author.

30. Michel Foucault, reported by Jacques Donzelot, interview with the author.

31. Deleuze wrote a handsome afterword entitled "L'ascension du social." Gilles Deleuze, "L'ascension du social," afterword to Jacques Donzelot, *La police des familles*, 213–20. English translation: Gilles Deleuze, "The Rise of the Social," in Jacques Donzelot, *The Policing of Families*, trans. Robert Hurley (Baltimore: Johns Hopkins University Press, 1997), ix–xvii.

32. Alain Joubert, *Michel Foucault, une journée particulière* (Lyon: Aedelsa Editions, 2004).

33. Reprinted in Gilles Deleuze, *L'île déserte et autres textes. Textes et entretiens 1953–1974*, ed. David Lapoujade (Paris: Minuit, 2002), translated as *Desert Islands and Other Texts (1953–1974)*, trans. Mike Taormina (New York: Semiotexte, 2003), 204–5.

34. Ibid. 286.

35. Claude Mauriac, *Mauriac et fils* (Paris: Grasset, 1986), 388.

36. The companie républicaine de sécurité, or CRS.

37. Gilles Deleuze, Paris VIII archives, BDIC.

38. See Didier Eribon, *Michel Foucault*.

39. Gilles Deleuze, "Les intellectuels et le pouvoir," *L'Arc* 49 (4 March 1972), translated as "Intellectuals and Power" in Michel Foucault, *Language, Counter-Memory, Practice*.

40. Ibid. 289.

41. Judith Revel, interview with the author.

42. Dosse, *Gilles Deleuze and Félix Guattari: Intersecting Lives*, chapter 15, "The CERFI at Work," 267–83.

43. Gérard Soulier, interview with the author.

44. Much later on it became known that this democratic figure and state attorney was, in fact, a Stasi agent.

45. Claude Mauriac, *Mauriac et fils*, 294.

46. Gilles Deleuze, letter to James Miller (7 February 1990). In James Miller, *The Passion of Michel Foucault* (New York: Anchor Books, 1993), 298.

47. See Dosse, *Gilles Deleuze and Félix Guattari: Intersecting Lives*, chapter 20, "The Year of Combat: 1977," 362–78.

48. Miller, *The Passion of Michel Foucault*, 449n41.

49. Gilles Deleuze, "Grandeur de Yasser Arafat," *Revue d'Études Palestiniennes* 10 (Winter 1984), 41–3. Reprinted in Gilles Deleuze, *Two Regimes of Madness, Texts and Interviews 1975–1995*, ed. David Lapoujade, trans. Ames Hodges and Mike Taormina (New York: Semiotext, 2007), under the title "The Importance of Being Arafat," 241–5. For a more precise translation, see Gilles Deleuze, "The Grandeur of Yasser Arafat," trans. Timothy Murphy, in *Discourse* 20:3 (Fall 1998), 30–3.

50. Michel Foucault, *Le Monde* (17–18 October 1986). Reprinted in *Dits and écrits*, 2:96.

51. Jacques Donzelot, interview with the author.

52. Ibid.

53. See Dosse, *Gilles Deleuze and Félix Guattari: Intersecting Lives*, chapter 10, "'Psychoanalysm' Under Attack," 183–205.

54. Jacques Donzelot, interview with the author.

55. Michel Foucault, *La volonté de savoir* (Paris: Gallimard, 1976), translated as *The History of Sexuality, Volume 1: An Introduction*, trans. Robert Hurley (New York: Pantheon, 1978).

56. Gilles Deleuze, "Désir et plaisir," in *Magazine Littéraire* 325 (October 1994), 59–65; reprinted in Gilles Deleuze, *Two Regimes of Madness*, 122-34. A translation, by Daniel W. Smith, appears in this volume, 223–31, under the title "Desire and Pleasure."

57. Gilles Deleuze, "Desire and Pleasure," in this volume, 227 (translation modified).

58. Ibid. 228.

59. Miller, *The Passion of Michel Foucault*, 297.

60. David Rabouin, "Entre Deleuze et Foucault: Le Jeu du Désir et du Pouvoir," *Critique* 637/638 (June–July 2000): 475–90.

61. Ibid. 485.

62. Michel Foucault, interview with Gérard Raulet, "Structuralisme et post- structuralisme," *Telos* 16:55 (Spring 1983), 195–211. Reprinted in Michel Foucault, *Dits et écrits*, 4:445.

63. Eric Alliez, interview with the author.

64. Gilles Deleuze, Paris VIII seminar (21 January 1986), Bibliothèque nationale de France sound archives.

65. Ibid.

66. Jacques Donzelot, interview with the author.

67. Gilles Deleuze, "Désir et plaisir," in *Deux régimes de fous*, 113.

68. Paul Veyne, "Le dernier Foucault et sa morale," *Critique* 471/472 (August–September 1986), 940n1.

69. Hervé Couchot, "Philosophie et vérité: quelques remarques sur un chassé-croisé," *Concepts* 8 (2004), 29.
70. Gilles Deleuze, "Desire and Pleasure," in this volume, 224 (translation modified).
71. Michel Foucault, introduction to his seminar at the Collège de France (11 January 1978), public recording, quoted in Couchot, "Philosophie et vérité," 39n1.
72. Couchot, "Philosophie et vérité," 43.
73. Thomas Bénatouïl, "Deux usages du stoïcisme: Deleuze et Foucault," in Frédéric Gros and Carlos Lévy, *Foucault et la philosophie antique* (Paris: Kimé, 2003), 31.
74. Gilles Deleuze, *The Logic of Sense*, 179.
75. Gilles Deleuze, Paris VIII Foucault seminar (6 May 1986), Bibliothèque nationale de France sound archives.
76. Ibid.
77. Michel Foucault, *L'usage des plaisirs* (Paris: Gallimard, 1984), 90, translated as *The Use of Pleasure: The History of Sexuality, Volume 2*, trans. Robert Hurley (New York: Random House, 1985).
78. Matthieu Potte-Bonneville, interview with the author.
79. Judith Revel, interview with the author.
80. Gilles Deleuze, Paris VIII Foucault seminar, Bibliothèque nationale de France audio archives.
81. "Kant is the first to have defined the human being in relation to the split which divides each one of us." Kant brought about the development of modern philosophy by differentiating two heterogeneous dimensions and by insisting on the irreducible disjunction between receptivity and spontaneity, between intuitions and concepts, and by making finiteness into a constitutive principle: "With Kant, something came to light which could not be seen beforehand." Ibid.
82. Gilles Deleuze, "Un portrait de Foucault," interview with Claire Parnet (1986), in Gilles Deleuze, *Pourparlers*, 140, translated as "A Portrait of Foucault" in Gilles Deleuze, *Negotiations*, 103.
83. Judith Revel, "Foucault lecteur de Deleuze: de l'écart à la différence," *Critique* 591/592 (August–September 1996), 734.
84. See Dosse, *Gilles Deleuze and Félix Guattari: Intersecting Lives*, chapter 2, "La Borde: Between Myth and Reality," 40–54.
85. Judith Revel, interview with the author.
86. Ibid.
87. Michel Foucault, *The Archaeology of Knowledge*, trans. A. M. Sheridan (London: Tavistock, 1972), 10.
88. Gilles Deleuze, interview with Raymond Bellour and François Ewald, *Le Magazine Littéraire* (September 1988), 24.
89. "Necessarily, we must dismiss those tendencies that encourage the consoling play of recognitions. We need to break into pieces everything that enables the consoling game of recognitions. Knowledge, even under the banner of history, does not depend on 'rediscovery' and it emphatically excludes the 'rediscovery of ourselves.' History becomes 'effective' to the degree that it introduces discontinuity into our very being – as it divides our emotions, dramatizes our instincts, multiplies our bodies and confronts

them with themselves . . . This is because knowledge is not made for understanding, but for cutting." Michel Foucault, "Nietzsche, généalogie, histoire" (1971), in *Dits et écrits*, 2:147–8, translated as "Nietzsche, Genealogy, History," in Foucault, *Language, Counter-Memory, Practice*, 154 (translation slightly modified).

90. Ibid.
91. Michel Foucault, *Les mots et les choses* (Paris: Gallimard, 1966), 343, translated as *The Order of Things: An Archaeology of the Human Sciences* (New York: Vintage, 1970), 331.
92. Gilles Deleuze and Claire Parnet (1977) *Dialogues*, trans. Hugh Tomlinson and Barbara Habberjam (New York: Columbia University Press), 80.
93. Gilles Deleuze and Felix Guattari, *A Thousand Plateaus*, trans. Brian Massumi (Minneapolis: University of Minnesota Press, 1987), 79. 20 November 1923 is linked to galloping inflation in Germany after 1918: "The curtain falls on 20 November 1923," wrote J. K. Galbraith in *Money: Whence It Came, Where It Went*, rev. ed. (New York: Houghton Mifflin, 1995).
94. Friedrich Nietzsche, *Untimely Meditations*, trans. R. J. Hollingdale (Cambridge: Cambridge University Press, 1983).
95. Gilles Deleuze, *The Logic of Sense*, 53.
96. Ibid. 54.
97. Michel Foucault, "The Discourse on Language," in *The Archaeology of Knowledge*, 215–37: 220.
98. Ibid. 231.
99. Deleuze and Guattari, *A Thousand Plateaus*, 262.
100. "Not being inferior to the event, becoming the child of one's own events." Deleuze and Parnet, *Dialogues*, 62–3.
101. Ibid. 49.
102. Gilles Deleuze, "Un nouvel archiviste" (1970) and "Ecrivain non: un nouveau cartographe" (1975), revised versions printed in Gilles Deleuze, *Foucault*, trans. Sean Hand (New York: Continuum, 2006), 11–30, 31–51.
103. Gilles Deleuze, interview with Didier Eribon (1986), in *Pourparlers*, 129, translated as "Life as a Work of Art" in *Negotiations*, 94.
104. Ibid.
105. Deleuze, *Foucault*, 43.
106. Gilles Deleuze, Paris VIII Foucault seminar (17 December 1985), French National Library sound archive.
107. Gilles Deleuze, Paris VIII Foucault seminar (6 May 1986), French National Library sound archive.
108. Ibid.
109. Mathieu Potte-Bonneville, interview with the author.
110. Frédéric Gros, "Le Foucault de Deleuze: une fiction métaphysique," *Philosophie* 47 (September 1995), 53–63.
111. Ibid. 54.
112. Ibid. 63.
113. Frédéric Gros, interview with the author.
114. Robert Maggiori, "Gilles Deleuze–Michel Foucault: une amitié philosophique," *Libération* (2 September 1986).

115. François Regnault, interview with the author.

116. Gilles Deleuze, "Qu'est-ce qu'un dispositif?," in *Michel Foucault philosophe* (Paris: Seuil, 1989), 185–95, translated as "What is a Dispositif?" in *Michel Foucault Philosopher*, ed. and trans. T. Armstrong (New York: Routledge, 1991).

117. Gilles Deleuze, Paris VIII Foucault seminar (26 November 1985), Bibliothèque nationale de France sound archive.

118. Ibid.

119. Ibid.

120. Gilles Deleuze, Paris VIII Foucault seminar (22 April 1986), Bibliothèque nationale de France sound archive.

121. Ibid.

122. Michel Foucault, *Death and the Labyrinth: The World of Raymond Roussel*, trans. Charles Ruas (New York: Doubleday, 1986).

123. Raymond Roussel, *Comment j'ai écrit certains de mes livres* (Paris: UGE 10/18, 1977).

124. For example, Roussel would generate from the sentence "Les lettres du blanc sur les bandes du vieux billard [The white letters on the cushions of the old billiard table]" the punning and homonymic sentence "Les lettres du blanc sur les bandes du vieux pillard [Letters by a white man about the hordes of the old plunderer]." He would then write a story linking these two concepts.

125. Gilles Deleuze, "Postscript on Control Societies," in *Negotiations*, 178.

126. Ibid.

127. Gilles Deleuze, Paris VIII Foucault seminar (8 April 1986), Bibliothèque nationale de France sound archive.

128. Ibid.

129. Deleuze, "Postscript on Control Societies," 180.

130. Ibid. 182.

CHAPTER 2

Theatrum Philosophicum

MICHEL FOUCAULT

I must discuss two books of exceptional merit and importance: *Difference and Repetition* and *The Logic of Sense.*[1] Indeed, these books are so outstanding that they are difficult to discuss; this may explain, as well, why so few have undertaken this task. I believe that these words will continue to revolve about us in enigmatic resonance with those of Klossowski, another major and excessive sign, and perhaps one day, this century will be known as Deleuzian.

One after another, I should like to explore the many paths that lead to the heart of these challenging tests. As Deleuze has said to me, however, this metaphor is misleading: there is no heart, but only a problem – that is, a distribution of notable points; there is no center but always decenterings, series, from one to another, with the limp of a presence and an absence – of an excess, of a deficiency. Abandon the circle, a faulty principle of return; abandon our tendency to organize everything into a sphere. All things return on the straight and narrow, by way of a straight and labyrinthine line. Thus, fibrils and bifurcation (Leiris's marvelous series would be well suited to a Deleuzian analysis).

Overturn Platonism: what philosophy has not tried? If we defined philosophy at the limit as any attempt, regardless of its source, to reverse Platonism, then philosophy begins with Aristotle; or better yet, it begins with Plato himself, with the conclusion of the *Sophist* where it is impossible to distinguish Socrates from the crafty imitator; or it begins with the Sophists who were extremely vocal about the rise of Platonism and who ridiculed its future greatness with their perpetual play on words.

Are all philosophies individual species of the genus "anti-Platonic"? Would each begin with a declaration of this fundamental rejection? Can they be grounded around this desired and detestable center? Should we instead *say* that the philosophical nature of a discourse is its Platonic differential, an element absent in Platonism but present in the discourse itself? A better formulation would be: It is an element in which the effect of absence is induced in the Platonic series through a new and divergent series (consequently, its function in the Platonic series is that of a signifier both excessive and absent); and it is also an element in which the Platonic series produces a free, floating, and excessive circulation in that other discourse. Plato, then, is the excessive and deficient father. It is useless to define a philosophy by its anti-Platonic character (as a plant is distinguished by its reproductive organs); but a philosophy can be distinguished somewhat in the manner in which a phantasm is defined, by the effect of a lack when it is distributed into its two constituent series-the "archaic" and the "real" – and you will dream of a general history of philosophy, a Platonic phantasmatology, and not an architecture of systems.

In any event, here is Deleuze. His "reversed Platonism" consists of displacing himself within the Platonic series in order to disclose an unexpected facet: division.[2] Plato did not establish a weak separation between the genus "hunter," "cook," or "politician," as the Aristotelians said; neither was he concerned with the particular characteristics of the species "fisherman" or "one who hunts with snares,"[3] he wished to discover the identity of the true hunter. *Who is?* and not *What is?* He searched for the authentic, the pure gold. Instead of subdividing, selecting, and pursuing a productive seam, he chose among the pretenders and ignored their fixed cadastral properties, he tested them with the strung bow, which eliminates all but one (the nameless one, the nomad). But how does one distinguish the false (the simulators, the "so-called") from the authentic (the unadulterated and pure)? Certainly not by discovering a law of the true and false (truth is not opposed to error but to false appearances), but by looking above these manifestations to a model, a model so pure that the actual purity of the "pure" resembles it, approximates it, and measures itself against it; a model that exists so forcefully that in its presence they sham vanity of the false copy is immediately reduced to nonexistence. With the abrupt appearance of Ulysses, the eternal husband, the false suitors disappear. *Exeunt* simulacra. Plato is said to have opposed essence to appearance, a higher world to this world below, the sun of truth to the shadows of the cave (and it becomes our duty to bring essences back into the world, to glorify the world, and to place the sun of truth within man). But Deleuze locates Plato's singularity in the delicate sorting, in this fine operation that precedes the discovery of essence precisely because it calls upon it, and tries to separate malign simulacra from the masses *[peuple] of* appearance. Thus it is useless to attempt the reversal of Platonism by reinstating the rights of appearances, ascribing to them solidity and meaning, and bringing them closer to essential forms by lending them a conceptual backbone: these timid creatures should not be encouraged to stand upright. Neither should we attempt to rediscover the supreme and solemn gesture that established, in a single stroke, the inaccessible Idea. Rather, we should welcome the cunning assembly that simulates and clamors at the door. And what will enter, submerging appearance and breaking its engagement to essence, will be the event; the incorporeal will dissipate the density of matter; a timeless insistence will destroy the circle that imitates eternity; an impenetrable singularity will divest itself of its contamination by purity; the actual semblance of the simulacrum will support the falseness of false appearances. The sophist springs up and challenges Socrates to prove that he is not the illegitimate usurper.

To reverse Platonism with Deleuze is to displace oneself insidiously within it, to descend a notch, to descend to its smallest gestures – discreet, but *moral* – which serve to exclude the simulacrum; it is also to deviate slightly from it, to open the door from either side to the small talk it excluded; it is to initiate another disconnected and divergent series; it is to construct, by way of this small lateral leap, a dethroned para-Platonism. To convert Platonism (a serious task) is to increase its compassion for reality, for the world, and for time. To subvert Platonism is to begin at the top (the vertical distance of irony) and to grasp its origin. To pervert Platonism is to search out the smallest details, to descend (with the natural gravitation of humor) as far as its crop of hair or the dirt under its fingernails – those things that were never hallowed by an idea; it is to discover the decentering it put into effect in order to recenter itself around the Model, the Identical, and the Same; it is the decentering of oneself with respect to Platonism so as to give rise to the play (as with every perversion) of surfaces at its border. Irony rises and subverts; humor falls and perverts.[4] To pervert Plato is to side with the Sophists' spitefulness, the unmannerly gestures of the Cynics, the arguments of the Stoics, and the fluttering chimeras of Epicurus. It is time to read Diogenes Laertius.

We should be alert to the surface effects in which the Epicurians take such pleasure:[5] emissions proceeding from deep within bodies and rising like the wisps of a fog – interior phantoms that are quickly reabsorbed into other depths by the sense of smell, by the mouth, by the appetites, extremely thin membranes that detach themselves from the surfaces of objects and proceed to impose colors and contours deep within our eyes (floating epiderm, visual idols); phantasms of fear or desire (cloud gods, the adorable face of the beloved, "miserable hope transported by the wind"). It is all this swarming of the impalpable that must be integrated into our thought: we must articulate a philosophy of the phantasm construed not through the intermediary of perception of the image, as being of the order of an originary given but, rather, left to come to light among the surfaces to which it is related, in the reversal that causes every interior to pass to the outside and every exterior to the inside, in the temporal oscillation that always makes it precede and follow itself – in short, in what Deleuze would perhaps not allow us to call its "incorporeal materiality."

It is useless, in any case, to seek a more substantial truth behind the phantasm, a truth to which it points as a rather confused sign (thus, the futility of "symptom-atologizing"); it is also useless to contain it within stable figures and to construct solid cores of convergence where we might include, on the basis of their identical properties, all its angles, flashes, membranes, and vapors (no possibility of "phenom-enalization"). Phantasms must be allowed to function at the limit of bodies; against bodies, because they stick to bodies and protrude from them, but also because they touch them, cut them, break them into sections, regionalize them, and multiply their surfaces; and equally, outside of bodies, because they function between bodies according to laws of proximity, torsion, and variable distance – laws of which they remain ignorant. Phantasms do not extend organisms into the imaginary; they topologize the materiality of the body. They should consequently be freed from the restrictions we impose upon them, freed from the dilemmas of truth and falsehood and of being and nonbeing (the essential difference between simulacrum and copy carried to its logical conclusion); they must be allowed to conduct their dance, to act out their mime, as "extrabeings."

The Logic of Sense can be read as the most alien book imaginable from *The Phenomenology of Perception*.[6] In this latter text, the body-organism is linked to the world through a network of primal significations which arise from the perception of things, while, according to Deleuze, phantasms form the impenetrable and incorporeal surface of bodies; and from this process, simultaneously topological and cruel, something is shaped that falsely presents itself as a centered organism and distributes at its periphery the increasing remoteness of things. More essentially, however, *The Logic of Sense* should be read as the boldest and most insolent of metaphysical treatises on the simple condition that instead of denouncing metaphysics as the neglect of being, we force it to speak of extrabeing. Physics: discourse dealing with the ideal structure of bodies, mixtures, reactions, internal and external mechanisms, metaphysics: discourse dealing with the materiality of incorporeal things – phantasms, idols, and simulacra.

Illusion is certainly the misfortune of metaphysics, but not because metaphysics, by its very nature, is doomed to illusion, but because for too long it has been haunted by illusion and because, in its fear of the simulacrum, it was forced to hunt down the illusory. Metaphysics is not illusory – it is not merely another species of this particular genus – but illusion is a metaphysics. It is the product of a particular metaphysics that designated the separation between the simulacrum on one side and the original and the perfect copy on the other. There was a critique whose task was to unearth metaphysical illusion and to establish its necessity; Deleuze's metaphysics, however, initiates the necessary critique for the disillusioning of phantasms. With this grounding, the way is cleared for the advance of the Epicurean and materialist series, for the pursuit of their singular zigzag. And it does not lead, in spite of itself, to a shameful metaphysics; it leads joyously to metaphysics – a metaphysics freed from its original profundity as well as from a supreme being, but also one that can conceive of the phantasm in its play of surfaces without the aid of models, a metaphysics where it is no longer a question of the One Good but of the absence of God and the epidermic play of perversity. A dead God and sodomy are the thresholds of the new metaphysical ellipse. Where natural theology contained metaphysical illusion in itself and where this illusion was always more or less related to natural theology, the metaphysics of the phantasm revolves around atheism and transgression. Sade and Bataille and, somewhat later, the/palm upturned in a gesture of defense and invitation, Roberte.[7]

Moreover, this series of liberated simulacrum is activated, or mimes itself, on two privileged sites: that of psychoanalysis, which should eventually be understood as a metaphysical practice since it concerns itself with phantasms; and that of the theater, which is multiplied, polyscenic, simultaneous, broken into separate scenes that refer to each other, and where we encounter, without any trace of representation (copying or imitating), the dance of masks, the cries of bodies, and the gesturing of hands and fingers. And throughout each of these two recent and divergent series (the attempt to "reconcile" these series, to reduce them to either perspective, to produce a ridiculous "psychodrama," has been extremely naive), Freud and Artaud exclude each other and give rise to a mutual resonance. The philosophy of representation – of the original, the first time, resemblance, imitation, faithfulness – is dissolving; and the arrow of the simulacrum released by the Epicureans is headed in our direction. It gives birth – rebirth – to a "phantasmaphysics."

Occupying the other side of Platonism are the Stoics. Observing Deleuze in his discussion of Epicurus and Zeno, of Lucretius and Chrysippus, I was forced to conclude that his procedure was rigorously Freudian. He does not proceed – with a drum roll – toward the great Repression of Western philosophy; he registers, as if in passing, its oversights. He points out its interruption, its gaps, those small things of little value neglected by philosophical discourse. He carefully reintroduces the barely perceptible omissions, knowing full well that they imply an unlimited negligence. Through the insistence of our pedagogical tradition, we are accustomed to reject the Epicurean simulacra as useless and somewhat puerile; and the famous battle of Stoicism, which took place yesterday and will reoccur tomorrow, has become cause for amusement in the schools. Deleuze did well to combine these tenuous threads and to play, in his own fashion, with this network of discourses, arguments, replies, and paradoxes, those elements that circulated for many centuries throughout the Mediterranean. We should not scorn Hellenistic confusion or Roman platitudes but listen to those things said on the great surface of the empire; we should be attentive to those things that happened in a thousand instances, dispersed on every side: fulgurating battles, assassinated generals, burning triremes, queens poisoning themselves, victories that invariably led to further upheavals, the endlessly exemplary Actium, the eternal event.

To consider a pure event, it must first be given a metaphysical basis.[8] But we must be agreed that it cannot be the metaphysics of substances, which can serve as a foundation for accidents; nor can it be a metaphysics of coherence, which situates these accidents in the entangled nexus of causes and effects. The event – a wound, a victory-defeat, death – is always an effect produced entirely by bodies colliding, mingling, or separating, but this effect is never of a corporeal nature; it is the intangible, inaccessible battle that turns and repeats itself a thousand times around

Fabricius, above the wounded Prince Andrew.[9] The weapons that tear into bodies form an endless incorporeal battle. Physics concerns causes, but events, which arise as its effects, no longer belong to it. Let us imagine a stitched causality: as bodies collide, mingle, and suffer, they create events on their surfaces, events that are without thickness, mixture, or passion; for this reason, they can no longer be causes. They form, among themselves, another kind of succession whose links derive from a quasi-physics of incorporeal – in short, from metaphysics.

Events also require a more complex logic.[10] An event is not a state of things, something that could serve as a referent for a proposition (the fact of death is a state of things in relation to which an assertion can be true or false; dying is a pure event that can never verify anything). For a ternary logic, traditionally centered on the referent, we must substitute an interrelationship based on four terms. "Marc Antony is dead" *designates* a state of things; *expresses* my opinion or belief; *signifies* an affirmation; and, in addition, has a *meaning*: "dying." An intangible meaning with one side turned toward things because "dying" is something that occurs, as an event, to Antony, and the other toward the proposition because "dying" is what is said about Antony in a statement. To die: a dimension of the proposition; an incorporeal effect produced by a sword; a meaning and an event; a point without thickness or substance of which someone speaks, which roams the surface of things. We should not restrict meaning to the cognitive core that lies at the heart of a knowable object; rather, we should allow it to re-establish its flux at the limit of words and things, as what is said of a thing (not its attribute or the thing in itself) and as something that happens (not its process or its state). Death supplies the best example, being both the event of events and meaning in its purest state. Its domain is the anonymous flow of discourse; it is that of which we speak as always past or about to happen, and yet it occurs at the extreme point of singularity. A meaning-event is as neutral as death: "not the end, but the unending; not a particular death, but any death; not true death, but as Kafka said, the snicker of its devastating error."[11]

Finally, this meaning-event requires a grammar with a different form of organization,[12] since it cannot be situated in a proposition as an attribute (to be *dead*, to be *alive*, to be *red*) but is fastened to the verb (to die, to live, to redden). The verb, conceived in this fashion, has two principal forms around which the others are distributed; the present tense, which posits an event, and the infinitive, which introduces meaning into language and allows it to circulate as the neutral element to which we refer in discourse. We should not seek the grammar of events in temporal inflections; nor should we seek the grammar of meaning in fictitious analysis of the type: to live = to be alive. The grammar of the meaning-event revolves around two asymmetrical and hobbling poles: the infinitive mode and the present tense. The meaning-event is always both the displacement of the present and the eternal repetition of the infinitive. To die is never localized in the density of a given moment, but from its flux it infinitely divides the shortest moment. To die is even smaller than the moment it takes to think it, and yet dying is indefinitely repeated on either side of this widthless crack. The eternal present? Only on the condition that we conceive the present as lacking plenitude and the eternal as lacking unity: the (multiple) eternity of the (displaced) present.

To summarize: At the limit of dense bodies, an event is incorporeal (a metaphysical surface); on the surface of words and things, an incorporeal event is the *meaning* of a proposition (its logical dimension); in the thread of discourse, an incorporeal meaning-event is fastened to the verb (the infinitive point of the present).

In the more or less recent past, there have been, I think, three major attempts at conceptualizing the event: neopositivism, phenomenology, and the philosophy of history. Neopositivism failed to grasp the distinctive level of the event; because of its logical error, the confusion of an event with a state of things, it had no choice but to lodge the event within the density of bodies, to treat it as a material process, and to attach itself more or less explicitly to a physicalism ("in a schizoid fashion," it reduced surfaces into depth); as for grammar, it transformed the event into an attribute. Phenomenology, on the other hand, reoriented the event with respect to meaning: either it placed the bare event before or to the side of meaning – the rock of facticity, the mute inertia of occurrences – and then submitted it to the active processes of meaning, to its digging and elaboration; or else it assumed a domain of primal significations which always existed as a disposition of the world around the self, tracing its paths and privileged locations, indicating in advance where the event might occur and its possible form. Either the cat whose good sense precedes the smile or the common sense of the smile that anticipates the cat. Either Sartre or Merleau-Ponty. For them, meaning never coincides with an event; and from this evolves a logic of signification, a grammar of the first person, and a metaphysics of consciousness. As for the philosophy of history, it encloses the event in a cyclical pattern of time. Its error is grammatical; it treats the present as framed by the past and future: the present is a former future where its form was prepared; it is the past to come, which preserves the identity of its content. On the one hand, this sense of the present requires a logic of essences (which establishes the present in memory) and of concepts (where the present is established as a knowledge of the future), and on the other, a metaphysics of a crowned and coherent cosmos, of a hierarchical world.

Thus, three philosophies that fail to grasp the event. The first, on the pretext that nothing can be said about those things which lie "outside" the world, rejects the pure surface of the event and attempts to enclose it forcibly – as a referent – in the spherical plenitude of the world. The second, on the pretext that signification only exists for consciousness, places the event outside and beforehand, or inside and after, and always situates it with respect to the circle of the self. The third, on the pretext that events can only exist in time, defines its identity and submits it to a solidly centered order. The world, the self, and God (a sphere, a circle, and a center): three conditions that make it impossible to think through the event. Deleuze's proposals, I believe, are directed to lifting this triple subjection that, to this day, is imposed on the event: a metaphysics of the incorporeal event (which is consequently irreducible to a physics of the world), a logic of neutral meaning (rather than a phenomenology of signification based on the subject), and a thought of the present infinitive (and not the raising up of the conceptual future in a past essence).

We have arrived at the point where the two series of the event and the phantasm are brought into resonance – the resonance of the incorporeal and the intangible, the resonance of battles, of death that subsists and insists, of the fluttering and desirable idol: it subsists not in the heart of man but above his head, beyond the clash of weapons, of fate and desire. It is not that they converge in a common point, in some phantasmatic event, or in the primary origin of a simulacrum. The event is that which is invariably lacking in the series of the phantasm – its absence indicates its repetition devoid of any grounding in an original, outside of all forms of imitation, and freed from the constraints of similitude. Consequently, it is disguise of repetition, the always-singular mask that conceals nothing, simulacra without dissimulation, incongruous finery covering a nonexistent nudity, pure difference.

As for the phantasm, it is "excessive" with respect to the singularity of the event, but this "excess" does not designate an imaginary supplement adding itself to the bare reality of facts; nor does it form a sort of embryonic generality from which the organization of the concept gradually emerges. To conceive of death or a battle as a phantasm is not to confuse them either with the old image of death suspended over a senseless accident or with the future concept of a battle secretly organizing the present disordered tumult; the battle rages from one blow to the next, and the process of death indefinitely repeats the blow, always in its possession, which it inflicts once and for all. This conception of the phantasm as the play of the (missing) event and its repetition must not be given the form of individuality (a form inferior to the concept and therefore, informal), nor must it be measured against reality (a reality that imitates an image); it presents itself as universal singularity: to die, to fight, to vanquish, to be vanquished.

The Logic of Sense tells us how to think through the event *and* the phantasm, their severed and double affirmation, their affirmation of disjunction. Determining an event on the basis of a concept, by denying any importance to repetition, is perhaps what might be called knowing *[connaitre]*; and measuring the phantasm against reality, by going in search of its origin, is judging. Philosophy tried to do both; it dreamed of itself as a science, and presented itself as a critique. Thinking, on the other hand, would amount to effectuating the phantasm in the mime that produces it at a single stroke; it would make the event indefinite so that it repeats itself as a singular universal. Thinking in the absolute would thus amount to thinking through the event *and* the phantasm. A further clarification: If the role of thought is to produce the phantasm theatrically and to repeat the universal event in its extreme point of singularity, then what is thought itself if not the event that befalls the phantasm and the phantasmatic repetition of the absent event? The phantasm and the event, affirmed in disjunction, are the object of thought *[le penser]* and thought itself *[la pensée]* on the surface of bodies they place the extra being that only thought can think through; and they trace the topological event where thought itself is formed. Thought has to think through what forms it, and is formed out of what it thinks through. The critique-knowledge duality is perfectly useless: thought says what it is.

This formulation, however, is a bit dangerous. It connotes equivalence and allows us once more to imagine the identification of an object and a subject. This would be entirely false. That the object of thought *[le penser]* forms thought *[la pensée]* implies, on the contrary, a double dissociation: that of a central and founding subject to which events occur while it deploys meaning around itself; and of an object that is a threshold and point of convergence for recognizable forms and the attributes we affirm. We must conceive of an indefinite, straight line that (far from bearing events as a string supports its knots) cuts and recuts each moment so many times that each event arises both incorporeal and indefinitely multiple. We must conceptualize not the synthesizing and synthesized subject but rather a certain insurmountable fissure. Moreover, we must conceptualize a series, without any original anchor, of simulacra, idols, and phantasms which, in the temporal duality in which they are formed are always the two sides of the fissure from which they are made signs and are put into place as signs. The fissure of the I and the series of signifying points do not form a unity that permits thought to be both subject and object, but they are themselves the event of thought *[la pensée]*and the incorporeality of what is thought *[le penser]*, the object of thought *[le penser]* as a problem (a multiplicity of dispersed points) and thought *[la pensée]* as mime (repetition without a model).

This is why *The Logic of Sense* could have as a subtitle: *What Is Thinking?* A question that Deleuze always inscribes twice through the length of his book – in the text of a stoic logic of the incorporeal, and in the text of a Freudian analysis of the phantasm. What is thinking? Listen to the stoics, who tell us how it might be possible to have thought about *what is thought*. Read Freud, who tells us how *thought* might think. Perhaps we arrive here for the first time at a theory of thought that is entirely disburdened of the subject and the object The thought-event is as singular as a throw of the dice; the thought-phantasm does not search for truth, but repeats thought.

In any case, we understand Deleuze's repeated emphasis on the mouth in *The Logic of Sense*. It is through this mouth, as Zeno recognized, that cartloads of food pass as well as carts of meaning ("If you say cart, a cart passes through your mouth"). The mouth, the orifice, the canal where the child intones the simulacra, the dismembered parts, and bodies without organs; the mouth in which depths and surfaces are articulated. Also the mouth from which falls the voice of the other giving rise to lofty idols that flutter above the child and from the superego. The mouth where cries are broken into phonemes, morphemes, semantemes: the mouth where the profundity of an oral body separates itself from incorporeal meaning. Through this open mouth, through this alimentary voice, the genesis of language, the formation of meaning, and the flash of thought extend their divergent series.[13] I would enjoy discussing Deleuze's rigorous phonocentrism were it not for the fact of a constant phonodecentering. Let Deleuze receive homage from the fantastic grammarian, from the dark precursor who nicely situated the remarkable facets of this decentering:

Les dents, la bouche
Les dents la bouchent
L'aidant la bouche
Laides en la bouche
Lait dans la bouche, etc.

The Logic of Sense causes us to reflect on matters that philosophy has neglected for many centuries: the event (assimilated in a concept, from which we vainly attempted to extract in the form *of a fact,* verifying a proposition, of *actual experience,* a modality of the subject, of *concreteness,* the empirical content of history); and the phantasm (reduced in the name of reality and situated at the extremity, the pathological pole, of a normative sequence: perception – image – memory – illusion). After all, what most urgently needs thought in this century, if not the event and the phantasm?

We should thank Deleuze for his efforts. He did not revive the tiresome slogans: Freud with Marx, Marx with Freud, and both, if you please, with us. He analyzed clearly the essential elements for establishing the thought of the event and the phantasm. His aim was not reconciliation (to expand the farthest reaches of an event with the imaginary density of a phantasm, or to ballast a floating phantasm by adding a grain of actual history); he discovered the philosophy that permits the disjunctive affirmation of both. Even before *The Logic of Sense,* Deleuze formulated this philosophy with completely unguarded boldness in *Difference and Repetition,* and we must now turn to this earlier work.

Instead of denouncing the fundamental omission that is presumed to have inaugurated Western culture, Deleuze, with the patience of a Nietzschean genealogist, points to the variety of small impurities and paltry compromises.[14] He tracks down the minuscule, repetitive act of cowardice and all those features of folly, vanity, and complacency which endlessly nourish the philosophical mushroom – what Michel Leiris might call "ridiculous rootlets." We all possess good sense, we all make mistakes, but no one is dumb (certainly, none of us). There is no thought without goodwill; every real problem has a solution, because our apprenticeship is to a master who has answers for the questions he poses; the world is our classroom. A whole series of insignificant beliefs. But in reality, we encounter the tyranny of goodwill, the obligation to think "in common" with others, the domination of a pedagogical model, and most important, the exclusion of stupidity – the disreputable morality of thought whose function in our society is easy to decipher. We must liberate ourselves from these constraints; and in perverting this morality, philosophy itself is disoriented.

Take difference. It is generally assumed to be a difference *from or within* something; behind difference, beyond it – but as its support, its site, its delimitation, and consequently, as the source of its mastery – we pose, through the concept, the unity of a group and its breakdown into species in the operation of difference (the organic domination of the Aristotelian concept). Difference is transformed into that which must be specified within a concept, without overstepping its bounds. And yet, above the species, we encounter the swarming of individualities. What is this boundless diversity which eludes specification and remains outside the concept, if not the resurgence of repetition? Underneath the ovine species, we are reduced to counting sheep. This stands as the first form of subjectivation: difference as specification (within the concept) and repetition as the indifference of individuals (outside the concept). But subjectivation to what? To common sense which, turning away from mad flux and anarchic difference, knows how, everywhere and always in the same manner, to recognize what is identical; common sense extracts the generality of an object while it simultaneously establishes the universality of the knowing subject through a pact of goodwill. But what if we gave free rein to ill will? What if thought freed itself from common sense and decided to function only in its extreme singularity? What if it made malign use of the skew of the paradox, instead of complacently accepting its citizenship in the *doxa*? What if it conceived of difference differentially, instead of searching out the common elements underlying difference? Then difference would disappear as a general feature that leads to the generality of the concept, and it would become – a different thought, the thought of difference – a pure event. As for repetition, it would cease to be the dreary succession of the identical, and would become displaced difference. Thought is no longer committed to the construction of concepts once it escapes goodwill and the administration of common sense, concerned as it is with division and characterization. Rather, it produces a meaning-event by repeating a phantasm. The morally good will to think within common sense thought had the fundamental role of protecting thought from its genital singularity.

But let us reconsider the functioning of the concept. For the concept to master difference, perception must apprehend global resemblances (which will then be decomposed into differences and partial identities) at the root of what we call "diversity." Each new representation must be accomplished by those representations which display the full range of resemblances; and in this space of representation (sensation – image – memory), likenesses are put to the test of quantitative equalization and graduated quantities, and in this way the immense table of measurable differences is constructed. In the corner of this graph, on its horizontal axis where the smallest quantitative gap meets the smallest qualitative variation, at this zero point, we encounter perfect resemblance, exact repetition. Repetition which, within the concept, was only the impertinent vibration of identities, becomes, within a system of representation, the organizing principle for similarities. But *what* recognizes these similarities, the exactly alike and the least similar – the greatest and the smallest, the brightest and the darkest – if not good sense? Good sense is the world's most effective agent of division in its recognitions, its establishment of equivalences, its sensitivity to gaps, its gauging of distances, as it assimilates and separates. And it is good sense that reigns in the philosophy of representations. Let us pervert good sense and allow thought to play outside the ordered table of resemblances; then it will appear as the vertical dimension of intensities, because intensity, well before its gradation by representation, is in itself pure difference: difference that displaces and repeats itself, contracts and expands; a singular point that constricts and slackens the indefinite repetitions in an acute event. One must give rise to thought as intensive irregularity. Dissolution of the Me.

A last consideration with respect to the table of representation. The meeting point of the axes is the point of perfect resemblance, and from this arises the scale of differences as so many lesser resemblances, marked identities: differences arise when representation can only partially present what was previously present, when the test of recognition is stymied. For a thing to be different, it must first no longer be the same; and it is on this negative basis, above the shadowy part that delimits the same, that contrary predicates are then articulated. In the philosophy of representation, the relationship of two predicates, like red and green, is merely the highest level of a complex structure: the *contradiction* between red and not-red (based on the model of *being* and *nonbeing*) is active on the lowest level; the non identity of red and green (on the basis of a *negative* test of *recognition*) is situated above this; and this ultimately leads to the *exclusive* position of red and green (in the table where the *genus* color is *specified*). Thus for a third time, but in an even more radical manner, difference is held fast within an oppositional, negative, and contradictory system. For difference to have a place, it was necessary to divide the "same" through contradiction, to limit its infinite identity through nonbeing, to transform its indeterminate positivity through the negative. Given the priority of the same, difference could only arise through these mediations. As for the repetitive, it is produced precisely at the point where the barely launched mediation falls back on itself; when, instead of saying no, it twice pronounces the same yes, and when, instead of distributing oppositions into a system of definitions, it turns back indefinitely to the same position. Repetition betrays the weakness of the same at the moment when it can no longer negate itself in the other, when it can no longer recapture itself in the other. Repetition, at one time pure exteriority and a pure figure of the origin, has been transformed into an internal weakness, a deficiency of finitude, a sort of stuttering of the negative – the neurosis of dialectics. For it was indeed toward dialectics that the philosophy of representation was headed.

And yet, how is it that we fail to recognize Hegel as the philosopher of the greater differences and Leibniz as the thinker of the smallest differences? In actuality, dialectics does not liberate differences; it guarantees, on the contrary, that they can always be recaptured. The dialectical sovereignty of the same consists in permitting differences to exist but always under the rule of the negative, as an instance of nonbeing. They may appear to be the successful subversion of the Other, but contradiction secretly assists in the salvation of identities. Is it necessary to recall the unchanging pedagogical origin of dialectics? What ceaselessly reactivates it, what causes the endless rebirth of the aporia of being and nonbeing, is the humble classroom interrogation, the student's fictive dialogue: "This is red; that is not red. At this moment, it is light outside. No, now it is dark." In the twilight of an October sky, Minerva's bird flies close to the ground: "Write it down, write it down," it croaks, "tomorrow morning, it will no longer be dark."

The freeing of difference requires thought without contradiction, without dialectics, without negation; thought that accepts divergence; affirmative thought whose instrument is disjunction; thought of the multiple – of the nomadic and dispersed multiplicity that is not limited or confined by the constraints of the same; thought that does not conform to a pedagogical model (the fakery of prepared answers) but attacks insoluble problems – that is, a thought which addresses a multiplicity of exceptional points, which is displaced as we distinguish their conditions and which insists upon and subsists in the play of repetitions. Far from being the still incomplete and blurred image of an Idea that would, from on high and for all time, hold the answer, the problem lies in the idea itself, or rather, the Idea exists only in the form of a problem: a distinctive plurality whose obscurity is nevertheless insistent, and in which the question ceaselessly stirs. What is the answer to the question? The problem. How is the problem resolved? By displacing the question. The problem escapes the logic of the excluded third, because it is a dispersed multiplicity; it cannot be resolved by the clear distinctions of a Cartesian idea, because as an idea it is obscure-distinct; it seriously disobeys the Hegelian negative because it is a multiple affirmation; it is not subjected to the contradiction of being and nonbeing, since it is being. We must think problematically rather than question and answer dialectically.

The conditions for thinking of difference and repetition, as we have seen, have undergone a progressive expansion. First, it was necessary, along with Aristotle, to abandon the identity of the concept, to reject resemblance within representation, and simultaneously to free ourselves from the philosophy of representation; and now, it is necessary to free ourselves from Hegel – from the opposition of predicates, from contradiction and negation, from all of dialectics. But there is yet a fourth condition, and it is even more formidable than the others. The most tenacious subjectivation of difference is undoubtedly that maintained by categories. By showing the number of different ways in which being can express itself, by specifying its forms of attribution, by imposing in a certain way the distribution of existing things, categories create a condition where being maintains its undifferentiated repose at the highest level. Categories dictate the play of affirmations and negations, establish the legitimacy of resemblances within representation, and guarantee the objectivity and operation of concepts. They suppress anarchic difference, divide differences into zones, delimit their rights, and prescribe their task of specification with respect to individual beings. On one side, they can be understood as the a priori forms of knowledge, but, on the other, they appear as an archaic morality, the ancient decalogue that the identical imposed upon difference. Difference can only be liberated through the invention of an acategorical thought. But perhaps invention is a misleading word, since in the history of philosophy there have been at least two radical formulations of the univocity of being – those given by Duns Scotus and Spinoza. In Duns Scotus's philosophy, However, being is neutral, while for Spinoza it is based on substance; in both contexts, the elimination of categories and the affirmation that being is expressed for all things in the same way had the single objective of maintaining the unity of being. Let us imagine, on the contrary, an ontology where being would be expressed in the same fashion for every difference, but could only express differences. Consequently, things could no longer be completely covered over, as in Duns Scotus, by the great monochrome abstraction of being, and Spinoza's modes would no longer revolve around the unity of substance. Differences would revolve of their own accord, being would be expressed in the same fashion for all these differences, and being would be no longer a unity that guides and distributes them but their repetition as differences. For Deleuze, the noncategorical univocity of being does not directly attach the multiple to unity itself (the universal neutrality of being, or the expressive force of substance); it puts being into play as that which is repetitively expressed as difference. Being is the recurrence of difference, without there being any difference in the form of its expression. Being does not distribute itself into regions; the real is not subordinated to the possible; and the contingent is not opposed to the necessary. Whether the battle of Actium or the death of Antony were necessary or not, the being of both these pure events – to fight, to die – is expressed in the same manner, in the same way that it is expressed with respect to the phantasmatic castration that occurred and did not occur. The suppression of categories, the affirmation of the univocity of being, and the repetitive revolution of being around difference – these are the final conditions for the thought of the phantasm and the event. We have not quite reached the conclusion. We must return to this "recurrence," but let us pause a moment.

Can it be said that Bouvard and Pecuchet make mistakes?[15] Do they commit blunders whenever an opportunity presents itself? If they make mistakes, it is because there are rules that underline their failures and under certain definable conditions they might have succeeded. Nevertheless, their failure is constant, whatever their action, whatever their knowledge, whether or not they follow the rules, whether the books they consulted were good or bad. Everything befalls their undertaking – errors, of course, but also fires, frost, the foolishness and perversity of men, a dog's anger. Their efforts were not wrong; they were totally botched. To be wrong is to mistake a cause for another; it is not to foresee accidents; it may derive from a faulty knowledge of substances or from the confusion of necessities with possibilities. We are mistaken if we apply categories carelessly and inopportunely, but it is altogether different to ruin a project completely: it is to ignore the framework of categories (and not simply their points of application). If Bouvard and Pecuchet are reasonably certain of precisely those things which are largely improbable, it is not that they are mistaken in their discrimination of the possible but that they confuse all aspects of reality with every form of possibility (this is why the most improbable events conform to the most natural of their expectations). They confuse or, rather, are confused by the necessity of their knowledge and the contingency of the seasons, the existence of things, and the shadows found in books: an accident, for them, possesses the obstinacy of a substance, and those substances seized them by the throat in their experimental accidents. Such is their grand and pathetic stupidity, and it is incomparable to the meager foolishness of those who surround them and make mistakes, the others whom they rightfully disdain. Within categories, one makes mistakes; outside of them, beyond or beneath them, one is stupid. Bouvard and Pecuchet are acategorical beings.

These comments allow us to isolate a use of categories that may not be immediately apparent; by creating a space for the operation of truth and falsity; by situating the free supplement of error, categories silently reject stupidity. In a commanding voice, they instruct us in the ways of knowledge and solemnly alert us to the possibilities of error, while in a whisper they guarantee our intelligence and form the a priori of excluded stupidity. Thus we court danger in wanting to be freed from categories; no sooner do we abandon them than we face the magma of stupidity and risk being surrounded not by a marvelous multiplicity of differences but by equivalences, ambiguities, the "it all comes down to the same thing," a leveling uniformity, and the thermodynamism of every miscarried effort. To think in the form of the categories is to know the truth so that it can be distinguished from the false; to think "acategorically" is to confront a black stupidity and, in a flash, to distinguish oneself from it. Stupidity is contemplated: sight penetrates its domain and becomes fascinated; it carries one gently along and its action is mimed in the abandonment of oneself; we support ourselves on its amorphous fluidity; we await the first leap of an imperceptible difference, and blankly, without fever, we watch to see the glimmer of light return. Error demands rejection – we can erase it; we accept stupidity – we see it, we repeat it, and softly, we call for total immersion.

This is the greatness of Warhol with his canned foods, senseless accidents, and his series of advertising smiles: the oral and nutritional equivalence of those half-open lips, teeth, tomato sauce, that hygiene based on detergents; the equivalence of death in the cavity of an eviscerated car, at the top of a telephone pole and at the end of a wire, and between the glistening, steel blue arms of the electric chair. "It's the same either way," stupidity says, while sinking into itself and infinitely extending its nature with the things it says of itself; "Here or there, it's always the same thing; what difference if the colors vary, if they're darker or lighter. It's all so senseless – life, women, death! How stupid this stupidity!" But, in concentrating on this boundless monotony, we find the sudden illumination of multiplicity itself – with nothing at its center, at its highest point, or beyond it – a flickering of light that travels even faster than the eyes and successively lights up the moving labels and the captive snapshots that refer to each other to eternity, without ever saying anything: suddenly, arising from the background of the old inertia of equivalences, the zebra stripe of the event tears through the darkness, and the eternal phantasm informs that soup can, that singular and depthless face.

Intelligence does not respond to stupidity, since it is stupidity already vanquished, the categorical art of avoiding error. The scholar is intelligent. It is thought, though, that confronts stupidity, and it is the philosopher who observes it. Their private conversation is a lengthy one, as the philosopher's sight plunges into this candleless skull. It is his death mask, his temptation, perhaps his desire, his catatonic theater. At the limit, thought would be the intense contemplation from close up – to the point of losing oneself in it – of stupidity; and its other side is formed by lassitude, immobility, excessive fatigue, obstinate muteness, and inertia – or, rather, they form its accompaniment, the daily and thankless exercise which prepares it and which it suddenly dissipates. The philosopher must have sufficiently ill will to play the game of truth and error badly: this perversity, which operates in para doxes, allows him to escape the grasp of categories. But aside from this, he must be sufficiently "ill humored" to persist in the confrontation with stupidity, to remain motionless to the point of stupefaction in order to approach it successfully and mime it, to let it slowly grow within himself (this is probably what we politely refer to as being absorbed in one's thoughts), and to await, in the always-unpredictable conclusion to this elaborate preparation, the shock of difference. Once paradoxes have upset the table of representation, catatonia operates within the theater of thought.

We can easily see how LSD inverts the relationships of ill humor, stupidity, and thought: it no sooner eliminates the supremacy of categories than it tears away the ground of its indifference and disintegrates the gloomy dumbshow of stupidity; and it presents this univocal and acategorical mass not only as variegated, mobile, asymmetrical, decentered, spiraloid, and reverberating but causes it to rise, at each instant, as a swarming of phantasm-events. As it slides on this surface at once regular and intensely vibratory, as it is freed from its catatonic chrysalis, thought invariably contemplates this indefinite equivalence transformed into an acute event and a sumptuous, appareled repetition. Opium produces other effects: thought gathers unique differences into a point, eliminates the background and deprives immobility of its task of contemplating and soliciting stupidity through its mime. Opium ensures a weightless immobility, the stupor of a butterfly that differs from catatonic rigidity; and, far beneath, it establishes a ground that no longer stupidly absorbs all differences but allows them to arise and sparkle as so many minute, distanced, smiling, and eternal events. Drugs – if we can speak of them generally – have nothing at all to do with truth and falsity; only to fortune-tellers do they reveal a world "more truthful than the real." In fact, they displace the relative positions of stupidity and thought by eliminating the old necessity of a theater of immobility. But perhaps, if it is given to thought to confront stupidity, drugs, which mobilize it, which color, agitate, furrow, and dissipate it, which populate it with differences and substitute for the rare flash a continuous phosphorescence, are the source of a partial thought – perhaps.[16] At any rate, in a state deprived of drugs, thought possesses two horns: one is ill will (to baffle categories) and the other ill humor (to point to stupidity and transfix it). We are far from the old sage who invests so much goodwill in his search for the truth that he can contemplate with equanimity the indifferent diversity of changing fortunes and things; far from the irritability of Schopenhauer, who became annoyed with things that did not return to their indifference of their own accord. But we are also distant from the "melancholy" that makes itself indifferent to the world, and whose immobility – alongside books and a globe – indicates the profundity of thought and the diversity of knowledge. Exercising its ill will and ill humor, thought awaits the outcome of this theater of perverse practices: the sudden shift of the kaleidoscope, signs that light up for an instant, the results of the thrown dice, the destiny of another game. Thinking does not provide consolation or happiness. Like a perversion, it languidly drags itself out; it repeats itself with determination upon a stage; at a stroke, it flings itself outside the dice box. At the moment when chance, the theater, and perversions enter into resonance, when chance dictates a resonance among the three, then thought becomes a trance; and it becomes worthwhile to think.

The univocity of being, its singleness of expression, is paradoxically the principal condition that permits difference to escape the domination of identity, frees it from the law of the Same as a simple opposition within conceptual elements. Being can express itself in the same way, because difference is no longer submitted to the prior reduction of categories; because it is not distributed inside a diversity that can always be perceived; because it is not organized in a conceptual hierarchy of species and genus. Being is that which is always said of difference; it is the *Recurrence* of difference.[17]

With this term, we can avoid the use of both *Becoming* and *Return*, because differences are not the elements – not even the fragmentary, intermingled, or monstrously confused elements – of an extended evolution that carries them along in its course and occasionally allows their masked or naked reappearance. The synthesis of Becoming might seem somewhat slack, but it nevertheless maintains a unity – not only and not especially that of an infinite container but also the unity of fragments, of passing and recurring moments, and of the floating consciousness that recognizes it. Consequently, we are led to mistrust Dionysus and his Bacchantes even in their state of intoxication. As for the Return, must it be the perfect circle, the well-oiled millstone that turns on its axis and reintroduces things, forms, and men at their appointed time? Must there be a center and must events occur on its periphery? Even Zarathustra could not tolerate this idea:

"Everything straight lies," murmured the dwarf disdainfully. "All truth is crooked, time itself is a circle."

"Spirit of Gravity," I said angrily, "you do treat this too lightly."

And convalescing, he groans:

"Alas! Man will return eternally, abject man will return eternally."

Perhaps what Zarathustra is proclaiming is not the circle; or perhaps the intolerable image of the circle is the last sign of a higher form of thought; perhaps, like the young shepherd, we must break this circular ruse – like Zarathustra himself, who bit off the head of a serpent and immediately spat it away.

Chronos is the time of becoming and new beginnings. Piece by piece, Chronos swallows the things to which it gives birth and which it causes to be reborn in its own time. This monstrous and lawless becoming – the endless devouring of each instant, the swallowing-up of the totality of life, the scattering of its limbs – is linked to the exactitude of rebeginning. Becoming leads into this great, interior labyrinth, a labyrinth no different in nature from the monster it contains. But from the depths of this convoluted and inverted architecture, a solid thread allows us to retrace our steps and to rediscover the same light of day. Dionysus with Ariadne: you have become my labyrinth. But Aeon is *recurrence* itself, the straight line of time, a splitting quicker than thought and narrower than any instant. It causes the same present to arise – on both sides of this indefinitely splitting arrow – as always existing, as indefinitely present, and as indefinite future. It is important to understand that this does not imply a succession of present instances which derive from a continuous flux and that, as a result of their plenitude, allow us to perceive the thickness of the past and the horizon of a future in which they, in turn, become the past. Rather, it is the straight line of the future that repeatedly cuts the smallest width of the present, that indefinitely recuts it starting from itself. We can trace this schism to its limbs, but we will never find the indivisible atom that ultimately serves as the minutely present unity of time (time is always more supple than thought). On both sides of the wound we invariably find that the schism has already happened (and that it had already taken place, and that it had already happened that it had already taken place), and that it will happen again (and in the future, it will happen again): it is

less a cut than a constant fibrillation. Time is what repeats itself; and the present –
split by this arrow of the future that carries it forward by always causing its swerv-
ing on both sides – endlessly recurs. But it recurs as singular difference; and the
analogous, the similar, and the identical never return. Difference recurs; and being,
expressing itself in the same manner with respect to difference, is never the universal
flux of Becoming; nor is the well-centered circle of the identical. Being is a Return
freed from the curvature of the circle; it is Recurrence. Consequently, three deaths
of Becoming, the devouring Father-mother in labor; of the circle, by which the gift
of life passes to the flowers each springtime; of recurrence – the repetitive fibrillation
of the present, the eternal and dangerous fissure fully given in an instant, affirmed
in a single stroke once and for all.

By virtue of its splintering and repetition, the present is a throw of the dice. This
is not because it forms part of a game in which it insinuates small contingencies or
elements of uncertainty. It is at once the chance within the game and the game itself
as chance; in the same stroke, both the dice and rules are thrown, so that chance
is not broken into pieces and parceled out but is totally affirmed in a single throw.
The present as the recurrence of difference, as repetition giving voice to difference,
affirms at once the totality of chance. The univocity of being in Duns Scotus led to
the immobility of an abstraction, in Spinoza it led to the necessity and eternity of
substance; but here it leads to the single throw of chance in the fissure of the present. If being always declares itself in the same way, it is not because being is one but
because the totality of chance is affirmed in the single dice throw of the present.

Can we say that the univocity of being has been formulated on three different
occasions in the history of philosophy, by Duns Scotus and Spinoza and finally by
Nietzsche – the first to conceive of univocity as returning and not as an abstraction
or a substance? Perhaps we should say that Nietzsche went as far as the thought
of the Eternal Return; more precisely, he pointed to it as an intolerable thought.
Intolerable because, as soon as its first signs are perceived, it fixes itself in that image
of the circle which carries in itself the fatal threat that all things will return – the
spider's reiteration. But this intolerable must be considered because it exists only as
an empty sign, a passageway to be crossed, the formless voice of the abyss whose
approach is indissociably both happiness and disgust. In relation to the Return,
Zarathustra is the *Fursprecher*, the one who speaks for. . ., in the place of. . ., marking the spot of his absence. Zarathustra is not Nietzsche's image but his sign. The
sign (which must be distinguished from the symptom) of rupture: the sign closest
to the intolerability of the thought of the return, "Nietzsche" allowed the eternal
return to be thought. For close to a century the loftiest enterprise of philosophy has
been directed to this task, but who has had the arrogance to say that he has seen it
through? Should the Return have resembled the nineteenth century's conception of
the end of history, an end that circled menacingly around us like a phantasmagoria
at the final days? Should we have ascribed to this empty sign, imposed by Nietzsche

as an *excess*, a series of mythic contents that disarmed and reduced it? Should we have attempted, on the contrary, to refine it so that it could unashamedly assume its place within a particular discourse? Or should this excessive, this always-misplaced and displaced sign have been accentuated; and instead of finding an arbitrary meaning to correspond to it, instead of constructing an adequate word, should it have been made to enter into resonance with the great signified that today's thought supports as an uncertain and controlled ballast? Should it have allowed recurrence to resound in unison with difference? We must avoid thinking that the return is the form of a content that is difference; rather, from an always-nomadic and anarchic difference to the unavoidably excessive and displaced sign of recurrence, a lightning storm was produced which will bear the name of Deleuze: new thought is possible; thought is again possible.

This thought does not lie in the future, promised by the most distant of new beginnings. It is present in Deleuze's texts — springing forth, dancing before us, in our midst; genital thought, intensive thought, affirmative thought, acategorical thought — each of these an unrecognizable face, a mask we have never seen before; differences we had no reason to expect but which nevertheless lead to the return, as masks of their masks, of Plato, Duns Scotus, Spinoza, Leibniz, Kant, and all other philosophers. This is philosophy not as thought but as theater — a theater of mime with multiple, fugitive, and instantaneous scenes in which blind gestures signal to each other. This is the theater where the laughter of the Sophist bursts out from under the mask of Socrates; where Spinoza's modes conduct a wild dance in a decentered circle while substance revolves about it like a mad planet; where a limping Fichte announces "the fractured I // the dissolved self"; where Leibniz, having reached the top of the pyramid, can see through the darkness that celestial music is in fact a *Pierrot lunaire*. In the sentry box of the Luxembourg Gardens, Duns Scotus places his head through the circular window; he is sporting an impressive mustache; it belongs to Nietzsche, disguised as Klossowski.

NOTES

1. Gilles Deleuze, *Différence et répétition* (Paris: Presses Universitaires de France, 1968), translated as *Difference and Repetition*, trans. Paul Patton (New York: Columbia University Press, 1994; Deleuze, *Logique du sens* (Paris: Minuit, 1969), translated as *The Logic of Sense*, trans. Mark Lester with Charles Stivale, ed. Constantin V. Bourdas (New York: Columbia University Press, 1990).
2. Deleuze, *Difference and Repetition*, 126–8; *Logic of Sense*, 253–6.
3. Plato, *The Sophist*, trans. F. M. Cornford, in *Plato: The Collected Dialogues*, ed. E. Hamilton and H. Cairns (Princeton: Princeton University Press, 1961), 957–1017.
4. On the rising of irony and the plunging of humor, see Deleuze, *Difference and Repetition*, 5, and *Logic of Sense*, 134–41.
5. Deleuze, *Logic of Sense*, 266–79.

6. Merleau-Ponty, *La Phénoménologie de la perception* (Paris: Gallimard, 1945), translated as *The Phenomenology of Perception*, trans. Colin Smith (London: Routledge & Kegan Paul, 1962).
7. A character in Klossowski's *Les Lois de l'hospitalité* (Paris: Gallimard, 1965).
8. Deleuze, *Logic of Sense*, 6–11.
9. Fabricius was a Roman general and statesman (d. 250 BC). Prince Andrew is a main character in Tolstoi's *War and Peace*.
10. Deleuze, *Logic of Sense*, 12–22.
11. Maurice Blanchot, *L'Espace littéraire* (Paris: Gallimard, 1955), cited in Deleuze, *Difference and Repetition*, 112; see also Deleuze, *Logic of Sense*, 148–53.
12. Deleuze, *Logic of Sense*, 148–53.
13. On this subject, see Deleuze, *Logic of Sense*, 185–233. My comments are, at best, an allusion to these splendid analyses.
14. This entire section considers, in a different order from that of the text, some of the themes that intersect within *Difference and Repetition*. I am, of course, aware that I have shifted accents and, far more important, that I have ignored its inexhaustible riches. I have reconstructed one of several possible models. Therefore, I will not apply specific references.
15. A reference to the protagonists of Gustave Flaubert's novel, *Bouvard and Pécuchet*, trans. T. W. Earp and G. W. Stonier (Norfolk, CT: New Directions, 1954).
16. "What will people think of us?" [Note added by Gilles Deleuze.]
17. On these themes, see Deleuze, *Logic of Sense*, 162–8, 177–80, and *Difference and Repetition*, 35–43, 299–304.

CHAPTER 3

Michel Foucault's Main Concepts

GILLES DELEUZE

For Daniel Defert

Foucault refers to his work as "studies in history," though he does not see it as "the work of an historian." He does the work of a philosopher, but he does not work on the philosophy of history. What does it mean to think? Foucault has never dealt with any other problem (hence his debt to Heidegger). And the historical? It is formations which are stratified, made up of strata. But to think is to reach a non-striated material, somewhere between the layers, in the interstices. Thinking has an essential relation to history, but it is no more historical than it is eternal. It is closer to what Nietzsche calls the Untimely: to think the past *against* the present – which would be nothing more than a common place, pure nostalgia, some kind of return, if he did not immediately add: "*in favor*, I hope, of a time to come." There is a becoming of thought which passes through historical formations, like their twin, but which does not resemble them. Thinking must come from the outside of thought, and yet at the same time be engendered from within – beneath the strata and beyond them. "To what extent the task of thought thinking its own history can liberate thought from what it thinks in silence and enable it to think differently."[1] "Thinking differently" informs the work of Foucault along three different axes, discovered one after the other: 1) strata as historical formations (archaeology), 2) the outside as beyond (strategy), and 3) the inside as a substratum (genealogy). Foucault often took pleasure in underlining the turning points and the ruptures in his own work. But these changes in direction rightfully belong to this kind of work, just as the ruptures belong to the method, in the construction of the three axes, i.e. the creation of new coordinates.

1. STRATA OR HISTORICAL FORMATIONS: THE VISIBLE AND THE UTTERABLE (SAVOIR)

Strata are historical formations, both empirical and positive. They are made of words and things, seeing and speaking, the visible and the utterable, planes of visibility and fields of legibility – content and expression. These last terms we may borrow from Hjelmslev, provided we do not confuse content with the signified, nor expression with the signifier. Content has its own form and substance: for example, the prison and its inmates. Expression also has a form and a substance: for example, criminal law and "delinquency." Just as criminal law as a form of expression defines a field of utterability (the propositions of delinquency), so the prison as a form of content defines a place of visibility ("panoptics," the surveillance of everything at every moment without being seen). This example is drawn from the last major analysis of strata which Foucault conducted in *Discipline and Punish*. But such an analysis was already present in *The History of Madness*: the asylum as a place of visibility, and the medicine of psychology as a field of utterances. In the meantime, Foucault writes *Raymond Roussel* and *The Birth of the Clinic*, more or less together. The first shows how the work of Roussel is divided into two parts: inventions of visibility by machines, and productions of utterances through "procedures." The second shows how the clinic and then pathological anatomy lead to variable partitions between the visible and the utterable. Foucault will draw his conclusions in *The Archaeology of Knowledge*, where we find a general theory of the two elements of stratification: the forms of content, or nondiscursive formations; and the forms of expression, or discursive formations. In this sense, that which is stratified constitutes Knowledge (the lesson of things and the lesson of grammar) and is subject to archaeology. Archaeology does not necessarily refer to the past, but to strata, such that our present has an archaeology of its own. Present or past, the visible is like the utterable: it is the object not of phenomenology, but of epistemology.

To be sure, words (*mots*) and things (*choses*) are rather vague terms to designate the two poles of knowledge, and Foucault will admit that the title *Les Mots et les Choses* [English translation: *The Order of Things*] should be taken ironically. The task of archaeology is to discover a genuine form of expression which cannot be confused with linguistic units, no matter what they are: words, phrases, propositions, or speech-acts. We know Foucault will discover this form in a totally original conception of the "utterance," defined as a function that intersects diverse units. But an analogous operation holds for the form of content: the visible, or units of visibility, is not to be confused with visual elements, whether qualities, things, objects, or amalgams of action and reaction. In this respect, Foucault constructs a function which is no less original than his "utterance." Units of visibility are not the forms of objects, not even those forms which would be revealed in the contact between light and things. Instead, they are forms of the luminous, luminous forms, created by light itself, allowing things and objects to subsist only as ashes, reflections, or sparkles (*Raymond Roussel*, but maybe *Manet* as well). Thus the task of archaeology is twofold: to "extract," from words and language, "utterances" that correspond to each stratum, but also to "extract" from things and vision, units of visibility, the visible. Of course, from the beginning, Foucault singles out the primacy of utterances, and we will see why. Furthermore, in *The Archaeology of Knowledge*, the planes of visibility will receive only a negative definition, "non-discursive formations," situated in a space that is merely complimentary to the field of utterances. Nevertheless, despite the primacy of utterances, the visible remains irreducibly distinct from it. Knowledge has two irreducible poles, and there also exists an "archaeology of seeing." The primacy of one in no way implies a reduction. When we neglect his theory of the visible, we mutilate the conception which Foucault had of history, and we mutilate his thought, the conception he had of thinking. Foucault never stopped being fascinated by what he saw, just as he was by what he heard or read. Archaeology in his conception is an audiovisual archive (beginning with the history of science). And in our own time, the joy Foucault secretly takes in the utterance is necessarily linked to his passion for seeing. Voice and Eyes.

This is because utterances are never directly legible or even utterable, although they are not hidden. They become legible and utterable only in relation to certain conditions which make them so, and which constitutes their inscription on an "enunciative support." The condition is that "there be some (a little) language," that is, a mode of being of language on each stratum, a variable way in which language is, is full, and is gathered (*The Order of Things*). Words must thus be pried open, split apart, either phrases or propositions, to grasp the way in which language appears in each stratum, understood as the dimension which provides "some" language and which conditions the utterances. If we cannot rise to the level of this condition, we will not find utterances, but will instead bump up against the words, phrases and propositions which seem to conceal them (so it is with sexuality, in *La Volonté de Savoir*). On the other hand, if we can rise to this condition, we understand that every age says all it can say, hides nothing, silences nothing, in terms of the language at its disposal: even in politics, but especially in politics, even in sexuality, but especially in sexuality – in the most cynical or the crudest language. The same goes for the visible. The units of visibility are never hidden, but they too have conditions without which they remain invisible, although in plain sight. Hence one of Foucault's themes: the visible invisible. In this instance, the condition is light, that "there be" some light, variable according to each stratum or historical formation: a way of being of light, which causes the units of visibility to emerge as flashes and sparkles, a "second light" (*Raymond Roussel*, but also *The Birth of the Clinic*). Things and objects must now in turn be pried open to grasp the way in which light appears on each stratum and conditions the visible: this is the second aspect of the work of Raymond Roussel, and more generally, the second pole of epistemology. An age sees only what it can see, but sees all it can, independently of any censorship and repression, in terms of the conditions of visibility, just as an age utters all it can. There are no secrets whatsoever, although nothing is immediately visible, nor immediately legible.

This research into conditions constitutes a kind of neo-Kantianism in Foucault, but with two differences which Foucault formulates in *The Order of Things*: 1) the conditions are those of real experience and not of possible experience, thus being on the side of the "object," not on the side of a universal "subject"; and 2) they have to do with historical formations or strata as *a posteriori* syntheses, and not with the *a priori* syntheses of all possible experience.

But Foucault's neo-Kantianism lies in a Receptivity constituted by the units of visibility along with their conditions, as well as a Spontaneity constituted in turn by the units of utterablity along with their own conditions. The spontaneity of language, and the receptivity of light. Receptive here does not mean passive, since there is just as much action and passion in what light makes visible. Nor does spontaneous mean active, but rather the activity of an "Other" that acts on the receptive form (so it is in Kant, where the spontaneity of "I think" acts on the receptive beings which represent this spontaneity to themselves as other). In Foucault, the spontaneity of the understanding, the cogito, is replaced by the spontaneity of language (the "being there" of language), whereas the receptivity of intuition is replaced by the receptivity of light (space-time). Now the primacy of utterance over the visible is easily explained: *The Archaeology of Knowledge* indeed lays claim to a "determinant" role for utterances as discursive formations. But the units of visibility are no less irreducible, because they refer to a form of the "determinable," which will not allow itself to be reduced to a form of determination. This was Kant's great problem: the mutual adaptation of two forms, or of sorts of conditions, different by nature.

In his transformation of Kant, Foucault makes some essential claims, one of which I believe is this: from the beginning, there exists a *difference of nature* between the visible and the utterable, although they are inserted in one another and ceaselessly interpenetrate one another as they compose each stratum or knowledge. It is perhaps this aspect, this first aspect which attracts Foucault to Blanchot: "speaking is not seeing." But whereas Blanchot insists on the primacy of speaking as determinant, Foucault (despite hasty first impressions) maintains the specificity of seeing as determinable. Between speaking and seeing, there is no isomorphism, and no conformity, although there exists a mutual presupposition, and the utterable has primacy of the visible. *The Archaeology of Knowledge* indeed insists on this primacy, but will add: "In vain do we say what we see; *what we see never resides in what we say*, and we vainly try to make others see, through imagery, through metaphor and comparison, what we are seeing; the place where imagery, metaphor, and comparison shine in all their radiance is not the place which our eyes unfold; it is rather the place defined by the successions of syntax."[2] The two forms do not have the same formation, the same "genealogy," in the archaeological sense of the word *Gestaltung*. *Discipline and Punish* will provide the final great demonstration of this difference between seeing and speaking: an encounter occurs between the utterances of "delinquency," which depend on a new regime of penal utterances, and the prison as the form of content which depends on a new regime of visibility; the two are different by nature, they do not have the same genesis, nor the same history, although they encounter one another on the same stratum, helping and reinforcing one another, though their alliance can be broken at certain moments. Here we see Foucault's method assume its historical meaning and development: the "play of truth" between what we see and what we say, delinquency as utterance, the prison as visibility. But early on in his work, as I mentioned, Foucault had done a similar analysis in a different case (*The History of Madness*): the asylum as a place of visibility, mental illness as an object of utterance, and the two having different geneses, indeed a radical heterogeneity, but enjoying a mutual presupposition on the same stratum, even if they should be forced to brake their alliance on some other stratum.

On each strata, or in each historical formation, certain phenomena of capturing and holding can be found: series of utterances and segments of the visibility are inserted in one another. Forms of content like the prison, like the asylum, engender secondary utterances which produce or reproduce delinquency and mental illness; but also, forms of expression like delinquency engender secondary contents which are vehicles of the prison (*Discipline and Punish*). Between the visible and its luminous condition, utterances slip in; between the utterable and its language condition, the visible works its way in (*Raymond Roussel*). This is because each condition has something in common: each constitutes a space of "rarity," of "dissemination," littered with interstices. Thus the particular way in which language is *gathered* on a stratum (its "being there") is at the same time a space of *dispersion* for those utterances stratified in language. Similarly, the particular way in which light is gathered is at the same time a space of dispersion for the units of visibility, the "ashes," the "glimpses," of a second light. It is a mistake to think that Foucault is primarily interested in imprisonment. Such environments merely perform the conditions of visibility in a certain historical formation; they didn't exist before, and they won't exist after. Imprisonment or not, these spaces are forms of exteriority, either language or light, in which utterances are disseminated and the visible dispersed. This is why utterances can slip into the interstices of seeing, and the visible, into the interstices of speaking. We speak, we see and make see, at the same time, although they are not the same thing and the two differ in nature (*Raymond Roussel*). And from one stratum to another, the visible and the utterable are transformed at the same time, although not according to the same rules (*The Birth of the Clinic*). In short, each stratum, each historical formation, each positivity, is made up of the interweaving of determinant utterances and determinable units of visibility, in as much as they are heterogeneous, though this heterogeneity does not prevent their mutual insertion.

2. STRATEGIES OR THE NON-STRATIFIED (POWER): THINKING THE OUTSIDE

The coadaptation of the two forms is in no way impeded, but that is not enough. Coadaptation must be positively engendered, through a moment comparable to what Kant called "schematism." We are now on a new axis. This new axis has to do with power, and no longer with knowledge. The preceding determinations are found on this new axis, only now it is a mutual presupposition between power and knowledge, a difference of nature between them, and the primacy of power. But it is no longer a question of the relation between two forms, as it was with knowledge. Now it is a question of *power relations*. The essence of force is to be sought in its relation to other forces: form affects other forms, and is affected by them. Consequently, Power (with a capital 'P') does not express the dominance of a class, and does not depend on a State apparatus, but "is produced at every point, or rather in every relation from point to point."[3] Power flows through the ruling class no less than through those who are ruled, in such a way that classes result from it, and not the reverse. The State or Law merely effects the integration of power. Classes and the State are not forces, but subjects which align forces, integrate them globally, and perform the relation of forces, on and in the strata. These agents of stratication presuppose power relations prior to any subject and object. This is why power is exercised before being possessed: it is a question of strategy, "anonymous strategies," "almost mute," and blind. One cannot say that a social field is self-structuring, or that it is self-contradictory. A social field strategizes, it is self-strategizing (hence a sociology of strategies, as in the work of Pierre Bordieu). This is also why power introduces us to a realm of "microphysics," or presents itself a complex of micro-powers. Therefore, we should distinguish the strategy of forces from the stratification of forms which flows from it. But from one to the other, there is no enlargement, or inversely, miniaturization: there is heterogeneity.

In this celebrated Foucauldian thesis, can we not see a kind of return to natural law? But with this one difference: it has nothing to do with law, a too global notion, nor with Nature, another global term too heavily freighted. Rather, a Nietzschean inspiration is behind this thesis, as Foucault's article on Nietzsche demonstrates. And later on, if Foucault opposes every manifestation of what he considered facile and hasty conceptions of repressive power, it is because power relations are not so easily determined by simple violence. The relation of one force to another consists in the way in which one force affects the others, and is affected by them; in which case, we can draw up a list of "functions": sample and subtract, enumerate and control, compose and increase, etc. Force itself is defined by a double capacity, to affect and be affected, hence it is inseparable from its relation to other forces which, on every occasion, determine or fulfill these capacities. We thus see something like a receptivity of force (a capacity to be affected) and a spontaneity of force (a capacity to affect). Now, however, receptivity and spontaneity no longer have the same meaning as they did a while ago with respect to the strata. On the strata, seeing and speaking were each composed of already-formed substances and already formalized functions: prisoners, students, soldiers and workers were not the same "substance," precisely because locking up, teaching, lighting and laboring were not the same function. Power relations, however, mix and blend non-formed materials and non-formalized functions: for example, some body, or some population, over which is exercised a general function of control and sectorization (independently of the concrete forms which the strata impart to them).

In this sense, Foucault can say, or at least he does so once in a crucial passage of *Discipline and Punish*, that a "diagram" expresses a relation of force or power: "a functioning abstracted from any obstacle, resistance, or friction . . . and which should be detached from any specific use."[4] For example, a disciplinary diagram that defines modern societies. But other diagrams act on societies with other stratifications: the diagram of sovereignty, which functions by means of sampling rather than sectorization; or the pastoral diagram, which has to do with a "flock" and assumes "grazing" as its function . . . One of the more original aspects of the diagram is its being a place of mutations. The diagram is not exactly outside the strata, but *it is the outside of the strata*. It is between two strata as the place of mutations which enables the passage from one stratum to the other. Thus power relations constitute the power in a diagram, whereas the relations of forms define the knowledge in an archive. Foucault's genealogy is no longer a simple archaeology of forms that appear in a stratum; it now becomes a strategy of forces on which the stratum itself depends.

His study of stratified relationships of knowledge culminates in the *Archaeology*. The study of strategic relations of forces or power begins in earnest in *Discipline and Punish* and is further developed in *The Will to Knowledge*. Between the two, there is both irreducibility, reciprocal presupposition and a certain predominance of the latter. "Diagrammatism" will play a role similar to Kant's schematism but in a completely different way: the receptive spontaneity of forces accounts for the receptivity of visible forms, the spontaneity of utterable statements and their correlation. The relationships between forces *occur* in the strata, which would have nothing to embody or actualize without them. Inversely, without the strata actualizing them, the relationships of forces would remain transitive, unstable, fleeting, almost virtual, and would not take shape. We can understand this by referring to *The Archaeology of Knowledge*, which already suggested "regularity" was a property of the utterance. Regularity for Foucault does not designate frequency or probability but a curve connecting singular points. The relationships of forces indeed determine singular points, singularities as affects, such that a diagram is always a discharge of singularities. It is like in mathematics where the determination of singularities (nodes of force, focal points, method of steepest descent, etc.) is distinguished from the slope of the curve passing nearby. The curve initiates the relationships of force by regularizing them, aligning them, making the series converge, tracing a "general line of force" connecting singular points. When he defines the utterance as a regularity, Foucault notes that curves or graphs are utterances and that utterances are the equivalent of curves and graphs. Thus the utterance is essentially related to "something else," something of a different nature that cannot be reduced to the meaning of the sentence or the referent of the clause: they are the singular points of the diagram next to which the *curve-utterance* is traced in language and becomes regular or legible. And maybe the same should be said of visibilities. In that case, paintings organize the singularities from the point of view of receptivity, by tracing lines of light that make them visible. Not only Foucault's thought but his style proceed by curve-utterances and painting-descriptions (*Las Meninas* or the description of the Panopticon; all of the remarkable descriptions Foucault introduced into his texts). Thus a theory of descriptions is just as crucial for him as a theory of utterances. And these two elements result from the diagram of forces that is actualized in them.

We could present things in the following way: if a force is always in relation to other forces, the forces necessarily refer to an irreducible Outside made up of indivisible distances through which one force acts on another or is acted on by another. Only from the outside does a force confer on others or receive from other forces the variable affectations that only exist at a certain distance or in a certain relationship. Forces are therefore in a perpetual becoming that doubles history or rather envelops it, according to a Nierzschian conception: "emergence designates a place of confrontation," states the article on Nietzsche, "not a closed field where a struggle takes place," but "a non-place, a pure distance" that only acts in the interstices.[5] An outside more distant than any external world and even farther than any form of exteriority. The diagram is such a non-place, constantly disturbed by changes in distance or by changes in the forces in relation. It is only a place for mutation. While seeing and speaking are forms of exteriority, each exterior to the other, then thinking addresses an outside that no longer has any form. Thinking means reaching non-stratification. Seeing is thinking, speaking is thinking, but thinking takes place in the gap, in the disjunction between seeing and speaking. This is Foucault's second meeting point with Blanchot: thinking belongs to the Outside to the extent that the latter, this "abstract storm," surges into the interstice between seeing and speaking. Blanchot's article takes up where the Nietzsche article leaves off. The call of the outside is a constant theme for Foucault and means that thinking is not the innate exercise of a faculty but must happen to thought. Thinking does not depend on an interiority uniting the visible and the utterable but takes place under the intrusion of the outside that carves the interval: "*thought of the outside*" as a roll of the dice, as a discharge of singularities.[6] Between two diagrams, between two states of diagrams, there are mutations, reworkings of the relationships of forces. Not because anything can connect to anything else. It is more like successive drawings of cards, each one operating on chance but under external conditions determined by the previous draw. It is a combination of randomness and dependency like in a Markov chain. The component is not transformed, but the composing forces transform when they enter into relation with new forces. The connection therefore does not take place by continuity or interiorization but by reconnection over the breaks and discontinuities. The formula of the outside is the one from Nietzsche quoted by Foucault: "the iron hand of necessity shaking the cup of chance."[7]

The theme of the "death of man" in *The Order of Things* can be explained in this way. Not only does the concept of man disappear, and not because man "surpasses" himself, but the component forces of man enter into new combinations. They did not always compose man, but for a long rime, during the classical period, they were in relationship with other forces in such a way as to compose God and not man, such that the infinite was first in relation to the finite and thought was thought of the infinite. Then they composed man, but to the extent that they entered into relationship with another type of forces, obscure forces of organization of "life," "production" of wealth, "filiation" of language that were able to reduce man to his own finiteness and to give him a History to make his own. But when these forces appear at a third draw, new compositions must arise and the death of man connects to the death of God to make room for other ashes or other utterances. In short, man only exists on a stratum depending on the relationships of forces taking place on it. Thus the outside is always the opening of a future where nothing ends because nothing has started, but everything changes. *The diagram as the determination of a group of relationships of force* does not exhaust forces, which can enter into other relationships and other compositions. The diagram as comes from the outside but the outside is not to be confused with any diagram as it constantly "draws" new ones. Force in this sense possesses a potential in relation to the diagram in which it is caught, like a third power distinct from its power to affect or be affected. This third power is *resistance*. In fact, a diagram of forces presents, alongside the singularities of power corresponding to its relationships, singularities of resistance, "points, nodes, foci" that in turn act on the strata in order to make change possible. Moreover, the last word in the theory of power is that resistance comes first, since it has a direct relationship with the outside. Thus a social field resists more than it strategizes and the thought of the outside is a thought of resistance (*The Will to Knowledge*).

3. THE FOLDS OR THE INSIDE OF THOUGHT (DESIRE)

We must therefore distinguish between the formalized relationships on the strata (Knowledge), the relationships of forces at the diagram level (Power), and the relationship with the Outside, the absolute relationship, as Blanchot says, which is also a non-relationship (Thought). Does that mean there is no inside? Foucault subjects interiority to constant and radical critique. But what of an inside that is deeper than any internal world just as the outside is farther than any external world? Foucault often returns to the theme of the *double*. The double for him is not a projection of the interior but, on the contrary, a fold of the outside, like in embryology for the invagination of tissue. For Foucault – and for Raymond Roussel – the double is always a "*doublure*" in every sense of the word.[8] If thought continues to "hold" onto the outside, how could the outside not appear inside as what it does not think or cannot think: an unthought in thought, says *The Order of Things*. This unthought is the infinite for the classical age but, starting in the nineteenth century, the dimensions of finiteness begin to fold the outside and develop a "depth," a "thickness pulled back into itself," an inside of life, work and language. Foucault takes up the Heideggerian theme of the Fold, the Crease, in his own way. He sends it in a completely different direction. A crease in the outside, be it the fold of the infinite or the folds of finiteness, imposes a curve on the strata and forms their inside. Becoming the doubling [*doublure*] of the outside or, as it was already put in the *History of Madness*, being "inside the outside."[9]

Perhaps there is not the rupture between recent books by Foucault and his earlier work as many have said and he himself suggested. There is instead a re-evaluation of them all according to this axis or dimension: the inside. *The Order of Things* already asked the question of the unthought as well as the question of the subject: "What do I have to be, me who thinks and who follows my thought, to be what I do not think, for my thought to be what I am not?"[10] The inside is an outside operation; it is a *subjectivation* (which does not necessarily mean an interiorization). If the outside is a relationship, the absolute of relationships, then the inside is also a relationship, the relationship becoming subject. *The Use of Pleasure* gives it its name: "the relationship of self to self." If force receives a dual power from the outside, the power to affect (other forces) and to be affected (by other forces), how could there not ensue a relationship between force and itself? Perhaps this is the element of "resistance." At this point, Foucault rediscovers the affection of self by self as the greatest paradox of thought: the relationship with oneself forms an inside that is constantly derived from the outside.

Here again, it is necessary to show how the relationship with the outside comes first and yet how the relationship to self is irreducible and takes places along a specific axis. The subject is always constituted, the product of a subjectivation, but it appears in a dimension that opposes all stratification or codification. Consider the historical formation of the Greeks: using the light that was their own and with the utterances they invented, they actualized the relationships of force of their diagram and it led to the city-state, the family, but also eloquence, games, everywhere where at that moment the domination of one over another could take place. At first glance, the domination of self by self, or Virtue as morality, is only another example: "Ensuring the direction of one's self, managing one's house, participating in the government of the city-state are three practices of the same type."[11] And yet the relationship to the self *does not let itself be aligned* according to the concrete forms of power or be subsumed in an abstract diagrammatic function. One might say that it only develops by *detaching itself* from relationships with others, by "disconnecting itself" both from the forms of power and the functions of virtue. It is as if the relationships of the outside folded to make a double [*doublure*] and allow a relationship to the self to arise that develops according to a new dimension. *Enkrateia* is "a power exercised over oneself in the power one exercises over others"[12] (how could one claim to govern others if one could not govern oneself?), to such an extent that the relationship to the self becomes the primary internal regulator in relation to the constitutive powers of politics, the family, eloquence or games, and even virtue itself. Government of others is reflected, doubled or submits in a government of the self that relates force to itself and not to another force. Maybe the Greeks invented this dimension, at least as a partially autonomous dimension (an aesthetic conception of existence).

Foucault's thesis seems to be this: among the Greeks, the relationship to self found the opportunity to occur in sexuality. This is because the sexual relationship or affect is inseparable from the two poles that constitute its terms: spontaneity-receptivity, determinant-determinable, active-passive, masculine role-feminine role. But because of its violence and expenditure, sexual activity will only exercise its determinant role if it is able to regulate itself, to affect itself. Thus sexuality is the matter and test of the relationship to self.

From this point of view, the relationship to self occurs in three forms: a simple relationship with the body as a Dietetics of pleasures or affects (governing oneself sexually to be able to govern others); a developed relationship, with the spouse, as the Economy of the household (governing oneself to be able to govern the spouse, for the wife to attain good receptivity); finally a *redoubled* relationship with the young man as the Erotics of homosexuality or pederasty (not only governing oneself, but making the boy govern himself by resisting the power of others). What seems essential to me in this presentation of the Greeks is that there is no necessary connection, only an historical encounter between the relationship to self, which would more likely tend towards the food model, and sexual relations, which provides the terms and the material. Therein lies the difficulty Foucault had to surmount: he started, he says, by writing a book on sexuality, *The Will to Knowledge*, but without reaching the Self. Then he wrote a book on the relationship to self but it did not arrive at sexuality. He had to reach the point or the moment when the two notions were balanced, with the Greeks. From there, the entire history of the Inside could be developed: how the connection between the relation to self and sexual relations became increasingly "necessary" on the condition that the value of the relationship to self, the terms of sexual relations, the nature of the ordeal and the quality of the material changed. This led to Christianity with the substitution of flesh for the body, desire for pleasure ... The Greeks certainly did not lack either individuality or interiority. But it is a long history, the history of modes of subjectivation as they formed the constantly reworked genealogy of the desiring subject.

The inside takes on many figures and modes depending on the way the folds are formed. Desire. Isn't desire the inside in general, or the mobile connection between the inside and the two other features, the outside and the strata? If it is true that the inside is formed by a crease in the outside, then there is a *topological relationship* between them. The relationship to self is homologous to the relationship with the outside and all the contents of the inside are in relation with the outside. "The interior of the exterior, and vice versa," said *Madness and Civilization. The Use of Pleasure* speaks of isomorphism. Everything is done through the strata, which are relatively exterior settings and therefore relatively interior. The stratified formations place the absolute outside and inside derived from it in contact; or inversely, they unfold the inside on the outside. The entire inside is actively present for the outside at the edge of the strata. Thinking combines the three axes; it is a constantly changing unity. There are three types of problems here or three figures of time. The strata delve into the past in vain; they only extract successive presents from it, they are in the present (what is one seeing, what is one saying at this moment?). But the relationship with the outside is the future, possible futures depending on the chances for transformation. The inside, for its part, condenses the past in modes that are nor necessarily continuous (for example, Greek subjectivity, Christian subjectivity. . .). *The Archaeology of Knowledge* raised the problem of long and short durations, but Foucault seemed to consider primarily relatively short durations in the domain of knowledge and power. With *The Use of Pleasure* he discovered long durations, starting with the Greeks and the Fathers of the Church. The reason for this is simple: we do not save the knowledge that is no longer useful for us or power that is no longer exercised, but we continue to serve moralities in which we no longer believe. In each moment, the past accumulates in the relationship to self while the strata carry the changing present and the future comes into play in the relationship to the outside. Thinking means taking residence in the strata in the present which serves as a limit. But it is thinking the past as it is condensed in the inside, in the relationship with the self. Thinking the past against the present, resisting the present, not for a return, the return to the Greeks for example, but "in favor, I hope, of a time to come." Foucault's work was created by inventing a topology that actively puts the inside and outside in contact on the stratified formations of history. It is up to the strata to produce layers that show and tell something new; but it is also up to the relationship of the outside to call the powers in place into question, and it is up to the relationship with the self to inspire new modes of subjectivization. Foucault's work abruptly stops at this final point. His interviews are a full part of his work because each one is a topological operation that involves us in our current problems. His work has led thought to discover an entirely new system of previously unknown coordinates. It paints the most beautiful paintings of light in philosophy and traces unprecedented curves of utterances. It reconnects with the great works that have changed what thinking means for us. Its transformation of philosophy has only begun.

NOTES

1. Michel Foucault, *The History of Sexuality: The Use of Pleasure, Volume 2*, translated by Robert Hurley (New York: Vintage, 1990).
2. Michel Foucault, *Let Mots et les choses* (Paris: Gallimard, coll. Bibliothèques des sciences humaines, 1966), 25, translated as *The Order of Things: An Archaeology of the Human Sciences* (New York: Random House, 1970), 9.
3. Michel Foucault, *La Volonté de savoir* (Paris: Gallimard, coll. Bibliothèque des histoires, 1976), 122, translated by Robert Hurley as *The History of Sexuality: An Introduction (The Will to Knowledge)* (New York: Vintage, 1990), 93.
4. Michel Foucault, *Surveiller et punir* (Paris: Gallimard, coll. Bibliothèque des histoires, 1975), 207, translated by Alan Sheridan as *Discipline and Punish: The Birth of the Prison* (New York: Random House, 1977), 205.
5. Michel Foucault, "Nietzsche, Genealogy, History," in *The Foucault Reader*, ed. P. Rabinow (New York: Pantheon, 1984), 76–100.
6. Michel Foucault, "The Thought of the Outside," in *Aesthetics, Method and Epistemology*, ed. James Faubion (New York: The New Press, 1998), 137–47.
7. The Nietzsche quote comes from *Daybreak*, aphorism 130.
8. Translator's note: *Une doublure* can refer to a double, replica, understudy, stand-in, stunt-person, or the linking of a piece of clothing.
9. Michel Foucault, *Histoire de la folie à l'âge classique* (Paris: Gallimard, 1972, reprint), 22, translated by Robert Howard as *Madness and Civilization: A History of Insanity in the Age of Reason* (New York: Vintage, 1988), 31.
10. Foucault, *The Order of Things*, 322.
11. Foucault, *The Use of Pleasure*, 76.
12. Ibid. 79.

CHAPTER 4

When and How I Read Foucault[1]

ANTONIO NEGRI

TRANSLATED BY KRIS KLOTZ

The journal *Aut Aut*[2] – the first journal in Italy that took an interest in Michel Foucault – published an article in its final 1978 issue that I had written one year earlier, called "On the Method of the Critique of Politics."[3] In this text, I discussed the influence that Foucault's work had had up to this point on the thought of the Italian revolutionary left, for which I had been a militant in the 1970s. Foucault's latest work had been *Discipline and Punish*, translated into Italian in 1976. At that time, I had begun to work again on Marx, and on the *Grundrisse* in particular. In fact, between 1977 and 1978, I taught a course on "Marx beyond Marx" at ENS Ulm on the invitation of Althusser.[4]

I recall this information because it is important to highlight the overlap between my reading of Foucault and a period of my work when I tried to summarize a lengthy "revisionist" interpretation of Marx. This revision was not at all a rejection of Marx, as was often the case at the end of the 1970s. On the contrary, it fully adhered to the fundamental concepts of political economy and it was undertaken within a revolutionary militancy.

Why, then, was I interested in Foucault? At this time, the social and political "movements" that were contesting the current political situation in Italy were experiencing an intense conflict with the Italian Communist Party (ICP) and the trade unions. The latter were in the process of establishing an alliance with the forces of the right concerning social and parliamentary grounds. They called this alliance "the historical compromise." The ICP insisted on the hypothesis that the proletariat could henceforth conquer the sovereign power,[5] and that left-wing forces could not be picky when confronting this series of difficult but necessary compromises. In sum, politics was autonomous and indifferent to values; only force counted. For the ICP, as I understood it, the cult of sovereignty and the "reason of State" went hand in hand. How could we demystify this idea, which was so bizarre for the communists, that power and sovereignty corresponded to autonomous regions, that they represented indifferent instruments – in brief, that they formed a veritable transcendental plane? And that struggle could only emerge from this transcendental plane? We thought, on the contrary, that the materiality of power and of political construction was extremely well-determined, character-ized by neoliberal politics, and that this condition was anything but indifferent. In order to resist, we therefore had to refuse: we had to denounce this so-called indifference of power and affirm a critical and materially-determined perspec-tive. We had to deny indifference because each and every one of us represented a *difference* – determined, real, politically defined, and incapable of appearing other than we were. With Foucault, we could say: "The human being is not characterized by a certain relationship to truth, but he possesses, as belonging properly to him, a truth both offered and hidden."[6]

However, this was not sufficient for transforming the rejection of a foreseen political disaster – the disaster of the politics of the Italian left – into the construc-tion of a new horizon of struggles. It was necessary to reorganize our analysis and to rethink our own organization. We had to give to this moment of conscience a capacity to expand, and to provide it with an unheard-of theoretical foundation. And Foucault could provide us invaluable assistance with this.

Immediately, it had seemed to us that Foucault was situated within an "ontolog-ical" tradition of French thought that had not yielded to the sirens of a philosophy of life and action. In my reading, I had moved from Foucault's essay on Binswanger to his essay on Kant's *Anthropology* and to his work on Weizsaecker,[7] then to the *History of Madness* and *The Birth of the Clinic*. My article highlighted, on the one hand, the power of a relation perceived between ontology and anthropology. On the other hand, it highlighted the fact that the construction of the historical object was always extremely realistic, because the historical object was never removed from something that could be given outside of immediate experience. As Althusser had noted, it resulted from "absolutely unexpected temporalities" and "novel logics."[8] In freeing himself from the Kantian "schematism of Reason," or from Husserlian intentionality, Foucault constructed the historical object, it seemed to me, within a concrete horizon that was made of struggles and strategies.

At that time, I wrote: "the horizon of strategy, of the ensemble of strategies, cor-responds to the intersection of the will to know and concrete data, to the intersec-tion of the rupture and the limit of the rupture. Every strategy is a struggle, every synthesis is a limit. Here, there is more cunning than in Reason, there is more con-creteness than in the Idea. Power is finally brought back to the network of acts that constitute it."[9] I added: "Of course, these acts are concealed by the ambiguity that power represents in itself. But this does not preclude the affirmation that reality, at every instant, presents itself as divided. It does not preclude that heteronomous ends can be affirmed; nor that we must abandon the one-dimensional characteriza-tion of what we have before us. All of this is not precluded, because what changes is the perspective on things, which modifies and revitalizes research. This is a way of being inside reality and repeating there this act of existence and of separation, which belongs to us and which characterizes all subjects who are acting in history. Struggles are what envelop needs and points of view, perspectives and the will, desires and expectations. Synthesis is delegated to nothing and no one. Science is freed from what commanded it and offers itself to action, to concrete contingency[10] and to practical determination."[11]

What happens, then, regarding this decision? Something that is both elementary and incredibly difficult. It is a matter of pushing this experience of history towards truth, of pushing the description of *historia rerum gestarum* to *res gestae*.[12] We must reconquer the totality in order to deny it (*das Ganz ist un-Wahr*[13]). But we must do so because power in itself cannot comprehend life, the perspective of singularities, or the apparatus [*dispositif*] that is organized by desire.

At the end of the 1950s, I worked a lot on German historicism. In fact, my doctorate thesis was devoted to *Historismus*.[14] Dilthey, in particular, captured my attention, especially the singular *Kulturpolitik* that constituted the space of his inquiries. I rediscovered Burckhardt and Nietzsche much more than I would have expected. In these works, there were "epochs" within which knowledge organized itself in a unitary manner, but which always came to pieces. They were discontinuous epochs. Could we not refer to them, by means of archaeology, as to an "episteme"? At the same time, both the "epoch" of the analyses of *Historismus* and the "episteme" of Foucault could sometimes seem more stable than the founding decision that traversed them and more stable than our ability to rediscover this decision. In this blockage of the process, *Kultur* tended to transform itself into *Zivilisation* in the work of the historicists. Similarly, the "living" episteme – what Foucault later called biopolitics – tended to be reabsorbed in the constricted network of biopower.

The *episteme*: it was extremely difficult to understand this notion in a non-structuralist manner, at a time when we were observing the apex of this method that had spread throughout the human sciences. In fact, this is how we interpreted *The Order of Things*[15] when it was published. Nearly ten years later, the same fate was reserved for *Discipline and Punish*.[16] The fixation of the analysis of Foucault on the image of the Panopticon, for example, impeded the movement of this work and the analysis of knowledge to which it was otherwise devoted. Production seemed to be dominated by a sort of unproductive circulation. The Panopticon subsumed production and got lost somewhere between the formalism of a philosophical tradition of action ("without object") and the concretism of a philosophy of structure ("without subject"). Between *historia rerum gestarum* and *res gestae*, we had the impression of a sort of closed circuit without the possibility of exit. Bizarrely, all the openings that Foucault proposed, and that I briefly tried to recall above, were blocked.

And yet, it is where this blockage appeared at its strongest, in the analyses of *Discipline and Punish,* that everything ended up being reopened. The terms used by Foucault to name this new economy of power were about to divide into "bio-politics" and "biopower." Before this distinction was introduced, we had characterized this economy precisely as a "Panopticon," which was mixed together with the exploitation of life and the employment of the physical force of individuals, with the management of their bodies and with the control of their needs; in sum, with the normalization of what human beings are and do. As a result of this division of terms, our reading of Foucault was completely modified and revitalized. We had to think both biopower and biopolitics. And, instead of thinking of the two notions as equivalent and indistinct, we had to consider them as different. It was by insisting on the distinction between biopower and biopolitics that I was able to incorporate Foucault's work into the heart of my own investigations.

The problem was the following: So long as we ignored the distinction between biopower and biopolitics, resistance to the harnessing and management of life seemed impossible. Exteriority was no longer guaranteed and a counter-power could amount to nothing more than the symmetrical and inverse reproduction of that from which it sought to free itself. For this reason, the "liberal" interpreters of Foucault felt authorized. Starting from Foucault's analysis of the normative management of a living being organized into populations, they developed a political conception of the actuarial management of life, a classification of individuals into desubjectifying [*désubjectivant*] and homogeneous macro-systems.

But one could also dissociate biopower and biopolitics, and make of the latter the affirmation of a potency [*puissance*] of life against the power [*pouvoir*] over life. One could locate in life itself – in the production of affects and languages, in social cooperation, in bodies and desires, in the invention of new modes of life – the space of a creation of a new subjectivity that immediately amounted to an instance of desubjection [*désassujettissement*]. This is what we did.

Some will say that the opposition between potency [*puissance*] and power [*pouvoir*] owes more to Spinoza than to Foucault. Regarding my own work, this is certainly evident. At that time, I had begun to work on the philosopher of Amsterdam and I was going to publish *The Savage Anomaly* some years later.[17] But I remain convinced that this distinction between power and potency is also very well-suited to Foucault. When Foucault wrote, at the end of *Disciple and Punish*: "In this central and centralized humanity, the effect and instrument of complex power relations, bodies and forces subjected [*assujettis*] by multiple apparatuses [*dispositifs*] of 'incarceration,' objects for discourses that are them-selves elements of this strategy, we must hear the rumbling of battle,"[18] we had to hear the sound of what was already at work, the sound of what could not be reduced to the solitary noise of the Panopticon. That is, we had to avoid reduc-ing potency to power.

This brings us to an interview with Foucault, published in the journal *Aut Aut* in 1978: "Regarding the simplistic reduction of my analyses to the mere metaphor of the Panopticon, I believe that we can respond at two levels. We can say: let us compare what they attribute to me to what I have said. Here it is easy to show that my analyses of power are by no means reducible to this figure, not even in the book where they went looking for it, that is, *Discipline and Punish*. In fact, if I showed that the Panopticon has been a utopia, a type of pure form elaborated at the end of the eighteenth century in order to provide the most convenient formula for a constant, immediate and total exercise of power, and if I therefore revealed the birth, the formulation of this utopia, its *raison d'être*, it is also true that I immediately showed that it was precisely a utopia that had never functioned such as it was described, and that the whole history of the prison – its reality – consists precisely in always falling short of this model."[19] For us, Foucault's clairvoyance became evident with the publication of *Discipline and Punish*. Of course, we were way down in the "little province" of Italy, but we were conscious of it nonetheless. And, in my own article from 1977, I cited this other passage from Foucault: "Now, the study of this microphysics presupposes that the power exercised [on the body] cannot be conceived as a property, but as a strategy . . . . Moreover, this power is not applied purely and simply, as an obligation or interdiction, to those who 'do not have it;' it invests them, it is transmitted by them and through them. . . . This means that these relations descend into the depths of society, that they are not localized in the relations of the State to its citizens or on the border between classes, and that they do not settle for reproducing – at the level of individuals, bodies, gestures, and comportments – the form of the law or government. This means that even if there is continuity (these relations are, in fact, articulated on this form according to a whole series of complex components), there is neither analogy nor homology, but a specificity of mechanism and modality. Finally, they are not unequivocal. They define innumerable points of confrontation, centers of instability, each of which contains its risks of conflict, of struggles, and of an at least temporary inversion of force relations. The reversal of these 'micropowers' does not therefore obey the law of all or nothing; it is not acquired once and for all by a new control of the apparatuses [*appareils*] nor by a new functioning or a destruction of institutions. Nonetheless, none of its localized episodes can be inscribed in history except by the effects that it induces on the whole network in which it is caught."[20]

It was at this moment that, from within the very difficult struggles that were taking place in Italy and in response to Foucault's investigations, I wrote a small book, *Dominio et sabotaggio*,[21] in which I insisted emphatically on the antagonistic and "agonistic" conception of power. It was especially in this period that the antagonism of class struggle could begin to be understood, on the basis of the "micro-conflictuality" henceforth involved in socialization (both of capital and the workforce). And that's how the concept of the "social worker"[22] emerged in my work.

We must, then, go beyond the promises of the dialectic and consider power not as a property but as a strategy. In my 1977 article, I therefore made a lengthy digression on what seemed to me to be the state of the critique of political economy in its most dynamic moments, that is, on all the Ricardian movements that were surpassing Keynesianism. And I lingered at length on Piero Sraffa.[23] In his *Production of Commodities by Means of Commodities*,[24] he showed how potencies [*puissances*] determined new value and produced innovation from within the circulation of commodities, thus updating Marx's account of this theme and the theme of transformation. I highlighted the theoretical importance of the developments Sraffa made regarding Ricardian circulation. I also recalled the anecdote of the encounter, or confrontation, between Sraffa and Wittgenstein, after which the latter turned away from the thought of the *Tractatus*. Piero Sraffa had in fact remarked to his Cambridge colleague that the problem that he himself had, concerning the critique of political economy, was of the same nature as Wittgenstein's, concerning logic. It was necessary to try to identify a point of transformation (that is, of innovative production) within the circulation of commodities (for the economist) or within linguistic circulation (for the philosopher). At the moment when, for Wittgenstein, "every possibility of transformation was in crisis, and the solutions that he foresaw did not satisfy him – because an enormous amount of suffering and experience put these solutions in question, Sraffa made a Neapolitan gesture, a sign of contempt with his hands,[25] and asked ironically, 'what is the symbolic translation of this?' They say that this anecdote lies behind the discovery of a new field of inquiry on the production of signs by means of other signs, beyond the sphere of their pure circulation and the static universe of their movements. It hardly matters whether or not the episode is true, as long as the anecdote works. Production of signs by means of other signs, production of commodities by means of other commodities: isn't this the victory of a new political economy, which understands production from within circulation? Doesn't Sraffa's apparently irrational proposition prevail?"[26] And doesn't the anecdote correspond to what Foucault already proposed to do when he spoke of "putting in question our will to truth; restoring to discourse its character as an event; finally removing the sovereignty of the signifier"?[27]

Is all of this sufficient? Can one speak of truth without also speaking immediately of *praxis*, of resistance? In 1977, my response was the following: ". . . this is not sufficient. Nor is it sufficient for Foucault, it seems. In his "Preface" to Bruce Jackson's book,[28] he proposes an interpretation of the world as a space in which command, exclusion, and violence circulate, and proposes a very critical image of capital similar to the prison. At the same time, he is struck, surprised, and excited by the formidable reality of revolt, by the independence, communication, and auto-valorization that are born from within the prisons themselves. The idea and the reality of power, of law, of order, which traverse the prisons and bind together the most terrifying experiences in the prisoners' stories, begin here to waver. Events, in their serial and regular character, open onto new conditions of possibility. There is nothing dialectical about this. The dialectic, with its false rigor, imprisons the imagination of possibility. There is no static reversal but rather the opening of a horizon. The analytic *logic* of separation, precisely because it is drawn to a close, opens up a strategy of separation. Separation and reversal only become real in strategy. The world of self-valorization is henceforth opposed to the world of the valorization of capital. Possibility is transformed into potency. Am I forcing this Spinozist idea of possibility understood as potency on Foucault's thought? Perhaps. . . . Everything happens as if the Foucauldian analyses were not only "searching," so to speak, for critical outcomes but also for a sort of stability in the effective character of the obtained results. Yet, this methodological "mobility," which seduces us so much, which is adapted so well to the quality of intellectual work that is required by capital today, and which is intrinsic to current revolutionary modalities and ends, poses a problem: can it stand on its own, or must it necessarily be incarnated in the concrete determination of the historical process, of potency [*puissance*] against power [*pouvoir*], of the proletariat against capital? This introduces a problematic framework, to which only the real movement of things is likely to give a response. Whatever the response, we must be thankful to Foucault for having formulated this set of questions."[29]

At the end of 1983, I arrived in France after a long period of incarceration in Italy. Around the time of Foucault's death I resumed contact with Gilles Deleuze, with whom I discussed Foucault at great length. I had to get past the reservations that some of Deleuze's friends and collaborators had about Foucault. I immersed myself, then, in the genius and inspiration[30] that presided over the writing of his *Foucault*[31] (of course, I am not using these terms in the sense that they are used in the history of philosophy; nothing could be farther from the work of Deleuze and Foucault than that). It seems to me that this book definitively overcame the impasse between "subjectivity without object" and "structure without subject," whose topography I tried rapidly to describe (and which should doubtlessly be understood as a "loss of identity" for the French philosophy of the 1950s).[32] This overcoming was not an *Aufhebung*; it contained nothing dialectical (As Foucault said, "The theme of universal mediation is, I believe, only a way of eliding the reality of discourse.")[33] This book definitively surpassed the tradition of French spiritualism that had restricted truth to the figure of the individual-subject, that had reduced action to love and annulled the positivity of existence through psychology. Actually, well before recounting the history of the encounter between the "episteme" and the innovation that it entails, Deleuze offered the "apparatus" [*dispositif*] of this overcoming to Foucault. It is for this reason that he was able to speak of it from then on with so much pertinence. As for us, who looked to grasp the bigger picture of this extraordinary overcoming of the French philosophical tradition (which occurred within this tradition's own borders) and who attempted to realize the hegemonic "confirmation" of this overcoming (which Foucault and Deleuze authorized throughout the field of philosophy, including outside of Europe), we were going to have to wait for the publication, some years later, of Foucault's courses at the Collège de France. Nonetheless, we had already understood that if the twentieth century became Deleuzian, the twenty-first would doubtlessly be Foucauldian.

Some have made great efforts, however, to try to block the way to the conversion of the Foucauldian project – beyond biopower, through biopolitics – to the production of subjectivity. At the very beginning of the 1990s, I taught a seminar at the Collège International de Philosophie, and I recall an intense confrontation between François Ewald and Pierre Macherey. The polemic concerned individualism, different determinations of freedom, and the meaning of ethics in Foucault's work. Neither saw that it is actually the singularity that Foucault opposed to individualism, that one had to look for a freedom in ethics that was not only spiritual but also bodily, and that his ontology was productive. Consequently, they did not really understand that the sovereignty from within which biopower takes root (be it liberal or socialist) is not the only basis upon which ontology can be constructed and measured. For Foucault, in contrast, sovereignty was subsumed – that is, analyzed and deconstructed – under biopolitics, based on the relation between different productions of subjectivity.

This is what Foucault wrote: "When one defines the exercise of power as a mode of action upon the action of others, when one characterizes it by the 'government' of men by other men – in the most extensive sense of the word – one includes an important element: freedom. Power is exercised only on 'free subjects,' insofar as they are 'free' (understanding by this term individual or collective subjects who have before them a field of possibility in which several behaviors, several reactions, and diverse modes of comportment can take place). Where the determinations are saturated, there is no relation of power. Slavery is not a power relation when man is in chains (in this case, it is a matter of a physical relationship of constraint), but only when he can move around and, if worst comes to worst, escape. There is not, then, a mutually exclusive confrontation of power and freedom . . . The relation of power and freedom's disobedience therefore cannot be separated. The central problem of power is not that of 'voluntary servitude" (how can we desire to be slaves?). At the heart of the power relation, ceaselessly provoking it, there is the recalcitrance of the will and the intransigence of freedom."[34] This text is from 1980. From this moment, everything that Foucault would develop would be situated from within this perspective. In fact, it is a matter, I believe, of incessantly deepening the materialist character of the analysis of historical determinations, and of deepening the content of the episteme in the passage from "archaeology" to "genealogy." It is also a matter of looking deeper into this idea of the potency of the "production of subjectivity," which can happen within resistances and rebellions, or within the expression and critique of political democracy.

79

I would like to cite for the final time a brief passage from my 1977 article, published one year later in *Aut Aut*: "When Marx reaches the definition of the capitalist society (that is, the intuition that the development of capital, in the name of an inherent necessity, overtakes every limit of historical prediction and thereby imposes the modification of its own categories of operation), he requires, at that time, the implementation of a new representation (*Neue Darstellung*), a new and better-adapted exposition. In the Marxian thematic, the *Neue Darstellung* is of course not only a new exposition of contents, it must also be a new identification of subjects, and consequently a new methodological foundation. Today, we are in the middle – or perhaps beyond – this preliminary phase that Marx had foreseen, and that his critical path required. *We are witnessing, then, an original and fertile disruption of the scientific horizon of the revolutionaries – and for that we must also be thankful to Foucault.* This categorical disruption, this resolute innovation of method issues in certain fundamental tasks – tasks that it is a matter of taking up directly, by insisting on the structural complexity of capitalist civilization, on the radicalism of the destructive project, on the sectarian partiality of the scientific strategy that we implement, and on the offensive character of the tactical consequences that result from this. What is certain is that we are already far advanced in this development. *The intensity of the approach and the fecundity of the Foucauldian method belong to things already done and to tasks to be accomplished.*

"However, like always, the reasons for a choice or task, the foundations of a method, are not based only on the identification of a historical transition. Ontology is denser than History.[35] As we have seen, the method is renewed by the specificity of the exposition of the contents. But, in this contemporary phase, we must say even more: the method (as apparatus [*dispositif*], as production of subjectivity, as *praxis*) determines the specificity of the contents. The method needs to be rooted in the ontology of a grasp of a historical existence that belongs to the radicalism that the world shows us. Try, then, to read with the simplicity of the dialectical method or of its paradoxical alternatives some of the great problems of (the critique of) political economy and of politics. At best, you will only come away empty-handed! Today, in contrast, truth shows its complexity through the thousands of developments that introduce revolution to the critical process. To follow these developments – to articulate, against power, the infinitely complex interconnection of autonomies and independences, of autonomy and autonomies, of possibilities and potency; to explicate this process as the source, and simultaneously as the catastrophe, of adverse power, we need the method, and its ontological plenitude, that will permit this work. Today, the method of the critique of political economy and of politics attempts to approximate this method, both in its multiple and diversified activity and in the complexity of the semantic function that this method determines. For this, we should be thankful to Foucault."[36]

Indeed, thanks to Foucault.

NOTES

1. This article was originally translated from Italian into French by Judith Revel for the volume *Michel Foucault* (Paris: L'Herne, 2011), 199–206. The original Italian appears in Negri's *Il comune in rivolta: Sul potere costituente delle lotte* (Verona: Ombre Corte, 2012), 67–77. I have worked primarily from Revel's translation, but have consulted the Italian throughout (translator's note).

2. *Aut Aut*, one of the most important and prestigious journals in Italy for philosophy, the human and social sciences, psychoanalysis, and aesthetic criticism, was founded in 1954 by Enzo Paci, who was its director until his death in 1976. From 1968, Pier Aldo Rovatti and Salvatore Veca served as editors of the journal. Rovatti, a student of Paci, is also one of the principal translators and scholars of Foucault's work. For a brief period (1974–6), Rovatti and Paci served as co-directors, after which Rovatti became the sole director of the journal (Revel's note).

3. Antonio Negri, "Sul metodo della critica della politica," *Aut Aut* 167–8 (September–December 1978), 197–212. Reprinted in Negri, *Macchina Tempo* (Milan: Feltrinelli, 1982), 70–84.

4. See Antonio Negri, *Marx oltre Marx. Quadern di lavoro sui Grundrisse* (Milan: Feltrinelli, 1979), translated into French as *Marx au-delà de Marx. Cahiers de travail sur les Grundrisse* (Paris: Bourgois, 1979), and into English as *Marx Beyond Marx: Lessons on the Grundrisse*, trans. Harry Cleaver, Michael Ryan and Maurizio Viano (New York: Autonomedia, 1992).

5. Negri uses both *potere* and *potenza* throughout this article, which are equivalent to the French *pouvoir* and *puissance*, respectively. Both are often rendered in English as "power," but in order to mark the distinction between them I translate the former as "power" and the latter as "potency." Negri elaborates on the distinction below (translator's note).

6. Michel Foucault, *Histoire de la folie à l'age classique* (Paris: Gallimard, 1972), 548–9, translated into English as *History of Madness*, trans. Jonathan Murphy and Jean Khalfa (New York: Routledge, 2006), 529. Translation slightly modified.

7. Michel Foucault, "Introduction," in L. Binswanger, *La Rêve et l'existence* (Bruges: Desclée de Brouwer, 1954); "Introduction à l'Anthropologie," in E. Kant, *Anthropologie du point de vue pragmatique* (Paris, Vrin, 2008). (Foucault's translation of Kant's text was published in 1964 by Vrin, but without Foucault's introduction. The introduction, which was in fact Foucault's secondary thesis, remained at the library of the Sorbonne and was only added to the work three years ago) (Revel's note). Translated into English in Foucault, *Introduction to Kant's Anthropology*, trans. Roberto Nigro and Kate Briggs (Los Angeles: Semiotext(e), 2008).

8. On this point, see P. Vilar, "Histoire marxiste, histoire en construction. Essai de dialogue avec Althusser," *Annales. ESC* 28:1 (1973), 165–98, translated into English as "Marxist History, a History in the Making: Towards a Dialogue with Althusser," *New Left Review* I:80 (July–August 1973).

9. Negri, *Macchina Tempo*, 74. We translate from the original Italian edition, unpublished in France (Revel's note).

10. Negri plays here on the distinction between the terms *déterminatezza* and *determinazione*, which are rendered in French as *contingence* (literally, the determined character of a thing) and *détermination*. (Revel's note).

81

11. Negri, *Macchina Tempo*, 74.
12. In other words, "the *history* of what happened" and "what *actually* happened (translator's note)."
13. Play on the Hegelian formula that Negri inverts here as "The Whole is not true" (Revel's note).
14. Antonio Negri, *Saggi sullo storicismo Tedesco. Dilthey e Meinecke* (Milan: Feltrinelli, 1959).
15. Michel Foucault, *Les Mots et les choses* (Paris: Gallimard, 1966). I read the book in French as soon as it came out, but it was quickly translated into Italian by P. Pasquino: M. Foucault, *Le Parole e le cose* (Milan: Rizzoli, 1967). See also the invaluable collected volume *Les Mots et les choses de Michel Foucault. Regards critiques 1966–1968* (IMEC/Presses universitaires de Caen, 2009).
16. Michel Foucault, *Surveiller et punir. Naissance de la prison* (Paris: Gallimard, 1975). (The Italian translation by Alcesti Tarchetti also came out quickly: M. Foucault, *Sorvegliare e punier. Nascita della prigione* (Turin: Einaudi, 1976).
17. Antonio Negri, *L'anomalia selvaggia. Potere e Potenza in Baruch Spinoza* (Milan: Feltrinelli, 1981), translated into French as *L'Anomalie sauvage. Pussiance and pouvoir chez Baruch Spinoza* (Paris: PUF, 1982), and into English as *The Savage Anomaly: The Power of Spinoza's Metaphysics and Politics*, trans. Michael Hardt (Minneapolis: University of Minnesota Press, 1981).
18. Foucault, *Surveiller et punir*, 315. Slightly modified version of *Discipline and Punish: The Birth of the Prison*, trans. Alan Sheridan (New York: Vintage, 1995), 308.
19. Michel Foucault, "Precisazioni sul potere. Riposta ad alcuni critici" (conversation with P. Pasquino, Feb. 1978), *Aut Aut* 167–8 (September–December 1978), 3–11, translated in French as "Précisions sur le pouvoir. Réponses à certains critiques" in Foucault, *Dits et Écrits* III:238 (Paris: Gallimard, 1976–9), 628. Slightly modified version of "Clarifications on the Question of Power," in *Foucault Live* (New York: Semiotext(e), 1996), 257.
20. Foucault, *Surveiller et punir*, 315. Slightly modified version of *Discipline and Punish*, 26–7.
21. Antonio Negri, *Il Dominio e il sabotaggio: sul metodo marxista della trasformazione sociale* (Milan: Feltrinelli, 1978).
22. For Negri, the passage from the figure of the mass worker to the social worker is, at the end of the 1970s, the attempt to describe the substitution of the classical figure of the worker (who is desubjectified and reduced to the pure physical force of his arms, within a chain in which he is at every moment permutable or replaceable) with that of the social worker, who integrates the elements of socialization essential to the process of production and is resubjectified on this basis. In fact, what Negri describes as the figure of the mass worker corresponds well to the pages of *Discipline and Punish* devoted to the regulation of the construction and management of productive space; while the social worker represents a new figure, stemming from the post-1968 struggles, and which is at the origin of a "micro-conflictuality" spread throughout the social fabric (Revel's note).
23. Piero Sraffo (1898–1983) was an Italian economist, considered the founder of neo-Ricardianism (Revel's note).
24. P. Sraffa, *Production of Commodities by Means of Commodities: Prelude to a critique of economic theory* (Cambridge: Cambridge University Press, 1960), translated into

French as *Production de marchandises par des marchandises. Prélude à critique des théories économique* (Paris: Dunod, 1999).

25. In fact, Sraffa did what the Italians call *fare le fiche*. He made a fist and inserted his thumb through his index and middle fingers, which is popularly perceived as indicating the form of the feminine sex (*fica*) and is traditionally understood as a sign of contempt and dissatisfaction (Revel's note).

26. Negri, *Macchina Tempo*, 82.

27. Michel Foucault, *L'Ordre du discours* (Paris: Gallimard, 1970), 53. In English, reprinted as the appendix to *The Archaeology of Knowledge*, trans. A. M. Sheridan Smith (New York: Vintage, 2010), 229. Translation slightly modified.

28. Michel Foucault, "Preface" to B. Jackson, *Leurs prisons. Autobiographie de prisonniers américains* (Paris: Plon, 1975), reprinted in *Dits et Écrits*, II:144.

29. Negri, *Macchina Tempo*, 82.

30. The original Italian is *l'aria di quel capolavoro*, literally "the air of that masterpiece" (translator's note).

31. Gilles Deleuze, *Foucault* (Paris: Éditions de Minuit, 1986). English translation: *Foucault*, trans. Seán Hand (Minneapolis: University of Minnesota Press, 1988).

32. V. Descombes, *Le Même et l'autre* (Paris: Éditions de Minuit, 1980).

33. Foucault, *L'Ordre du discours*, 50. Slightly modified translation of *The Archaeology of Knowledge*, 228.

34. Michel Foucault, "The Subject and Power," in H. Dreyfus and P. Rabinow, *Michel Foucault: Beyond Structuralism and Hermeneutics* (Chicago: University of Chicago Press, 1983), 221–2. Translation slightly modified. French translation in Foucault, *Dits et Écrits*, IV:306, 237–8.

35. In French in the original (Revel's note).

36. Negri, *Macchina Tempo*, 83–4. Emphasis in the original (Revel's note).

PART II

Method and Critique

CHAPTER 5

Critical Problematization in Foucault and Deleuze: The Force of Critique without Judgment

COLIN KOOPMAN

"One thing haunts Foucault – thought . . . To think means to experiment and to problematize."

(Gilles Deleuze on Michel Foucault in 1986, 116)

"The freeing of difference requires thought without contradiction, without dialectics, without negation . . . We must think problematically rather than question and answer dialectically."

(Michel Foucault on Gilles Deleuze in 1970, 359)

THE FORCE OF CRITIQUE

In a 1972 conversation concerning the role of philosophy in the work of social critique, Michel Foucault and Gilles Deleuze put forward a conception of critical theory that resonates widely throughout the varied terrains of their work. At the heart of the conception they constructed together in "Intellectuals and Power" is a radical revisioning of the work that philosophy should expect of itself insofar as philosophy can legitimately expect itself to engage present social, cultural, ethical and political problems. Foucault and Deleuze clearly expected such engagements of themselves. Much of their work is located, in different ways of course, at the interface of the sciences of the human and the politics of ourselves. How we take ourselves to be known, as subjects of, say, psychiatric normalization or biological specification or economic calculation, raises questions for how we take ourselves to be related to one another, for example as shared agents and subjects of governance. In engaging such problems, Foucault and Deleuze recognized, or at least affirmed,

87

the need for a new conception of philosophical practice. Foucault concisely captured the specific difference in the 1972 discussion when he said that, "theory does not express, translate, or serve to apply practice: it is practice . . . it is an activity conducted alongside those who struggle for power, and not their illumination from a safe distance."[1] To this Deleuze replied with his now-famous statement that, "A theory is exactly like a box of tools."[2] But what does it mean to construe the work of theory, or what I would just prefer to call the work of philosophy, as a box of tools, as a practical instrumentality whose primary purpose is that of functional engagement in a local struggle? What conception of philosophy is at work here? And how can those who find this conception attractive develop philosophical practices with the aim of fashioning philosophical tools, rather than conceiving of philosophy in some grander, possibly even hyperbolic, style?

Consider a prefatory image to these questions insofar as they could be taken as questions about philosophical engagement. There is a famous photograph of Foucault and Deleuze portraying Deleuze on the left beside a young official, who appears to be a policeman, placing a gloved hand on his back, and Foucault on the right making a very emphatic face to someone else who is just out of frame, but possibly also a cop as indicated by another gloved hand reaching from out of the frame right into the heart of the picture in order to lay itself on the chest of the bald philosopher. The image itself is a tumult. One need not know anything about its context to be able to see it as exemplifying philosophy as a work of critical engagement. Here is philosophy becoming an explosive box of tools. Interestingly, in the background of the photograph, standing a few feet behind Foucault and Deleuze, and squarely between the two of them within the composition of the image, stands Jean-Paul Sartre. In one sense Sartre was the paradigm of the engaged philosopher for Foucault's and Deleuze's generation. Among the most important engaged intellectuals in the decades in which they were young upstart philosophers, Sartre must have given Foucault and Deleuze a great deal of confidence in their many attempts to bring their philosophy to bear on the demands of their day. But in another sense Sartre is most certainly not the model of that which relayed between Foucault and Deleuze in their practice of philosophy. For on one reading Sartrean philosophy was all about bringing the lessons of existentialist phenomenology to bear on the realities of social practice. Sartre, as it were, applied the insights of philosophical theory to the realities of political and social practice. Sartre was, on any accounting, an engaged philosopher. This no doubt thrilled younger philosophers of Foucault's and Deleuze's generation. But, they must have been asking themselves all the while, must we model our engagement after Sartre, or should we search out some other way of putting philosophy into contact with politics? They sought different ways of making a difference. In Foucault and Deleuze, and between them, philosophical critique became a practical enactment of philosophy within social contexts. The possible difference from Sartre, and it is crucial for understanding not only Foucault and

Deleuze but also for how we might activate them midst the perils of our own present, is between applying philosophical insight in contexts of practical engagement and constructing philosophical insight through and also for the work of practical engagement. The latter, I shall argue, is the model offered us by Foucault and Deleuze (leaving Sartre now to the side though he will make an oblique return below in my discussion of French Hegelianism). This difference, I shall argue, has everything to do with a metatheoretical watershed for which Deleuze and Foucault are paradigmatic figures.

In the vicinity of that range of philosophic thought that is somewhere between Foucault and Deleuze we find a crucial philosophical watershed for the twentieth century. This is the divide between a negative dialectics that would ceaselessly pursue the work of *contradiction* and an experimental methodology that would engage its reality by way of a work of *problematization*. The separation between a dialectical and an experimental methodology represents a decisive divide in our philosophical present. For this divide has everything to do with the possibilities open to philosophical engagement in the present. If our work of critique is to engage the realities in which we find ourselves, then much hangs out how we vision and implement the work of critique. Critical engagement, according to Foucault and Deleuze, has everything to do with a new role for "the intellectuals" vis-à-vis "the powers" in which we so often find ourselves implicated. The classical role of the intellectual was to speak the truth to power by telling power how it ought to be organized – laying down a law of justice or a rule of morality, for instance. For Foucault and Deleuze, something else was always at stake – Deleuze captured this in "The Intellectuals and Power" dialogue when he said to Foucault that, "you were the first to teach us a fundamental lesson, both in your books and in the practical domain: the indignity of speaking for others."[3] A philosophical labor that would be critical without speaking for others, telling them what they ought to do, has everything to do with a mode of philosophy that would be critical without being judgmental. This, for Foucault and Deleuze, points directly to the basic divide between a negative dialectics of contradiction and the productive work of experimentation.

CRITICAL, IMMANENT, EXPERIMENTAL, PROBLEMATIZING

One way in which Foucault and Deleuze have been important for the philosophical transformations of the past half century, and thus why they remain important for us today, concerns their practice of philosophy as a mode of experimental immanent critical problematization. There are four terms in my attribution. Each of them is crucial for understanding both Foucault and Deleuze.

First, Foucault and Deleuze are Kantians in that for them philosophy is *critical* philosophy. Second, there are different ways of taking up the project of a critical inquiry into conditions of possibility, and Foucault and Deleuze remained rigorously *immanent* in their pursuit of critique. Third, while others have pursued the work of immanent critique through the facilities of a negative dialectics of contradiction, Foucault and Deleuze by contrast rigorously avoided the negative work of contradiction in favor of pursuits facilitated by an *experimental* methodeutic. Fourth, within the space of experimentation one might experiment with an eye toward the stabilizations gained by answering a question, or one might with Foucault and Deleuze experiment with the different aim of destabilization as facilitated by posing a problem, or *problematizing*. I shall detail each of these four cuts in turn in order to situate the stakes for us today of learning through Foucault and Deleuze's philosophical mode of experimental immanent critical problematization.

Critique as a mode of philosophy

With respect to the first decisive cut, Foucault and Deleuze here follow the familiar contours of the Kantian critical project. Their shared debt to a certain aspect of Kantian philosophy has not been recognized often enough. Foucault and Deleuze inherited from Kant the work of critique. Critique was Kant's philosophical alternative to the unending philosophical vacillations that were the promises of early modern philosophy, perhaps paradigmatically the back and forth between metaphysics and skepticism. Critique for Kant meant an interrogation of limits or bounds, which Kant most often figured as conditions of possibility. A critical philosophy is a philosophy that asks of its objects of inquiry, "What makes this possible?" This question is radically different in form from the classical philosophical interrogation of definitions most famously taking the form of, "What is this?" Whereas the metaphysicians are brazen in their answer to the classical question of definition, the skeptics are skittish.

One of Kant's key insights was that any response to the definitional question leaves philosophy painfully out of touch with what is actually going on with respect to its objects of inquiry, a pain that can only be removed by pressing philosophy into different modalities. Definition has its place, to be sure, but the delusion of metaphysics and skepticism is the delusion that definition is everything. What Kant taught us was that only someone under the sway of that particular illusion would muster the bravado to think themselves capable of knowing what really is, and for the same reason that only someone under the sway of that illusion would feel disappointment in not being able to know what really is. Kant's project was thus an attempt to get philosophy out from under the sway of that picture, so that it could see itself instead as inquiry into the conditions of possibility of whatever objects of inquiry present themselves to us. The philosophical promise of the critical philosophy was that of a critique of judgment, which can only be understand as an inquiry into the conditions of possibility of judgment such that the work of a critique of judgment must itself rigorously refrain from judging.[4] The promise of critique, then, is the promise of a philosophical labor that is preparatory for judgment without itself being judgmental.

Immanence as a mode of critique

This brings us to the second decisive cut. The force of the Kantian project persists for us today only insofar as that project has been subjected to severe revision in the wake of Kant. Critique in Kant's own hands, though full of the promise of the evasion of metaphysics, finds itself falling again and again back into a philosophical mode that is hardly distinguishable from metaphysics. This is because Kant could not help but forward his project of critique as one of specifically transcendental critique, that is critique that concerns itself with objects which can be thought, or cognized, a priori.[5] One familiar way of glossing the work of transcendental critique concerns the scope and modality of a priori thought, such that the work of critique would concern that which is universal in scope and necessary in modality. In Kant's unmodest hands, then, the project of critique comes to be identified with transcendental critique, and thereby cannot avoid slipping back into the metaphysics which it wanted to show us the way out of. To put this in other terms, Kant had wanted to perform a critique of judgment without himself undertaking to judge but could not but help himself to the vast range of judgments enacted by his own transcendental perspective.

It is important to recognize the lengths to which Kant went in order to avoid lapsing back into a dogmatic metaphysics. Kant wanted to be rigorous about avoiding the transcendence of metaphysics, and so he invented the idea of transcendental critique by explicitly distinguishing the transcendent and the transcendental.[6] For Kant, a transcendent principle contrasts to an immanent one in that it passes beyond the limits of possible experience, while the transcendental use of a principle contrasts to an empirical use in employing a principle to extend beyond the limits of experience. Kant tells us that a principle that commands the transgression or disruption of limits of the empirical is transcendent, but that a transcendental use of a principle that takes us beyond these limits without commanding their removal is not itself transcendent. The distinction is quite fine. But it fails to hold up in Kant's own critical philosophy, for instance where he transcendentally invokes the immortality of the soul from the perspective of moral reason but insists that this is not the assertion of a transcendent principle concerning immortality from the perspective of speculative reason.[7]

The sway of metaphysics, the stretch of its shadow, proves just enormous. Metaphysics is like a shark – you cannot play games with it. You need to either keep away or accept that you could get bit. Kant thought he could dip into the seas and stay safe simply because he was not calling into question the limit between the uncertain ocean and the safety of land. But as soon you use reason transcendentally to wade out into the waters beyond, you cannot cry foul when metaphysics sees you as actually trying to transcend. From the perspective of the shark there is no difference between the shy swimmer who only wants to test the waters for a second and the fish who lives there all the time. That is why metaphysics swallowed Kant. Some contemporary philosophers take the voraciousness of metaphysics as a sign that it is unavoidable, using this view to argue against the basic promise of the Kantian critical project – but these metaphysical revivalisms, no matter how rigorously argued and exquisitely developed, are throwbacks that we should guard against.[8] That the critical promise is difficult to deliver on does not mean we should just give up – my view is that Foucault and Deleuze offer us a unique way of appreciating the continuing force and viability of the Kantian project.

Deleuze and Foucault, on my reading, did manage to avoid the bite of metaphysics. They are part of a long tradition of critical philosophy which would severely reject the tendencies of transcendental critique in favor of the initial promise of a purely immanent critique. Foucault expressed this well in his "What Is Enlightenment?" essay named after a famous essay by Kant of the same title: "The point is to transform the critique conducted in the form of necessary limitation into a practical critique that takes the form of a possible crossing. Criticism is no longer going to be practiced in the search for formal structures with universal value but, rather, as a historical investigation into the events that have led us to constitute ourselves and to recognize ourselves as subjects of what we are doing, thinking, saying. In that sense, this criticism is not transcendental, and its goal is not that of making a metaphysics possible: it is genealogical in its design and archaeological in its method."[9] Note the specific contrasts here: Foucault is cautious about the quintessential Kantian ideas of necessary limitation, formal structure, universal value, transcendental critique, and metaphysics, contrasting these to his own genealogical-archaeological mode of critique. For Foucault, then, critique would be an inquiry into immanent conditions of possibility rather than a search for transcendental conditions of possibility. For Foucault, the work of critique would, for example, take the form of inquiries into how we have been made into the subjects we are by processes that are immanent to and wholly within the history of our very modes of subjectivation. Deleuze sought to transform the Kantian project from within in quite similar terms, looking to rescue an immanent critique of judgment from the judgmental tendencies of a critique turned transcendental: "Kant did not invent a true critique of judgment; on the contrary, what the book of this title established was a fantastic subjective tribunal."[10]

There are many ways, after Kant, of attempting to shift critique from the search for transcendental conditions to the search for immanent conditions. This is, perhaps most famously, a Hegelian project, for it is Hegel who described philosophy as the work of "observ[ing] the subject matter's own immanent development."[11]

To be sure, there is much of Hegel behind Foucault and Deleuze. But Hegel is not the only possible source for their turn to immanence. The idea of an immanent critique, which would ask the question of conditions of possibility from a perspective wholly immanent to that which is conditioned, was perhaps Hume's before it was either Hegel's or Kant's. Kant's pride of place in the history of modern philosophy depends, of course, on Kant's own reading of Hume as a skeptic who woke him from the slumbers of dogmatism. But what if Hume was not a skeptic? What if Hume was rather something like what we today would call a naturalist or even a pragmatist? Hume's famous claims to the effect that the conditions of knowledge are located in habit and custom were, to be sure, skeptical with respect to the metaphysicians, but they were also more positively a suggestion about how we might take up immanent inquiries into the conditions of contemporary cultural forms. Hume himself undertook such immanent inquiries, perhaps most provocatively in his massive six-volume *History of England*, a book that few philosophers read today, and which quite a few Hegelians even manage to forget as an alternative to *geistesgeschichte* historiography in the grand style.[12]

This is not the place to offer a counter-narrative of the history of modern philosophy, though I will remark tangentially that it is quite plain that such a counter-narrative is now badly in need of telling. The point of pointing out, however hesitatingly, Hume's precedent for the project of immanent critique is to motivate two related thoughts, both of which are crucial for understanding at least part of what is at work in Foucault and Deleuze.[13] The first thought is that, though Foucault and Deleuze took up critique in the manner of the project of immanent critique and Hegel is our most famous exemplar of immanent critique, perhaps nonetheless Hegel may not be the best guide to the work that immanent critique does in Foucault and Deleuze. As I discuss below, their well-known departures from Hegel are nothing less than startling, once one grasps their full force. These departures may be part of a longer counter-tradition in philosophy that reaches back behind Hegel, and even behind Kant himself. This brings me to the second thought, which concerns that to which Foucault and Deleuze are reaching back. If we needed to give more flesh to the idea of immanent critique, we might refer to it under the headings of cultural critique, or even empirical critique. It is a practice of critique that takes as its concern those ever-moving shapes of cultural norms and forms in which we find ourselves enmeshed in ever-evolving ways. Cultural critique is immanent critique because it is an inquiry into conditions of culture from a point of view that is also located within the culture whose conditions are being investigated. Thinking through Hume here helps us see how Foucault and Deleuze are offering immanent cultural critique in a mode that is also empirical. In invoking the empirical here my primary connotation is not that of empiricist epistemology. Rather, the empiricism I invoke is the empiricism of inquiry and of investigation. It is the empiricism of severe patience – the mode of the obsessive whose only obsession is that they need to see for themselves. It is no surprise that empiricism and skepticism are often linked in the history of modern philosophy, for the empiricist is just the philosopher who is obsessive about finding out and thus skeptical of the brazen confidence of the rationalist who is content to go on reasoning alone. Putting the point this way helps make plain how Deleuze and Foucault were reacting against a Kantian inflation of reason not so much by turning to a Hegelian absolute immanence as by returning to a Humean empirical immanence. What are the empirical conditions, scrutable for those who care to look, of the evolving forms and norms of our cultural milieus? Answering this question does not require assuming a philosophical point of view that is outside of, or transcendental with respect to, that which we are asking after.

Experimentation as a mode of immanent critique

This brings me to the third cut, which I shall argue is *the most decisive moment* in the metaphilosophical shift enacted by, and between, Foucault and Deleuze. On my reading, Foucault and Deleuze are for us today crucial figures in a tidal shift in twentieth-century philosophy found across a diversity of traditions. This is a shift in the basic categories of thought with which philosophy does its work. Those who forwarded it achieved a drastic departure from the philosophical inheritances that have long dominated much of modern philosophy, including contemporary philosophy from the early decades of the twentieth century in both Anglo-American and Continental variants. I shall here reference that shift by way of a contrast situated in what we might call the methodeutic (though perhaps logic is an equally fecund term here) operative in the work of critique. On a standard account, the work of critique proceeds by way of a dialectical methodeutic of contradiction. The seachange that was Deleuze and Foucault was at its most radical in its departure from the dialectics of contradiction in its effort to attain what I will call a methodeutic of experimentation.

Experimentation is my term, not Foucault's or Deleuze's, though it is in ample usage throughout their works.[14] One might think that a term more in keeping with Deleuze's vocabulary might be "difference" and a term closer to Foucault's might be "transgression." And yet I find these terms misleading in some fundamental way, at least without sufficient prefatory explanation. A better term, drawing on what I regard as the central aspect of Foucault and Deleuze, would be a "problematization."[15] But I refrain from that more precise term at this juncture because I regard problematization as one possible aspect of what I am calling experimentation. One can take up the project of critique through experimentation and work in a mode that is not at its core problematizational. For instance, one might work not so much to problematize as to reconstruct, in the sense of problem-solving. Both Foucault and Deleuze took up an experimental approach to immanent critique *primarily* in a problematizational mode. Before explicating the term of problematization, however, it is crucial to understand the broader shift in methodeutic that is at play here, because that broader shift helps us gain a grip on how experimentation represents that sea-change of a departure from the inheritance, still with us today, of a dialectics of contradiction.

It is here where Hegel, or to be perfectly precise, a certain reading of Hegel, is perhaps most important for understanding Foucault and Deleuze. For the shift toward experimentation is brought into clear relief against the background of a Hegelian negative dialectics of contradiction. It is, however, important to be explicit at the outset that my differentiation of Foucault's and Deleuze's innovation is paired not so much with the work of Hegel himself as with the inheritances of Hegel*ian* philosophy against which Foucault and Deleuze (and others) were writing in their mid-century French context. My effort here is not so much to make sense of Hegel himself as it is to make sense of what Foucault and Deleuze (but especially Deleuze given how little Foucault wrote directly about Hegel himself) must have thought about Hegel such that they would mount the challenges they offered to a certain Hegel*ianism*. I take it that much recent revisionist work in Hegel scholarship has done a good deal to revise the received interpretations of Hegelian philosophy against which Foucault was working.[16] That noted, this revisionist scholarship does nothing to impinge the importance of the Deleuzian and Foucaultian departure from prominent brands of Hegelian philosophy, nor do Deleuze's and Foucault's philosophical revision do anything to impinge contemporary revisionist scholarship that stands in a good position to benefit from their criticisms of certain metaphilosophical modalities.

Why, then, the importance of a certain Hegelianism? The philosophical context in which Foucault and Deleuze were educated (mid-twentieth century French philosophy) was one that was widely, if not almost everywhere, characterized by a sturdy brand of Hegelian dialectics often passed down to us today in textbook glosses about theses, antitheses and syntheses. This, at least, was what Foucault and Deleuze themselves suggested, or rather how they experienced the conditions of their own philosophical maturation.[17] For both, the dominant French Hegelian system was best exemplified in Jean Hyppolite's and Alexander Kojève's widely-celebrated readings of Hegel's *Phenomenology of Spirit* – and neither of these readings were terribly far from the popular model of Sartrean philosophy, whose politics of engagement I briefly noted at the outset.[18] These and other readings made use above all of Hegel's negative dialectics to make sense of the meaning of the historical tragedies of the early twentieth century, recouping them under the banner of a theory of dialectical progress – these were the core themes that were taken up in influential ways by existentialist, Marxist and Freudian inflections of Hegelianism.[19]

What all of this suggests is that Foucault and Deleuze were centrally concerned to reject the dominant program(s) of negative dialectics characteristic of their

philosophical milieu and that operated this rejection so by restructuring many
of the basic categories structuring philosophical thought itself. What Foucault
and Deleuze found most objectionable in French Hegelianism was its reliance on
Hegel's image of thought cast in terms of the work of contradiction and its opera-
tionalization through determinate negation.[20] These ideas had offered the French
Hegelians a way of accounting for the meaningfulness of determinate historical
transformation. Such an account was very badly needed as the Second Great War
drew to a close and the French Hegelians saw the logic of contradiction as the most
promising strategy. But for Foucault and Deleuze such an approach needed to
answer the prior question of whether or not there are other routes to a critique of
our present than by way of contradiction and negativity. It would be their gain to
suggest that there are. What had been operative in French Hegelianism such that
contradiction appeared to be the only route to immanence?

An answer to this difficult question can be approached by a consideration of
Hegel's lack of place for indeterminacy, or to state that differently, Hegel's figuring
indeterminacy as itself a lack. In a crucial moment at the outset of *The Philosophy of
Right*, Hegel makes plain his refusal to think indeterminacy as a positive category.
Considering the possibility that the will might be through and through free, or
entirely undetermined, Hegel claims, all too effortlessly, that, "The essential insight
to be gained here is that this initial indeterminacy is itself a determinacy."[21] The
broader point here is that every indeterminacy is always already a kind of determination – the indeterminate just is that which is *taken as* indeterminate, which is to
say it is just that which is *determined* as indeterminate. For Hegel there is, as such,
no positivity role for indeterminacy to play in the motion of thought. Behind every
indeterminacy there is a determination, indeed a whole host of historical determinations, lurking. To put this differently, for Hegel everything that is, is determinate.
It is in virtue of this that Hegel is reliant on the category of contradiction and the
operator of negation to put thought into motion. If everything that is already is
determinate, then the flow of determination can take place only by way of the
negation of contradictory determinations – philosophy always starts with what is
determinate and identical with itself, and from there derives difference by way of
the negativity of contradiction. The only place for movement in such a view is the
movement of negation because everything is determinate and so anything can be
overcome only by way of its negation – the pain or suffering of motion is always
the painfulness or sufferance of negativity. By contrast, if philosophy were to give a
positive status or role to the indeterminate as such in its operations, then it would
be possible for thought and reality to gain their motion by way of relations not all
reducible to the labor of the negative.

To the French Hegelian image of philosophy as dialectically pursuing the negative work of the mechanism of *contradiction*, Foucault and Deleuze replied with a
practice of philosophy as the pursuit of emerging cultural-empirical forms by way

of *experimentation*, one aspect of which would involve the severe work of problematization. The methodeutic of experimentation does not negate the dialectics of contradiction, but it differs from it. The point is of course not that there are no contradictions, but only that the relation of contradiction cannot explain everything when it comes to transformations of thought and practice. The grand bloated assumption of Hegelian dialectics is simply that determinate conflicts are bound to resolve themselves, that is, that they will eventually grow into contradictions and as if by their own internal force lead to the work of determinate negation. Two differences, companion to one another in the same sense that they are companion in French Hegelianism, are crucial for Foucault and Deleuze: first, the introduction of a positive idea of indeterminacy, and second, an expansion of the range of relations whereby transformation takes place.

The first crucial difference is this: whereas contradiction works only with determinacy, experimentation also works with a second level of indeterminacy. The category of the indeterminate, which figures most prominently in Foucault and Deleuze in their idea of problematizations, is outside of the sway of the operations of determinacy. There are many ways of figuring the indeterminate. Psychologically, we might think of it in terms of the state of doubt, which is neither belief that *x* nor belief that *not x*. Semantically, we might think of it in terms of vagueness, which is neither the meaning of *x* nor the meaning of *not x*. Politically, we might think of it in terms of that which is fraught, which is a zone of neither *justice* nor *injustice*. However we figure it, the first crucial difference, to repeat, is the status of the indeterminate as a positive category in its own right. On the view I am attributing to Foucault and Deleuze, the indeterminate serves as a background against which determinations are made, or within which determinations are generated. It is this background that gives relief and contour to foreground determinations.

To put the point in a somewhat different idiom for a moment, indeterminacy refers to a general rulelessness out of which emerge determinate rules, such that these determinate rules possess whatever specific ruleishness they have only against the backdrop of the indeterminacy out of which they emerged. Without an indeterminate backdrop against which rules gain the specific determinacy that they have, rules cannot gain determinacy. The only other option would be to insist that rules have their determinacy in themselves, such that they are self-sufficient – but this of course requires the strong foundationalist claim that rules are sufficient for their own application, which is to say that rules carry within themselves rules for their own application. There is, of course, yet a third option, namely that rules have their determinacy purely by way of their relation to other determinate rules such that a general economy of rules is sufficient for ruleishness – but this strong coherentist claim, which seems to be the upshot of Hegel's own dialectics, must fail to confront the problem of ruleishness as such and why we do not just as well regard purported determinations as the scandalous pose of the absolutely indeterminate.[22]

Experimentation thus adds a whole new level of analytics not possible within the dialectics of contradiction. There is, as there always was, the level of determination which is conceived as a kind of plane on which there are a variety of positions standing in all kinds of differential relations to one another, including presumably relations of opposition or contradiction, though there is no reason at all to privilege specifically those relations as if they are the only ones that matter. Beneath this level of determinations and their relations there is a whole other level of the indeterminate problematization that makes possible the elaboration of the plane on which these positions and oppositions can stand in any sort of relation whatsoever.

This brings us to the second crucial difference. In experimentation there is an idea of an indeterminate problematization which is itself a set of positive conditions of possibility for the elaboration of differing determinations, such that within the conditions of an indeterminate problematization we can specify a multiplicity of relations between determinations, all of these relations and determinations assuming their form against the broader backdrop of motivating indeterminacy that is productive of them. So, whereas contradiction can only work by way of a logic of deduction (which invokes necessity and is subtractive), experimentation introduces a more primary logic of abduction (which invokes contingency and is tentatively additive). In an experimental methodeutic, problems do not already contain within them (as if deductively) the responses that would constitute a determination, but rather these responses must be contingently elaborated (as if abductively) on the basis of the problematic conditions. Experimentation thus does not contradict the category of deductive contradiction within a plane of determination, but rather works to obviate the rather simplistic idea that contradiction can account for, as if with the deductive rigor of complete closure, all logical relations and all practical transformations.

In other words, experimentation rather than contradiction is able to more squarely confront the vicissitudes of practical transformation. That, of course, would be the decisive gain here. This will come as no surprise for anyone who accepts the truism that practices can perfectly well sustain conflicts that theory deems to be contradictions. Within the space of a problematization a given determination may of course conflict with another determination, and yet these frictions, and indeed the underlying problem itself, can thereby persist. All this seems flatly impossible within a dialectics of contradiction, because a contradiction simply must give rise to a determinate negation, and hence a reconfiguration of the practical situation. On the logic of experimentation, it is possible to affirm that there are of course *dramatic reconfigurations* of practical reality, and yet at the same time observe that there is just as well *the dramatic and stubborn persistence* of entrenched patterns of practical friction. Experimentation help us understand why, for example, there can be for we moderns no such thing as a solution or resolution to such intractable problems as punishment, sexuality or madness. Is this observation

98

premised on the pessimistic assumption that these are permanent problems of humanity? Of course not. There will one day emerge other problematizations, just as these problematizations emerged for us so that we now emerge within them. But it is a pretense of the philosopher to think that we can predict these emergent problematizations as if they would be the deductive result of the determinate negation of present contradictions. The emergence of a problematization, the coming into being of a complex indeterminate assemblage, is an entirely contingent affair. We can, after the fact, write the history of such an emergence, but it will not be a history that proceeds by way of determinate negation. It is not, for example, as if the modern punitive regime of imprisonment is somehow a determinate negation of the preceding regime of torture. The problematization, in each case, is quite different. The work of imprisonment and torture is determined on the basis of entirely different zones of indetermination. Imprisonment and torture are therefore not opposed or contradictory regimes of punishment, but are rather regimes of punishments who have their origins in quite different, perhaps even incommensurable, underlying problematizations.

Problematization as a mode of experimental immanent critique

We can now finally turn to the last of the four cuts I am attributing to Foucault and Deleuze, namely the cut within an experimental methodeutic between a mode of problematization and a mode of construction. As I have been describing it, an experimental philosophy operates with at least two terms: problems and responses, or questions and answers, or doubts and beliefs, or (the terms I have been employing thus far) determinacy and indeterminacy, or (my preferred terms) *inquisitive problematizations* and *responsive reconstructions*.[23] Though experimentation has two aspects, critical analysis for Foucault and Deleuze was in the main diagnostic and problematizing rather than prognostic and responsive – or at least this is true of what is best (in the sense of most fecund) in both Foucault and Deleuze.[24] Experimental immanent critique in their work involves diagnosing the problems and pathologies, the fractious frictions, and cracked conflicts of the present.

Problematization is at the center of the Foucaultian and Deleuzian alternative to contradiction. Stating the point with more strength, I would assert that the basic watershed between the negativity of contradiction and the problematicity at the heart of experimentation is the precise location of the *central philosophic achievement* of both Foucault and Deleuze. It will thus be worth our while to tarry for awhile with these shared conceptions of problematization – I will then turn in the final section to a brief consideration of the responsive aspects of Foucault's and Deleuze's ethical-political works. But before turning to Foucault and Deleuze themselves, it will be useful to briefly situate the crucial achievement I am ascribing to both.

According to the standard narrative, the break from negative dialectics for which Foucault and Deleuze are representative has everything to do with the importance of Nietzsche over and against Hegel.[25] I want to suggest, however, that the story of a Nietzsche-versus-Hegel contest is perhaps overplayed, even if it is quite true. Insofar as the proper Foucaultian and Deleuzian alternative to negative dialectics is their shared emphasis on problematization, then it simply cannot be located through Nietzsche alone.[26] Hegelian negativity is indeed opposed by Nietzschean affirmativism – and yet Deleuze's affirmativism was not really central for Foucault. Hegelian historical totality is also opposed by Nietzschean particularism – however, Foucault's fine genealogies do not really appear in Deleuze. Now all that said, the standard focus on Nietzsche is of course understandable insofar as Deleuze and Foucault themselves were wont to emphasize the importance of Nietzsche for their thinking. My claim is just that Nietzsche is overrated when positioned as the sole influence on their shared philosophical gain, at least if we locate that gain in terms of the substitution of productive problematization for negative contradiction. In Deleuze's case the more important influence for this idea is to be found in Bergson (and in other unexpected figures including Leopold von Sacher-Masoch), while in Foucault's case an influence can be sought in Canguilhem (and of course in Deleuze himself).[27] Nietzsche is not as nothing for these ideas, but he may be much less than the standard narratives have supposed.

PROBLEMATIZATION IN DELEUZE AND FOUCAULT

I shall begin with Deleuze and from there move to Foucault by way of a famous comment the latter offered about the specific importance of the work of the former.[28] Useful beginning points can be found in both philosophers by way of overarching claims for the importance of problematization for the work of philosophy itself. In Deleuze's case, the overarching claim is offered in his co-authored *What Is Philosophy?* where he and Guattari famously identify philosophy with "the discipline that involves *creating* concepts."[29] Less famous, though no less important, is their further claim that "All concepts are connected to problems without which they would have no meaning."[30] The obvious inference that we can draw is that for Deleuze problematicity is a condition of the very work of philosophy itself. This, to be sure, is a strong claim, and one that is surely underemphasized, even if dutifully acknowledged often enough, in commentaries.[31] A thorough examination of Deleuze's own contributions to philosophy, however, will bear out this claim – wherever Deleuze does philosophy, there is always a sense of the problematization that is at work.

To explore the reach of problematization across Deleuze's thought, we can begin with the history of philosophy writings in the early 1960s as a prelude to their finer crystallization in his master works from the final years of that decade. The most obvious starting point, at least according to the standard narrative, is Deleuze's 1962 book on Nietzsche, *Nietzsche and Philosophy*. This is often taken to be a key source in these matters as I have been discussing them insofar as Deleuze's main target in this book is without a doubt the Hegelian dialectics of contradiction. Deleuze is decisive on this score in the book's conclusion: "There is no possible compromise between Hegel and Nietzsche . . . Three ideas define the dialectic: the idea of a power of the negative as a theoretical principle manifested in opposition and contradiction; the idea that suffering and sadness have value, the valorization of the 'sad passions', as a practical principle manifested in splitting and tearing apart; the idea of positivity as a theoretical and practical product of negation itself."[32] Throughout the book, Deleuze returns time and again to this theme of Nietzsche's gains over the dialectics of contradiction. And yet while Deleuze is clearly critical of Hegel, it is not always as clear what form his own positive alternative, rooted in a reading of Nietzsche, would take. The clearest suggestion that Deleuze offers suggests the importance of a category of difference: "If the speculative element of the dialectic is found in opposition and contradiction this is primarily because it reflects a false image of difference . . . For the affirmation of difference as such it substitutes the negation of that which differs."[33] Deleuze's affirmativism in his book on Nietzsche is an impressive provocation. But in the final analysis it is not clear why an affirmation of difference is advantaged over a dialectics of contradiction, nor is it clear how affirmation does not just in the end collapse back into negation insofar as affirmation and negation are but two opposed modes of determination. What Deleuze lacks in this book, perhaps because it was Nietzsche's lack before him, was an account of the problematic and the indeterminate as that which is generative of difference such that we can recognize the dialectics of contradiction as genuinely reductive of differences that matter.

It would not be until his book on Bergson in 1966 that Deleuze would develop an account of problematic indeterminacy in sufficient detail and thereby definitively institute his break from a certain Hegelianism. As a first piece of evidence for my argument about Bergson's importance concerning these matters consider a pair of short precursor essays published by Deleuze as early as 1956. Bergson is the topic, and the titular figure, of both. Through these essays we realize that Deleuze had already stated the core themes for which his Nietzsche book would become famous many years later: "Internal difference will have to distinguish itself from *contradiction, alterity,* and *negation*. This is precisely where Bergson's method and theory of difference are opposed to the other theory, the other method of difference called dialectic."[34] As for what exactly is wrong with Hegel: "difference has been replaced by the play of determination" such that for Hegel everything that is, as we saw above, is determinate.[35] And what exactly is productive with Bergson: "Everything comes back to Bergson's critique of the negative: his whole effort is aimed at a conception of difference without negation."[36] Indeed Deleuze would here already locate in Bergson a key idea of indeterminacy: "Not only is vital difference not a determination, but it is very much the opposite: it is indetermination itself."[37] The crucial theme of indeterminacy is even more prominent in the second of these two essays, which is perhaps more properly described as more of an encyclopedia entry on Bergson. Deleuze there writes, in the final paragraph, that, "When Bergson . . . speaks to us of indeterminacy, he does not invite us to abandon reason but to reconnect with the true reason of the thing in the process of being made, the philosophical reason that is not determination but difference . . . The method was profoundly new."[38]

What in 1956 Deleuze figures in terms of indeterminacy, would assume more specificity in his 1966 book on Bergson, where the idea of the problematic would first come into the fore in his thought. It is clear in the final chapter of this book that Deleuze is posing Bergsonian evolution as an alternative to Hegel eschatology.[39] Three ideas in Bergson's account of development are key for Deleuze in his counter to Hegel: problematicity, difference and temporality.[40] The first and root of these ideas is that of the problem as a category with positive status, the idea of problems as productive. The productiveness of problems, of course, has everything to do with their indeterminacy, that is with their being problems to which we do not yet have solutions, even if problems are the conditions of possibility of determinate solutions. For Deleuze, the first and essential gain of Bergson is thus the act of "the stating and creating of problems."[41] This category of the problematic has everything to do with the very possibility of a definitive break from a dialectics of negative contradiction – the category of the problem, unlike the category of the affirmation, cannot be reprogrammed into the category of negation because the problematic, as indeterminate, is precisely what would be incapable of a negation insofar as any and every negation, just like any and every affirmation, must be determinate. Hence Hegel's insistence, cited above, on the determinacy even of that which appears indeterminate – the Hegelian system can achieve totality only insofar as everything in the totality is determinate. The very idea of a category of suspense holds the Hegalian dialectics of contradiction in abeyance. Bergson's problems suspend determinacy. In so doing, Deleuze's Bergson manages to put a hold on Hegel, and without trying to engage in the impossible task of refuting Hegel that Deleuze's Nietzsche too often undertakes and of course inevitably fails at.

An even more under-discussed source of Deleuze's conception of problematization can be located in the work of Sacher-Masoch, who is the central focus of a number of early essays by Deleuze, including a very long introduction to Masoch's *Venus in Furs* published under the title *Coldness and Cruelty*. In his writings on Masoch, Deleuze develops an alternative conceptualization of indeterminacy by way of a reading of masochistic suspense. To understand this point, it is crucial to first note that Deleuze's central argument in the book is that masochism is a specific literary and clinical mode, such that it is a mistake to unify it with sadism as its paired opposite through that ill-conceived concept of sadomasochism championed by Krafft-Ebbing, Freud, and others.[42] Whereas the sadistic technique operates by way of "negation", the masochistic employs the altogether different logic of "disavowal" or "suspense": "The fundamental distinction between sadism and masochism can be summarized *in the contrasting processes of the negative and negation on the one hand, of disavowal and suspense on the other.*"[43] Deleuze is unambiguous about the refusal to collapse suspense into negation: it is "an entirely different operation," one in which the motion of thought "consists neither in negating nor even destroying, but rather in radically contesting the validity of that which is: it suspends belief in and neutralizes the given in such a way that a new horizon opens up beyond the given and in place of it."[44] Masochistic suspense, in short, sets in motion a critical operation that is indeterminate through and through, it does not negate nor affirm, but presses beyond judgment in order to hold judgment in abeyance, so as to open up indeterminacies, and through that the possibility of new horizons of determination. If the "problem" is for Deleuze the Bergsonian name for indeterminacy, then "disavowal" and "suspense" are its Masochistic names. Perhaps Masoch was more central for Deleuze's development of problematization, which is to say for Deleuze's break from the Hegelian dialectics of contradiction, than is typically credited. Even at the methodological level Deleuze carefully notes Masoch's own employment of the category of the problematic.[45] Deleuze's book on Masoch, it ought to be remembered, was published only one year before *Difference and Repetition* while Deleuze's first essay on Masoch was published the year before *Nietzsche and Philosophy*. Perhaps, after all, Masoch and Bergson matter more to Deleuze than we have been inclined to think, overshadowed as they are in our imagination by figures who tend to strike for us sexier poses, namely Nietzsche.

Deleuze's critique of the negative dialectics of contradiction may have begun in creative rereading of Bergson and Masoch, but it would not fully crystallize into the alternative of experimental problematization until those two monuments of late sixties French philosophy, Deleuze's *Difference and Repetition* of 1968 and *The Logic of Sense* of 1969.[46] Dan Smith argues that Deleuze, in *Difference and Repetition*, "attempts to develop a new concept of dialectics, which is more or less synonymous with the concept of 'problematics.'"[47] Smith here affirms a point about which I aim only to be more emphatic, namely the *centrality* of the notion of problematization for Deleuze's philosophical *achievements*. I would argue that the notion of problematization is the *greatest gain* in Deleuze's philosophical works of the 1960s. That notion also constitutes his point of steadiest contact with Foucault's philosophical interventions in the 1960s and 1970s. Their import is in part a function of the depth of the departure they mark from the inherited dialectics of contradiction which remain with us today.

This is not the occasion on which to follow the intricate contours of Deleuze's arguments in *Difference and Repetition* and *The Logic of Sense*. The centrality of the notion of problematization in those books is rather my concern. And for these purposes I shall remain merely summary. In so doing, there will be, I confess, an immense reservoir of things to say about the role of problematization in these two books which I will not here touch on. A fuller exploration would, no doubt, complicate aspects of my argument. Such complications would be welcome, in part because they would help us specify the differences between Foucault and Deleuze. For now, however, my emphasis is on the resonances, or repetitions and relays, between Foucault and Deleuze.

Difference and Repetition begins with a critique of Hegel or what Deleuze calls "a generalized anti-Hegelianism" in which "difference and repetition have taken the place of the identical and the negative, of identity and contradiction."[48] There is a long and difficult path from these opening remarks on the book's first page to Deleuze's mysterious remark in the book's conclusion concerning "ideal problem-constellations in the sky."[49] Along that path we find ample evidence of the centrality of problematization for the skyward push beyond Hegel. One key moment involves Deleuze's takeover of the concept of dialectics itself: "*Problems are always dialectical*: the dialectic has no other sense, nor do problems have any other sense."[50] Whereas in previous work he had explicitly countered his use of Nietzsche against Hegel's "dialectics",[51] he now uses the Bergsonian notion of problems to reinvest dialectics from the inside as an effort in experimentation rather than contradiction. Another key moment concerns the problem of movement, always central to Deleuze, Bergson, Hegel, and indeed every prominent corner of modern philosophy: "Practical struggle never proceeds by way of the negative but by way of difference and its power of affirmation, and the war of the righteous is for the conquest of the highest power, that of deciding problems by restoring them to their truth, by evaluating that truth beyond the representations of consciousness and the forms of the negative, and by acceding at last to the imperatives on which they depend."[52] The negative, Deleuze tells us here, is but a shadow of the problematic.[53] The negative, in other words, is but a "false problem",[54] an idea that Deleuze had already developed in detail in the book on Bergson.[55]

The Logic of Sense follows a rather different, albeit related, trajectory from that laid out by Deleuze in his book from just one year prior. Whereas *Difference and Repetition* begins with an assault directly on Hegel, *The Logic of Sense* seems more innocent, though perhaps that just means it is more cunning. Deleuze here opens with a discussion not of philosophical giants, but of confounding miniatures, specifically the children's stories of Lewis Carroll. The philosophical concern of the book, as stated by Deleuze on the first page, is that of "events, pure events" and a related notion of "becoming."[56] This book ends, once again, with the sky, now in the form of "the thunderbolt of the univocal" and the fleetingness of the shock of the event that "is, of course, quickly covered over by everyday banality."[57] Between these two citations Deleuze does much to let the reader feel the thunder of the event. The argument is even more complex and circuitous than in his prior work, though perhaps this is appropriate for his subject matter. Allow me to once again just draw attention to two key moments along the pathway of the book. First, Deleuze's striking assertion that "The mode of the event is problematic."[58] The thunder that shakes meaning and disrupts our banal everydayness has something to do with the problematic, which thus functions as a kind of condition of transformative reorganization, or a condition of becoming. Later, we find another moment in which Deleuze is precise about the positive status of the problematic, which is seemingly an incoherent idea even on his own account. In the section of the book on logical genesis, Deleuze writes that, "The problem in itself is the reality of the genetic element, the complex *theme* which does not allow itself to be reduced to any propositional *thesis*."[59] As I read Deleuze here, the point is that problems are not determinate theses, but rather indeterminate themes, and as such are generative. On the next page, in a passage worth quoting at length, Deleuze writes:

That the problem does not exist outside of the propositions which, in their senses, express it means, properly speaking, that the problem *is not*: it inheres, subsists, or persists in propositions . . . This nonbeing, however, is not the being of the negative; it is rather the being of the problematic, that we should perhaps write as (non)-being or ?-being. The problem is independent of both the negative and the affirmative; it nevertheless does have a positivity which corresponds to its position as a problem.[60]

It would be difficult to find as clear and precise a statement against the Hegelian logic of contradiction as that.

Foucault thought so too. In a famous review of Deleuze's *Difference and Repetition* and *The Logic of Sense* published in 1970 he wrote: "The freeing of difference requires thought without contradiction, without dialectics, without negation; thought that accepts divergence; affirmative thought whose instrument is disjunction; thought of the multiple . . . We must think problematically rather than question and answer dialectically . . . And now, it is necessary to free ourselves from Hegel – from the opposition of predicates, from contradiction and negation, from all of dialectics."[61] Deleuze repaid the positive half of the compliment (the half emphasizing the productivity of problems) years later when he wrote that for Foucault, "To think means to experiment and to problematize."[62] And more proximately, Deleuze voiced the negative half of the compliment (the half expressing skepticism about contradiction) in a now-published letter to Foucault written in response to *The Will to Know*: "Indeed it seems to me that another of Michel's great innovations in the theory of power is that a society does not contradict itself, or hardly does so. Yet his answer is: it strategizes itself, it makes up strategies."[63]

It would be a terrible mistake to think that Deleuze was here co-opting Foucault. The centrality of problematization for the work of philosophy was, to be sure, as much Foucault's gain as it was Deleuze's. In one interview we find Foucault claiming that, "Neither the dialectic, as the logic of contradictions, nor semiotics, as the structure of communication, can account for the intrinsic intelligibility of conflicts . . . 'Dialectic' is a way of evading the always open and hazardous reality of conflict by reducing it to a Hegelian skeleton."[64] For Foucault, as for Deleuze, the diacritic of philosophy does not consist in ferreting out the contradictions, furtive but structural (even at times orphic) within complex social assemblies, but rather in casting a light, at once clarifying and intensifying (even at times dazzlingly bright), on the persisting problematizations at the heart of who we are. In Foucault's work, this point came to be about what we, in the history of our present, take to be irremediably problematic. What are the problems we cannot but feel the force of? Over what, and why, are we constantly anxious and inevitably distraught? What are the problems with which we wrap and warp our lives in burning intensities? These questions, and this focusing of questions around problematizations, were Foucault's central devices for freeing himself from a certain French Hegelianism all wrapped up in negative dialectics. But what, we ought to ask, is problematization positively for Foucault?

A useful departure point for considering the centrality of problematization in Foucault is the following overarching remark, striking in its sweep, from a late interview in 1984: "The notion common to all the work that I have done since *History of Madness* is that of problematization, though it must be said that I never isolated this notion sufficiently. But one always finds what is essential after the event; the most general things are those that appear last. It is the ransom and reward for all work in which theoretical questions are elaborated on the basis of a particular empirical field."[65] This is a decidedly strong claim. And Foucault realizes it. And yet he persists. I propose to take Foucault at his word here. Problematization indeed was one of his most constant and lasting preoccupations. On this reading, that is, on Foucault's own reading of himself, *History of Madness* is an investigation of the problematization of madness in a particular historical field, *Discipline and Punish* an investigation of the problematization of crime and punishment in the eighteenth and nineteenth centuries, and *The Will to Know* a problematization of the emergence of the fraughtness we all feel today about sex and sexuality.[66] We can find problematization in all of Foucault's major works even if would it not crystallize into the explicit concept that it became before a number of interviews and lectures from the early 1980s. And where we find problematization at work we are not so likely to find Nietzsche so much as other figures, including Canguilhem but of course also Deleuze himself. I have traced all of this elsewhere before, offering the requisite citations of all those pages in books ranging from *History of Madness* and *The Birth of the Clinic* to *Discipline and Punish* and *The Will to Know* as well as in the late lecture courses where Foucault regularly employs the idea of the problematic as an analytical category – having said well more than enough about problematization elsewhere, then, allow me here to just remain summary.[67]

Foucault's clearest statements of problematizations can be found in the late interviews. In a discussion with Paul Rabinow published under the title "Polemics, Politics, and Problematizations" Foucault was prompted by the following useful question: "What is a history of problematics?" In the course of his reply, Foucault offers this instructive remark: "For a domain of action, a behavior, to enter the field of thought, it is necessary for a certain number of factors to have made it uncertain, to have made it lose its familiarity, or to have provoked a certain number of difficulties around it."[68] Foucault is here naming the provocation of the indeterminate. His claim is that the emergence of new thought, the motion of practice, is contingent upon the problematic that precedes it. His next claim is even more striking: "To one single set of difficulties, several responses can be made. And most of the time different responses actually are proposed. But what must be understood is what makes them simultaneously possible: it is the point in which their simultaneity is rooted; it is the soil that can nourish them all in their diversity and sometimes in spite of their contradictions."[69] A problematization, Foucault is here unambiguous, is capable of supporting contradictory responses. These contradictions, of course, may be felt as conflict and tension but they do not automatically give rise to the negation of one another, nor to the negation of the underlying problematic. Understanding that every determination is elaborated in response to a specific indeterminate problematization helps us account for the stubborn persistence of conflict. Thus Foucault says of his genealogies, "The work of a history of thought would be to rediscover at the root of these diverse solutions the general form of problematization that has made them possible – even in their very opposition."[70] Foucault did not here name the Hegelianism against which he and Deleuze were writing. But he did not need to. It would have been obvious to anyone of his milieu.

The genealogical inflection of experimental problematization in Foucault helps elucidate a crucial aspect of the work of problematization which is perhaps not quite as visible in Deleuze as in Foucault, though to be sure it can be read through the latter back into the former. In Foucault's work it is clear that problematization is both an act of inquiry and an object of inquiry – problematization is at once something that the critical philosopher undertakes and something that the critical philosopher takes as the object of their critique. This dual role of problematization is a source of its fecundity. The best way of making sense of it in Foucault's case is to regard him as simultaneously describing and intensifying the problematizations that are his concern. We do not need Foucault to know that we are all anxious about sexuality. And yet Foucault's genealogies of sexuality serve to provoke, stir, and shake up that anxiety, thus intensifying what we all already knew to be there.

It is with respect to this double status of problematization that it offers a mode of critique that at once avoids judgment and yet at the same time exerts a pull on us. A problematization does not tell us, Foucault is clear enough, that sexuality, or biopower, or discipline are bad (nor, of course, good). And yet a problematization exposes us to the fractures and fraughtnesses that are always already underway for us in these domains. It is in this sense that problematization is a critical operation that does its work without always falling under the sway of determinate judgment. The point, again, is not that determination is bad (for that would itself be just another determination). The point, rather, is that the work of immanent critique needs a richer conception of how it functions, such that sometimes it might work to make normative determinations and yet at other times work to intensify the indeterminate background out of which all normative determinations are made. This is why Foucault could confidently say:

> A critique does not consist in saying that things aren't good the way they are. It consists in seeing on what type of assumptions, of familiar notions, of established, unexamined ways of thinking the accepted practices are based . . . To do criticism is to make harder those acts which are now too easy. Understood in these terms, criticism (and radical criticism) is utterly indispensable for any transformation.[71]

It was precisely here, with respect to the work of transformation and the energy of transition, where Deleuze and Foucault needed to break from the classical dialectics that would reduce all becoming to the negative work of contradiction.

For both Deleuze and Foucault, then, the work of experimental problematization offered a path beyond the stalemates of mid-century French philosophy, above all the stalemate of a dialectics of contradiction that would find its way only through belaboring the pain of the negative. Deleuze and Foucault challenge us to consider a wider array of operations playing out on the planes of determinacy in which we find ourselves situated. An experimental dialectics that makes room for the productiveness of the indeterminate was the crucial gain of both. In Deleuze's work with Guattari, subsequent to the texts I have treated here, this would come to figure most prominently in his productive theory of desire and above all the notion of the unconscious as a productive even if indeterminate factory. In Foucault's work, the space of indeterminacy would perhaps figure most prominently in his remarkable ability to hold together that which other theorists insisted was contradictory, thus enabling us to glimpse through him the possibility that repression and liberation, or power and freedom, function all so often as conflicted pairings that cannot be reduced to contradictions. For both, it is crucial that a certain vagueness is a condition of possibility of who we are, because it shows that indeterminacy is already an aspect of who we might yet become.

CRITIQUE WITHOUT JUDGMENT

The central achievement of thought that emerges between Foucault and Deleuze is their enactment of problematization as a mode of critique without judgment. Thus they maintain with severity the crucial promise of the critical philosophy – the promise that was not delivered on by Kant, by Hegel, by Marx, by Freud, and so many others too, of course. The work of Deleuze and Foucault is a work that would maintain the critique of judgment by decisively departing from the prevailing winds of the dialectic. Where too often the work of critical philosophy has assumed forms that would speak directly to reality in the form of a determinate judgment, Foucault and Deleuze keep critique separate so that philosophy can make room for itself without descending to the role of arguing for or against determinate positions within the realities it takes as its task.

I take the work of problematization to be the most important point of resonance between Foucault and Deleuze. Their deep sympathies in this respect take us further in the pursuit of their broader philosophical projects than do other familiar terms all too commonly used to lump them together. We hear much about "Continental Philosophy" (which is hopelessly vague albeit a factual sociological descriptor, though ironically not on the Continent so much as in America) and "French Philosophy" (which confusedly even if only unwittingly proposes to identify philosophical positions with national membership). But these are clearly too rudimentary to be useful as explanatory concepts, let alone as sorting tools. More promisingly, we hear appellations or accusations of "Postmodernism" (which is thankfully now out of fashion) or "Poststructuralism" (which is still very much the going favorite). But my claim is that the gains of Foucault and Deleuze need not be sought, indeed should not be sought, in some -ism that would name some new region of philosophy into which we all must march. I would situate both Foucault and Deleuze more humbly, as proposing and enacting philosophical methodologies, for instance genealogy and archaeology or symptomatology and schizoanalysis. These methods of critical problematization do not need a misplaced -ism to back them up and ground them. What they need, rather, are contemporary philosophers today, you and me, picking up these methods and putting them to work in the context of *newer* inquiries into *emergent* norms and forms. The only way to make use of Foucault and Deleuze is to use them to go beyond where they themselves could have gone. They could not go where we can go today – because our world is decisively different from theirs. Locating that difference means working at that temporal stitch that holds together but keeps separate where we are today and where they were yesterday.

The crucial gain for making that stitch has to do with a mode of critique that does not judge. The press of thought beyond judgment was central for both Foucault and Deleuze, and could be central again today for us.

In Foucault's case, we should not neglect his repeated claims to the effect that problematizations are not an attempt at determinate affirmation or negation, but rather an attempt to make visible an indeterminate background field in virtue of which specific determinations can come to be elaborated. In an interview with Paul Rabinow and Hubert Dreyfus, Foucault says, "You see, what I want to do is not the history of solutions . . . I would like to do the genealogy of problems, or *problématiques*. My point is not that everything is bad, but that everything is dangerous, which is not exactly the same thing as bad. If everything is dangerous, then we always have something to do. So my position leads not to apathy but to a hyper- and pessimistic activism."[72] For Foucault, the work of problematization is a way of outflanking the invitation to judgment. Interviewers were always asking Foucault for his opinions on what to do. They were asking, in other words, for Foucault to offer determinate solutions to the problems he was posing. But if the difficult labor of posing problems was their primary work, then these questions are confused. Consider another interview with interlocutors at Berkeley, in which Foucault found himself responding to questions along these lines: "Listen, listen . . . How difficult it is! I'm not a prophet; I'm not an organizer; I don't want to tell people what they should do. I'm not going to tell them, 'This is good for you, this is bad for you!' I try to analyze a real situation in its various complexities, with the goal of allowing refusal, and curiosity, and innovation."[73] There are countless such remarks by Foucault scattered throughout his interviews, lecture courses, and other occasional writings: "It's amazing how people like judging. Judgment is being passed everywhere, all the time."[74]

Deleuze too was often asked to stake himself to a position, a view, or an opinion. It is ironic that so many intellectuals are invited to solve problems in virtue, presumably, of simply being well-known intellectuals, as if being well-disciplined in a specific field automatically translates to a kind of universality of intellect.[75] Like Foucault, Deleuze had the better wisdom to resist these constant invitations. In one interview he quipped, "Intellectuals are wonderfully cultivated, they have views on everything. I'm not an intellectual, because I can't supply views like that, I've got no stock of views to draw on . . . It's really good not having any view or idea about this or that point. We don't suffer these days from any lack of communication, but rather from all the forces making us say things when we've nothing much to say."[76] A striking line near the end of *Anti-Oedipus* confirms this stance, in this case an orientation toward political critique without taking a political position: "Schizoanalysis *as such* has strictly no political program to propose . . . Schizoanalysis is something that does not claim to be speaking for anything or anyone."[77]

There is, of course, much in the work of both Foucault and Deleuze that cannot be accounted for in terms of this exposition of the work of critique beyond judgment. Suffice it to say that Foucault and Deleuze, though they agreed on much, did not of course agree on everything. What resonates most between the work of both, I have argued, is also that which constitutes their greatest philosophical achievement for our present philosophical moment: the potentiality of a work of critical philosophy that finally frees itself from the tempting sway of the judgmental orientation of contradiction in order that thought might find its way to the experimental orientation of problematization and reconstruction. It is this idea above all that we should hold on to, work through, and work over. To learn to philosophize in this mode would be invigorating for the contemporary work of critique. It would give us a fresh set of challenges. For pronouncements we could substitute problems. For answers we could substitute questions. For rigidified pride we could substitute unrelenting curiosity. For philosophy as an announcement of what is obligatory, we could at long last substitute philosophy as an instrumentality for transformative engagement. All of this might, though surely only in fits and starts, contribute toward conditions for the re-engagement of philosophy with practice, thus recomposing the tenuous relationship between we "intellectuals" and the "powers" toward which we supposedly speak. And though we may fail in all of this, should we not at least allow ourselves to try? The experiment itself would be worth the effort.[78]

NOTES

1. Foucault in Deleuze and Foucault (1972, 207–8).
2. Deleuze in Deleuze and Foucault (1972, 208). Though this famous remark is Deleuze's (it is often incorrectly attributed to Foucault), it is worth noting that in a later 1977 interview (and not only there) Foucault indicates his broad agreement with this claim by explicitly appropriating the metaphor of philosophy as providing tools: "What we have to present are instruments and tools that people might find useful. By forming groups specifically to make these analyses, to wage these struggles, by using these instruments or others: this is how, in the end, possibilities open up" (Foucault 1977a, 197).
3. Deleuze in Deleuze and Foucault (1972, 208).
4. As Kant specifies the project of *The Critique of Pure Reason*, "Such a critique is therefore a preparation, so far as may be possible, for an organon, and so presumably not an organon itself" (1787, A12/B26).
5. Kant writes, "I entitle *transcendental* all knowledge which is occupied not so much with objects as with the mode of our knowledge of objects insofar as this mode of knowledge is to be possible a priori. A system of such concepts might be entitled transcendental philosophy" (1787, A11/B25).
6. See Kant (1787, A296/B352–3).
7. See for instance Kant (1787, B424).
8. See, for instance, Meillasoux (2006), which is without doubt the gold standard for the recent revivals of speculative and ontological philosophy.
9. Foucault (1984a, 315); translation lightly modified from *EW1*.

10. Deleuze (1993a, 126).
11. Hegel (1821, §2, 12).
12. I borrow the term *geistesgeschichte* from Rorty (1984).
13. On Hume as a precedent for Deleuze see, of course, Deleuze's 1953 book on Hume (*Empiricism and Subjectivity*) as well as discussion by Smith (2001, 62ff.). I am still awaiting a good discussion of Hume's precedent for Foucault.
14. "I am an experimenter and not a theorist," Foucault once quipped (1978, 240). "[E] xperimentation on oneself, is our only identity, our single chance for all the combinations that inhabit us," Deleuze once cryptically proclaimed (1977, 11).
15. See Smith (2006, 107).
16. See for instance Zambrana (2012).
17. Deleuze provocatively wrote of Hyppolite in one of his first publications: "In the wake of this fruitful book by Jean Hyppolite [*Logic and Existence*], one might ask whether an ontology of difference couldn't be created that would not go all the way to contradiction, since contradiction would be less and not more than difference" (1954, 18). Foucault similarly spoke to an interviewer much later of having "to free myself from the dominant influences in my university training in the early fifties – Hegel and phenomenology . . . The work of Jean Wahl and the teaching of Jean Hyppolite. It was a Hegelianism permeated with phenomenology and existentialism, centered on the theme of the unhappy consciousness" (1978, 246).
18. The most influential texts were Kojève (1947) and Hyppolite (1946). A useful intellectual history of mid-century French Hegelianism, focusing in the final chapter on its meanings for both Foucault and Deleuze, is Roth (1988). See on Sartre's connections here work by Flynn (1997).
19. Though my overt focus here is on French Hegelianism (and its composites of dialectical history and existential phenomenology), it would not be inaccurate to suggest that it was really Freudo-Hegelianism, Marxo-Hegelianism, and of course Freudo-Marxism that were Deleuze and Foucault's biggest targets. In his reviews of *Difference and Repetition* and *The Logic of Sense*, Foucault applauded as follows: "We should thank Deleuze for his efforts. He did not revive the tiresome slogans: Freud with Marx, Marx with Freud, and both, if you please, with us" (1970, 355). Later, in his preface to the English translation of *Anti-Oedipus* where he describes Deleuze and Guattari as setting fire to their shared philosophical inheritance, suggesting that their book enacts an incineration of "Marx and Freud in the same incandescent light." Further down the page he wryly notes, "*Anti-Oedipus* is not a flashy Hegel" (Foucault 1977a, xii). Deleuze in his book, *Foucault*, would repay the compliment (or at least part of it) years later: "It is as if, finally, something new were emerging in the wake of Marx" (Deleuze 1986, 30). There are, of course, countless other instances in Foucault and Deleuze where Freud and Marx, and through them a certain Hegel, are displaced.
20. It may be useful to consider the core elements of negative dialectics. Two elements are central: the relation of *contradiction* and its corollary motion of *negation*. Tom Rockmore concisely summarizes the place of these two elements in Hegel's dialectic, which he argues "consists in relativizing opposites and in thinking the unity of contraries . . . what causes the concept to change and propels it from phase to phase is the negative or

negation that it contains and that develops from within it" (Rockmore 1992, 112–13). On this very standard reading, the dialectic works to relate concepts by way of its central category of contradiction or opposition. A relation of contradiction is one that cannot be withstood and maintained. It is therefore a specification of conditions under which the terms of the contradiction must suffer determinate negation. This should not be construed as one term negating the other. Rather it is their contradictory relation which is negated, involving not so much the negation of one term and the affirmation of another as the negation of the contradictory opposition itself, and with it the entirety of involved terms. Thus, for example, the class interests of the capitalist accumulators and the persisting laboring are in contradiction with one another. It is this contradiction, and not the capitalists or the laborers taken by themselves as they are for themselves, that generates the negative outflow. What emerges after this negation is determinately engendered in the negation itself, which is to say that what emerges after negation is on the basis of negation itself. What will emerge is itself based on the determinate negation of that which constituted the contradiction. We should not expect some radically new third term to suddenly appear. Thus, the communes of the proletariat can be seen as the form that labor will assume on the basis of the determinate negation of capitalist accumulation in the context of the contradiction between capital and labor. The contradiction between capital and labor just would not, on a Hegelian logic, give rise to some radically new third term, such as a reinvigoration of religiosity. Nor would the emergent third term be identical with one of the two terms at work in the contradiction. The proletarian communes are not to be identified with those who labor in the context of capitalism. The negative work of contradiction thus preserves both continuity (against radicality) and progress (against stasis). It shows how history *moves* (rather than jumps) *forward* (rather than sideways). This progressive and continuous nature of the dialectic of the concept is, as is well known, absolutely crucial to Hegel's presentation of his account of the absolute.

21. Hegel (1821, §34, 40); see this point of Hegel's in another of his idioms in Hegel (1807, §92, 59).

22. The path between foundationalism and coherentism that Deleuze and Foucault are together navigating would profit much from comparison to the kind of Wittgensteinean remarks I am offering here.

23. One reason why it is worth being precise about the duality of experimentation is because this point helps us see that a philosophical tradition that emphasized experimental reconstruction rather than experimental problematization would find itself perfectly at home with Foucault and Deleuze, in part because any such tradition would share their side of the basic watershed. One such tradition worth mentioning insofar as it nicely, though for some quite unexpectedly, pairs with Foucault and Deleuze in this way is that of philosophical pragmatism, for which the core categories of the motion of thought are also problematizations and reconstructions. For a discussion of the relationship between Foucault's genealogy and pragmatism generally see Koopman (2011), or at greater length the final chapters of both Koopman (2009) and Koopman (2013). For one instance of Deleuze's own positive remarks about pragmatism see Deleuze (1993b, 86).

24. My reading strategy here is forthrightly normative and selective rather than descriptive and exhaustive – above all my effort is to read what is *best* in Foucault and Deleuze. I accept that there are other aspects of Foucault, and especially Deleuze, that are not problematizational in this sense – my argument is simply that these are not the best aspects of their work and do not represent what we today should take from them. I make this argument in the final section below, but for a criticism of this aspect of Foucault's work see Koopman (2013, Chapter 6), and on Deleuze albeit briefly see Koopman (2013, Chapter 2).

25. There are numerous works employing this standard story: one worth mentioning in the present context, because it elaborates the usual narrative in connection with a discussion of French Hegelianism, is Roth (1988).

26. Roth, to stick with just the one example, makes the argument that, for Foucault and Deleuze, "Nietzsche . . . replaces Hegel as the locus of philosophical authority" (1988, 190), an argument which leads him to the conclusion that Deleuze and Foucault be read primarily as implementing a philosophical "delegitimation" (1988, 189–224). But delegitimation would of course simply be an instance of negative determination, thus essentially repeating Hegel, whereas my claim is that Deleuze and Foucault institute their break by moving beyond determination into the sphere of the indeterminate. On my reading, problematization is a proper alternative to both legitimation and delegitimation. Roth is, I think, led down the path of this misreading by adhering too closely to the standard narrative of placing all the emphasis on Nietzsche – his account is only typical insofar as it completely ignores Bergson and Canguilhem in this respect (neither name features in the index, which is perhaps surprising for a well-researched and professional intellectual history of the dominant Hegelian episode in mid-century French philosophy).

27. Much has been made of these influences for both thinkers, but my point is just that the literature overwhelmingly emphasizes Nietzsche. I do not here develop this suggestion regarding Canguilhem as a precursor for Foucaultian problematization, but any such development surely would involve a careful look at the closing paragraphs of Foucault's homage to Canguilhem in Foucault (1985) as well as Foucault's undeveloped but interesting claim about Canguilhem that, "Many of his students were neither Marxists nor Freudians nor structuralists, and I am speaking of myself" (1983a, 437).

28. Why begin with Deleuze? Mainly for convenience. In approaching these texts, we might adopt a typical procedure of according priority by way of chronology. This, at least, has the advantage of making the exposition manageable, though perhaps at the cost of being somewhat misleading if it implicates an invocation of that confounding category of intellectual history known as "influence." While it is undeniable that Deleuze arrived at a self-conscious statement of the work of experimentation before Foucault, there is in fact no real need to attribute priority to either Deleuze or Foucault on this matter, and indeed no real gain in doing so. Deleuze was the first to get here only in the sense that he was the first to state these matters with meta-philosophical clarity in his works of the 1960s, in such books as his 1962 *Nietzsche and Philosophy* and his 1966 *Bergsonism.* As for Foucault, the operations of experimental thought is already clearly on display in his

History of Madness project published in 1961, though that book of course sorely lacks the kind of self-reflective apparatus that Deleuze already had up and running in his book of the next year.

29. Deleuze and Guattari (1991, 5).
30. Deleuze and Guattari (1991, 16).
31. Patton (2000, 21) is one exception in making a strong claim on behalf of the centrality of problems for Deleuze.
32. Deleuze (1962, 195).
33. Deleuze (1962, 196).
34. Deleuze (1956a, 38).
35. Deleuze (1956a, 42).
36. Deleuze (1956a, 42).
37. Deleuze (1956a, 40).
38. Deleuze (1956b, 31).
39. Deleuze (1966, 106–13).
40. Deleuze (1966, 14).
41. Deleuze (1966, 14).
42. Deleuze writes, "It is too readily assumed that the symptoms only have to be transposed and the instincts reversed for Masoch to be turned into Sade, according to the principle of the unity of opposites" (1967, 13).
43. Deleuze (1967, 35).
44. Deleuze (1967, 31).
45. See Deleuze (1967, 53) discussing Masoch's own self-reflections published as Appendix I to the cited edition.
46. On the relation of these two monuments to the historical works preceding them, Dan Smith and John Protevi note: "Deleuze's historical monographs were, in a sense, preliminary sketches for the great canvas of *Difference and Repetition* (1968), which marshaled these resources from the history of philosophy in an ambitious project to construct a 'philosophy of difference.'" (Smith and Protevi 2012, online).
47. Smith (2001, 69); cf. (2006, 107). Note however a crucial difference in exposition here: I depart from Smith in his retention of the idea of a "new dialectics" as a label for what Deleuze and Foucault are doing, preferring instead to specify the difference in terms of an alternative to dialectics altogether. Smith's approach has the merits of remaining perhaps closer to Deleuze's own terminology, as suggested in my discussion of *Difference and Repetition* on the next page. However, I find Deleuze's terminology needlessly confused, and do not see how the two-sided dialectic could be reinvested in a manner that would break its attachment to contradiction and opposition. Foucault, for his part, as shown in the ensuing discussion, never sought to recuperate the notion of the dialectic. Perhaps I am here only playing Foucault to Smith's Deleuze. I thank Adina Arvatu for helpful conversation on this point.
48. Deleuze (1968, xix).
49. Deleuze (1968, 284).
50. Deleuze (1968, 179).
51. Cf. Deleuze (1962).

52. Deleuze (1968, 208).
53. Cf. Deleuze (1968, 202, 208).
54. Deleuze (1968, 207).
55. Deleuze (1966, 15–21).
56. Deleuze (1969, 1).
57. Deleuze (1969, 249).
58. Deleuze (1969, 54).
59. Deleuze (1969, 122).
60. Deleuze (1969, 123).
61. Foucault (1970, 358–9).
62. Deleuze (1986, 116).
63. Deleuze (1977, 127).
64. Foucault (1976, 116).
65. Foucault (1984b, 257); for another remark to almost exactly the same effect, see Foucault (1983c, 171).
66. See Foucault (1984b, 257).
67. See Koopman (2013, 46, 132).
68. Foucault (1984c, 117).
69. Foucault (1984c, 118).
70. Foucault (1984c, 118).
71. Foucault (1981, 456).
72. Foucault (1983b, 256).
73. Foucault (1980b, 13).
74. Foucault (1980a, 323).
75. I am of course here riffing on Foucault's distinction between the "specific intellectual" and the "universal intellectual" in Foucault (1977c, 127).
76. Deleuze (1988, 137).
77. Deleuze and Guattari (1972, 380).
78. For discussion of ideas integral to the arguments herein, or for comments on earlier drafts of this essay, I thank Adina Arvatu, Thomas Nail, Dan Smith, and (with an additional note of thanks for his so many other modes of intellectual and scholarly stimulation) Nicolae Morar.

BIBLIOGRAPHY

Deleuze, Gilles (1954) "Jean Hyppolite's *Logic and Existence*," in Deleuze, *DI*.
Deleuze, Gilles (1956a) "Bergson's Conception of Difference," in Deleuze, *DI*.
Deleuze, Gilles (1956b) "Bergson, 1859–1941," in Deleuze, *DI*.
Deleuze, Gilles (1962) *Nietzsche and Philosophy*, trans. Hugh Tomlinson (New York: Columbia University Press, 2006).
Deleuze, Gilles (1966) *Bergsonism*, trans. Hugh Tomlinson and Barbara Habberjam (New York: Zone Books, 1991).
Deleuze, Gilles (1967) *Coldness and Cruelty*, in Deleuze and Sacher-Masoch, *Masochism* (New York: Zone Books, 1991).

Deleuze, Gilles (1968) *Difference and Repetition*, trans. Paul Patton (New York: Columbia University Press, 1994).

Deleuze, Gilles (1969) *The Logic of Sense*, trans. Mark Lester and Charles Stivale (New York: Columbia University Press, 1990).

Deleuze, Gilles (1977) "Desire and Pleasure" (written in 1977 and first published in 1994), in Deleuze, *Two Regimes of Madness: Texts and Interviews, 1975–1995* (New York: Columbia University Press, 2007).

Deleuze, Gilles (1986) *Foucault*, trans. Seán Hand (Minneapolis: University of Minnesota Press, 1988).

Deleuze, Gilles (1988) "On Philosophy," interview with Raymond Bellour and Françis Ewald, in Deleuze, *Negotiations* (New York: Columbia University Press, 1995).

Deleuze, Gilles (1993a) "To Have Done with Judgment," in Deleuze, *ECC*.

Deleuze, Gilles (1993b) "Bartleby; or, The Formula," in Deleuze, *ECC*.

Deleuze, Gilles (*DI*): *Desert Islands, and Other Texts, 1953–1974* (Los Angeles: Semiotext(e), 2004).

Deleuze, Gilles (*ECC*): *Essays Critical and Clinical*, trans. Daniel W. Smith and Michael A. Greco (Minneapolis: University of Minnesota Press, 1997 [book first published in French 1993]).

Deleuze, Gilles and Foucault, Michel (1972) "Intellectuals and Power," in Deleuze, *DI*.

Deleuze, Gilles and Guattari, Felix (1991) *What Is Philosophy?*, trans. Hugh Tomlinson and Graham Burchell (New York: Columbia University Press, 1994).

Deleuze, Gilles and Parnet, Claire (1977) *Dialogues*, trans. Hugh Tomlinson and Barbara Habberjam (New York: Columbia University Press).

Flynn, Thomas R. (1997) *Sartre, Foucault, and Historical Reason, Volume One: Toward an Existentialist Theory of History* (Chicago: University of Chicago Press).

Foucault, Michel (1970) "Theatrum Philosophicum," in Foucault, *EW2*.

Foucault, Michel (1976) "Truth and Power," in Foucault, *EW3*.

Foucault, Michel (1977a) "Confinement, Psychiatry, Prison," in Foucault, *Politics, Philosophy, Culture: Interviews*, ed. Lawrence D. Kritzman (London: Routledge, 1988).

Foucault, Michel (1977b) "Preface" to Gilles Deleuze and Felix Guattari, *Anti-Oedipus*, trans. Robert Hurley, Mark Seem and Helen Lane (Minnepolis: University of Minnesota Press, 1983 [orig. pub. 1972]).

Foucault, Michel (1977c) "Truth and Power," interview with Fontana and Pasquino, in Foucault, *EW3*.

Foucault, Michel (1978) "Interview with Michel Foucault," in Foucault, *EW3*.

Foucault, Michel (1980a) "The Masked Philosopher," in Foucault, *EW1*.

Foucault, Michel (1980b) "Power, Moral Values, and the Intellectual," interview by Michael Bess in *History of the Present* 1–2 (Spring 1988), 11–13.

Foucault, Michel (1981) "So Is It Important to Think?," interview with Didier Eribon, in Foucault, *EW3*.

Foucault, Michel (1983a) "Structuralism and Post-Structuralism," interview with Gérard Raulet, in Foucault, *EW2*.

Foucault, Michel (1983b) "On the Genealogy of Ethics: Overview of Work in Progress," interview with Paul Rabinow and Hubert Dreyfus, in Foucault, *EW1*.

Foucault, Michel (1983c) *Fearless Speech*, ed. Joseph Pearson (Los Angeles: Semiotext(e), 2001).

Foucault, Michel (1984a) "What is Enlightenment?," in Foucault, *EW1*.

Foucault, Michel (1984b) "The Concern for Truth," interview with François Ewald, in Foucault, *Politics, Philosophy, Culture: Interviews and Other Writings, 1977–1984*, ed. Lawrence Kritzman (New York: Routledge, 1988).

Foucault, Michel (1984c) "Polemics, Politics, and Problematizations," interview with Paul Rabinow, in Foucault, *EW1*.

Foucault, Michel (1985) "Life: Experience and Science," in Foucault, *EW2*.

Foucault, Michel (*EW1*): *Essential Works, Volume 1: Ethics, Subjectivity, and Truth*, ed. Paul Rabinow (New York: New Press, 1997).

Foucault, Michel (*EW2*): *Essential Works, Volume 2: Aesthetics, Method, and Epistemology*, ed. James Faubion and Paul Rabinow (New York: New Press, 1998).

Foucault, Michel (*EW3*): *Essential Works, Volume 3: Power*, ed. James Faubion and Paul Rabinow (New York: New Press, 2000).

Grace, Wendy (2009) "Faux Amis: Foucault and Deleuze on Sexuality and Desire," *Critical Inquiry* 36, 52–75.

Hegel, G. W. F. (1807) *The Phenomenology of Spirit*, trans. A. V. Miller (Oxford: Oxford University Press, 1977).

Hegel, G. W. F. (1821) *The Philosophy of Right*, trans. Alan White (Newburyport: Focus Philosophical Publishing, 2002). [References are to Hegel's section numbers followed by page number in the cited edition.]

Hyppolite, Jean (1946) *Genesis and Structure of the Phenomenology of Spirit* (Evanston: Northwestern University Press, 1979 [orig. pub. 1946]).

Kant, Immanuel (1787) *Critique of Pure Reason*, trans. Norman Kemp Smith (New York: Saint Martin's Press, 1965).

Kojève, Alexandre (1947) *Introduction to the Reading of Hegel: Lectures on the Phenomenology of Spirit*, ed. Allan Bloom (Ithaca: Cornell University Press, 1980 [orig. pub. 1947]).

Koopman, Colin (2009) *Pragmatism as Transition: Historicity and Hope in James, Dewey, and Rorty* (New York: Columbia University Press).

Koopman, Colin (2011) "Genealogical Pragmatism: How History Matters for Foucault and Dewey," *Journal of the Philosophy of History* 5:3, 533–61.

Koopman, Colin (2013) *Genealogy as Critique: Foucault and the Problems of Modernity* (Bloomington: Indiana University Press).

Meillasoux, Quentin (2006) *After Finitude: En Essay on the Necessity of Contingency*, trans. Ray Brassier (New York: Continuum, 2008).

Patton, Paul (2000) *Deleuze and the Political* (New York: Routledge, 2003).

Rockmore, Tom (1992) *Before and After Hegel: A Historical Introduction to Hegel's Thought* (Berkeley: University of California Press).

Rorty, Richard (1984) "The Historiography of Philosophy: Four Genres," in Richard Rorty, J. B. Schneewind and Quentin Skinner (eds.), *Philosophy in History* (Cambridge: Cambridge University Press).

Roth, Michael S. (1988) *Knowing and History: Appropriations of Hegel in Twentieth-Century France* (Ithaca: Cornell University Press, 1988).

Smith, Daniel W. (2001) "Hegel: Deleuze, Hegel, and the Post-Kantian Tradition," in Smith, *Essays on Deleuze*, 2012.

Smith, Daniel W. (2006) "Dialectics: Deleuze, Kant, and the Theory of Immanent Ideas," in Smith, *Essays on Deleuze*, 2012.

Smith, Daniel W. (2012) *Essays on Deleuze* (Edinburgh: Edinburgh University Press).

Smith, Daniel W. and Protevi, John (2012) "Gilles Deleuze," in *Stanford Encyclopedia of Philosophy*, at http://plato.stanford.edu/entries/deleuze/. Accessed April 2016.

Zambrana, Rocío (2012) "Hegel's Legacy," *The Southern Journal of Philosophy* 50:2, 273–84.

CHAPTER 6

Foucault's Deleuzian Methodology of the Late 1970s

JOHN PROTEVI

We will explore the Deleuzian nature of Foucault's differential historical methodology in the mid-to-late 1970s. We will track formulations that suggest the key concept of *Difference and Repetition*: individuation as the integrating of a differential field or "multiplicity."[1]

In *Discipline and Punish* (1975), Foucault uses "war" (or at least "battle") as a "model" for understanding social relations:

> Now, the study of this micro-physics presupposes that the power exercised on the body is conceived not as a property, but as a strategy, that its effects of domination are attributed not to 'appropriation,' but to dispositions, maneuvers, tactics, techniques, functionings; that one should decipher in it a *network of relations*, constantly in tension, in activity, rather than a privilege that one might possess; that one should take as its model a perpetual battle rather than a contract regulating a transaction or the conquest of a territory. (DP 35F / 26E; emphasis added)[2]

As a result of conducting his genealogy of the war model in "*Society Must Be Defended*," Foucault comes to nuance his use of "war" in *History of Sexuality, Volume 1*,[3] where war is no longer seen as a grid of intelligibility that reveals a regime of truth governing a particular historical discourse. Rather, it is seen as a practical option for "coding" the multiplicity of force relations, that is, an optional and precarious "strategy" for integrating them:

> Should we turn the expression around, then, and say that politics is war pursued by other means? If we still wish to maintain a separation between war and politics, perhaps we should postulate that this *multiplicity of force relations* can be

coded – in part but never totally – either in the form of 'war,' or in the form of 'politics'; this would imply two different strategies (but the one always liable to switch into the other) for *integrating* these unbalanced, heterogeneous, unstable, and tense force relations. (HS1, 123F / 93E; emphasis added)

Thus at this point Foucault has "power" as the grid of intelligibility for social relations and "war" as an active strategy of political practice; looking at the social field in terms of power lets us see war as a possible strategy for integrating a multiplicity of force relations, whereas power "itself" can only be seen if we look at it *as* such a multiplicity: "It seems to me that power must be understood in the first instance as the *multiplicity* of force relations immanent in the sphere in which they operate and which constitute their own organization" (HS1, 121–22F / 92E; emphasis added).

So, in HS1 the "multiplicity of force relations" is the grid of intelligibility for power, which is in turn the grid of intelligibility of the social field. These successive grids of intelligibility reveal a dynamic social ontology, an interactive realism, in which war is a strategy for action in the social field, a way of integrating the multiplicity of force relations that constitute that field and thereby constituting the protagonists of political history as engaged in a "war by other means." The looping effect or self-fulfilling prophecy here should be clear: it's almost a cliché to say that naming yourself and others as warriors tends to create the reality in which others treat you as such and you respond in kind since they have just proved your point.

It's important not to confuse his historical realism with Foucault's celebrated genealogical analysis of the constitution of the objects of the human sciences, to which he compares his analysis of the constitution of the objects of the liberal and neoliberal power-knowledge *dispositifs* and their regimes of truth (e.g., various forms of *homo economicus*). I qualify the ontological status of these objects as "interactively realist" in the sense that they are not dependent on a human subject or intersubjective community, but are, in Foucault's terms, "marked out in reality" as a result of the *dispositif* of practices that constitute them (NB 21–22F / 19E). "Interactive realism" is basically the same as what Ian Hacking calls, in an update to his important essay "Making Up People," the "looping effect" of a "dynamic nominalism."[4] That is to say, the interaction of the constituting practices and the constituted objects is extended in time and is structured by feedback loops, so that the expectation of an action increases the probability of that action. We also know this phenomenon by two other terms: "self-fulfilling prophecy" and "methodology becomes metaphysics," as when a policy based on an assumption creates the conditions that produce behavior conforming to that assumption.[5]

With the shift to "governmentality" in *Security, Territory, Population* and *Birth of Biopolitics*, there is still the Nietzschean–Deleuzian concept of integration of a multiplicity of differential elements and relations as embedded in the interplay of power and resistance in practices, but there is a change in the nature of the relata; it is no longer "force" relations, but relations of "actions," as we read in "The Subject and Power": power is the "action on the action of others." Thus with governmentality, we still find a differential field, but one of actions rather than forces: "to govern . . . is to structure the possible field of action of others."[6]

In STP and NB the grid of intelligibility is governmentality, which prevents us from hypostasizing the state as a substance, and lets us avoid what Foucault will call "state phobia." In an important passage in *Naissance* Foucault concentrates on the "statification" of governmental practices. But this does not mean starting by analyzing the "essence" of the state and then trying to deduce current practices of state governmentality as accidents accruing to the substance defined by that essence. For Foucault, "the state does not have an essence"; it is not "an autonomous source of power" (NB 79F / 77E). Rather it is only the "effect, the profile, the mobile shape [*découpe mobile*] of a perpetual statification [*étatisation*] or perpetual statifications [*étatisations*] in the sense of incessant transactions which modify, or move, or drastically change, or insidiously shift" multiple practices such as finance, investment, decision-making, control, and relations of local/central authorities (NB 79F / 77E). The state has no essence; it is not a substance with changing properties, but is an individuation of what Deleuze would call an Idea, a multiplicity, a system of differential elements and relations involved in "incessant transactions."[7] Foucault continues with his nominalist anti-essentialism: "The state has . . . no interior. The state is nothing else but the mobile effect of a regime of multiple governmentalities" (NB 79F / 77E).

Foucault's move to governmentality as the horizon for examining the state enables a nominalist anti-essentialism that, in seeing concrete states as individuations of a multiplicity, outflanks the "state phobia" against which he rails in both its left- and right-wing manifestations. A genealogy tracks individuations as the integration of a multiplicity of heterogeneous differential elements and relations, as opposed to a causal and substantialist narrative, which Foucault will call a "genetic analysis." By focusing on the integration of a multiplicity we can replace a "genetic analysis through filiation with a genealogical analysis . . . which reconstructs a whole network of alliances, communications, and points of support" (STP 123F / 117E).[8] For instance, a genealogy of military discipline connects it to a series of problems – floating populations, commercial networks, technical innovations, models of community management – problems which are the very ones out of which certain state organs emerge as a "stratifying" solution. Thus we see military discipline is an integrator of a differential field, being composed of "techniques with operative value in multiple processes"; the state does not provide the horizon for understanding this multiplicity, for it is itself immanent to it (STP 123 F / 119E).

In naming his differential historical methodology, Foucault insists upon the difference between a genealogy and a "genetic" analysis, which proceeds by identifying a unitary source that splits into two.[9] To establish intelligibility, he asks, "could we not . . . start not from unity, and not even from . . . duality, but from the *multiplicity* of extraordinarily diverse processes" (STP 244F / 238E; emphasis added). Foucault continues that establishing the intelligibility of these processes would entail "showing [*montrant*] phenomena of coagulation, support, reciprocal reinforcement, cohesion and *integration*" (STP 244F / 238–239E; emphasis added).

So by having a differential grid of intelligibility we see the revealed reality of the statification process is differential; in the classic Deleuzian manner, the integration of a multiplicity produces an emergent effect: "in short it would involve showing the bundle [*faisceau*] of processes and the network [*réseau*] of relations that ulti-mately induced as a cumulative, overall effect, the great duality" (STP 244F / 239E). Foucault's notion of individuation as integration of a differential field is clear as he concludes this very important passage:

> At bottom, maybe intelligibility in history does not lie in assigning a cause that is always more or less a metaphor for the source. Intelligibility in history would perhaps lie in something that we could call the constitution or composition of effects. How are overall, cumulative effects composed? . . . How is the state effect constituted on the basis of a thousand diverse processes. . .? [*Comment se com-posent des effets globaux, comment se composent des effets de masse? Comment s'est constitué l'effet Etat à partir de mille processus divers. . .?*]" (STP 244F / 239E)

It's the processes that constitute the state as their effect, not Foucault as subject of knowledge; Foucault's contribution is to provide the grid of intelligibility that reveals this individuation as integration of a differential field at work in historical reality.

In *Sécurité*, Foucault's differential method provides us with a genealogy of the modern state on the basis of the history of governmental reason. In the nineteenth century we see the breakup of the administrative state's police apparatus into dif-ferent institutions: economic practice; population management; law and respect for freedom; and the police (in the contemporary sense of a state apparatus that intervenes to stop disorder). These are added to the diplomatic-military apparatus (STP 362F / 354E). But it's crucial to see that the administrative state's police apparatus that is here broken up was itself differential; it was not a unitary source. It arose with *raison d'Etat*, which is itself "something completely different [which] emerges in the seventeenth century" (STP 346F / 338E). The administrative state emerges from a "cluster [*faisceau*] of intelligible and analyzable relations that allow a number of fundamental elements to be linked together [*lier*] like the faces of a single polyhedron" (STP 346F / 338E).

We note the by now familiar Deleuzian language of the linking together of differential elements and relations.[10] Foucault here lists four elements: the art of government thought as *raison d'Etat*; competition of states while maintaining

European equilibrium; police; and the emergence of the market town and its problems of cohabitation and circulation (each of these is a differential field of multiple processes and practices). So police is part of a larger *dispositif*, and is itself concerned with a multiplicity of all the factors going into providing for the being and well-being of men, that well-being which, in a fascinating phrase, Foucault qualifies as a "well-being beyond being [*ce bien-être au-delà de l'être*]" (STP 335F / 328E).[11] More precisely, police integrates relations between the increase of those forces and the good order of the state (321F / 313E). Police does not deal with things but with "forces" that arise from adjusting the relations among the rates of increase of multiple processes. As noted before, here we see forces as elements of the state as analyzed by *raison d'Etat*.

With *Naissance*, Foucault enriches his discussion of novelty in history with a more explicit focus on the notion of "regimes of truth." Identifying the novelty of liberalism and neoliberalism entails using as a grid of intelligibility the institution of "regimes of truth," which are defined in terms reminiscent of those for "episteme" in earlier works: "the set of rules enabling one to establish which statements in a given discourse can be described as true or false" (NB 37F / 35E; SD 145F / 163–64E). For instance, the question of liberalism is that of a new "regime of truth as the principle of the self-limitation of government" (NB 21F / 19E). Compared to *raison d'Etat*, classical liberalism constitutes a new question, the self-limitation of the government to allow the natural mechanisms of exchange markets to operate, just as *raison d'Etat* asked about the "intensity, depth, and attention to detail" of governing for the sake of the maximum growth of power of the state (NB 21F / 19E).

We will conclude our discussion of Foucault's differential methodology with a problematic text. Concerning the establishment of the market as the site of veridiction for liberalism as a governmental practice, Foucault insists that we not look for "the cause" of this novel constitution. Instead, if we are to understand this historical novelty we have to understand the "polygonal or polyhedral relationship" between multiple elements which are themselves changing rates of change of heterogeneous processes: "a new influx of gold . . . a continuous economic and demographic growth . . . an intensification of agricultural production" (NB 35F / 33E). This is a clear example of a Deleuzian multiplicity: a system of differentially linked processes exhibiting changing rates of change. Foucault follows up by claiming that in order to "establish the intelligibility [*effectuer . . . la mise en intelligibilité*]" of the process by which the market became a site of veridiction one must "put into relation the different phenomena [of "influx of gold," "continuous economic and demographic growth," and "an intensification of agricultural production"] [*la mise en relation de ces différent phénomènes*]" (NB 35F / 33E; translation modified).

So far so good; rendering something intelligible comes from the integration of a multiplicity that preserves the heterogeneity of the processual elements. Foucault continues on with an odd bit of quasi-ontological modal analysis that is the key for our understanding of the realist ontological status of the regime of truth as that which is revealed by a grid of intelligibility (as opposed to the interactively real status of the objects of a regime of truth). Establishing the intelligibility of the process by which the market became a site of veridiction is a matter of "showing how it was possible [*Montrer en quoi il a été possible*]." We do not have to show that the establishment of such a site of veridiction "would have been necessary [*qu'il aurait été nécessaire*]"; this would be a "futile task." Here is the key: neither do we have to show of the process that "it is a possibility [*un possible*], one possibility in a determinate field of possibilities [*un des possibles dans un champ déterminé des possibles*]." Rather, to establish the intelligibility of a historical novelty consists in "simply showing it to be possible [*Que le réel soit possible, c'est ça sa mise en intelligibilité*]" (NB 35F / 34E; translation modified at several points).

This is difficult to reconcile with Deleuze, given his well-known adoption of the Bergsonian critique of the possible-real relation as opposed to the virtual-actual relation (*Bergsonisme* 99–101F / 96–98E; DR 272–74F / 211–12E).[12] Nonetheless, we might be able to salvage something by focusing on Foucault's denial that the establishment of the intelligibility of a historical novelty consists in showing it is one possibility in a determinate field of possibilities. For that's Deleuze's main target in adopting Bergson. The virtual as differential field gives rise to actual entities – its differentiated state passes through individuation and dramatization on the way to differenciation – but is not itself composed of actual individuated/differenciated entities; at most it consists in potentials for individuation processes that are triggered at critical points in the relations of other processes – hurricanes are individuated at critical points in the relations of wind and water currents provoked by temperature and pressure differences. This seems to resonate with Foucault's denial of a "determinate field of possibilities" in which the novelty under consideration was an individuated member. So as long as Foucault insists that intelligibility entails the putting into relation of multiple processes we can see the phrase "showing it was possible" in terms of establishing the differential field of processes (influx of gold, economic and demographic growth, etc.) out of which the market as site of veridiction was actualized. What we can say is that Foucault's showing a regime of truth as an immanent historical reality meets Deleuze's requirement that one show the conditions of genesis of "real experience" (DR 200F / 154E) in the integration, resolution or actualization of a differential field.

NOTES

1. Foucault does not mention integration in "Theatrum Philosophicum," though he does discuss multiplicity. See *Dits et Ecrits I* (Paris: Gallimard Quarto edition, 2001), 958 and *Language, Counter-Memory, Practice* (Ithaca: Cornell University Press, 1977), 185.

2. Michel Foucault, *Surveiller et punir* (Paris: Gallimard, 1975), translated by Alan Sheridan as *Discipline and Punish* (New York: Vintage, 1979).

3. Michel Foucault, *Histoire de la sexualité, tome 1: La volonté de savoir* (Paris: Gallimard, 1976), translated by Robert Hurley as *The History of Sexuality, Volume 1: An Introduction* (New York: Random House, 1978).

4. Ian Hacking, "Making Up People," in *Reconstructing Individualism: Autonomy, Individuality, and the Self in Western Thought*, ed. Thomas Heller, Morton Sosna and David Wellbery (Stanford: Stanford University Press, 1986). The updated version to which I refer was published in the *London Review of Books* 28:16 (17 August 2006); only this version contains the phrase "looping effect."

5. For an article examining just such a looping effect in contemporary practices based on the assumptions of Rational Choice Theory producing the neoliberal *homo economicus*, see Elinor Ostrom, "Policies that Crowd out Reciprocity and Collective Action," in Herbert Gintis, Samuel Bowles, Robert Boyd and Ernst Fehr, *Moral Sentiments and Material Interests: The Foundations of Cooperation in Economic Life* (Cambridge, MA: MIT Press, 2005), 253–75.

6. Foucault's differential methodology accords with his desire to avoid positing a transhistorical constant, a "universal" that is simply treated differently in different epochs (NB 4F / 2–3E; 64F / 63E). To take a famous example, in *Surveiller et punir*, it is never the case that he wants to examine how the prison changes from absolutism to liberalism. That would be a closet substantialist metaphysics in which the prison is a substance that receives different properties. Foucault analyzes this substantialist model as "historicism" (NB 5F / 3E). Foucault instead proposes a genealogy of constitutive practices; we are accustomed to calling this his "nominalism." From this perspective, the absolutist monarch didn't have prisons at his disposal. He had a mechanism, enclosure, which was put to a certain function: enclosure for protection to await later punishment. If we had to give a name to the place, the building, where the enclosure happened, it would be better to call it a "jail." You only get prisons with a new *dispositif*, where the mechanism of enclosure is put to a different function, punishment (and penitence, and rehabilitation, etc.).

7. With "incessant transactions" we have a strong echo of the Deleuzian notion of a multiplicity as a structure of continuous variation. Relatively implicit in DR (e.g. 326F / 253E), continuous variation is a major concept throughout *Mille Plateaux*.

8. Can we go outside the state? There is an immediate problem: is not the state the totalizing field for all these "outsides" of institutions, functions and objects? Can we ever get outside such a horizon for social being (STP 123F / 119E)? Again, the focus in a genealogy is on the different means of integrating a multiplicity of socio-economic processes and governmentality practices. Foucault suggests that studying military discipline is not a matter of studying state control of its military institution, for this would be a substantialism entailing the study of different accidental properties surrounding the unchanging essence of the state and its army.

9. We see here a merely terminological difference with Deleuze. In DR, the conditions of real experience (not merely possible experience) form an "intrinsic genesis" (200F / 154E). But insofar as this genesis is the integration of a differential field, we see that "genesis" in DR is

equivalent to "genealogy" for Foucault, albeit that Deleuze works in an ontological register and Foucault in an epistemological register.

10. The editor of *Naissance* notes the appearance of similar language defining a genealogy in terms of "singularity" and "multiple determining elements" in a roughly contemporaneous essay by Foucault (NB 50n8F / 49n8E).

11. Is the mere "being" of men here just physical survival that forces men back onto themselves in desperate selfishness, while "well-being" allows for productive relations among men? So that free sociality is dependent on a guarantee of the necessities of life? In another context, we might attempt to draw out the classic questions of the relations of *oikos* and *polis*, of necessity and freedom, from this small phrase of Foucault's.

12. Gilles Deleuze, *Le Bergsonisme* (Paris: PUF, [1966] 1997), translated by Hugh Tomlinson and Barbara Habberjam as *Bergsonism* (New York: Zone Books, 1988).

CHAPTER 7

Deleuze's Foucault: *A Metaphysical Fiction*[1]

FRÉDÉRIC GROS

TRANSLATED BY SAMANTHA BANKSTON

Before all else, we need to acknowledge a previously held, reprehensible position: for a long time Deleuze's book on Foucault[2] seemed to consist of a dogmatic rigidity that did not manage to break into the enthusiasm of what Foucault said. From cover to cover the book seemed *ridiculous* to us. It seemed far, so far from Foucault's actual work, and with a menacing sort of passion we thought about *demonstrating* that in his book Deleuze had committed nothing more than a work of fiction. The reception of Deleuze's presentation at the conference, "Michel Foucault, Philosopher,"[3] only reinforced these poorly conceived convictions.

There was enough that could be found in Deleuze's interviews, which were collected in *Negotiations, 1972–1990*,[4] to reverse these initial opinions, but the turning point took place elsewhere. For instance, previously unpublished notes were published by *le Magazine littéraire*,[5] where he expressed exemplary honesty, and a sincere desire to *understand* Foucault. François Ewald calls for a discussion in their exchange. That was really it, but even more: there is a kind of sensitivity in their encounter from the very start. It is with *scrupulous hesitation* that Deleuze realizes what he understood; in other words, *what he had already transformed.*

It was not a case of simply repeating the old refrain: in his book, like all of his others, Deleuze talks about, above all, Deleuze. It is *Deleuze's* Nietzsche, Spinoza, Bergson, and finally Foucault that is to be found. There is a facility in invoking the charm and secrecy in the delusional projections of these tendentious interpretations. Because, above all, Deleuze wants to *understand* Foucault, but understanding for him is not commentary, and it's not staying as faithful as possible to what Foucault said, as if attempting to disambiguate his line of thought. To understand is not to explicate, clarify, or *to lay bare.* There is a double movement in the practice through which Deleuze gives thought to Foucault's work, a double movement that provides his book with quite a foreign tone (what we took in our naiveté to be blind dogmatism).

Understanding an author for Deleuze is to first *ground* her in a certain way. Grounding an author is not anchoring her in an initial intuition, nor is it building up her system. Rather, it consists in revealing the inherent metaphysics of a particular work (even more so, he puts the work into play as a possibility for life). The second movement of understanding (though alchemy wants this to be the same thing) is a movement of reverie. For Deleuze, understanding an author is to be able to *dream* her: knowing how to direct her thought along the twists and turns that thought takes. It's not a matter of going back and digging up the thought of an author by insisting on the furrows that the works tracked out (a pedestrian exercise of historical, academic commentary), but trying to navigate an author by following the current of a thought, even if it's known that the direction no longer even belongs to this thought *as such* (instead, it's constituted as a precise echo): an oceanic practice of philosophical commentary, which is, without a doubt, the most faithful kind of treason.[6] What is summoned in Deleuze is not the historical Foucault, but nor is it a redoubling of Deleuze (it is the opposite of narcissism to dream along foreign coordinates). What Deleuze summons is Foucault's double: that which Foucault *is*, if he had been a metaphysician.

It was only in listening to the recorded lectures that Deleuze gave on Foucault at the University of Paris VIII from 1985–6 that enabled us to take account of this dimension.[7] In the recordings we find no dogmatism; his voice isn't even certain: it *searches*. Deleuze *posits* formulas ("the archive is audio-visual", "one must fold the line from the outside in order to escape death", etc.) about which one doesn't even think to ask whether the words are *Foucault's* or *Deleuze's*: they are like dimensions of a metaphysical dream *out of Foucault*, and Deleuze *stretches* and explores while even wondering where the dream can lead him. And after having *thrown* these formulas like philosophical dice that are left to be read, and the hesitations of the final faces of the dice (the *formulas*) cease, we hear Deleuze turn them around and around again, folding them, and not like a secret that is revealed, but like an enigma that is deployed according to its own dimension. And in order to think even more, Deleuze incessantly *risks* other formulas, and by risking them he *takes a stand*.

When reading Deleuze's book, we hadn't seized upon this *uncertainty* that ran through it, and thus it's important to note that a linear succession of affirmations suffocates the book. This text requires performing an extremely slow type of reading: each formula must be able to be experienced as an interrogation, an invitation, an expectation. The extreme coldness, disengaged from what is said, is inversely the ardent risk of continuing *another's dream*.

What can even indicate the fact that when speaking about Foucault Deleuze is simultaneously talking about his close, *living* friend? The extreme dryness is not there to (only) conjure pathos, because at each moment Deleuze employs the very means of his process. Penetrating the *metaphysical intimacy* of beings that are known and loved is a very strange practice, which is undoubtedly more distressing than learning or unveiling the *private* secrets of their life. What's more, in his book and seminars, Deleuze traces the *extreme curb of a fate*. It's extreme not because it would take the appearances of an adventurous epic, but because, even further than any sketch of an interior life, it's at this point that he teaches us what is at the very heart of all existence: his philosophy.

In brief, if it is decidedly true that Deleuze narrates a systematic dream (the dream of Foucault as a metaphysician), we would simply want to resituate the *steps* of this dream, as a path is reconstituted by a reminder of limits: and each step afterward will rediscover the missing links, or the complications of folds, in the dispersed writings of Deleuze.

THE STRATA OF KNOWLEDGE

The audio-visual archive

What we find in the first act are "strata", historical formations of knowledge. Knowledge is about seeing and speaking, what is seen and what is stated, evidence and visibility. And this is the first Deleuzian affirmation of Foucault: "the archive is audio-visual." History will be the exact determination for each era's "distribution of the visible and the articulable" and its knowledge.[8] It is not a history of mentality and ideas, but a history of the visible and the enunciated, while their combination shapes "knowledge." Or even still, it's a history of "machinic processes" (how is the visible extracted?) and "enunciated procedures" (how are enunciations produced?), which, when combined, enable a history of "procedures of truth."[9]

Light and language

This visibility and enunciation, pursued by Deleuze, depend neither on subjective nor objective syntheses for their distribution: they are not rooted in the synthetic act of a pure ego, no more than the materiality of socio-historical conditions. They are familiar with the transcendental: it's the "there is", "there is" light for visibility, and "there is" language for enunciation. With that, Foucault constitutes an ontology: it is in the light-Being, in the language-Being, that the enunciated and the visible come to find their conditions of possibility. What speaks for Foucault is not the "I" as the ultimate foundation (personology), nor the "signifier" as an organizing latency (structuralism), nor even the "World", even given in its native coldness (phenomenology).[10] What speaks is language-Being. But at the same time Deleuze adds that if we can even talk about ontology it is an "historical" ontology: language-Being and light-Being are inseparable in the determinate way by which they resemble ("fall" on) the visible and the enunciated. There are a priori conditions that only exist as historical regimes of enunciation, a historical machine of visibility: assemblages that are always immanent. In other words, and more to the point: there is not a light-Being or language-Being that can be given in ordinary experience. There is *nothing* prior to knowledge, prior to "these combinations of the visible and the articulable on each strata, at each historical formation."[11]

The non-relation

Deleuze continues to remark that after all, for Foucault, these two forms (Deleuze talks about forms of exteriority: Light and Language define the spaces of *dispersal* for the seen and the enunciated) are irreducible, and even *outside one another*. This is the great principle announced in Blanchot: to speak is not to see. Deleuze firmly insists on this disjunction: here, he sees the definite refusal of all phenomenological intentionality.

This disjunction of Seeing and Speaking simultaneously constitutes Foucault's Kantianism:[12] there is an irreducibility between the forms of Receptivity (the visible or intuition) and the forms of spontaneity (the enunciated or the understanding). And Foucault's Kantianism explains the primacy of enunciation over visibility:[13] enunciation remains a determiner.

This irreducibility of the visible in Foucault affirms his stance from all analytic philosophy, while the primacy of enunciation sets him apart. It's thus through his Kantian bias that Deleuze begins to demarcate the precision of Foucault's thought.

The passage

Meanwhile, this irreducibility poses a problem: how is it possible to understand, if speaking is not seeing, if one can see that which is spoken about, and say what one sees? So, Deleuze evokes the Bataillean grasp between seeing and speaking (statements slip between visibility and their conditions), but at the same time he understands that reason for such a formation of the irreducibility must be sought elsewhere.[14] Thus, it's necessary to invoke a second axis, which is not itself a form, but which returns reason to historical formations from the union-separation of seeing and speaking as forms of exteriority.

STRATEGIES OF POWER

Power as non-formal and non-stratified

Thus, we need an element that is not itself a form, but from which the systemic stratifications of knowledge can be understood, as long as they still contain a central inconsistency. The non-formal, the non-stratified, is a *relation of forces*.

This time Foucault's Nietzscheanism is laid bare: the power relation is given as a relation of forces.[15] Force is thus thought as that which is multiple[16] in its own essence, related in essence to another force. To think about power as a relation of forces is to note its relative specificity with all relations of violence: power is a force relation acting on another force, thus *non-formal*, while violence is *deforming*. Force relations do not open up to a perpetual chaos, but are introduced according to given historical configurations. For Deleuze, this singular, historical introduction of force relations constitutes a *diagram*:[17] such as discipline (where the formula equals imposing some task to some multiplicity).

According to Deleuze, we must be able to understand Foucault's great theses from that point. On the one hand, force, as long as it belongs to its essence of relating to another force, can have the power to affect, and the power to be affected. It can easily be seen that this double postulation makes the duality of seeing and speaking echo. But this simple *return* is not enough: a *passage* is necessary. Force relations as such are non-formal, and above all they are virtual: first they are actualized in stratifications. Force relations are multiple, moving, molecular, and virtual ("evanescent games"): they only begin to truly exist by being integrated into molar instances, what Deleuze immediately designates as institutions or *milieus of knowledge* (the family, school, the factory) – this means stratified forms where force relations become consistent and stable (and are capable of being reproduced). For example, "For sexuality, the molar instance around which micro-sexual relations are actualized and integrated is sex." To illustrate Foucault's thesis, Deleuze appeals to Proust, sketching sexless molecular sexuality below two acknowledged levels of sexuality (normal heterosexuality and guilty homosexuality): the body and its pleasures.

The concrete instance that integrates force relations (introduced simply by the diagram) is also termed a "dispositif" by Deleuze. This can be said another way: at the level of the *diagram* (example: discipline) function is not formalized, nor is substance formed (imposing some task to some multiplicity). The *dispositif* only knows formalized functions (instructing, correcting, enforcing work, etc.) and formed substances (the student, the son of a family, the worker, etc.). The passage from the dispositif to the diagram is a passage from "a compact stratification to a diffuse strategy": it's in this movement from one to the other that the true method of exploration must exhaust itself on the social field.

What represents knowledge for Foucault is now better understood: a process of integration of force relations in molar instances. There is no need to pose the problem of *primacy* between power and knowledge, since knowledge integrates the force relations that constitute its *immanent cause*. "In what sense is there a primacy of power over knowledge, or power relations over relations of knowledge? It's because they would have nothing to integrate if there weren't differential power relations. It is true that such relations would be evanescent, embryonic or virtual, without the operations that integrate them."[18]

Differenciation of force relations

But every actualization is differenciation at the same time that it is integration: it's in the very movement of its actualization that divergence operates. As stated previously, it is the essence of force to re-enter into a relation with another force: every force is the power to affect (presupposing a *function*) and to be affected (presupposing a *material*). It's along these two directions that force relations are actualized in the difference of light-beings (machines) and language-beings (enunciations). Deleuze shows how the enunciated integrates force relations: the enunciation AZERT[19] (the first letters on a French keyboard) assumes a force relation between fingers, letters, and touches ("AZERT standardizes relations between letters and the French language – frequency and vicinity – and relations of fingers"). The same goes for luminosity (the description of *Las Meninas* shows how the lines of light intersect to culminate in the force relation between two dominant singularities – painting and the king).

This is where Deleuze situates the second turning point in Foucault: since after having exposed the principles of the actualization of forces, it can even be said that the determination of the being has been settled: everything finds its reason (or non-reason) of being. And that's what leads to the following question: but can we escape Power? Or are we condemned like determined particles to our presence? Is there an opposition to power? From where can resistance arise? How can mutations of the diagram be explained?

The passage to Foucault's third conceptualization is not like the passages from formations of knowledge to non-formal power. What was required then was a systematicity that had to be completed. What is needed now is the urgency of an ethical attitude.

Modes of Subjectification

The line from the Outside: one dies

It was in Kant that we discovered the irreducibility of spontaneity and receptivity of (stratified) historical formations of knowledge. Then there was Nietzsche for the first movement of force relations, and finally, we discover Heidegger for the fold.

In other words, employing an approach that becomes increasingly risky, one moved from forms of exteriority to the Outside of forces, in order to finally reach the *line from the Outside*. It can also be said that one passes from epistemology to ontology in order to unfold ethics.

One must understand how this line from the Outside is possible and beyond power. Occasionally, Deleuze identifies with Blanchot's "one dies", which Blanchot situated in literature and is the space delivered by the movement of writing. It is a line of death, not in the sense that it would be inert; on the contrary, it is tra-versed by movements of unfathomable violence. To depict this, Deleuze provides the image of the line of the whale in Herman Melville's *Moby Dick*.

Foucault's fascination with Bichat is thus better understood, which is already expressed in *The Birth of the Clinic*: the line from the Outside would be death that is coextensive with life, and is thus *as if one could only escape power in a confrontation with death*.

This Outside, if we follow the direction that is already set out by Blanchot, is Distant, more distant than any milieu of exteriority. This is why it is simultaneously nearer than any milieu of interiority. We're going quickly, but what is given to us as simple, sophisticated inversions, is carried out carefully by Deleuze in the extreme slowness of an enigma that not so much uncovers its revealed content, but rather the vastness of its secret. The equivalence between absolute distance and proximity is nonetheless ontologically immediate.

In the line of "one dies", Deleuze shows how Foucault devotes himself to bend-ing it and folding it on itself: this is the solution of life. Because, this line from the Outside is strictly speaking *unlivable*: "the line must cause a fold on pain of death." Only Artaud would have attempted to make the bed with his poems. In accor-dance with Deleuze and Leiris, Foucault would have also opposed being surrounded by folds, and Roussel distances them: "the choice between death and memory").[20] Henceforth, the question is: what happens when the line from the Outside is folded?

Subjectification as folding

For Deleuze, the first effect of this line is to produce an Inside: an inside of the Outside, an inside closer than any milieu of interiority. The thought of an inside would be the folding from Outside, and this is what connects Foucault, Blanchot, and Heidegger, according to Deleuze. This is where Deleuze cites the chapter from *The Order of Things* on the analytic of finitude, in particular: the folding of the line from the Outside (or the "oceanic line") is what constitutes an Inside, as well as the unthought of Thought. And this would then be finitude: the *result* of a fold (it wouldn't know in any case how to be a constituent if there is only a *historical* folding of the oceanic line in it). This Inside as a fold from the Outside is its double: a double that is not an external projection of a primary interiority, but repetition (through invagination) of the Inside. There is an empirical-transcendental pair as well as a fold of words in Roussel's writings ("Foucault is always protected from Heidegger by Roussel").

There's another specific detail in Foucault this time, which Deleuze realizes when considering the final texts. That of positing that the folding of the line from Inside produces a subjectivity, which the Greeks understood first: "Who invented creating the fold rather than confronting the void? This is the Greeks' idea."[21]

In sum, they invented the subject, and invented the subject as a fold of force on itself. Certainly, the *Greek diagram* of forces permitted it, even demanded it: to be a free man and to be able to govern others first necessitates knowing how to govern oneself. This is what Deleuze called the Greek "disengagement." By the function of the Greek diagram, only the free man can govern other free men, but the free man who is capable of governing free men will be the one who knows how to govern himself, which is a "very curious operation, which refers neither to the domain of knowledge, nor the domain of power."

It is thusly that the self arises as a fold, an auto-affectation of force: "force is folded on itself, bent on the self. There was a subjectification." Foucault does not rediscover the subject: he states a new thought of subjectification as the folding from Inside. The self-relation is announced in its irreducibility to stratifications of knowledge and to diagrams of power, even if the folds of subjectifications cease to be taken up in the wake of power-knowledge. From there incessant metamorphoses arise, and out of which the political, rather than resistance, arises: because subjectification is precisely a *knot*. It is known that knots (of subjectification), if they assure the regular weaving of lines (of power and knowledge), can also introduce a tension within them that it will cause them to break.

We never wanted to indicate by the chapter title that Deleuze produced a fiction, except by following the first impulse of a metaphysical dream of Foucault. What is established at each step is a new *image of thought*: to think is to speak *and* see (it's not knowing, and it's not *relating* words and things, concepts and realities); thinking is to convey singular and *risky* force relations (it's not about stating sovereign necessities); finally, thinking is *folding*, bending the line from Inside on itself (it's not unbending the full interiority of consciousness).

There is an extreme coherence of Deleuze's reading in Foucault's work. This coherence doesn't only stick to the symphonic character imposed on the three established movements of a Foucauldian meditation; that is, to the dramatic scansion. Without a doubt, it also sticks to the fact that when reading Foucault Deleuze rediscovers knowledge from his reading of Bergson. This was already accomplished with the postulation of two pure forms (seeing and speaking) that find their common principle in non-formal force relations (always conveyed by a singular irreducibility), which are only actualized by being differenciated. Finally, in his third act of fiction, Deleuze delivers thought from a subjectification as a constitution of "absolute memory." This is memory without psychological interiority, like the memory that had conjured Bergson: this would be the line from the Outside's operation of the fold. After all, this is what is at stake when conceiving of thought as folding: seeing the very source of time within it.

This reference to Bergson is masked but points to the distant path that follows the twists and turns of fiction. Therefore, one can still dream along with Deleuze: to dream of Foucault and find a fraternal double in Bergson.

NOTES

1. This article was initially published in French in the journal *Philosophie* 47 (1995), 53–63. All cited texts have been translated by Samantha Bankston.
2. Gilles Deleuze, *Foucault* (London: Athlone Press, 1988).
3. *Michel Foucault philosophe*, international conference, Paris, 9–11 January 1988, Seuil, 1989, 185–95.
4. Gilles Deleuze, *Negotiations, 1972–1990* (New York: Columbia University Press, 1995).
5. Gilles Deleuze, "Desire and Pleasure," in Arnold I. Davidson (ed.), *Foucault and His Interlocutors* (Chicago: University of Chicago Press, 1997), 183–92.
6. One would unmistakably find an echo of this practice in what Foucault understands by the "repetition of a question" in relation to Kant's interrogation of the Enlightenment.
7. These recordings can be consulted in the Foucault Center at the Saulchoir library, 34 bis, rue de la Glacière, Paris, in the 13th arrondissement. The cited passages without references from the work are extracts from audiotapes.
8. Deleuze, *Foucault*, p. 42.
9. Ibid. p. 54.
10. For these three denunciations, see: Ibid. p. 48.
11. Ibid. p. 42.
12. However, Deleuze strongly notes Foucault's differences from Kant, Ibid. p. 58.
13. Deleuze saw evidence of this primacy in the organization of *The Archaeology of Knowledge*, which only accorded a marginal position to the "non-discursive."
14. Deleuze recalls that in the same way Kant called for the necessity of a *third instance* (the schema of the imagination) to co-adapt the determinable and determination.
15. "Foucault's definition seems very simple: power is a relation of forces," Ibid. p. 59.
16. According to Deleuze, the differential element of forces in Nietzsche is the "will," where a will is related to another force in order to command or obey.
17. For a definition of a diagram, see: Ibid. p. 61.
18. Ibid. p. 68.
19. Translator's note: AZERT is the French keyboard's equivalent of QWERTY on the standard Anglophone keyboard.
20. Ibid. p. 82.
21. "The Greeks are the first doubling," Ibid. p. 83.

PART III

Convergence and Divergence

CHAPTER 8

Speaking Out For Others: Philosophy's Activity in Deleuze and Foucault (and Heidegger)

LEONARD LAWLOR AND JANAE SHOLTZ

There are many obvious intersections between Deleuze and Foucault: the relation of desire and pleasure; the structures of *agencement* and *dispositif*; and, the self-relation as the fold. These intersections are especially evident and determinable insofar as Deleuze wrote about Foucault and Foucault wrote about Deleuze. Yet, it is remarkable that *both* Deleuze and Foucault, each at the end of his life, wrote about philosophy itself. Of course, Deleuze's last great book (written with Guattari), appearing in 1991, is called *What is Philosophy?*[1] Yet, Foucault's last two courses at the Collège de France from 1982 to 1984 aim to answer the same question.[2] This final intersection of Deleuze and Foucault's thinking in the question of philosophy seems to have gone largely unnoticed. So, the question that we are going to address here is: what is philosophy for both Deleuze and Foucault? There is, however, a more precise way to formulate this question. On the one hand – this is a Deleuzian way to formulate the problem – the problem is the relation of philosophy to historical contingency. That is, today philosophy finds itself in the territory of capitalism. On the other hand – this is a Foucaultian way – the problem is the relation of philosophy to power. That is, philosophy always finds itself in a particular relation to power. Both ways of expressing the problem imply that essentially the problem amounts to this: what is philosophy's "reality" (to use Foucault's terminology [CF-GSO1, 211/229]), or what is philosophy "use" (to use Deleuze's terminology [QPh, 14/8–9]). In short, what is philosophy's activity?

It seems that the answer we find in late Deleuze and in late Foucault consists in a certain way of speaking. Philosophy's activity is linguistic. As we see in Deleuze and Guattari's *What is Philosophy?*, philosophy's use is "speaking for others" (*parler pour les autres*), and if we look at Foucault's final courses at the Collège de France its reality consists in what the ancient Greeks called "*parrēsia*" (speaking frankly, fearless speech, or even outspokenness). As we shall see, these two philosophical linguistic utterances are connected. In *What is Philosophy?*, Deleuze and Guattari argue that speaking for others arises when we are before the intolerable suffering of others. This standing before them, in their suffering, fills us with the shame at being human all too human. Thus the feeling of shame motivates us to speak for them. This speaking for them, however, takes us beyond the merely linguistic. Speaking for them requires *parrēsia*; it requires that we speak frankly, that we speak out, and then, as Foucault would say, speaking for requires, beyond the passivity of the feeling of shame, the activity of courage. The use of philosophy comes to light when we convert shame into courage. Then we see that philosophy has a reality insofar as it affects a change in reality. As Deleuze and Guattari say, what is at issue in speaking for is "becoming" (QPh, 105/109).[3] On the basis of the feeling of shame we must become other, enter into our own conversion of speaking and acting. We then speak for others so that they become other, so that they escape from their suffering and agony. We speak frankly and become outspoken when we take the risk to address the tyrant, the risk to expose the most naked and excessive uses of power, as those found for instance in the prisons.

There are two problems with which we must deal in order to understand the conversion of shame into courage (based on the association of "speaking for" with *parrēsia*). On the one hand, if it is indeed the case that what is at issue in speaking for is becoming, then we must re-examine the problem of return or *the* return (as in Nietzsche's eternal return doctrine) as we find it in the early Deleuze and Foucault. The return necessary concerns the future, the future of what is coming and of what is other. Foucault himself indicates that the problem of the return is at the center of both his own thinking and Deleuze's when he says, in "Theatrum Philosophicum," that "Time is what repeats itself; and the present . . . does not stop recurring. . . . Being is a Return [*Retour*] freed from the curvature of the circle; it is Recurrence [*Revenir*]. . . [freed] from the law of the Same."[4] Now, twice in this review essay, Foucault praises Deleuze for not denouncing metaphysics "as the forgetfulness of being." The allusion to Heidegger is obvious. Thus, we think that, if the project of determining the activity of philosophy for the later Deleuze and Foucault requires that we go back to the earlier problem of return, then the earlier problem of return requires us to look at the criticisms Deleuze and Foucault level at Heidegger's thought.[5] Heidegger's thought seems to express precisely the idea against which early Deleuze and Foucault fight: the idea of circular return. Immediately, we can say that philosophy's activity is not a circular return – not a return to an origin or foundation – as if it amounted to a promise being fulfilled. Thus philosophy's reality, its deed, its use, must amount to going beyond historical contingency without returning to a prior condition or it amounts to going beyond the current regime of power within which it finds itself without returning to that prior regime. Its activity or reality must consist in a creative repetition that returns without end.

The second problem then appears on the basis of this concept of unlimited return. The very idea of speaking for others seems to imply a form of representation: when I speak for you, I represent you, and then I mediate you with me and with others on the basis of a reductive and homogenizing identity, similarity, and resemblance. In other words, when I speak for you, it looks as though your singularity disappears; you never appear as an event. There is only the repetition of a general concept. The representation then looks to be precisely a circular return. In fact, as early as the 1968 *Difference and Repetition*, Deleuze denounces speaking for others; he says, "The misfortune in speaking is not speaking, but speaking *for others* or representing something" (DR, 74/52). The problem becomes more acute when we look at the 1972 exchange between Deleuze and Foucault called "Intellectuals and Power." There, Deleuze says, "We laughed at representation, saying it was over, but we didn't follow this '*theoretical* conversion' through – namely, theory demanded that those involved finally speak on their own account, *practically*." As is well known, Deleuze claims in "Intellectuals and Power" that Foucault was the first to teach us the fundamental lesson of "the indignity of speaking for others."[6] How is it possible to reconcile this early indignity with speaking for others with Deleuze (and Guattari's) later endorsement of "speaking for" in *What is Philosophy?* Although we are not certain, it seems that it was Foucault and Deleuze's involvement in "Le Groupe d'Information sur les Prisons" in 1971–2 that allowed them to start to think of "speaking for" in a new way. The GIP's independence from any political party and from any enterprise (like a sociological study or a judicial inquest) freed the prisoners from representing something like a social type. The questionnaire that the GIP used, in particular, allowed the inmates to speak on their own account. Yet, the GIP spoke too, not only through the way the questionnaire was worded but also through its own publications. What the GIP did then in its publications was make the voices of the inmates "resound." Freed from representing a general concept, a social type, or a moral universal, this resonance looks to be more like a creative repetition. So, we are going to examine the GIP documents as a kind of *verification* of our interpretation of the late endorsement of "speaking for" and its association to *parrēsia*. Before we come to this "verification" through the GIP documents, we must take up the problem of the return in Deleuze and Foucault in relation to Heidegger. Through Heidegger, we shall be able to see that the conversion of shame into courage gives us a glimpse of how philosophy calls us to go over man.[7] We start with Heidegger and Deleuze.

I. RETURN IN DELEUZE, FOUCAULT – AND HEIDEGGER

Deleuze's most extensive early discussion of Heidegger appears in Chapter 1 of *Difference and Repetition*.[8] As is well-known, in this chapter, Deleuze attempts to liberate difference from the demands of "the concept in general." The concept in general (or representation) leads us to conceive difference only for or in relation to something that serves as its foundation or ground. Indeed, difference becomes nothing but the negation of the foundation, a negation which, when it is itself negated, returns difference to the foundation from which it derived. In other words, in the representational concept of difference, difference is nothing but a bare repetition of the foundation; the dialectic is always circular. In this conception, difference relates negatively back to a foundation, which is the abstract identity of the concept (the third term of mediation). Therefore, difference is no longer conceived in terms of itself or "in itself," hence the title of *Difference and Repetition*'s first chapter. It is within the context of this reconception of difference and its relation to negation that Deleuze introduces his note on "Heidegger's Philosophy of Difference." In the note Deleuze makes five points.

Here are the five points in brief. The *first point* is that the "not" in Heidegger does not express the negative; rather the "not" expresses the difference between being and beings. The *second point* is that the difference between being and beings is not the "between" in the ordinary sense.[9] Instead, it must be understood as "the fold," the "Zwiefalt." Difference understood as the fold is constitutive of being. In other words, being, in Heidegger, differentiates the being off from a sort of background of obscurity. In this way, Deleuze gives a new sense to Heidegger's expression "ontological difference": being is the active "differenciator" of beings (DR 90/65; see also DR 154/117).[10] The *third point* is that the "ontological difference corresponds to the question." In other words, Deleuze makes an equivalency between being and questioning. As equivalent to a question, being actively constitutes beings as differences, as if they were so many different answers to a question that remains open and consequently unanswerable. As a kind of nonbeing, difference (or the question) – this is the *fourth point* – "is not," as Deleuze says, "an object of representation."[11] The "turn beyond metaphysics," according to Deleuze, amounts to insisting that metaphysics cannot think "difference in itself." The Heideggerian "turn," for Deleuze, is a resistance to conceiving difference as a third term "between" being and beings, it is a "stubborn" resistance to mediation. Finally, the *fifth point*: "Difference cannot, therefore, be subordinated to the Identical or the Equal, but must be thought as the Same, in the Same." Through the Same, Heidegger is trying to think a "gathering" that is not reducible to empty indifferent oneness.

It seems that Deleuze intends these five points to show how certain readings of Heidegger are really misunderstandings (probably he has in mind those of Sartre and Merleau-Ponty). In particular, Deleuze's five points aim to outline a more accurate reading of the Heideggerian "not": "the Heideggerian NOT refers not to the negative in being, but to being as difference; it refers not to negation but to the question." Deleuze's defense of Heidegger is so strong here that he says that he considers the Heideggerian "correspondence" between difference and the question, between the ontological difference and the being of the question, "fundamental."

Despite this attachment to Heidegger's thought, Deleuze suggests that Heidegger's own formulas for the "not" might be to blame for the misunderstandings of his later work. Indeed, through a series of questions, Deleuze distances himself from Heidegger's thinking. In particular, Deleuze is not certain that speaking of the Same (or gathering), rather than Identity, is really enough to think original difference.[12] Deleuze asks, "Is Sameness enough to disconnect difference from all mediation?" The distance, however, that Deleuze takes from Heidegger's thought really comes down to the status of the being (*das Seiende* or *l'étant*), not the status of being (not *das Sein* or *l'être*). The question for Deleuze is the following: "Does Heidegger make the conversion by means of which being [*l'être*] must be said only of difference and in this way being [*l'être*] revolves around the being [*l'étant*]?" In other words, "Does Heidegger conceive the being [*l'étant*] in such a manner that the being [*l'étant*] is removed from all subordination in relation to the identity of representation?" Deleuze concludes, "It seems not, given [Heidegger's] interpretation of Nietzsche's eternal return" (DR 91/66).[13]

Whether or not Deleuze's claim about Heidegger's interpretation of Nietzsche's eternal return doctrine is correct – in *Difference and Repetition* (but already in the 1962 *Nietzsche and Philosophy*),[14] it is clear that Deleuze thinks that Heidegger does not understand the eternal return doctrine – it tells us a lot about how Deleuze conceives his own thinking in relation to that of Heidegger. When Heidegger interprets the eternal return doctrine as being "metaphysical," Deleuze thinks that Heidegger is claiming that the return of the eternal return is a founded repetition. That is, it is the repetition of an identity that predetermines all the answers to the question, as if for Nietzsche the repetition was a repetition of permanence, as if for Nietzsche repetition did not produce a multiplicity of new answers, as if for Nietzsche therefore there was no true becoming. In contrast, what Deleuze sees in the eternal return doctrine is a very specific kind of repetition, one that, as he says, "makes a difference" (DR 85/60). The repetition to which the eternal return refers, in Deleuze's interpretation of Nietzsche, is a repetition that repeats no identity. It is a foundationless repetition. It is foundationless insofar as it repeats the being (*l'étant*), but the being – an individual thing – is not conceived as copy of an original or of a model. The being is conceived as a singularity or as an event. A singular event, for Deleuze, is a true "commencement" so that the repetition of the eternal return is a "recommencement." Being based in a commencement, in an event, the recommencement is not determined. Therefore the recommencement – the return of the eternal return – has the potential to produce more differences, more events, more novelties, more answers to the question (DR 258–61/200–2). The repetition is creative.[15] Therefore, insofar as Deleuze thinks that Heidegger does not understand Nietzsche's eternal return doctrine, he thinks the real issue between his own thinking and that of Heidegger is the idea of foundation: founded repetition versus unfounded repetition. Heidegger, for Deleuze, remains attached to "the primacy of the Same" (DR 188n1/321n11). As we shall now see, Foucault also thinks that Heidegger remains attached to the primacy of the same.

The main occurrence of Heidegger's name in Foucault appears *The Order of Things*, in Chapter Nine, "Man and his Doubles."[16] Although "Man and his Doubles" is among the most difficult texts Foucault ever wrote, its basic idea is well known: the idea of man. Unlike human nature in the Classical Age which is correlated "term by term" to nature, man in the Modern Age is defined by a kind of ambiguity or doubling of finitude. First and foremost, man's finitude appears to him in the positive content of certain disciplines such as biology and man's finitude appears to him in the way man knows in these disciplines.[17] In other words, finitude is repeated from the positive content of knowledge into the conditions for that positive knowledge. In Chapter Nine, after having defined "man's primary characteristic" as repetition (the repetition of the positive and the fundamental), Foucault then extends the repetition of finitude into three other "doubles" that define man: "the transcendental repeats the empirical, the *cogito* repeats the unthought, the return of the origin repeats its retreat" (OT 326/316).

It is in the section that concerns this fourth repetition, the retreat and return of the origin, that we find the one occurrence of Heidegger's name. The section overall, however, concerns man's relation to the origin. Foucault provides a tripartite description of this relation. *First*, Foucault speaks of the origin retreating from man into the past. In Modern thought, according to Foucault, man always finds himself alive against the background of life, labor, and language that began long ago. In short, man's origin is the "already begun" (OT 341/330). The "already begun" means that man is not "contemporaneous" with the origin. Because of this non-contemporaneity, it is not possible to attribute, according to Foucault, an origin to man. Then *second*, because man seems to have no origin, to be virtually outside of time, he also appears to be that being from which all the chronologies of life, labor, and language have derived. Therefore, the origin of things always retreat or withdraws to a beginning earlier than man, while man retreats from things as that from which all the durations of things can begin. This double retreat, however, makes possible, according to Foucault, a "third retreat" (OT 343/332). So, *third*, taking up the *task* to call into question everything that pertains to time, Modern thought contests the origin of things in order to discover the "origin without either origin or beginning."[18] Time then would be, as it were, "suspended" in thought – in the sense that making this timeless origin be visible thought would seem to have made time stand still. And yet, thought itself would not be able to escape from time because it is not contemporary with the originless origin of time. In the Modern Age, thought can never be contemporary with the origin. However, as Foucault stresses, the suspension of time in thought is able to make the relation of thought and origin "flip over." Previously, the origin withdrew from thought into the past; now, however, it withdraws from thought going out into the future.

In other words, after finding itself coming too late for the origin, thought now projects the origin out in front as what is still to be thought. Although Foucault does not say this, the task for thinking that aims at suspending time amounts to Heidegger's retrieval of the meaning of being as time. According to Foucault, however, this retrieval is a retrieval of the same.[19]

As with Deleuze's claim about Heidegger's interpretation of the eternal return doctrine, with Foucault we cannot find one clear argument to support the claim that Heideggerian retrieval is a retrieval of the same.[20] A clue seems to appear, however, when Foucault says in "Man and his Doubles" that "[the origin] is promised to [man] in an imminence that will perhaps be forever snatched from him" (OT 345/334-5). The clue seems to be this: it is difficult to conceive promising in any other way than as something to be kept; as something to be kept, a promise must be fulfilled.[21] Then as something to be fulfilled, it seems that promising must always be based in a lack. The same dominates this retrieval or return or repetition because the promising, to which Foucault seems to be referring, is conceived as a deficiency (OT 353/342).[22] The withdrawal of the origin produces a deficiency, but the deficiency, it seems, produces something like an outline or a figure in relief that the future will fill in. In other words, what is to come is determined as what is going to fill in this lack. The still coming future will be the same as what was outlined with the withdrawal of the origin into the past. There seems, however, for Foucault, another and stronger step in this "argument," if we can call it an argument and if we understand it correctly. Foucault speaks of "the insurmountable relation of man's being to time" (OT 346/335). Thus it seems that the lack is a lack in "man's own being," which means that the return of the origin – promised and not yet fulfilled – is a fulfillment of *man's being*. Man is the figure in relief made by the withdrawal. The return of the origin therefore is a return of the same being as us. And then, we see that what is at issue in the question of return is really a going beyond or over man.

II. THE CONVERSION OF SHAME INTO COURAGE

Therefore, for both Deleuze and Foucault, as we just saw, Heideggerian repetition, return, or retrieval does not reach the true repetition, because Heidegger, it seems, conceives repetition as a repetition of the same. Thus the true repetition, for both Deleuze and Foucault, is what we called above a "creative repetition." The phrase "creative repetition" seems to be contradictory since repetitions repeat and therefore cannot be creative. Yet, one can understand the phrase if one thinks of the artwork. An event such as the writing of *Hamlet* was based in no determinate model, no exact foundation, and no self-identical origin; therefore its subsequent theater productions, while repetitions, are all able to be different. We know of course how important Oedipus and Hamlet are in Deleuze's *Difference and Repetition*. We know how important the tragic is in both early Deleuze and in early Foucault. The importance of tragedy and the artwork in Deleuze and Foucault means that both Deleuze and Foucault oppose the repetition of the same with the repetition of the different, and that opposition between same and different means that they oppose the being of man with the being of language.

There is no question that Foucault, in *The Order of Things*, opposes the being of language to the being of man.[23] There, Foucault notes that at the end of the Classical Age, language loses its status as the transparent medium between things and order, as the transparent medium between speaker and hearer. No longer occupying the middle, language, for Foucault, no longer functions transitively. Language no longer has a destination, an end or *telos* or *eschaton*. Then language no longer folds back over itself into a circle. The being of language in Foucault is "radical intransitivity." Through radical intransitivity, language is liberated from its finitude, allowing it to take on an indefinite potentiality (OT 313/300). It seems that for Foucault the indefinite potentiality of language (when it is liberated from transitivity) implies that language is capable of producing events. Thus, we must say that, despite Deleuze's so-called "vitalism," it is language that inspires his reflections on sense and event in *Difference and Repetition* and in *The Logic of Sense*. In fact, in *The Logic of Sense*, Deleuze says, "We will not ask therefore what the sense of an event is: the event is sense itself. The event belongs essentially to language, it *is* in an essential relation to language."[24] Always, however, for Deleuze, the linguistic event (sense or more generally a work, like an artwork) arises out of an affective encounter, out of the vision of what is "terrible," as "the soldier" sees in Stephen Crane's *The Red Badge of Courage*.[25] This vision of the terrible opens the way to go beyond or over the being of man.

Going over man brings us to the question of philosophy in the final Deleuze and Foucault. In *What is Philosophy?*, Deleuze (with Guattari) speaks of shame as one of the most powerful motives of philosophy (QPh 103/108). This shame is what one feels when confronted with the suffering of others. And for them, it seems that the shame in relation to the suffering of others (alluding apparently to Nietzsche, they call this "the shame at being human") motivates one to "speak for" (*parler pour*) others. But then Deleuze and Guattari ask: what does it mean to speak for others? They say that speaking for other is speaking "before" others. They change the preposition from "pour" to "devant." One feels shame when one stands "before" (*devant*) the victims of the Holocaust (and here of course they are speaking of Heidegger's political "mistake"). But beyond the feeling of shame "before" (*devant*) the suffering of others, they say that what is at issue in "speaking for" is becoming (QPh, 105/109). Here "devant" seems to change its meaning from "before" to "being in advance of." In advance of, for example, the animals who are suffering, one must become animal. In other words, from the shame before, one must take the first step in advance of the animals, and become animal. The change in meaning of the "devant" seems to imply that the ones who are becoming are the avant-garde. But then, Deleuze and Guattari return to the preposition "pour." One becomes animal "so that" – "pour que" – the animals become something else or other. The "pour que" of becoming puts the animals back in front and reduces we who are becoming to being only means. We who are becoming non-human, we who are speaking for others and before others who are suffering and in agony amounts to making, helping, or better, *letting* the animals become something else and something other. "Speaking for" tries to help them change so that they are no longer suffering or in agony. This speaking so that others become other is really what responsibility would be for Deleuze and Guattari. And it seems this kind of responsibility would require courage.

The speaking that helps others become other (others to come), then, leads us to Foucault. In his final courses at the Collège de France, Foucault, as we mentioned at the beginning, lectured on the ancient Greek notion of *parrēsia*, translated as "free-speech," "fearless speech," or even "outspokenness" (CF-GSO1, 61/63). In particular, in *The Government of Self and Others I*, Foucault stresses that *parrēsia* is *not* a performative utterance.[26] *Parrēsia* is always something *more* than a performative. As examples of performative utterances, Foucault speaks of "I baptize you" and "I apologize," but he could just as well have spoken of "I promise." In contrast to performative utterances such as "I promise" – here we see the connection to Heidegger – "there is," Foucault says, "*parrēsia* at the moment when the statement of [the] of truth constitutes an irruptive event opening up an undefined or poorly defined risk for the subject who speaks." Involving a non-defined or badly defined, indeed an unforeseeable, risk for the speaker, this kind of event provides no outline of what is coming. It is truly different from promising, and thus it is genuine becoming. But the undefined risk for the speaker means that the speaker must act *courageously*.[27] Therefore, if we combine these two ideas, one from the late Deleuze, one from the late Foucault – that is, respectively, speaking for and *parrēsia* – we can then convert the shame before intolerable suffering into the courage to speak out. In fact, as we shall see now, it is precisely this combination of ideas that animated Deleuze and Foucault's work in "Le Groupe d'Information sur les Prisons" in 1971–2.

III. SPEAKING OUT FOR PRISONERS

In order to verify the interpretation of "speaking for" and its association with *parrēsia* that we just presented, we are going to reconstruct the contours of what the GIP was, what it did, and what it accomplished. So, *first*, we must ask for what purpose was the GIP established. While its activities ran over 1971 and 1972, its roots go back to events in the autumn of 1970.[28] In September 1970 and then again in January 1971, several imprisoned members of a Maoist inspired movement called "Gauche prolétarienne" went on a hunger strike in order to be recognized as political prisoners (rather than being treated as common criminals.) Daniel Defert, who was a member of the group charged to prepare the lawsuits for the imprisoned (the group was called "Organisation des prisonniers politiques" [OPP]), proposed to Foucault to generate a commission of inquest concerning the prisons. It was "at this moment," as Foucault says, that he "concerned himself" with the prisons (DE1a, 1072). It seems that Foucault accepted Defert's proposal because such an inquest was the logical next step following *The History of Madness*: from the confinement of the mad to the imprisonment of common criminals and political dissidents. However, while Defert seems to have proposed a "commission of inquest" (making use of a judiciary term), Foucault created an "information group," hence the name he gave to the group: "Le groupe d'information sur les prisons."[29] As Foucault says in the "GIP Manifesto," which he read aloud on 8 February 1971, "Hardly any information has been published on the prisons. The prisons are one of the hidden regions of our social system, one of the black boxes of our life. We have the right to know, we want to know" (DE1a, 1043). Foucault's transformation of the inquest commission into an information group explains why Deleuze says, much later, after Foucault had died, in the short interview called "Foucault and Prison," that "Foucault had been the only one, not to survive the past [Deleuze mentions the past of May 1968], but to invent something new at all levels."[30] According to Deleuze, the GIP was an entirely new kind of group. Because the GIP was new, starting it was, as Deleuze says, "like taking a step into darkness" (TRM, 255/273).

What made the GIP entirely new, according to Deleuze, was its "complete independence." It was completely independent because it concerned itself only with the prisons; it was "localized" (TRM, 257/276–7). It was not based on an ideology, or, more precisely, it was not based in something like a universal moral value; it was not a totalizing movement.[31] It had nothing to do with a political party or a political enterprise. What was at issue for GIP was not a sociological study of prisons; it was not reformist; it did want to propose an ideal prison (DE1a, 1072). What was at issue for the GIP was "to let those who have an experience of the prison speak," "literally to hand over the speaking to the inmates" (DE1a, 1043 and 1072).[32] The inmates were to speak "on their own account" (*pour leur compte*) (DIS, 298/206), and "in their own name" (DIS, 293/209). As the GIP "Manifesto" says, "We shall not find the information [we are seeking] in the official reports. We are asking for information from those who, somehow, have an experience of the prison or a relation to it" (DE1a, 1043). Clearly, here we see that the GIP sought to avoid, as Deleuze says in "Intellectuals and Power," "the indignity of speaking for [*parler pour*] others" (DIS, 291/208).

In fact, the GIP tried to avoid the indignity of speaking for others by distributing a questionnaire to the inmates. The GIP was not allowed to distribute the questionnaire inside the prisons. So, every Saturday, Foucault tells us in an interview published in March 1971 (DE1a, 1046), he and other members of the GIP went to the visitor gate of La Santé Prison and distributed the questionnaire to the families of inmates who were waiting in line. The first Saturday, Foucault says, the families of the inmates gave the GIP members a cold welcome. The second time, people were still distrustful. The third time, however, was different. Someone said that "all that is just talk, it should have been done a long time ago." Then suddenly, exploding with anger, a woman starts to tell her entire story: she speaks of the visits, the money she gives to the inmate she is visiting, the wealthy people who are not in prison, she speaks of the filth in the prisons. Thus the woman speaks in her own name, on her own account. And, when she starts to tell her story, it seems that the GIP has suc-ceeded in letting those who have an experience of the prison speak. The GIP had given speech over to the inmates. As Deleuze says, "This was not the case before" (TRM, 259/277).

What was made known by the questionnaire? The questionnaire was com-posed of eleven sections. The section topics and the questions contained in them are not surprising. They concerned the conditions of visitations; conditions of the cells; the food; what sort of exercise; what sort of work; knowledge of rights; the types of discipline and punishments used in the prisons. However, two questions seem remarkable. On the one hand, under the category of "Visites," the question-naire asks whether its respondent can describe the conditions of visitations, and, in particular, "those conditions which appear to you to be the most intolerable." On the other hand, under the category of "Discipline," and after asking about solitary confinement, the questionnaire asks the respondent what is "most intolerable after being deprived of freedom." The apparently one extant copy of the GIP question-naire is, in fact, filled in by an unknown former inmate. In response to the question of what constitutes the most intolerable conditions of the visits, the former inmate had written that it is "the 'screws' [that is, the police] behind your back who are trying to see whether you expose family letters. It's shameful." The answer to the second question of what is most intolerable after solitary confinement is: "One is, all the same, on solid ground [after being freed from solitary confinement]. [But] one has suffered." These answers indicate that what the inmates spoke of was shame and suffering. It is the shame and the suffering in the prisons that was (and is still?) the intolerable.[33] The knowledge of intolerable shame and suffering explains why Deleuze says that Foucault "was very shocked by the results [of the questionnaire]. We found something much worse [than bad food and poor medical treatment], notably, the constant humiliation" (TRM, 255/273). The pamphlet that GIP pub-lished was called "Intolerable." And Foucault says in an interview that "simply, I perceive the intolerable" (DE1a, 1073).

We come now to the *second* question: what did the GIP do? This question itself contains two others questions that are inseparably connected. What did GIP do with the information about intolerable suffering, shame, and humiliation? What did the inmates and families become as a result of what GIP did? The two questions are inseparable because, as Foucault reports, the GIP wanted that "there is not too much difference between those making the inquiry and collecting the information and those who are responding to the inquiry and providing information" (DE1a, 1046). In a rare occasion, Foucault then speaks of an "ideal": "The ideal for us would be that the families communicate with the prisoners, that the prisoners communicate among themselves, that the prisoners communicate with public opinion. That is, we'd like to break apart the ghetto" (DE1a, 1046). All that the GIP was doing was providing the "means" (*moyens*), the means to express, the means to communicate, the means to make the information circulate "from mouth to ear, from group to group" (DE1a, 1046–7).[34] By being simply a "means" to express the intolerable in its "raw state" (DE1a, 1073), the GIP broke apart the ghetto-like difference, but it also made the intolerable "echo" (DE1a, 1045).[35] In "Foucault and Prison," Deleuze will also speak of the "echo" made by the GIP. In fact, he says that the GIP "amplified" the inmates' voices, its means made their voices "resound" (*retentissement*) (TRM, 261/280). In fact, in this late text, Deleuze says that "the goal of the GIP was less to make [the inmates] speak than to design a place where people would be forced to listen to them, a place that was not reduced to a riot on the prison roof, but would ensure that what they had to say passes through" (TRM, 259/277). The conclusion we must draw is that in the GIP, the ones doing the inquiry became "means," or, as Deleuze would say, "relays" for the voices of the inmates (DIS, 289/206–7). But then, moving to the side of the ones responding to the inquiry, we must notice that they too were no longer simply inmates or prisoners. In a 1972 text for *Le Nouvel Observateur*, Deleuze says the inmates themselves are judging the forms that their collective actions must take within the framework of the specific prison within which they find themselves (DIS, 285/204). In the same text, Deleuze recounts that a new kind of public gathering is taking place. It has nothing to do with "public confession" or with a "traditional town meeting." Instead, former prisoners are coming forward and saying what was done to them, what they saw, physical abuse, reprisals, lack of medical care (DIS, 286/205). In fact, Deleuze reports that at one such gathering the prison guards tried to shout down the former inmates. The inmates however silenced the prison guards by describing the brutality that each one had committed. The inmates used the very sentence that the prison guards had used to intimidate the inmates: "I recognize him" (DIS, 287/205). Thus, at the least, the inmates became speakers. But they also became writers by responding to the questionnaire. The importance of writing is seen in the fourth GIP pamphlet (from late 1972), which published, without correcting punctuation or spelling (that is, in their "raw state"), letters written from prison by a certain "H. M." In the short commentary that he wrote to accompany the publication of the letters, Deleuze claims that H. M.'s letter bear witness to complementary or opposed personalities, all of which, however, "are participating in the same 'effort to reflect'." In fact, Deleuze says that H. M.s correspondence "is exemplary because its heartfelt reflections express what a prisoner is exactly thinking" (DIS 341/244). Thus we must conclude that the amplification of the inmates' voices was done so that they became thinkers.

We come then to the third question: what then happened? As Deleuze says in "Foucault and Prison," the GIP was a "thought-experiment" but like all experiments it had mixed results (TRM, 255/273). On the side of the ones responding to the questionnaire, there were risks. Accompanying the uprisings that continued over the two year period, there was a rash of suicides in the prisons as a kind of last ditch protest. In fact, H. M. committed suicide and the fourth GIP pamphlet was devoted to suicides in the prisons. On the side of the ones collecting the information, the GIP side, there were risks too. In a 1971 interview Foucault speculated that the authorities might react to the GIP's actions by throwing all of its members in jail (DE1a, 1073). Most importantly, however, soon after the GIP was disbanded in 1972, the prison authorities clamped down on the prisons again. As Deleuze reports in "Foucault and Prison," Foucault came to believe that the GIP had been a failure (TRM, 261/279). Foucault had the impression that the GIP had served no purpose. "It was not repression," Foucault says in Deleuze's words, "but worse: it was as if someone speaks but nothing was said" (TRM, 258/277). Yet, Deleuze insists that the GIP had been a success in a different way. Although it did not succeed in bringing about long-lasting concrete changes in the French prisons, the GIP did produce "new conditions for statements." It was successful, according to Deleuze, insofar as it made possible "a type of statement about the prison that is regularly made by the inmates and the non-inmates, a type of statement that had been unimaginable before" (TRM, 261/280). In other words, we could say that the GIP's success appeared not in the prisons themselves, but in the statements, concepts, and books it made possible. For instance, the former inmate Serge Livrozet wrote a book called *De la prison à la revolte*, for which Foucault wrote a preface (DEa, 1262–7, also TRM, 258/276–7). While the GIP documents constantly state that they are not trying to raise the inmates' consciousness (*pas de prise de conscience*) (DEa1, 1044), and, while Foucault constantly says that the GIP is not providing the inmates with knowledge (DEa1, 1289), the GIP in fact gave the inmates and their families a new way of relating to themselves. The GIP not only was a relay for the inmates' voices, but also it was a relay for thinking.

We are now in a position to be able to summarize the three stages that we have just outlined. First, because the GIP was a localized and therefore non-totalizing movement, because it was specific to the prisons, it was freed from anything like a universal moral value or a general concept. As always, Deleuze and Foucault's thinking is opposed to generalities and universals. GIP was no different. The GIP was non-representational. It was merely an information group. Second, when the inmates and their families started to speak, their voices emerged not a representation of some abstract idea. Their voices emerged – the voices became audible and the inmates and their families became visible – as an event, as a singularity.[36] Their voices emerged as an event from the "darkness" of the background (*un fond*), from the depth (*la profondeur*), of the prisons. Their emergence was not grounded on the foundation of a principle (*pas de fondement*). They spoke not for another, but on their own account, or, to capture the French expression, they "spoke *for* their own account" (*parlent pour leurs comptes*). What did they say? They spoke of intolerable suffering and shame. Third, when the inmates and their families spoke of their intolerable suffering, the GIP also spoke and spoke out. However, since the voices of the inmates did not represent a type, because the GIP did not represent a universal, the GIP's speech did not represent the inmates. Even though the GIP gave, as they themselves said, to the inmates the "means to express themselves," the GIP did not mediate. Instead, as we saw, they "amplified" or made "resound" the inmates' voices. The GIP reacted to the intolerable by making or letting the inmates' voices "echo." In other words, when the GIP re-sounded the inmates' voices, it produced a foundationless repetition, a recommencement of a commencement. Amplifying the audibility and visibility of the inmates and their families, we find ourselves "before" (*devant*) them. In other words, through its means, the GIP opened a space in which we are forced to listen to the agony of others, in which we feel shame at being human, and then we find ourselves in a space in which we are forced to become intolerant of the intolerable. What is at issue is not representation, but becoming. Not only did the GIP communicate knowledge, it also communicated the feeling of intolerance. And, the echoing – "speaking out" (*parrēsia*) – required courage since it involved risks: the members of the GIP might find themselves imprisoned. But, as we saw thanks to Deleuze's "Foucault and Prison," Foucault thought that the GIP was a failure. The inmates spoke, the echo resounded, but it was like no one had said anything, it was as if no one had listened. Nevertheless, caused by "the moment" of the 1970–1 hunger strikes, by "the moment" when Defert asked Foucault to establish the group, the "effectuation," as Deleuze would say, left behind a "counter-effectuation." It left behind, as a kind of remainder, *works*. It left behind the book called *Discipline and Punish*; it left behind the concept called "power."[37]

IV. Conclusion: Philosophy's Activity as Speaking Out For Others

While Foucault gave us a new concept of power, it was Heidegger who led thought for the first time to originary finitude, and therefore he led us to what most opposes power: the experience of powerlessness. In "What is Metaphysics," Heidegger says that the feeling of anxiety places us "in utter impotence."[38] Nevertheless, he did not free repetition from the being of we who are finite, as if the repetitions out into the future – what Heidegger called "transcendence" – would return us to what we originally or properly were. Heidegger thereby restricted the potencies of repetition to the same. Yet, if it is the case that there is no proper being of us, if in other words the self-relation is open to endless reconfigurations (due to the experience of time being endless[39]), then repetition becomes, not transcendence, but the intransitive, or, as we said above, repetition becomes creative. The difference between transcendence and intransitivity leads us to compose several highly determinate formulas concerning the idea of return, formulas through which we can distinguish Heidegger's thought from that of Foucault and Deleuze. First, we must think of return not as a memory of the origin, and not even as the forgetfulness of the origin, but as "counter-memory," as what effectuates itself against what is remembered, making a difference.[40] Second, we must think of return not as a promise fulfilled, but as amplification, as a kind of "refrain" that endlessly varies itself.[41] And, finally, we must think of return not as a return to being, but as the becoming of the beings. This formula of beings (including the beings called "man") becoming brings us to one more: we must define philosophy not by the feeling of anxiety before the nothing of one's own death which demands of you to become what you properly are – but by the feeling of shame before the intolerable suffering of others which demands of you to become other than how you find yourself. This difference between the feeling of anxiety and shame explains why Heidegger, unlike Foucault and Deleuze, never felt the need to speak out for prisoners. Even though he wrote about power, Heidegger never spoke out for the powerless. Thus he never spoke frankly, he never spoke out *as a means so that* the powerless would become other than what they are. Such outspokenness of course would have required courage. Although, as Deleuze claims (QPh, 104/108), Heidegger may have introduced shame into philosophy – he made philosophy compromise with the intolerable – he did not convert shame into courage. And even if this courageous speaking out for the powerless were to be a failure, even if no one were to listen, these utterances, these statements, these works, would still remain. They would remain as a call for a people to come and a land to come; they would call forth a world that is other and a life that is other.[42] In other words, the conversion of shame into courage is the primary genetic condition for philosophy. Only through this conversion to activity is philosophy able to have a reality and a use. Only through this conversion is philosophy able to call us to go beyond or over our existence as human all too human.

NOTES

1. Gilles Deleuze and Félix Guattari: *Qu'est-ce que la philosophie?* (Paris: Éditions de Minuit, 1991); translated into English by Hugh Tomlinson and Graham Burchell as *What is Philosophy?* (New York: Columbia University Press, 1994). Hereafter cited with the abbreviation QPh, with reference first to the French, then to the English translation.

2. Michel Foucault, *Le gouvernement de soi et des autres. Cours au Collége de France. 1982–1983* (Paris: Hautes Études Gallimard Seuil, 2008); English translation by Graham Burchell as *The Government of Self and Others. Lectures at the Collége de France, 1982–1983* (London: Palgrave MacMillan, 2010). Hereafter cited with the abbreviation CF-GSO1, with reference first to the French, then to the English translation. Michel Foucault, *Le courage de la vérité. Le gouvernment de soi et des autres II. Cours au Collège de France. 1984* (Paris: Hautes Études Gallimard Seuil, 2009); English translation by Graham Burchell as *The Courage of Truth. The Government of Self and Others II. Lectures at the Collège de France, 1983–1984* (London: Palgrave MacMillan, 2011). Hereafter cited with the abbreviation CF-GSO2, with reference first to the French, then to the English translation.

3. At a more general level, there seems to be three similarities between the way in which Deleuze conceives philosophy at the end of life and the way Foucault conceives philosophy at the end of his life. In his final courses at the Collège de France, Foucault seems to isolate three components of philosophy, as he understands it based on the study of ancient philosophy (that is, Plato, but especially the Stoics and the Cynics). First, philosophy is a way of living based in an *ascesis* or test. Second, philosophy has a linguistic aspect, which consists in frank-speaking or speaking out (*parrēsia*). And finally, philosophy has a complicated relation to political institutions: from a "necessary exteriority" it stands "over and against [*en face de*]" politics and speaks the truth (veridiction) (CF-GSO1, 264/286). ("Necessary exteriority" is an expression of the Cynical, anti-Platonic relation of philosophy and politics. The cynic Diogenes is not the philosopher-king. Instead, in relation to Alexander the Great, Diogenes calls himself a "dog." But even when Foucault discusses Plato's philosopher-king, he insists on a certain non-coincidence of philosophy and politics.) Similarly, for Deleuze, philosophy involves a conceptual persona who presents a way of life; the persona in particular presents the "pedagogy of the concept." Second, as we can see already (and this is what is best known about *What is Philosophy?*), philosophy involves a linguistic aspect, which is the creation of the concept. And finally, for Deleuze, philosophy has a complicated relation to political institutions: from a "utopia" or more precisely a non-place, it "takes the critique of its own time to its highest point" (QPh 95/99). For both Deleuze and Foucault, this critique from "the outside" is done, as Foucault would say, in the name of a life that is other and a world that is other, and, as Deleuze would say, in the name of a people to come and a land to come (QPh 105/109).

4. Michel Foucault, "Theatrum philosophicum," in *Dits et écrits I, 1954–1975* (Paris: Quarto Gallimard, 2001), 965 and 963; English translation by Donald F. Bouchard and Sherry Simon as "Theatrum Philosophicum," in Michel Foucault, *Essential Works of Foucault, 1954–1984* (Series Editor Paul Rabinow), *Volume 2: Aesthetics, Method, and Epistemology*, ed. James D. Faubion (New York: The New Press, 1998), 366 and 364, translation modified.

5. It is well known that in his final interview, Foucault says, "For me, Heidegger has always been the essential philosopher. My whole philosophical development was determined by my reading of Heidegger." Less well known – but we think equally important – is that fact that, when Deleuze in *What is Philosophy?*, speaks of "speaking for" (*parler pour*) the

illiterate, the aphasic, and the acephalous, this discussion, which is in effect the climax of Part I, occurs in the context of Deleuze describing how Heidegger brought shame into philosophy (QPh 104–5/108–9). See Michel Foucault, "Le retour de la morale," in *Dits et écrits, IV, 1980–1988* (Paris: NRF Gallimard, 1994), 703; English translation by Thomas Levin and Isabelle Lorenz as "The Return of Morality," in *Michel Foucault. Politics, Philosophy, Culture: Interview and other Writings, 1977–1984*, ed. Lawrence D. Kritzman (New York: Routledge, 1988), 250, translation modified. For Foucault's early studies, see Didier Eribon, *Michel Foucault*, trans. Betsy Wing (Cambridge, MA: Harvard University Press, 1991), 30–1; David Macey, *The Lives of Michel Foucault* (New York: Vintage, 1993), 34. The quotation with which I began is often cited. See Alan Milchman and Alan Rosenberg (eds.), *Foucault and Heidegger: Critical Encounters* (Minneapolis: University of Minnesota Press, 2003). Béatrice Han's essay in this volume is particularly interesting. Béatrice Han, "Foucault and Heidegger on Kant and Finitude," in Milchman and Rosenberg, *Foucault and Heidegger*, 127–62. See also Jean Zoungrana, *Michel Foucault. Un parcours croisé: Lévi-Strauss, Heidegger* (Paris: L'Harmattan, 1998). The section of our essay on Deleuze and Foucault's relation to Heidegger is based on Janae Sholtz and Leonard Lawlor, "Heidegger and Deleuze," in *The Bloomsbury Companion to Heidegger*, ed. Franvois Raffoul and Eric Nelson (London: Bloomsbury Academic, 2013), 417–24; and Leonard Lawlor, "Heidegger and Foucault," also in *The Bloomsbury Companion to Heidegger*, 409–16.

6. Gilles Deleuze, "Les intellectuels et le pouvoir," in *L'île déserte et autres textes. Textes et entretiens 1953–1974* (Paris: Minuit, 2002), 29; English translation by Michael Taormina as "Intellectuals and Power," in *Desert Islands and other Texts 1953–1974* (New York: Semiotext(e), 2004), 208 (translation modified). Hereafter *Desert Islands* will be cited with the abbreviation DIS, with reference first to the French, then to the English translation.

7. In *Nietzsche and Philosophy*, Deleuze says that the Nietzschean overman is defined by a different way of sensing: "The aim of critique is not the ends of man or of reason but finally the Overman, the overcome, overtaken man. The point of critique is not justification, but to feel otherwise [*de sentir autrement*]: another sensibility. See Gilles Deleuze, *Nietzsche et la philosophie* (Paris: Presses Universitaires de France, 1962), 108; English translation by Hugh Tomlinson as *Nietzsche and Philosophy* (New York: Columbia University Press, 1983), 94.

8. Gilles Deleuze, *Différence et répétition* (Paris: Presses Universitaires de France, 1968); English translation by Paul Patton as *Difference and Repetition* (New York: Columbia University Press, 1994). Hereafter cited with the abbreviation DR, with reference first to the French, then to the English translation.

9. Deleuze cites Heidegger's "Overcoming Metaphysics," in *The End of Philosophy*.

10. See also *The Fold* where Deleuze late in his career (1988) takes up again Heidegger's language of the *Zwiefalt* (TF 42/30).

11. Deleuze cites again "Overcoming Metaphysics." But here in the fourth point, he also cites Jean Beaufret's *Introduction to* Poème de Parmenide (Paris: Presses Universitaires de France, 1955), and Beda Alleman, *Hölderlin et Heidegger* (Paris: Presses Universitaires de France, 1954).

12. By focusing on the same (gathering), Deleuze's criticism of Heidegger is virtually identical to that of Foucault and that of Derrida. See Michel Foucault, *Les mots et les choses* (Paris: Tel Gallimard, 1966), 345; anonymous English translation as *The Order of Things* (New York: Vintage, 1970), 334. See Jacques Derrida, *Mémoires pour Paul de Man* (Paris: Galilée, 1988), 136; English translation by Cecile Lindsay, Jonathan Culler and Eduardo Cadava as *Memoires for Paul de Man* (New York: Columbia University Press, 1986), 141–2.

13. Here Deleuze cites Heidegger's interpretation of Nietzsche in *What is Called Thinking?*

14. Deleuze, *Nietzsche et la philosophie*, 211n1; *Nietzsche and Philosophy*, 220n31.

15. In *Difference and Repetition*, Deleuze calls what we are calling a "creative repetition" a "clothed" or disguised" repetition. See DR 114/84. Undoubtedly, with this description of recommencement (creative repetition), Deleuze seems to be very close to Heidegger's own reflections on the artwork, on the *Abgrund* (the foundationless), on the *Ereignis* (the event of propriation), and on another beginning. Indeed, the French word "recommencement" could be rendered in English as "another beginning."

16. Here is the occurrence: "This is why modern thought is devoted, from top to bottom, to its great preoccupation with return, to its concern with recommencement, to that strange, stationary disquietude which forces upon it the duty of repeating repetition. Thus from Hegel to Marx and Spengler we find the developing theme of a thought which, through the movement in which it accomplishes itself . . ., curves over upon itself. . . [and] achieves its circle. In opposition to this return . . ., we find the experience of Hölderlin, Nietzsche, and Heidegger, in which the return is given only in the extreme retreat of the origin." Foucault, *Les mots et les choses*, 345; English translation by A. M. Sheridan Smith as *The Order of Things* (New York: Vintage, 1970), 334. Hereafter cited with the abbreviation OT, with reference first to the French, then to the English translation. I have frequently modified the English translation.

17. In relation to the finite conditions of knowledge, we can say, using Kantian terminology, that man has no "intellectual intuition."

18. Foucault calls this "originless origin" the "rip" from which, itself having no chronology or history, time has issued forth (OT 343/332). "Rip" renders "déchirure," which probably is intended to render Heidegger's idea of a "Riss."

19. "Retrieval" renders "répétition" in French, "Wiederholung," in German. "Wiederholung" is a fundamental feature of Heidegger's thinking at the time of *Being and Time*. See GA 2, 2/BW, 1 and GA 2, 385/BW, 367. It organizes as well Heidegger's 1929 *Kant and the Problem of Metaphysics*. See GA 3, 204/KPM, 143.

20. In "Ariane s'est pendue," Foucault says that "[To think intensity] is to reject finally the great figure of the Same, which, from Plato to Heidegger, has not stopped locking Western metaphysics into its circle" (my translation). But here too, Foucault provides no explanation. See Michel Foucault, "Ariane s'est pendue," in *Dits et écrits I, 1954–1975*, 798.

21. This obvious conception of promise involves the idea of balance or justice, as if it were possible to fulfill the promise, balance it out, and do justice to it. Yet, perhaps it is possible to conceive promising on the basis of a fundamental disjunction, disjointure, or injustice. This unbalanced concept of the promise seems to be the

concept Derrida developed in his *Specters of Marx* (trans. Peggy Kamuf (New York: Routledge, 1995), 24). See also my earlier analysis of the promise in Derrida in Leonard Lawlor, *Derrida and Husserl* (Bloomington: Indiana University Press, 2002), 219, in particular.

22. See François Ewald, "Foucault and the Contemporary Scene," *Philosophy and Social Criticism* 25:3, 81–91, especially 83: "If there is an ethical line in Foucault – and there is one – it is fundamentally tied to the idea that one must combat this danger of repetition."

23. David Webb has made an important contribution to our understanding of Foucault's archaeology (although it could be argued that he over-emphasizes the mathematical and formal in Foucault and does not take account of Foucault's comments on literature). David Webb, *Foucault's Archaeology: Science and Transformation* (Edinburgh: Edinburgh University Press, 2013).

24. Gilles Deleuze, *Logique du sens* (Paris: Minuit, 1969), 34; English translation by Mark Lester with Charles Stivale, ed. Constantin Boundas as *The Logic of Sense* (New York: Columbia University Press, 1990), 22.

25. Deleuze, *Logique du sens*, 123; *The Logic of Sense*, 101.

26. This distinction between *parrēsia* and the speech act repeats and modifies the distinction between the statement (*l'énoncé*) and the speech act Foucault had made more than ten years earlier. See Michel Foucault, *L'archéologie du savoir* (Paris: NRF Gallimard, 1969), 105–15, and 121–6; English translation by A. M. Sheridan Smith as *The Archaeology of Knowledge* (New York: Pantheon, 1971), 79–87, and 92–6. The second set of pages concern the position of the subject of the statement.

27. Foucault is aware that *parrēsia* might fail. In particular, the history of the concept of frank-speech indicates that it is frequently confused with flattery, the "dangerous double" of *parrēsia* (CF-GSO1, 280/304).

28. See Macey, *The Lives of Michel Foucault*, 257–89; Eribon, *Michel Foucault*, 224–37; and James Miller, *The Passion of Michel Foucault* (New York: Anchor Books, 1993), 165–207.

29. See Michel Foucault, "Manifest du G.I.P.," document 86, in *Dits et écrits 1, 1954–1975* (Paris: Quarto Gallimard, 2001), 1042. Hereafter cited as DE1a; all English translations are my own. The small summary I just presented is based on the introduction to document 86. For a more detailed and important narrative of the entire GIP movement, see Phillippe Artières, Laurent Quéro and Michelle Zancarini-Fournel, *Le groupe d'information sur les prisons. Archives d'une lutte, 1970–1972* (Paris: IMEC, 2003), especially Part 1, and pp. 34–6.

30. Gilles Deleuze, "Foucault et les prisons," in *Deux régimes de fous* (Paris: Minuit, 2003), 254–5; English translation by Ames Hodges and Michael Taormina as "Foucault and Prison," in *Two Regimes of Madness* (New York: Semiotext(e), 2006), 272, translation modified. Hereafter *Two Regimes of Madness* will be cited with the abbreviation TRM, with reference first to the French, then to the English translation.

31. Not based in a universal truth – Foucault of course, like Heidegger, is interested only in the genesis of truth – the GIP leads Foucault to redefine the role of the intellectual. As is well known, Foucault says in "Intellectuals and Power" that "The role of intellectual

is no longer to situate himself 'slightly ahead' or 'slightly to one side' [of the oppressed] so he may speak the silent truth of each and all" (DIS, 290/207).

32. The French is: "Il s'agit de laisser la parole à ceux qui ont une expérience de la prison." See also "Intolerable 1," in Artières, Quéro, and Zancarini-Fournel, *Le groupe d'information sur les prisons*, 80: "The GIP (Prison Information Group) is not aiming to speak for the inmates of the different prisons. On the contrary, it aims to give to the inmates themselves the possibility of speaking, and to say what happens in the prisons. The purpose of the GIP is not reformist. We are not dreaming of the ideal prison. We wish that the prisoners say what is intolerable in the system of penal repression."

33. The first GIP bulletin, which collected some of the results of the questionnaire, also tells us that one inmate found that what was most intolerable about the visits was the distance established by the double bars in the meeting room, which forbids any intimacy. Another inmate said that what was most intolerable was not being able to kiss the kids.

34. Foucault uses the word "moyens" constantly in the interviews and statements concerning the GIP. And, even after the GIP had dissolved, Foucault still spoke of "moyen." See document 123, "L'intellectuel sert à rassembler les idées mais son savoir est partiel par rapport au savoir ouvrier," in DE1a, 1289–91, in particular, 1289.

35. Beside the audible image of the echo, Foucault also uses the image of "a genuine brush fire" (*un véritable feu de bruyère*) (DE1a, 1045).

36. For the "optics" of the GIP, see Michael Welch, "Counterveillance: How Foucault and the Groupe d'information sur les prisons Reversed the Optics," in *Theoretical Criminology*, 15:3 (2011), 301–13.

37. Michel Foucault, *Surveiller et punir* (Paris: Tel Gallimard, 1975), 227; English translation by Alan Sheridan as *Discipline and Punish* (New York: Vintage, 1995), 194. Here Foucault says, "We must cease once and for all to describe the effects of power in negative terms: it 'excludes,' it 'represses,' it 'pushes down,' it 'censors,' it 'abstracts,' it 'masks,' it 'conceals.' In fact, power produces; it produces reality; it produces domains of objects and rituals of truth. The individual and knowledge that is to be gained of him belong to this production."

38. (GA 9: 113/PM: 90).

39. That time is endless is really what Nietzsche's eternal return doctrine means. It is really what Foucault is trying to show in Chapter 9 of *The Order of Things* and what Deleuze is trying to show in both *Difference and Repetition* and *The Logic of Sense*. The claim about time being endless is developed in more detail in Leonard Lawlor, "What Happened? What is going to Happen? An Essay on the Experience of the Event," in *The Ends of History: Questioning the Stakes of History Reason*, ed. Amy Swiffen and Joshua Nicols (London: Routledge, 2013), 179–95.

40. Foucault introduces the notion of counter-memory in his 1971 "Nietzsche, Genealogy, History." See DE1a, document 84, 1004–24, in particular, 1021; English translation found in Michael Foucault, *Aesthetics, Method, and Epistemology. Essential Works of Foucault, 1954–1984*, ed. James D. Faubion (New York: The New Press, 1998), 369–91, in particular, 385.

41. Deleuze and Guattari introduce the notion of the refrain (the ritornello) in their 1980 *A Thousand Plateaus*. See Gilles Deleuze and Félix Guattari, *Mille plateaux* (Paris: Minuit, 1980), 381–433; English translation by Brian Massumi as *A Thousand Plateaus* (Minneapolis: University of Minnesota Press, 1987), 310–50. See also QPh, 26/21, where they speak of the concept as a "refrain" (*ritournelle*).

42. In a famous article, Gayatri Chakravorty Spivak criticizes Deleuze and Foucault's discussion in "Intellectuals and Power." See Gayatri Chakravorty Spivak, "Can the Subaltern Speak?," in *Colonial Discourse and Post-Colonial Theory: A Reader*, ed. Patrick Williams and Laura Chrisman (New York: Columbia University Press, 1994), 66–111. Spivak claims that Deleuze and Foucault do not recognize how representation works, its "double session" (p. 74). That is, following Derrida, she sees that representation contains an ambiguity between speaking for and presenting as in an artwork (p. 70). So, even if Deleuze and Foucault are trying to allow the inmates to speak on their own account, they cannot because "the subaltern" is always caught in (contaminated by) the ambiguity of representation, and therefore reduced ideologically. As she says at the end of her essay, "the subaltern cannot speak" (p. 104). Yet, if one looks at the GIP documents (in addition to "Intellectuals and Power"), it is clear that Foucault and Deleuze have tried in a very specific way to allow the inmates to speak on their own account. In particular, as we have tried to show, Foucault made the GIP be independent of any political party and therefore any ideology. In this way, he tried to free the inmates from general concepts that would reduce them. They could appear as a singularity, as an event. More importantly, both Deleuze and Foucault were aware of the risks involved in the GIP's practice of allowing the inmates to speak on their own account. There is no guarantee of success, and that lack of guarantee seems to be what Spivak is really asking for. But as a good Derridean, she should know that the enemy is good conscience. Insofar as success (complete liberation from ideology) is impossible, one is required to try to do more. Deleuze in particular is aware that what made GIP a true event is its counter-effectuation in works such as concepts and artworks. The work remains even if no one listened at its inception. Therefore our shame at being human remains too, and just as in Derrida, in Deleuze one is required to do more.

CHAPTER 9

Deleuze and Foucault: Political Activism, History and Actuality

PAUL PATTON

This chapter sketches an account of the relationship between Deleuze and Foucault that seeks to delve beneath the superficial view that they were fellow travelers in philosophy as in politics. It is inspired by the view that the more closely one looks at their work the more one sees differences between them. Before turning to some of their differences, I note some of the essential facts about their relationship.[1]

Deleuze and Foucault first met in 1952 although they did not become friends until a decade later, following a failed attempt by Foucault to have Deleuze appointed at the University of Clermont-Ferrand (Dosse 2010: 365). In 1963 Deleuze reviewed Foucault's *Raymond Roussel* (Deleuze 2004, 72–3). In 1966 he reviewed *Les Mots et les choses*, describing it as "a great book, brimming with new thoughts" (Deleuze 2004, 90–3). During the 1970s he published similarly celebratory reviews of *The Archaeology of Knowledge* (Foucault 1969, 1972; Deleuze 1970) and *Discipline and Punish* (Foucault 1975, 1977a; Deleuze 1975). These last two reviews reappeared in revised form as chapters in the book published after Foucault's death (Deleuze 1986, 1988).

During the 1960s they shared interests in the work of Nietzsche and Pierre Klossowski. Foucault published an essay on Klossowski in 1964 while Deleuze's "Klossowski or Bodies-Language" appeared in the journal *Critique* the following year before reappearing as an appendix to *Logique du sens* in 1969 (Foucault 1998, 123–35; Deleuze 1969, 1990). In 1966 Foucault and Deleuze became editors of the French edition of Colli-Montinari's *Complete Works of F. Nietzsche*. Their co-authored "General Introduction," published in 1967 expressed the hope that this edition would bring about a "return to Nietzsche" (Foucault 1994, Volume 1, 564). Deleuze's *Nietzsche and Philosophy* left a lasting impression on Foucault (Macey 1993, 109; Deleuze 1962, 1983). In his presentation at a conference organized by Deleuze at Royaumont Abbey in 1964, Foucault referred to Deleuze's analysis of the play of reactive forces (Foucault 1998, 277). He later referred to the importance of Deleuze's analysis for his own thinking about power and, in an interview published in 1983, referred again to Deleuze's 'superb book about Nietzsche' and to his role in the French rediscovery of Nietzsche during the 1960s (Foucault 1998, 438, 445). Deleuze's concept of a transcendental field of force relations forms the basis of Foucault's analysis of power in *The History of Sexuality, Volume 1* where he suggests that power must be understood "in the first instance as a multiplicity of force relations immanent in the sphere in which they operate," and as the processes by which these force relations are transformed, support or contradict one another, and as the strategies in which they take effect (Foucault 1978, 92–3). As such, power's condition of possibility "is the moving substrate of force relations which, by virtue of their inequality, constantly engender states of power" (Foucault 1978, 93). It follows that the power of a body resides not "in a certain strength we are endowed with" but in the fluctuating field of relations to other bodies. The power even of a single body is dispersed in such a manner that "power is everywhere, not because it embraces everything, but because it comes from everywhere" (Foucault 1978, 93).

In 1969, Foucault published a short review of *Différence et répétition* followed by a much longer article in 1970 on this book and its companion *Logique du sens* (Foucault 1994, Volume 1, 767–71; Foucault 1998, 343–68). The longer article begins with the much quoted remark that "perhaps one day, this century will be known as Deleuzian" (Foucault 1998, 343). Less frequently noted is the first part of this sentence in which Foucault places Deleuze's work in "enigmatic resonance" with that of Klossowki. Foucault's reading of Deleuze's books is framed by themes shared with Klossowski such as the overturning of Platonism and the revaluation of simulacra. At the same time, he points to the overriding concern of both books with the nature of thought. He notes that Deleuze's search for a new image and a new practice of thought requires abandoning the subordination of both difference and repetition to figures of the same in favor of a thought without contradiction, without dialectics and without negation. It requires a form of thought that embraces divergence and multiplicity: "the nomadic and dispersed multiplicity that is not limited or confined by the constraints of the same" (Foucault 1998, 358). It requires an acategorical thought and a univocal conception of being that revolves around the different rather than the same, following Deleuze's interpretation of Nietzsche's eternal recurrence. Whereas for Nietzsche's Zarathustra the thought of eternal recurrence remained intolerable, Foucault suggests that this thought, understood as the recurrence of difference, was enacted in Deleuze's texts. As a consequence of the "lightning storm" that bears the name of Deleuze, he writes, "new thought is possible; thought is again possible" (Foucault 1998, 367).

POLITICAL ACTIVISM

Deleuze and Foucault were deeply affected by the upheavals of May 1968, although neither was directly involved. In 1969, Foucault was responsible for Deleuze's appointment to the Philosophy Department at the newly established University of Paris VIII at Vincennes and they collaborated on a number of political activities throughout the early 1970s. These included the *Prisoner's Information Group* established by Foucault, and others, at the beginning of 1971 with the aim of publicizing the voices of those with direct experience of prisons, along with other campaigns such as the anti-racism movement inspired by the shooting of a young Algerian in the Paris neighbourhood known as the *Goutte d'Or* (Foucault 1994, Volume 2, 174–82; Defert and Donzelot 1976; Dosse 2010, 309–13). Deleuze participated in Foucault's seminar at the Collège de France in 1971–2 devoted to the case of Pierre Rivière. Both contributed to several issues of the journal *Recherches*, published by Guattari's *Centre d'études, de recherches et de formation institutionelles* (CERFI), including the infamous issue on homosexuality entitled *Trois milliards de pervers* (Guattari 1973).

The high point of their common political and theoretical engagement was undoubtedly the 'Intellectuals and Power' interview, conducted in March 1972 and published later that year in the issue of *L'Arc* devoted to Deleuze (Foucault 1977b, 205–17; Deleuze 2004, 206–13; Patton 2010a). They reject the Marxist idea that there is a single "totalising" relation between theory and practice in favor of a plurality of such relations. On their view, theory is neither the expression nor the translation of a practice while practice is neither the application of theory nor the inspiration of theory to come. Rather, theory is itself a local practice that operates as a relay from one practice to another, while practice forms a relay from one theoretical point to the next. Foucault suggests that it was one of the lessons of the upsurge of political action in France at the end of the 1960s that the masses have no need of enlightened consciousness produced by intellectuals in order to understand their situation. The problem is rather that their own forms of knowledge are blocked or invalidated. The role of the intellectual therefore consists of working within and against the order of discourse within which forms of knowledge appear or fail to appear. More generally, it consists of struggling against the forms of power of which he or she is both the object and the instrument.

Foucault considered existing theories of the state and state apparatuses, along with the theory of class power, associated with Marxism to be inadequate for understanding the nature of power and the forms of its exercise. He credited Deleuze's *Nietzsche and Philosophy* as well as his work with Guattari with advancing the manner in which this problem is posed (Foucault 1997b, 213; Deleuze 2004, 2011). He implicitly referred to his earlier comments about working within the order of discourse and knowledge in suggesting that identifying and speaking publicly about the centers of power within society is already a first step in turning power back on itself: "If the discourse of inmates or prison doctors constitutes a form of struggle, it is because they confiscate at least temporarily the power to speak on prison conditions – at present, the exclusive property of prison administrators and their cronies in reform groups" (Foucault 1977b, 214; Deleuze 2004, 211). Much of Foucault's work during the 1970s sought to develop new conceptual tools for understanding power and its relation to knowledge or theory. The opening lectures of his 1976 course at the *Collège de France* take up the question implicitly posed by his 1972 remarks about the relative lack of understanding of the nature of power and set out a series of heuristic principles designed to reorient the study of power away from the juridical, political and ideological apparatuses of the state and toward the material operations of domination and subjectification throughout society (Foucault 2003, 27–34). His 1982 essay, "The Subject and Power," which is in many ways a definitive statement of his considered views on the nature of power, offers much the same analysis of the totalization of micro-powers by a dominant or ruling power that he gave in the interview with Deleuze a decade earlier (Foucault 2000, 326–48).

While many of the points made in Deleuze and Foucault's 1972 interview reverberated throughout their publications in the years that followed, there were also signs of their future divergence. At one point, for example, Deleuze endorses and attributes to Foucault the idea that theory is "by nature opposed to power," even though Foucault has just suggested that theory always takes place within an order of discourse and knowledge that is governed by forms of power (Foucault 1977b, 208; Deleuze 2004, 208). Deleuze appears to understand "theory" to mean something like the conception of philosophy as the creation of concepts that he later described as "in itself" calling for "a new earth and a people that do not yet exist" (Deleuze and Guattari 1994, 108). Deleuze's understanding of power appears to rely on the repressive conception of power that Foucault soon came to challenge: he refers to the radical fragility of the system of power and its "global force of repression" (Foucault 1977b, 209; Deleuze 2004, 2008; *translations modified*). The publication of Foucault's *History of Sexuality, Volume 1*, which strongly criticized the repressive conception of power, marked the beginning of an increasing distance between them (Foucault 1976, 1978). A letter that Deleuze wrote to him in 1977, subsequently published as "Desire and Pleasure," set out a series of questions that reflected differences between Foucault's account of the formation of the Western apparatus of sexuality and Deleuze and Guattari's conception of assemblages of desire and power (Davidson 1997, 183–92; Deleuze 2007, 122–34). Some of these points bearing on the relation of desire to power and the primacy of movements of deterritorialization or lines of flight in any given assemblage were restated several years later in a footnote in *A Thousand Plateaus* (Deleuze and Guattari 1987, 530–1).

In response to questions from James Miller some years later Deleuze insisted that there was no single cause of their drifting apart, but a number of contributing factors: "The only important thing is that for a long time I had followed [Foucault] politically; and at a certain moment, I no longer totally shared his evaluation of many issues" (Miller 1993, 298). The issues on which their evaluations around this time diverged sharply included Israel–Palestine, the so-called "new philosophers" and the Croissant affair (Dosse 2010, 314). André Glucksmann's *La Cuisinière et le mangeur d'hommes* and Bernard-Henry Levy's *La barbarie à visage humaine* combined Foucaultian theses about the "Great confinement" with claims derived from Solzhenitsyn and other dissidents about Soviet totalitarianism (Glucksmann 1975; Levy 1977). In 1977 Foucault published a three-page review of Glucksmann's *Les Maîtres penseurs* in *Le Novel Observateur* that praised the book for tracing the origins of the Soviet Gulag to the manner in which nineteenth-century German philosophy linked the state and the revolution (Foucault 1994, Volume 3, 277–81). One month later, Deleuze published a denunciation of the "new philosophers" in which he expressed his disgust at their martyrology of the victims of the Gulag and accused them of trafficking in large empty concepts such as The Law, The Power, The Master and so on (Deleuze 2007, 139–47).

The Croissant affair involved one of the defense lawyers for the German *Red Army Faction* who, after having been charged with supporting a criminal organization and jailed on more than one occasion, fled to France in the summer of 1977 and applied for political asylum. After his arrest by French authorities in September 1977, Foucault, Deleuze and Guattari were among those who joined a Committee established to oppose his extradition and agitate for his release from prison. Their activities were to no avail as Croissant was finally extradited on 16 November. Foucault and Deleuze were among the small crowd of protesters outside *La Santé* prison when he was removed. Foucault published several pieces against the extradition of Croissant, but he refused to sign a petition circulated by Guattari and signed by Deleuze among others. Macey claims that a characterization in the petition of the West German state as "fascist" was unacceptable to Foucault (Macey 1994, 394). Eribon offers a milder version of what was unacceptable in the petition, suggesting that it presented West Germany as drifting towards "police dictatorship" (Eribon 1991, 260). Deleuze and Guattari's opinion piece in *Le Monde* on 2 November contains no characterization of the West German State as fascist nor any suggestion that it was becoming a police dictatorship, although it does take a critical stance toward "the German governmental and judicial model" which they describe as in "a state of exception" (Deleuze 2007, 149). Whatever may have been the text of the petition, Foucault preferred to restrict his support to the right of accused parties to legal representation. From this point on, Foucault and Deleuze rarely saw one another. Some years later, Deleuze wrote: "We worked separately, on our own. I am sure he read what I wrote. I read what he wrote with a passion. But we did not talk very often. I had the feeling, with no sadness, that in the end I needed him and he did not need me. Foucault was a very, very mysterious man" (Deleuze 2007, 286).

HISTORY AND ACTUALITY

In interviews that accompanied the publication, after Foucault's death in 1984, of his *Foucault* (1986, 1988), Deleuze expressed his great admiration for Foucault, describing him as responsible for "one of the greatest of modern philosophies" (Deleuze 1995, 94). He acknowledged that they employed different methods, but also pointed to strong affinities between their respective approaches to philosophy. These included a lack of interest in origins and a distaste for abstractions such as Reason, the Subject or Totality; a concern to analyze assemblages or apparatuses at varying levels of concreteness; a shared interest in cartographic description that sought to disentangle the various kinds of line that run through social and subjective space (Deleuze 1995, 86). Above all, he suggests, they shared an interest in seeking answers to a question peculiar to twentieth-century philosophy: 'How is it possible that something new is produced in the world?' (Deleuze 2007, 349). This common interest in the emergence of the new meant that both philosophers made extensive use of history and historical materials. However, in each case their relationship to history is an unconventional one that separates them from the practice of historians concerned to accurately record the past. In Deleuze's case, as he explained in his 1990 interview with Antonio Negri, he had become "more and more aware of the possibility of distinguishing between becoming and history" (Deleuze 1995, 170). In *What is Philosophy?* he explains this distinction by suggesting that philosophy creates concepts that express pure events, while history only grasps the event in its effectuation in states of affairs or lived experience: "the event in its becoming, in its specific consistency, in its self-positing as concept, escapes History" (Deleuze and Guattari 1994, 110). This distinction between becoming and history underpins his way of answering the question about the emergence of the new: it is the event in its becoming that is the condition of novelty or change in the world. The concepts that philosophy creates give expression to the pure event or eventness that is a part of every event but that also escapes or exceeds its actualization. Since history only refers to the event as actualized, the study of history can never really come to grips with the condition of possibility of newness in the world. For that, we need a different approach that Deleuze outlines with reference to Charles Péguy's *Clio* (Péguy 2002). Péguy shows us:

> that there are two ways of considering events, one being to follow the course of the event, gathering how it comes about historically, how it's prepared and then decomposes in history, while the other way is to go back into the event, to take one's place in it as in a becoming, to grow both young and old in it at once, going through all its components or singularities. (Deleuze 1995, 17–171)

The latter approach is the one followed by Deleuze and Guattari's philosophy when it creates concepts that express pure events or becomings, such as the concept of nomadic lines of flight. These pure events are the real object of philosophy precisely because they embody the conditions of the emergence of the new (Patton 2010a, 99).

Deleuze suggests that Foucault was also a philosopher for whom the study of historical materials was an important part of his method:

> Foucault's a philosopher who invents a completely different relation to history than what you find in philosophers of history. History, according to Foucault, circumscribes us and sets limits, it doesn't determine what we are, but what we're in the process of differing from; it doesn't fix our identity, but disperses it into our essential otherness. (Deleuze 1995, 94–5)

Deleuze's characterization of Foucault in this passages employs the same terms that he uses to describe his own conception of philosophy. Elsewhere, he suggests that their common interest in the emergence of the new was what separated them from the philosophical tradition that sought to discover the universal or eternal character of things: "We weren't looking for something timeless, not even the timelessness of time, but for new things being formed, the emergence of what Foucault called 'actuality.'" (Deleuze 1995, 86). However, such characterizations of Foucault's philosophy are misleading. They play down the differences between his conception of philosophy and that of Deleuze. They overlook the fact that he has a different relationship to history and a different usage of the term "actuality" (Patton 2010a; 2012a).

In *What is Philosophy?* Deleuze compares his own approach to philosophy with that of Nietzsche and Foucault in suggesting that what matters for all these philosophers is not so much the present but the actual, where this is understood to mean what we are in the process of becoming. He argues that, whereas he and Guattari identify becoming as the source of change, in the same way that Nietzsche identifies the untimely (*l'inactuel* or *l'intempestif*), for Foucault it is what he calls the actual (*actuel*) that fulfills this role. He does not mean *actuel* in the ordinary French sense of this word, which refers to that which is current or present, but rather *actuel* in the sense of Nietzsche's untimely. It is not a question of what already exists or is present in a given historical moment, but of what is coming about, of what is in the process of becoming. Thus, he argues that:

> Actuality is what interests Foucault, though it's what Nietzsche called the inactual or the untimely; it's what is *in actu*, philosophy as the act of thinking. (Deleuze 1995, 94–5)

166

Deleuze defends his assimilation of Foucault's *"actuel"* to Nietzsche's "untimely" and to his and Guattari's "becoming" by reference to a passage in *The Archaeology of Knowledge*, in which Foucault draws a distinction between the present (*notre actualité*) and "the border of time that surrounds our present, overhangs it and indicates it in its otherness" (Foucault 1972, 130). He suggests that this border between the present and the future is what Foucault means by the actual: "for Foucault, what matters is the difference between the present and the actual. The actual is not what we are but, rather, what we become, what we are in the process of becoming – that is to say, the Other, our becoming-other" (Deleuze and Guattari 1994, 112).

Deleuze is right to suggest that, in the passage from *The Archaeology of Knowledge*, Foucault draws a distinction between the present and the border of time that surrounds it and indicates its difference from what has gone before. However, he is wrong to suggest that this border is what Foucault calls the actual. Foucault does not use this term in the manner that Deleuze suggests. On the contrary, his text contrasts this border region with "our actuality":

> The analysis of the archive, then, involves a privileged region: at once close to us and different from our actuality, it is the border of time that surrounds our present, which overhangs it, and which indicates it in its otherness; it is that which, outside ourselves, delimits us. (Foucault 1972, 130, *translation modified*)[2]

Foucault's remark occurs in the context of a discussion of the overall system or arrangement of the different discursive practices present in a given society at a given time. Each discursive practice is defined by a set of rules that govern the emergence of things said (*énoncés*) in a given domain. These rules constitute a historical a priori of statements considered as events, that is, as things actually said. The totality of such sets of rules governing the discursive formations in a given culture at a given time is what Foucault calls the archive. This archive is "the law of what can be said, the system that governs the appearance of statements as unique events" (Foucault 1972, 129). Given that all statements, including those of the archaeologist of discourse, are subject to such rules governing what can be said, Foucault's problem here is to explain how and when it becomes possible to describe such an archive. It is clearly not possible to describe the archive within which we speak and write. However, it is possible to describe the archive of those discourses which are no longer our own. In this sense, a condition of possibility of the archaeology of discourse undertaken by Foucault is "the discontinuity that separates us from what we can no longer say and from that which falls outside our discursive practice" (Foucault 1972, 130). It is of this discontinuity, this difference, that Foucault speaks in referring to the "border of time" that surrounds our present (*notre actualité*).

The extent of Deleuze's creative misinterpretation of Foucault's remark from *The Archaeology of Knowledge* is even more apparent in the extended commentary on this passage that he gave in "What is a *Dispositif*?" (Deleuze 2007, 343–52). Here, Deleuze goes further than the mere transposition of the term "actuality" so that it becomes identified with the border of time that surrounds our present. He suggests that this border that surrounds the discursive present in which we speak and write is not simply a backward looking difference that allows us to identify and describe the archive of discursive practices that are no longer our own, but a difference endowed with a forward looking momentum. On his account, it acquires the positive meaning of a becoming, in the sense of what we will become in the future:

> The novelty of a *dispositif* in relation to those that precede it is what we call its actuality, our actuality. The new is the actual. The actual is not what we are but rather what we are becoming, what we are in the process of becoming, that is to say the Other, our becoming-other. In every dispositif we must distinguish what we are (what we are already no longer) and what we are becoming: *the part of history and the part of the actual.* History is the archive, the design of what we are and cease being while the actual is the sketch of what we will become. (Deleuze 2007, 350 *translation modified*)[3]

In Foucault's text, the border of time that separates us from what can no longer say is a becoming only in the most negative and minimal sense of the term. In Deleuze's commentary, it has been turned into the actual in the sense of what we are becoming or what we will become. This is clearly a forced interpretation of Foucault's text that, not surprisingly, proves difficult to reconcile with other aspects of his work.

A first problem is that we search in vain in his published works for analyses of what is coming about or we are becoming. In the terms of Deleuze's hypothesis, *Discipline and Punish* should have analyzed what prisons are in the process of becoming rather than confining itself to the analysis of the disciplinary techniques of power that they have embodied since the early nineteenth century. Deleuze's response to this problem is to suggest that we need to enlarge our understanding of Foucault's *oeuvre* to include not only his books but also his interviews. The books that address a particular archive, whether in relation to madness, the clinic, disciplinary power or sexuality, are only half the story: the other half is made explicit in the interviews that Foucault gave alongside the publication of his major works, in which he comments on the bearing of his historical studies on current problems. In this manner, Deleuze draws a distinction between Foucault's analysis of particular aspects of the archive, which are presented in his genealogical and archaeological studies, and his diagnoses of what the present is becoming, which are presented in interviews:

What are madness, prison, sexuality today? What new modes of subjectivation do we see appearing today that are certainly not Greek or Christian? . . . Foucault attached so much importance to his interviews in France and even more so abroad, not because he liked interviews but because in them he traced lines of actualization that required another mode of expression than the assimilable lines in his major books. The interviews are diagnoses. (Deleuze 2007, 352)[4]

However, since the appearance of "*Il faut défendre la société*" in 1997, the publication of Foucault's lectures makes this two-series partition of Foucault's work difficult to sustain (Foucault 2003; Patton 2012b). The lectures provide a third textual stratum alongside the books and interviews and occasional writings. For the most part, they continue Foucault's genealogical approach to the present. Although much of the lecture material remained in the form of exploratory exercises, tracing out problems, posing and sketching answers to questions that never found their way into the scholarly corpus of Foucault's published work, the lectures also included early drafts of historical analyses that found their way into books. For example, some elements of his 1972–3 course *Penal Theories and Institutions* reappeared in *Discipline and Punish*, just as parts of the final lecture of his 1975–6 course reappeared in the final chapter of *The History of Sexuality, Volume 1*. Moreover, in a manner that complicates Deleuze's distinction between the two parts of Foucault's oeuvre, Michel Senellart points out that the courses pursued their own forms of intervention in the social and political context in which they were written, thereby introducing the field of events (*l'événementiel*) into the order of theoretical discourse (Senellart 2011, 151).

Foucault's mode of engagement with the present in which the lectures were written changed over the course of the 1970s. Some courses do involve material that could be construed as analysis of the actual in Deleuze's future oriented sense of the term. For example, Foucault's 1978–9 lectures on neoliberal governmentality represent a quite different kind of response to a changed political context from those undertaken in 1976 or 1973. These lectures were delivered in the aftermath of the French legislative elections in March 1978, at which the Union of the Left narrowly failed to win a majority. Efforts to rethink the political orientation and strategies of the French left provide the background against which he raised a question about the nature of socialist governmentality at the end of his fourth lecture: "What would really be the governmentality appropriate to socialism? Is there a governmentality appropriate to socialism?" (Foucault 2008, 94). His answer was that if there is such a thing as socialist governmentality, it remained to be invented. Recent commentators have made much of his association with elements of the so-called "Second Left," a minority tendency within the Socialist Party.[5] The anti-statist "self-management" approach of this tendency shared some neoliberal concerns about the role of the state in governing social and economic life. It may well be an exaggeration to suggest that Foucault's 1979 lectures "should be read as a strategic endorsement of economic liberalism" (Behrent 2009a, 567; 2009b, 25). Nevertheless, the principle of abandoning techniques of discipline in favor of purely economic means of governing the behavior of individuals is one that Foucault appears to endorse (Patton 2010b, 212–14).

Given that these lectures were delivered at an early stage in the adoption of neoliberal policy and economic management by Western governments, they could well be construed as analysis of the actual in Deleuze's sense of the term, namely what we are in the process of becoming. Ironically, however, the content of Foucault's lectures on neoliberal governmentality takes him even further from the historical and political perspective that he formerly shared with Deleuze. The 1978–9 lectures are punctuated by a polemic against the "state phobia" shared by many in the French left during this period. State phobia involved an essentialist conception of the state as endowed with an inherent tendency to expand and dominate civil society and a corresponding suspicion of state power. Deleuze and Guattari's concept of the State as an apparatus of capture that is increasingly subordinate to the axiomatic of global capitalism is arguably no more than a sophisticated version of Marxist inspired state phobia. Foucault objects that such essentialist conceptions sustain forms of political analysis derived from first principles, thereby avoiding the need for empirical and historical knowledge of contemporary political reality. Part of his reason for undertaking the analyses of the principles of neoliberal government undertaken in these lectures was the fact that the post-war German state, which was founded on precisely these principles, served as a model for the reforms to public policy proposed in France during this period. At the very least, he argues, the quest for a distinctively socialist governmentality should be informed by knowledge of present political reality. In contrast to the widespread suspicion of the state on the left, he has no fundamental objection to government or to the institutions and policies that this implies. As he explained in a lecture to the *Société Française de Philosophie* the previous year, the critical attitude that he now considered to underpin his 'historicophilosophical' analyses of the present did not ask why we are governed at all but *how* we are governed.[6] The analysis of the principles of neoliberal governmentality undertaken in these lectures reflected a shift in the kind of critique that Foucault considered appropriate. He had moved away from the denunciation of the State towards a more nuanced political engagement with the question how power ought to be exercised. In a sense, to the extent that these lectures addressed what French government was in the process of becoming, they did conform to Deleuze's characterization of his approach to the present. The irony is that they did so at the expense of the fundamentally essentialist and repressive conception of state power to which Deleuze, at that time, remained committed.

NOTES

1. More detail on the elements of their relationship mentioned in this section is presented in Patton 2013.
2. The original reads: "L'analyse de l'archive comporte donc une région privilegiée : à la fois proche de nous, mais différente de notre actualité, c'est la bordure de temps qui entoure notre présent, qui le surplombe et qui l'indique dans son alterité ; c'est ce qui, hors de nous, nous délimite" (Foucault 1969, 172).
3. The original reads: "La nouveauté d'un dispositif par rapport aux précédents, nous l'appelons son actualité, notre actualité. Le nouveau, c'est l'actuel. L'actuel n'est pas ce que nous sommes, mais plutôt ce que nous devenons, ce que nous sommes en train de devenir, c'est-à-dire l'Autre, notre devenir-autre. Dans tout dispositif, il faut distinguer ce que nous sommes (ce que nous ne sommes déjà plus), et ce que nous sommes en train de devenir : *la part de l'histoire, et la part de l'actuel.* L'histoire, c'est l'archive, le dessin de ce que nous sommes et cessons d'être, tandis que l'actuel est l'ébauche de ce que nous devenons" (Deleuze 2003, 322).
4. Similar claims about the role of interviews as an integral part of Foucault's oeuvre are presented in Deleuze (1986, 115); Deleuze (1995, 106).
5. For example, Behrent claims that "Foucault's interest in neoliberalism appears to owe much to his attraction to the Second Left" (Behrent 2009a, 553). See also Behrent (2009b, 19–20); Senellart (2007, 371).
6. The critical question posed was "how not to be governed *like that,* by that, in the name of these principles, in view of such objectives and by means of such methods, not like that, not for that, not by them?" (Foucault 1996, 384).

BIBLIOGRAPHY

Behrent, Michael C. (2009a) "Liberalism Without Humanism: Michel Foucault and the Free-Market Creed, 1976–1979," *Modern Intellectual History* 6:3, 539–68.

Behrent, Michael C. (2009b) "A Seventies Thing: On the Limits of Foucault's Neoliberalism Course for Understanding the Present," in S. Binkley and J. Capetillo (eds.), *A Foucault for the 21st Century: Governmentality, Biopolitics and Discipline in the New Millennium* (Newcastle upon Tyne: Cambridge Scholars Publishing), 16–29.

Davidson, A. (ed.) (1997) *Foucault and his Interlocutors* (Chicago: The University of Chicago Press).

Defert, D. and Donzelot, J. (1976) "La charnière des prisons," *Le magazine littéraire* 112/113, 33–5.

Deleuze, G. (1962) *Nietzsche et la philosophie* (Paris: Presses Universitaires de France).

Deleuze, G. (1968) *Différence et répétition* (Paris: Presses Universitaires de France).

Deleuze, G. (1969) *Logique du sens* (Paris: Éditions de Minuit).

Deleuze, G. (1970) "Un nouvel archiviste," *Critique* 274 (March), 195–209.

Deleuze, G. (1975) "Ecrivain non: un nouveau cartographe," *Critique* 343 (December), 1207–27.

Deleuze, G. (1983) *Nietzsche and Philosophy*, trans. Hugh Tomlinson (Minneapolis: University of Minnesota Press).

Deleuze, G. (1986) *Foucault* (Paris: Éditions de Minuit).

Deleuze, G. (1988) *Foucault*, trans. Seán Hand, foreword by Paul Bové (Minneapolis: University of Minnesota Press).

Deleuze, G. (1990). *The Logic of Sense*, trans. Mark Lester with Charles Stivale, ed. Constantin Boundas (New York: Columbia University Press).

Deleuze, G. (1995) *Negotiations 1972–1990*, trans. Martin Joughin (New York: Columbia University Press).

Deleuze, G. (2003) *Deux régimes de fous et autres textes: textes et entretiens: 1975–1995*, ed. David Lapoujade (Paris: Minuit).

Deleuze, G. (2004) *Desert Islands and Other Texts 1953–1974*, ed. David Lapoujade, trans. Michael Taormina (New York: Semiotext(e)).

Deleuze, G. (2007) *Two Regimes of Madness: Texts and Interviews 1975–1995*, trans. Ames Hodges and Mike Taormina (New York: Semiotext(e) [Revised Edition]).

Deleuze, G. and Guattari, F. (1987) *A Thousand Plateaus: Capitalism and Schizophrenia*, trans. Brian Massumi (Minneapolis: University of Minnesota Press).

Deleuze, G. and Guattari, F. (1994) *What Is Philosophy?*, trans. Hugh Tomlinson and Graham Burchell (New York: Columbia University Press).

Dosse, F. (2010) *Gilles Deleuze and Félix Guattari: Intersecting Lives*, trans. Deborah Glassman (New York: Columbia University Press).

Eribon, D. (1991) *Michel Foucault*, trans. Betsy Wing (Cambridge, MA: Harvard University Press).

Foucault, M. (1969) *L'Archéologie du savoir* (Paris: Éditions Gallimard).

Foucault, M. (1972) *The Archaeology of Knowledge*, trans. A. M. Sheridan (London: Tavistock).

Foucault, M. (1975) *Surveiller et punir: Naissance de la prison* (Paris: Gallimard).

Foucault, M. (1976) *Histoire de la sexualité 1: La volonté de savoir* (Paris: Éditions Gallimard).

Foucault, M. (1977a) *Discipline and Punish*, trans. Alan Sheridan (London: Allen Lane/Penguin).

Foucault, M. (1977b). *Language, Counter-Memory, Practice: Selected Essays and Interviews*, ed. Donald F. Bouchard, trans. Donald F. Bouchard and Sherry Simon (Ithaca: Cornell University Press).

Foucault, M. (1978) *The History of Sexuality, Volume 1: An Introduction*, trans. Robert Hurley (London: Allen Lane/Penguin).

Foucault, M. (1994) *Dits et écrits*, tomes I–IV (Paris: Éditions Gallimard).

Foucault, M. (1996) "What is Critique?," in J. Schmidt (ed.), *What is Enlightenment?* (Berkeley and Los Angeles: University of California Press), 382–98.

Foucault, M. (1997) *Essential Works of Foucault 1954–1984, Volume 1, Ethics*, ed. Paul Rabinow, trans. Robert Hurley and others (New York: The New Press).

Foucault, M. (1998) *Essential Works of Foucault 1954–1984, Volume 2: Aesthetics, Method and Epistemology*, ed. James D. Faubion, trans. Robert Hurley et al. (New York: New Press).

Foucault, M. (2000) *Essential Works of Foucault 1954–1984, Volume 3: Power*, ed. James D. Faubion, trans. Robert Hurley et al. (New York: New Press).

Foucault, M. (2003) *"Society Must Be Defended": Lectures at the Collège de France 1975–1976*, ed. Mauro Bertani and Alessandro Fontana, trans. David Macey (New York: Picador).

Foucault, M. (2008) *The Birth of Biopolitics: Lectures at the Collège de France 1978–1979*, ed. Michel Senellart, trans. Graham Burchell (Houndmills, Basingstoke and New York: Palgrave Macmillan).

Glucksmann, A. (1975) *La Cuisinière et le mangeur d'hommes* (Paris: Éditions du Seuil).

Guattari, F. (ed.) (1973) *Trois Milliards de Pervers: Grand Encyclopédie des Homosexualités* (Paris: Recherches).

Levy, B.-H. (1977) *La barbarie à visage humaine* (Paris: Éditions Grasset).

Macey, D. (1993) *The Lives of Michel Foucault* (New York: Pantheon).

Miller, J. (1993) *The Passion of Michel Foucault* (New York: Doubleday).

Patton, P. (2010a) "Activism, philosophy and actuality in Deleuze and Foucault," *Deleuze Studies* 4: 2010 Supplement, *Deleuze and Political Activism*, 84–103.

Patton, P. (2010b) "Foucault and Normative Political Philosophy," in Timothy O'Leary and Christopher Falzon (eds.), *Foucault and Philosophy* (Oxford: Wiley-Blackwell), 204–21.

Patton, P. (2012a) "Deleuze, Foucault and History," in Bernd Herzogenrath (ed.), *Time and History in Deleuze and Serres* (London and New York: Continuum Press), 69–83.

Patton, P. (2012b) "From Resistance to Government: Foucault's Lectures 1976–1979," in C. Falzon, T. O'Leary and J. Sawicki (eds.), *A Companion to Foucault* (Oxford: Blackwell).

Patton, P. (2013) "Deleuze" entry in Leonard Lawlor and John Nale (eds.), *The Cambridge Foucault Lexicon* (Cambridge: Cambridge University Press).

Péguy, C. (2002) *Clio* (Paris: Éditions Gallimard).

Senellart, M. (2007) "Course Context," in Michel Foucault, *Security, Territory, Population: Lectures at the Collège De France, 1977–78*, ed. and trans. Michel Senellart, François Ewald and Alessandro Fontana (Basingstoke: Palgrave Macmillan), 369–401.

Senellart, M. (2011) "Le cachalot et l'écrevisse. Réflexions sur la rédaction des Cours au Collège de France," in P. Artières et al. (eds.), *Michel Foucault* (Paris: Éditions de L'Herne), 147–55.

CHAPTER 10

Becoming and History: Deleuze's Reading of Foucault

ANNE SAUVAGNARGUES

TRANSLATED BY ALEX FELDMAN

Deleuze returned often to the "admiration" and "affection" he felt for Foucault.[1] In the 1970s, he began to present Foucault as the contemporary philosopher who had done the most to reframe the question of history. Coming from a philosopher who insists so much on the opposition between becoming and history, this admiration invites notice. Deleuze, like Foucault, but also with him, and while discovering his thought, confronts this new way of dealing with empirical historicity: to take it epistemologically, in the form of the archive, without, for all that, renouncing the critique of linear chronology and of teleological or causal explanation. Starting, moreover, with his 1963 "Raymond Roussel or the Horror of the Void,"[2] Deleuze reviewed all of Foucault's major titles up through *Discipline and Punish* in 1975, and he developed lengthy analyses that would form the basis of the 1986 *Foucault.* We can thus follow in Deleuze's work itself a kind of journal of the theoretical surprises that Foucault's changes provoked. This attention to the work of the thinker of history is all the more fascinating in that history and the historical approach to philosophy are the object of express criticism in Deleuze. As a reader of Foucault, Deleuze puts into practice a theory of the crises of thought. He explores with Foucault a dimension of history whereby it can be understood not as the opposite of becoming, but as the necessary dimension of becoming's actualization.

Deleuze's project of understanding Foucault took place at the same time that both were moving in new intellectual directions, thanks, surely, to their contemporaneity and to their friendship and collusion in the 1970s, when they both discovered the field of the social. For Deleuze, the changes are visible in the writings with Guattari and in a new attention to the empirical fields of the social (*Anti-Oedipus*); whereas, in Foucault, the change is marked by the passage from the *Archaeology of*

Knowledge to the discovery of power in *Discipline and Punish*. As their thinking bent more and more toward the question of practices, the two thinkers also underwent a profound theoretical shake-up that was to result in a "pragmatics of multiplicities." If their trajectories, strictly linked during the period of the GIP,[3] diverge after 1975, Deleuze is no less attentive to the *History of Sexuality* of the 1980s, even if, for his own part, he critiques both sexuality and history: Foucault's approach forbids the treatment of sexuality as an invariant and transforms history into a process of subjectivation. As different, then, as the trajectories of the two authors are, they share a similar arc, traversing the fields of literature and then moving in the 1970s towards a pragmatics of thought and a philosophy of power. After a period of intense collaboration with Guattari that provisionally closed with *A Thousand Plateaus*, Deleuze devoted himself once again to studying philosophers (Spinoza, Foucault, Leibniz), but he also developed a new semiotic of the non-linguistic arts (*Bacon, Movement-Image, Time-Image, The Fold*); Foucault, on the other hand, took on the project of a *History of Sexuality*. Nevertheless, Deleuze affirmed no less than before that a great proximity links him to the work of Foucault:

> I am sure that he read what I wrote. I read what he wrote with a passion. But we did not talk very often. I had the feeling, with no sadness, that in the end I needed him and he did not need me.[4]

If the "need" each author had for the other was indeed asymmetrical, for Deleuze the need itself doubtless had to do with the vector of history. Deleuze approaches history by way of the relationship between the virtual and the actual, on a plane (*plan*) that he would qualify as metaphysical, whereas Foucault commits himself to the meticulous and empirical examination of a textual archive, something in which Deleuze was never interested. However, Deleuze does come to accord more and more attention to the form of the actual or the current (*l'actuel*) and to the question of history. If one compares the valorization of intensive becoming in *Difference and Repetition*, the interest in descriptions of singular assemblages (*agencements*) in *A Thousand Plateaus*, and the appearance of history in the group of works from the 1980s, with *Image-temps* and *Image-mouvement* in 1983 and 1985, *Foucault* in 1986, and *Le pli* in 1988 – then this change is something slowly breathed in, and not so much a transformation of the system. Each text is ever more concerned with the consistency and the consolidation of strata. In the work of Deleuze, a topological strip moves from a privilege of the virtual, of the becoming of constituted individuations, toward the phenomena of consolidation. Deleuze had distinguished in *Difference and Repetition* between actual and virtual modes of difference, opposing the becoming-intense of the virtual difference to the individual actualization and to the tendency to organization. The philosophy of difference insisted, then, on the virtual moment in order to counter the preeminence of the same and the similar, of common sense, of the image of thought. From *Anti-Oedipus* to *A Thousand Plateaus*, Deleuze conserves the critical accent that animates the descriptions of stratified modes, but he passes from a critique of organizations to a much more complex mode of interdependence between actual and virtual, between becoming and history. The body without organs or the capture of the wasp and the orchid explicitly underline becoming-intensive (cf. the 10th Plateau), but the theory of lines initiated in *Anti-Oedipus* and continued in *A Thousand Plateaus* allows us to think all material, social, or noetic bodies as "packets" or bundles of lines, as multiplicities assembling (*agençant*), at the same time, intensive vectors and actualizing vectors, becomings-intense and segments of organization. The virtual and the actual thereby become indiscernible and equally active at all the points of actualization. The great lesson of *A Thousand Plateaus* is that the phenomena of destratification (lines of flight) cannot be separated from the two relative modes of stratification, the molar lines with rigid segmentarity and the molecular lines with supple segmentarity that compose every assemblage.

The point is not that Deleuze abandons the privilege of the virtual that characterizes his first works, but rather than with Spinoza and the analysis of relations of force, with Marx, the decisive interlocutor of *Anti-Oedipus* and *A Thousand Plateaus*, and especially with Foucault, Deleuze accords a growing interest to the phenomena of stratification, to history, and to the empirical arrangement of assemblages that actualize a diagram of forces. It is with respect to Foucault that Deleuze passes imperceptibly from the preeminence of becoming to an interest in history, which appears now as "the stand-in double of a becoming."[5] In other words, history is no longer the reified image by which thought solidifies becoming, but rather the milieu of actualization that becoming needs in order to take form, with the result that the preeminence of the virtual henceforth implies the theorization of its real modes of actualization. Hence the interest for the phenomena of consolidation, which are no longer read only as doxical thicknesses (Nietzsche) or as tendencies to organization that are hostile to life (body without organs). Individuations no longer mark a decrease in intensity; actualization takes on a new interest, that of a taking of form that temporarily stabilizes relations of labile forces. Indeed, the best indication of this new status of history as actualization is the interest in forms. "In all of Foucault's work, there's a certain relation between form and forces that's influenced my work and was basic to his conception of politics, and of epistemology and aesthetics too."[6]

THE QUESTION OF HISTORY

With Foucault, "it is as if, finally, something new were emerging in the wake of Marx"[7]: history can be thought philosophically without being reduced to the "philosophy of history,"[8] that is, to a teleological discourse of the Hegelian type,

176

one which draws support from chronology in order to reduce it dialectically to the figures of the concept. Yet "Foucault never became a historian. Foucault's a philosopher who invents a completely different relation to history than what you find in the philosophers of history."[9] This "completely different" relation permits a consideration of "'epochs' or historical formations" as "multiplicities," complexes of forces in the process of becoming that "escape from both the reign of the subject and the empire of structure."[10] Foucault transforms the concept of history and at the same time disqualifies every phenomenology of history, every thought of the subject, but also every reading of historicity that is exclusively structural or topical.

What emerges in Foucault's writings is thus a new relationship to history, one that is also expressed by an "evolution" in Foucault's work itself. It is fascinating to follow in Deleuze's own texts the way in which he understands the changes in Foucault's trajectory. It is as though Deleuze is grappling with the "history of philosophy" of which he is so often critical: when it comes to Foucault, indeed, he ends up giving a new instruction manual for how to do it. An archivist and surveyor of Foucault's work, Deleuze searches for the "logic of this thought" that seems to him to be "one of the greatest modern philosophies."[11] Seeking to establish this thought in its dynamic ruptures as well as in its systematic equilibrium, he transforms his critique of the history of thought through this very reading.

Deleuze applies a double principle of method to Foucault: the principle of totality – to be interested in an author is to "take everything into account," according to a principle of systematic exhaustivity characteristic of Deleuze's first monographs. But for Foucault there is also a second principle, that of the dynamic tension of the system, a tension that does not exclude the diachronic and successive character of maturation. One could also say that, within the totality of a body of work, it is the *passages* that reorganize the problematics that become determinative.

> Here I'm trying to see Foucault's thought as a whole. By whole, I mean what drives him on from one level of things to another.[12]

In this regard, we can oppose Deleuze's reading of Kant[13] to the *Foucault* of 1986. The former stands out for its emphasis on a synchrony that places the three *Critiques* on exactly the same conceptual plane, whereas the latter conserves a theory of the dynamism of the system. Without letting go of the architectonic, Deleuze gives increasing importance to the "passages" that require a strict sense of chronology. Chronological order is not trivial, even if, of itself, it is insufficient: it is necessary and must be stablished at the outset with exactitude. At the conclusion of the 1964 Royaumont Colloquium, Deleuze was already insisting on such "normal scientific and critical requirements"[14] as the availability of both a reliable edition and a good chronology. At the moment when he accepted, with Foucault, the direction of the French edition of the *Complete Works* of Nietzsche, he praised the colossal labor undertaken by Colli and Montinari on the *Nachlass*, and he was in no way contemptuous of the scientific interest involved in this effort to arrange drafts, notes, fragments, and scattered projects in the most exact chronological sequence. Deleuze and Foucault defend the editorial choices of the *Complete Works* of Nietzsche, as well as its double system: to edit the posthumous notes in their chronological order and to unify them according to the "periods" established by the published works. Strict succession (the journal of fragments) and periodization of the works do not end up confining Nietzsche's thought to a linear progression. The attention to empirical succession instead readies the passage to an opening of the system. This attention thus is the best way to safeguard the variations and, in allowing the reader to grasp all the more closely Nietzsche's thought in the course of its becoming, it makes room for an open and plural systematicity suitable to his project.

> In fact, when a thinker like Nietzsche, a writer like Nietzsche presents several versions of the same idea, it goes without saying that this idea ceases to be the same . . . It was thus necessary to edit and publish the notebooks in their integrality and in chronological order, *in accordance with the periods that correspond to Nietzsche's published books.* Only in this way could the mass of unpublished works reveal their multiple meanings.[15]

Deleuze thus carries out a double displacement: against the necessity of chronological order, he counterposes its contingency; against the eternity or stability of the system, he counterposes the historicity of the investigation. Hence his extremely delicate position, which articulates history and becoming at each point of the succession, instead of opposing them frontally.

ANALYTIC AND DIAGNOSTIC

This subtle relationship between history and becoming explains the insistence with which Deleuze incorporates the *Dits et écrits* into Foucault's principal corpus of published works (*l'œuvre*). The innovation of this approach is that now principal works appear as a stratified formation, whereas the becoming of forces breathes in those circumstantial writings that, as reactions and solicitations, make up a journal of thought. Instead of opposing the principal works, untimely and inactual (*intempestive et inactuelle*), to succession as a creation torn from history, the former takes the form of a consolidated and historical archive, whereas the occasional writings are charged with becoming: they are assigned the task of inserting the enormous solidity of the principal body of works into political action. Here too Foucault's concepts allow Deleuze to modify his own practice as a reader. The distinction refers to that between knowing (*savoir*) and strategy, that is, to the passage from the

Archaeology of Knowledge to *Discipline and Punish*; the principal body of works thus falls under the realm of knowing, whereas the circumstantial set of things said and written (*dits et écrits*) belongs to the realm of strategy. Deleuze thus validates in its entirety the posthumous collection of *Dits et écrits* and grants them their full necessity. It is not a matter here of a relationship between the principal works (*l'œuvre*) and the "outside-the-*œuvre*" (*hors-d'œuvre*), to a *parergon*, but rather of two halves of a single conceptual apparatus: the closed and finished works belong to a history of thought, whereas the journal of punctual interventions signals the becoming of these works. This is a strong and original position. According to Deleuze, the published works of Foucault are stabilized around determinate archives (the general hospital of the seventeenth century, the clinic of the eighteenth century, the prison of the nineteenth century, then subjectivity in ancient Greece and Christianity); moreover, their finished character constitutes the works themselves as archives. It is in the other half of Foucault's body of works, says Deleuze, that we must look for the diagnostic:

> In every apparatus we must untangle the lines of the recent past from the lines of the near future: the archive from the current, the part of history and the part of becoming, *the part of the analytic and the part of the diagnostic*.[16]

Foucault formulates his analytic – let us note this Kantian vocabulary to which we will return later – in his regular works, where he constrains himself to formulating philosophical problems that he will treat in relation to a limiting material (the archive), thus reworking philosophy (as a history of rationality) as much as history (by way of a non-linear philosophy of history). The analytic, the archive, is determined philosophically by "extremely novel historical means."[17] The philosopher carries out the archaeology of stratified reason, that is, reason as it is given, positive, frozen in its historical process. But the apparatus (*dispositif*) is not historical without also being "actual or current" (*actuel*), in the sense in which Deleuze understands the term in Foucault, that is, as the equivalent of the "untimely" (*inactuel*) in Nietzsche,[18] for which he reserves the term becoming:

> [W]e have to distinguish between what we are (what we already no longer are) and what we are becoming: *the part of history, the part of currentness* [l'actuel].[19]

Foucault's published works, consolidated in systematic expositions, are both backward-looking and positive, belonging both to the historical – the relatively closed and accomplished state of an empirically given archive with an actualized and stabilized form – and to the analytical, the positivity of a definite structure. The occasional writings, both prospective and indicative, are doubly diagnostic: they inspect the present and signal the tension, within Foucault's thought itself, between doctrinal apparatus and possible becomings, between actualized forms and virtual forces. Systematic exposition then is reduced to history, whereas the chronological journal of interventions indicates becoming. The two faces of Foucault's work, history and becoming, analytic and diagnostic, translate the real movement of his thought in its historical inscription and its untimely value. In this manner, Deleuze believes he can escape both the reduction to history implicit in genesis and the idealist temptation of structure.

The chronological order of Nietzsche's fragments, much like the articulation of the analytic and the diagnostic in Foucault, allows us to pass judgment on this history of thought, which is both actualization of forms and becoming of forces. Of course, Deleuze, following Bergson and Nietzsche, opposes becoming to eternity as well as to history, insofar as the latter is objectified as a causal process on the model of an already-over. But if history is not reducible to this false teleology, it is rather actualization of forces; it archives and, in this archiving, conserves. The true temporality of the system is to be found not in chronologically fixed series (historical order) that correspond to what we have ceased to be, but rather to points of mutation, of disequilibrium that Deleuze calls becomings. Foucault is a great philosopher because he makes use of history in order to act, "as Nietzsche said, against the time, and thus on the time, in favor, I hope, of a time to come."[20] For Foucault, then, the chronological sequence of the occasional writings, far from exhibiting a reified history or objectifying a succession, marks out, on the contrary, the points of becoming in his thought. The sequence of the occasional writings thus does a better job of indicating the becomings of his thought, with their connections, erasures, crossing-outs, and points of incompleteness, than the full-length finished works, rigorously ordered as they are according to the philosophical examination of an archive. Just as, in Nietzsche, the chronological sequence of the posthumous writings injects becoming into the system, so too, in Foucault, the chronological sequence of the occasional *Dits et écrits*, of the things "said and written," injects becoming into the history of the closed works. The event, the crisis, the posthumous fragment, and the occasional writing all speak to the labor of becoming within the stratified totality of the corpus of works conceived as system or as historical succession. Hence the principle of an open totality, of a system in the process of becoming, a principle that integrates the lateral, occasional, and *minor* writings into the body of the ordinary publications (the normal, the major).[21] The posthumous works of Nietzsche and the circumstantial interventions of Foucault occupy the same function.

Foucault attached so much importance to his interviews in France and even more so abroad, not because he liked interviews, but because in them he traced lines of actualization that required another mode of expression than the assimilable lines in his major books. The interviews are diagnoses. It is similar for Nietzsche, whose works are difficult to read without the *Nachlass* that is contemporary to each. Foucault's complete works, as Defert and Ewald[22] imagine them, cannot separate the books that have left such an impression on us from the interviews that lead us toward a future, toward a becoming: strata and currentness.[23]

The strata of the systematic works must be therefore be completed by the cartographic plotting of actualities and current events that make up the circumstantial writings or the journal of ideas. From this point of view, the chronological reading takes on a new function as that which best attests the mutations of the open system. The body of an author's work must take into account its becomings as much as its history, and also its crises and its ruptures. To consider the body of work in its totality is to double it at each point with its virtual fractures. Diachrony is therefore no less indispensable than a systematic and achronological reading, but diachrony too remains insufficient to the extent that it does not double the constituted *form* of the conceptual apparatus, the relation of forces taken statically, with the *play of forces* effectuated therein, with the *diagram*.

THE CRISES OF THOUGHT

Empirical chronology renders the becoming of the system perceptible, and its modes of characteristic variation bring to light thought's lines of wandering (*lignes d'erre*).[24] Chronology also renders accessible the becoming of the idea, which passes through a textual cartography that includes readings and actions, accidents and encounters, and "points of bifurcation." The logic of thought is not a system in equilibrium, but a regime in becoming, where theoretical segments are confronted with practical forays and pragmatic stakes. These encounters make up what Deleuze calls the *crises* of thought, which expose this relation between forces and forms, becoming and history.

> A thought's logic isn't a stable rational system . . . A thought's logic is like a wind blowing on us, a series of gusts and jolts. You think you've got to port, but then you find yourself thrown back out onto the open sea, as Leibniz put it. That's particularly true in Foucault's case. His thought's constantly developing new dimensions that are never contained in what came before. So what is it that drives him to launch off in some direction, to trace out some – always unexpected – path? Any great thinker goes through crises; they set the tempo of the hours (*les heures*) of his thought.[25]

The crises of thought mark the becoming of the system. They must be simultaneously grasped at on the historical plane of successive actualization and on the virtual plane of coexistence. Hence the impression that Deleuze incessantly substitutes a "topos" for invention,[26] that he accentuates the logical aspect of development and smooths over the ruptures in a logical coexistence. But becoming doubles history, and Deleuze conceives the crises on the double plane of the actual and the virtual.

> There is certainly a succession of periods, but there are also coexistent aspects that accord with the three simultaneous elements of painting, which are perpetually present.[27]

This "perpetuity" of the problem, this "insistence" removed from succession, can give the impression that Deleuze sacrifices the mutations of the system to logic. On the one hand, Deleuze affirms the historicity of problems in an author, the pertinence of their exact mapping. The status of this historicity in becoming is not, however, due to succession, but rather depends on what Deleuze calls the problematic proper to an author – her "signature" or "formula" – which gives the principle of her style. Deleuze calls this a "diagram," fittingly borrowing the term from Michel Foucault in his review of *Discipline and Punish*. The diagram, "the presentation of relations between forces unique to a particular formation,"[28] characterizes the becoming that "doubles" the stratified formations of history on an intensive mode and reprises the characterization of the Idea as problem in *Difference and Repetition*. With respect to a work, the intensive diagram is not a permanent structure, a logical *topos*, or a preexisting form, but rather a virtual problem, a complex of forces. Moreover, the diagram, if it consists in non-formalized and non-formed forces, and if it insists upon intensive becoming, is, all the same, the object of a historical actualization.

> Not only can we differentiate diagrams, but we can also date the diagram of a painter, because there is always a moment when the painter confronts it most directly.[29]

The diagram is therefore indissociable from its actualization, which can indeed be assigned a date. In itself, as a problem, the diagram does not belong to the retrospective history of a thinker, but to her becoming. It explains this character of "crisis," this power of rupture, thanks to which a thought is not given once and for all but rather undergoes different periodizations. Mutations of thought require this double analysis, on the plane of history and on the plane of becoming: the succession of periods in Foucault's thought is not determined through a sense of history as causal succession, but is rather taken as a kind of creation, as rupture and becoming. The crisis indicates the becoming of the system and its historicity, just as much as it reveals its jolted and non-linear continuity.

It is what produces what Deleuze calls a "relinking,"[30] where "the 'cut' . . . constitutes . . . the ideal cause of continuity."[31] In this sense, "breaks are not lacunae or ruptures of continuity,"[32] for their fractures require a "redistribution" of the continuous, according to a new dimension that produces continuity from the contingent eruption of the fracture.

To explain the passage in Foucault's work from the writings devoted to social apparatuses (*dispositifs*) of confinement to the question of sexuality, and the theoretical difficulty that delayed the appearance of the second and third volumes of the *History of Sexuality* for eight years, Deleuze insists on the contingency of the investigations. Crisis marks intellectual labor as an adventure, a bumpy and unpredictable pursuit;[33] indeed, in *Difference and Repetition*, Deleuze writes, "This entire adventurous character of Ideas remains to be described."[34] This adventure is affected by external occasions and unforeseeable empirical encounters. Forces work on thought, making it be creative, even with respect to its own coordinates. There is thus a history and a becoming of thought, which produces "new coordinates," a history and a becoming that play out "successively" in Foucault's work. And when this body of work closes with Foucault's death, Deleuze organizes it according to three problems that respond both to the periodization of the works and to its logic. Foucault initially explores the strata as historical formations, thus elaborating an archaeology that develops as an archaeology of knowledge. Passing from the epistemological dimension of knowledge to the "outside" (*"dehors"*), to the forces in the process of becoming that supply the historical dimension of knowledge (*savoir*), Foucault discovers next the strategic dimension of the social, which leads him to pass from the analysis of knowledge to the strategies of power. The history of formations (knowledge) refers then to the examination of active (non-stratified) forces of power, which renews the question of history by thinking its political actualization as an insertion of the becoming of forces into the very heart of stratified forms. Finally, with the *History of Sexuality*, Foucault gives an account of the singular relationship that articulates the historical strata (knowledge) and the non-stratified forces (power) by setting up, as their "outside" of these forces and forms, the slow historical formation of a fold (*pli*) of subjectivity.[35]

The methodological concept of "crisis" is meant to be applicable both to development of the body of work and to its logic: from the dimension of knowledge to that of power, then from there to the fold of subjectivation, Deleuze systematically relinks the three periods of Foucault's work as three distinct dimensions. Crisis allows the transformation of the relationship between history and becoming since, on the plane of succession, there is no necessity, but rather unforeseeable crises (creation) – whereas on the plane of unforeseeable eruption, there is indeed necessity. Deleuze injects contingency into the chronological sequence, contingency that in turn permits the unexpected upsurge of the crisis as novelty.[36] For this reason, Deleuze always understands the "discovery of lines of subjectivation" in *The History of Sexuality* as a relaunching of Foucault's thought, not as a return to the subject or as a repentance.

> More than any other, this discovery came from a crisis in Foucault's thought, as if he needed to rework the map of apparatuses, find a new orientation for them to prevent them from closing up behind impenetrable lines of force . . . Leibniz expressed in exemplary fashion this state of crisis that restarts thought when it seems that everything is almost resolved: you think you have reached shore but are cast back out to sea.[37]

Crisis imposes this new orientation that changes the context, articulation, and cartography of preceding concepts and constitutes less a rupture or a modification of questions than a reconfiguration of the nature of a problem that the questions aim to explore. Whether it be a matter of the cinema and the crisis of the action-image,[38] of the baroque as "a long moment of crisis,"[39] or of Foucault's thought, the crisis articulates creation and determinateness, becoming and history, virtual and actual in thought. It is not that the dynamic caesura is reabsorbed into the static logic of a reconfiguration of the problem, a reconfiguration that would have been called for since the very beginning of the system. Between the deterministic anteriority-posteriority of a successive evolution of problems and a transformation by chance that would give everything over to the contingency of the investigation, Deleuze explores a "mixture of the aleatory and the necessary": no necessity in the succession, no contingency in the rupture, but rather the contingent eruption of the rupture into a succession (actualization) that attests the coexistence of a diagram of forces in the preceding theoretical formation, a diagram whose contingent actualization rekindles the system by creating a new dimension.

> Foucault always finds a new dimension or a new line in a crisis. Great thinkers are somewhat seismic; they do not evolve but proceed by quakes or crises.[40]

In sum, the static architectonic is nothing if it does not double itself in a dynamic mapping of the crises of thought. Deleuze can thus elaborate through Foucault a dynamics of systems of thought in disequilibrium where history doubles the becoming of the system at each point of actualization. The three axes of Knowledge, Power, and Subjectivity define both the community of a problem and a periodization of Foucault's work: these dimension are discovered successively, each layer opening onto the following, in accordance with a logic that is that of the crisis. *The Archaeology of Knowledge, Discipline and Punish,* and *The History of Sexuality* punctuate in this manner three different stages of Foucault's thought, which is "constantly developing new dimensions that are never contained in what came before":[41] not an epigenesis of the system, but a creation of dimension that reworks the preceding dimensions, according to a metastable and dynamic logic.

> His thought consists in tracing out and exploring one dimension after another in a way that has its own creative necessity, but no one dimension is contained in any other.[42]

THE STRATIFIED

Rather than oppose history and becoming, causal diachrony and virtual synchrony, what is important is to investigate how crisis injects breaks into succession while the contingent actualization of problems marks an event for the system: the double regime in Foucault of crises that shake up the analytic, of couplings and "expressions" that agitate the diagnostic, calls now for the analysis of the modes whereby forces are actualized in stratified forms.

For these reasons, Deleuze returns to the analysis of strata he had developed in the Third of the *Thousand Plateaus* written with Guattari. His aim now is to explore the dimension of knowledge (*savoir*) in Foucault. Instead of the great strata, the material, the organic, and the cultural, which made up together a universal history, the analysis now moves toward the Foucaultian archive. To be sure, the emphasis placed on the intensive is conserved: if the historical is a "stratified formation," "to think is to reach a non-stratified matter,"[43] "to reach the non-stratified,"[44] such that "thinking is no more historical than eternal," but thinking operates now "in an essential relationship with history."[45] Foucault is the inventor of this new figure of the historical, a relation to History without precedent that Deleuze writes in majuscule in order to underscore the difference with the older notion of successive causality. This genuinely new relationship with historical reality transforms its philosophical treatment.

> But History responds only because Foucault has managed to invent, no doubt in a way related to the new conceptions of certain historians, a properly philosophical form of interrogation which is itself new and which revives history.[46]

The "new coordinates" that are "successively" discovered in the work of Foucault – from the *Archaeology of Knowledge* to strategy and power and then to the genealogy of forms of subjectivations – constitute a complete reworking of the question of history along three essential lines. The first is epistemological. An epistemological relation is set up with history, consisting of the sort of operation on the empirical archive that characterizes Foucault's way of working. This operation determines knowledge as historical stratum, "the determination of the things visible and stable in each epoch"; it thus proposes a new history of thought. Knowledge is articulated in historical assemblages (*agencements*) that correlate statements (*énoncés*) and visibilities, doubly limiting the philosophy of history, which now becomes merely an epistemology of the empirical given and which must theorize the relation between the discursive and the non-discursive within the knowledge (*savoir*) of a period. Second, the relationship within knowledge between these two forms that are irreducible to one another, the two poles of the discursive and the non-discursive, of statements and visibilities, must be understood, in quite innovative fashion, as "capture." Deleuze applies to Foucault his own theory of capture, worked out with Guattari in *Kafka, Rhizome,* and *A Thousand Plateaus,* but submits it to a decisive change. Until then, he had understood it as the "capture of forces," whereas in *Foucault* it becomes the "capture of forms," a new relation between the discursive forms and the forms of the visibilities that define each period of knowledge. This move demonstrates Deleuze's interest for stratified forms. But, third, the relation between discourse and pragmatics must be inscribed in the heart of knowledge itself, which does not capture statements and visibilities without setting up, on a model qualified by Deleuze as neo-Kantian – and which is applicable to his own thought – a capture between forms of knowledge and forces of knowledge, between receptivity and spontaneity. The architectonic of the system doubles the history of the works: the capture of the visible and sayable forms of knowledge calls for capture between forms of knowledge and forces of power, which itself can only be grasped by a topological displacement that doubles the coordinates of knowledge (and the body of work up to the *Archaeology of Knowledge* in 1969) and the coordinates of power (*Discipline and Punish* of 1975) with a new axis of coordinates: the modes of subjectivation found in *The History of Sexuality.* For this reason, Deleuze constantly clarifies that this final move is by no means a "repentance" or a return to the subject, but rather an entirely new elaboration of the Form-subject with respect to the forces that compose this history of forms.

How does the dimension of knowledge renew the question of history? We have a relation of knowledge with history. Knowledge is the object of an "extraction" (epistemology) and not of a hermeneutic (phenomenology). Herein lies the merit of Foucault: his "principle of exteriority." "There is nothing before knowledge," and history is constituted by epistemology; there is "nothing underneath knowledge," no originary experience, but there do exist "things outside of knowledge."[47] Hence the strong affirmation that our relationship to history is not phenomenological but epistemological, an affirmation that transforms the status of history as much as that of knowledge, which becomes a "historical function," a practical assemblage (*agencement*), an "apparatus" (*dispositif*) of statements and visibilities[48] instead of subsisting in a purely intellectual dimension. As knowledge (*savoir*) becomes a practice, so too does history become a specific branch of knowing (*connaissance*).

The strata are "historical formations, positivities, or empiricities"[49] composed of two modes, seeing and saying, visibilities and statements. Knowledge (*savoir*), composed by these two "elements of stratification," "has two irreducible poles."[50] Each stratum of knowledge is thus composed of foldings of things visible and sayable, and it is the task of archaeology to "extract" them (Deleuze uses the same term in *Bacon* to characterize the logic of sensation). Consequently, epistemology supplants phenomenology in Foucault.

How does this epistemology, which extracts and produces history as a knowledge rather than an experience, proceed in the case of each of the two poles? Epistemology defines the "new" relation to history that escapes "the philosophers of history" and teleological discourses; yet it is also not simply the work done by the historian. It is a matter of "extracting" from the beds of sayabilities and visibilities their transcendental conditions. Here Foucault's neo-Kantian side is evident. The archive itself is not solely theoretical or enunciative; it is indissociable from visibilities, which do not themselves belong exclusively to the domain of vision, but are rather complexes of actions and passions, actions and reactions – multisensorial complexes that come to light.[51] Foucault lays bare, in a given "unity of the stratum"[52] at a moment of knowledge, the transcendental "conditions" of statements as well as those for visibilities. In short, statements and visibilities should not be confounded with things said or things seen. Statements (*énoncés*) must be "extracted" from words and visibilities from things. They must be plotted as conditions that are immanent but imperceptible, not hidden, but visible only through the operation of transcendental extraction.

For each of the two heterogeneous modes of the archive, the archaeologist exposes the transcendental conditions immanent to the given conditioned. If the conditioned is the inscribed or the given (to give two examples: for the form of the statement, legislation; for the form of visibility, the prison), the work of philosophy on the history of forms consists in a "dermatology" of strata or art of surfaces thanks to which the surface of inscription immanent to the inscribed can appear. Archaeology thus becomes the "constitution of a surface of inscription."[53] Deleuze calls attention to the Kantianism of this way of working: "this investigation of conditions constitutes a sort of neo-Kantianism in Foucault."[54] Yet this neo-Kantianism is to be understood through the reworking that Deleuze himself performed on Kant in *Difference and Repetition*. The transcendental is not a logical or mental possible that preexists that given; the conditions are not larger than the conditioned. "Real" and not "possible," although neither readable nor sayable, the conditions are virtual rather than actual. For this reason, "Statements are never directly readable or even sayable, although they are not hidden,"[55] for they are a real but virtual transcendental condition. The same holds for visibilities. These conditions can be called "empirical" precisely inasmuch as they are not transcendental in the Kantian sense of conditions of possibility belonging to the structure of human subjectivity. Instead, they are exposed directly in real experience. In this vein, Deleuze can speak of a transcendental empiricism during the period of *Difference and Repetition*. Real, they are not however actual, and from this point of view, they can be said to be "empirical" or given since they must be effectuated by epistemological extraction and do not precede it. The transcendental in Foucault is to be distinguished from the transcendental in Kant or in phenomenology: there is no reduction to a transcendental structure of lived experience. Consequently, there is nothing behind that which is said or seen, and each epoch says everything it can say. Nothing hidden, nothing anterior, no origin – but an effective condition that is not visible, real but not actual before its epistemological extraction that exhibits its transcendental immanence. The statements only become legible in relations with their "conditions," which "constitute their inscription in an 'enunciative' bedrock"[56] virtually demanded by them. This bedrock did not preexist their actualization, just as "an epoch does not preexist the statements that express it or the visibilities that fill it." Thus, "what Foucault takes from history is that determination of visible and articulable features [*des énonçables*] unique to each age which goes beyond any behavior, mentality, or set of ideas since it makes these things possible."[57]

Archaeology has "two poles," but "from one stratum to the other, the visibles and the stateables are transformed at the same time, although not according to the same rules." The transcendental conditions thus refer to this "capture" of the forms of saying and seeing, forms heterogeneous but simultaneous (statements are able "to slide themselves into the interstices of seeing" and the visibilities do likewise with saying), so much so that Deleuze insists at the same time on the heterogeneity and on indiscernibility of the two forms: "We speak, we see, and we make see, at the same time, although they are not the same thing and the two differ in nature."[58]

The work of Archaeology is not confined then to extracting transcendental conditions of seeing and speaking, but must also give an account of the modalities of their disjointed coexistence. Deleuze here takes up and applies to Foucault his own analysis of capture, which had served, from *Kafka* to *A Thousand Plateaus*, as a means to think a non-dialectical relation between several terms taken together as an ensemble in a "block of becoming." His principal example is the capture of the wasp and the orchid (developed, for example, in *Rhizome*), a capture that transforms both while maintaining their heterogeneity.

> In short, each stratum, each historical formation, each positivity, is made up of the interweaving of determinant utterances and determinable units of visibility, inasmuch as they are heterogeneous, though this heterogeneity does not prevent their mutual insertion.[59]

Capture, which serves to determine the neo-Kantianism of Foucault, assumes two connected functions: methodologically, it gives an account of the growth in dimensions that takes place within the body of work; philosophically, it exposes the relationship between history and becoming, or rather the manner in which the stratified forms are composed with the forces that remain exterior to them. *The Archaeology of Knowledge* adds to Foucault's earlier undertakings the distinction between discursive formations (statements) and non-discursive formations (milieu),[60] between which neither "correspondence," "isomorphism," "direct causality, nor symbolization"[61] can be established. In consequence, archaeology plays the role of a hinge between these two forms. From the *Archaeology* to *Discipline and Punish*, Deleuze notes the emergence of an assignable status for the non-discursive forms and the appearance of the form of visibility, which "haunts the entirety of Foucault's work" and which permits the determination of "the form of the visible in its difference from the form of the sayable." The problem then is to think the relation between these two forms that "do not cease to enter into contact, to insinuate themselves into each other, each tearing segments from the other,"[62] all the while remaining distinct, even as the statement takes a certain precedence over the visibility. Consider, for example, how at the beginning of the nineteenth century, the correlation between masses and population became visible at the same time that medical statements conquered new sayables. Capture formalizes this relationship between two forms that are both heterogeneous and yet concomitant. Sometimes Deleuze calls this relation a non-relation in order to underline its persistent heterogeneity without reducing it to a correspondence, a causality between sociology and ideology, or a subsumption under a superior "common" form." In this manner, Deleuze is close to the theory of capture in the Kantian schematism, which articulates the spontaneity of the categories and the receptivity of intuition, thought and sensibility, all the while maintaining their disjunction and difference in nature: "and yet, there is no common form, there is no conformity, not even correspondence,"[63] but rather "interlacing" (*entrelacs*) – almost a fold – "heterogeneity" and "co-adaptation" of forms[64] whose "mutual insertion" characterizes a historical stratum.

> In short, each stratum, each historical formation, each positivity, is made up of the interweaving of determinant utterances and determinable units of visibility, inasmuch as they are heterogeneous, though this heterogeneity does not prevent their mutual insertion.[65]

The general condition of statements in discursive formations not only refers back to their "capture" in non-discursive forms of visibility; this condition of the capture of forms also is revealed, alongside knowledge, as the play of forces of power. For "it is not enough that the co-adaptation of the two forms is not impeded; co-adaptation must be positively produced through a new instance comparable to what Kant called the 'schematism.'"[66] This new instance is power.

FROM HISTORY TO BECOMING

The historical stratum of the audiovisual archive of knowledge actualizes relations of forces. It is thus animated at each point by the relations of unstratified forces that constitute power. In passing from the figure of the archivist in *The Archaeology of Knowledge* to that of the surveyor in *Discipline and Punish*, knowledge acquires its practical dimension as assemblage (*agencement*) or apparatus (*dispositif*), and is to be understood as a practical theory of multiplicities. On the one hand, knowledge is led back to the forces that constitute it: Deleuze's enduring idea, already theorized in the first book on Nietzsche, is that forms are only relations of forces. Consequently, knowledge is indissociable from power and refers back to strategies, which are the dimension of its constitution. Deleuze is thus able to grasp the change in trajectory in Foucault's work – from the analysis of representations in the epistemological order characteristic of *The Order of Things* and the *Archaeology* to the analysis of punitive practices in *Discipline and Punish* – as an integration: relations of knowledges integrate relations of forces, and, as actualization, stratified knowledges actualize powers.[67] Furthermore, the relation between power and knowledge actualizes the relations of the forces of becoming in the forms of history. The stratified forms of knowledge are defined by way of power, itself defined as a diagram of forces, so that there is a "primacy" of strategic forces of power to stratified forms of knowledge; these forces, which remain on the side of knowledge and are irreducible to it, appear as knowledge's "outside." To define the diagram of power, Deleuze refers back to the definition given by Foucault himself: "A function that must be detached from every particular use" and from "every specific substance."[68] Deleuze specifies four properties: first, the diagram presents "the relations of forces proper to a formation"; next, it redistributes the "powers of affecting and being affected" that characterize relations of forces at a certain historical moment of actualization. Additionally, it is becoming and not form because, in the midst of the stratum, it is "a bubbling up of pure non-formalized function and pure unformed matters" – an intensive mode of relations of forces, of nude matter not yet endowed with qualities.[69] Finally, it is an "emission of singularities,"[70] so that it remains local and unstable, diffuse and non-localizable, because it is not incarnated in a determinate form but remains exterior to forms. These four definitions bring us back to the intensive nature of force and explain the primacy of power over knowledge: the constituted form flows out of the play of constituting forces.

Between power and knowledge, becoming of forces and history of forms, we must conceive the same type of capture as that which exists between the two forms of knowledge: "between power and knowledge, there is a difference of nature or a heterogeneity, but there is also mutual presupposition and capture."[71] Here we can conceive why history might hold out a positive interest, even as it is subordinated to becoming, not as a faulty concept, but rather as a constituted dimension of becoming: second, but well-founded. For power, in its labile and intensive dimension, is historically actualized and individuated by taking form in knowledge, even though it always presents the intensive side of knowledge. If the diagram is informal and always susceptible to transformation, it not, however, indeterminate or ahistorical. Taken from the point of view of the strata whose intensive outside it presents, the diagram is a becoming, but in itself, or from the point of view of other diagrams of forces, it in fact takes on a historical characterization, such that, for each historical form, a perfectly singular and dated diagram can be distinguished: Greek or Roman, disciplinary, or control-based. "Each stratified historical formation . . . refers back to a diagram of forces" that gives it an individuated sociohistorical existence.[72] The disciplinary diagram analyzed in *Discipline and Punish* is distinguishable from the earlier Sovereignty; the singularized diagrams are much like the "abstract machines" of *Anti-Oedipus* and *A Thousand Plateaus*: neither transhistorical universals nor abstract generic concepts, they determine an intensive face or side in coexistence, that is, a concomitant becoming in the strata. Indeed, we must admit that the diagram, differentiated in its singularity, presents in itself this vibration of history and becoming. Historical insofar as it determines a given strata and is singularized, independent but indissociable from the strata that it animates and that in turn impart to it a form, the diagram always presents the becoming of the strata. It is not "outside of" (*en dehors*) the strata but immanent to them, historical; it presents their intensive "outside" (*le dehors*), that which composes their informal becoming. For this reason, the "the list" of diagrams is "infinite, like that of the categories of power":[73] as many diagrams will be determined as the epistemological analyses of strata call for. The list of diagrams remains open, like that of the categories, with the result that it is even possible, for example, to define, according to the needs of the analysis, an "interstratic" diagram such as the Napoleonic one, intermediary between the strata of ancient sovereignty and that of the "new society of discipline that it prefigures." Individuated insofar as it doubles a particular stratum, the diagram is not for all that a formed individual, but rather a labile and moving complex of forces irreducible to any given form. In this way, Deleuze maintains the tension between history and becoming, actual and virtual – not only between knowledge and power, but within power itself.

Hence the preeminence of power over knowledge: the diagram is the "a priori of the historical formation," the condition of the relation between statements and visibilities of the audiovisual archive. It makes the subject a variable, a place, a subject-function, and it orders the theory of language in Foucault that Deleuze found so important and to which he always returned. Just as there is nothing beneath knowledge, so too is there no beginning of language, in the sense of an origin attributable to constituted subjects (Benveniste's linguistic personalism, for example), to the inscription of a signifier (the structural position), or to a pre-predicative experience.[74] The subject is determined by language and both are constituted by a historical a priori that correlates the noetic and the pragmatic within a stratum of knowledge irreducible to a founding consciousness; this a priori holds within a "regime" or an apparatus (*dispositif*) of power, just as visibilities hold to the "machines" explored in *A Thousand Plateaus*, arranging or assembling (*agençant*) power, social production, and rationality. "Just as statements are inseparable from regimes, visibilities are inseparable from machines,"[75] and these regimes and machines refer back to power as their transcendental condition. The result is that power appears as the transcendental condition of knowledge and as a fact, a "there is" irreducible to the formations and necessary for elucidating them, an "absolute that is nevertheless historical," a "historical a priori."[76] If the diagram is the a priori of the archive, "the a priori of history are themselves historical."[77]

For this reason, we must insist on the coexistence of becoming and history within the diagram of forces itself. As would be expected from the concept of capture, "between power and knowledge, there is a difference of nature or heterogeneity; but there is also mutual presupposition and capture."[78] Just as the diagram is determinative, so too does power take primacy over the form of knowledge, not only because knowledges, especially the human sciences, are "inseparable from the power relations which make them possible, and provoke forms of knowing (*savoirs*) which are capable to varying extents of crossing an epistemological threshold or of forming a definite body of knowledge (*connaissance*)."[79] Knowledge is thus worked over by relations of power. Better, it is power that produces the true as problem.[80] Indeed, the determining exteriority of relations of power guarantees that the Foucaultian approach to history is in fact an epistemology and not a phenomenology. Nothing is anterior to knowledge, the forces are not an undifferentiated in-itself or an antecedent experience, but the concrete element that knowledge puts into form. There is then "nothing under knowledge," but rather alongside it are relations of power, forces that do not fall under the domain of knowledge or what is integrated in its operations. Power exists therefore in the same way as the statement or the visibility, but alongside these forms, it guarantees the transcendental condition of knowledge: "Seeing and Saying are always already completely caught up in the power relations that they presuppose and actualize."[81] In this way, Foucault can substitute an epistemology for a phenomenology of knowledge: no originary experience serves as the originary ground of knowledge, but rather everything is bathed in a historical field of relations of forces.

> We can even say that if no original, free and savage experience lies beneath knowledge, as phenomenology would have it, it is because Seeing and Speaking are always already completely caught up within power relations which they presuppose and actualize.[82]

Capture thus defines the relation of heterogeneity but also of mutual presupposition that links power and knowledge. The relations of power remain "vanishing, embryonic or virtual" without the strata that integrate and stabilize them; the strata would have nothing to actualize without the "differential relations of power" that traverse them and destratify them. Capture lays bare this "non-relation," that is, an indirect relation that lies in the "interstice" of their difference of nature.[83] Herein lies the merit of the neo-Kantian version of capture: it ensures the relation of heterogeneity and presupposition between forms of knowledge and forces of power, just as much as it ensures the relation of forms of saying and seeing within knowledge. In this way, the diagram in Foucault is "an analogue of the Kantian schematism."[84]

> Foucault's diagrammaticism, that is to say the presentation of pure relations between forces or the emission of pure singularities, is therefore the analogue of Kantian schematism: it is this that ensures the relation from which knowledge flows, between the two irreducible forms of spontaneity and receptivity.[85]

The primacy of power follows from this. There is an "implication" between power and knowledge, but a "presupposition or condition" between knowledge and power.[86] In other words, the diagram needs the strata, which confer on it a certain stability, even though it is not reducible to the forms; it is also capable of communicating with other diagrams "according to another axis," that of the redistribution of forces, of their prospective capacity to change (resistance) or their inertial refusal to change (feudal segments that subsist in disciplinary societies, relations of forces conserved from earlier forms of domination). The diagram thus needs the forms: only the strata confer on it "a stability that it does not have on its own."[87] But force, for its part, is essentially plural and variable, with the result that the diagram, although it may well determine and relatively stabilize an historical ensemble of relations of forces, "does not exhaust the forces, which can enter into other relations and into other compositions."[88] For this reason, the diagram borders the stratified strata and conserves in them pockets of resistance or inertial strategic knots, cutting across the historical actuality of achronological becomings. Hence the primacy of becoming over history, which replays the primacy of forces to forms. "Becoming, change, and mutation concern the composing forces and not the composed forms."[89]

In consequence, the capture between stratified knowledge and unstratified power is assured by the third dimension of Foucault's work, the slow constitution of an interiority, as the folding of the outside of forces. Just as, in the opposition of becoming and history, we treated the break as a kind continuity and growth of dimensions, so too do the subjectivation processes characterizing the final part of Foucault's work show that forces, outside of the diagrams of power that they guarantee, are capable of producing an apparatus (*dispositif*) irreducible to knowledge and power: the dimension of the self, as produced interiority and historical subjectivation. This third dimension reinforces the interest in history. If "every form is a composite of relations of force," the task of philosophy – and in this it is different from the labor of historians – consists in asking, "the forces being given," "with what forms of the outside they entire into relation, and then what form is created as a result."[90] Foucault inaugurates a new philosophy of history that inspects the stratified forms under the light of the forces that traverse them and that confer upon them their actuality. For Deleuze, Foucault's contribution is this interest for forms, which is in no way incompatible with the preeminence of becoming: "that every form is precarious is evident since it depends upon relations of forces and on their mutations."[91] But this preeminence nevertheless require an epistemology of history and a diagnostic of forms: it is what permits the analysis of the archive, knowledges being doubled by powers on the new axis of the fold of subjectivation. Foucault's philosophy defines an anthropology in becoming.

> One needs to know with what other forces the forces within man enter into a relation, in a given historical formation, and what form is created as a result from this composite of forces.[92]

The relationship that Deleuze institutes between history and becoming is thus clarified. Dualism, he notes with respect to Foucault, can harden into difference of substance (Descartes) or of faculties (Kant); it can also be understood as a "provisional stage that is surpassed," as in Bergson or Spinoza. In Foucault, however, it is a matter of a "preparatory redistribution within a pluralism,"[93] a solution eminently valid as well for the relation between becoming and history. If "there is a history of assemblages (*agencements*), as there is a becoming of diagrams," if "the history of forms, the archive, is doubled by a becoming of forces, the diagram,"[94] history and becoming are not opposed to one another and are not superseded in a common form, but rather subsist in their heterogeneous but provisional distribution, which translates the co-existing modes of reality. They respond to the modal vibration of the actual and the virtual, composing the plural but immanent multiplicity of reality.

As the analysis of crisis showed, history, to the extent that it is a given and factual actualization, is the condition of determination of rupture, but in the sense of "negative conditions." History can nevertheless be taken as a determining condition, for every virtual is actualized, just as every actual is bordered by an intensive side or face. History is the condition of possibility of crisis, not the authority that legitimates it, explains it, or renders it necessary. Crisis escapes the historical, but requires history as its dimension of actualization.

194

History isn't experimentation, it's only the set of conditions, negative conditions almost, that make it possible to experience, experiment with, something beyond history. Without history, the experiments would remain indeterminate, divorced from any particular conditions, but the experimentation itself is philosophical rather than historical.[95]

Crisis thus ultimately proposes a theory of creation as well as a theory of history, and in this measure it is valid as method for a renewed history of philosophy. The principles of reading that Deleuze applies to Foucault flow from this method. A principle of exhaustivity: read everything, take everything, in a thought; a principle of historicity: be attentive to the crises and events, to the "hours of the thought"; to this is added the principle of experimentation: "Never interpret, experience, experiment."[96] According to the first principle, what counts in a work is the work as a whole (systematics). But according to the second, it is the passages by which a thought "will have been" (dynamics). According the third principle, thought's shakes and jolts, as well its very systematicity in the process of becoming, can only be grasped together from within the midst of its becoming. What Deleuze says of Foucault applies as much to the creativity of his own system as to the coexistence of becoming in history.

The thing is, his thought consists of tracing out and exploring one dimension after the other in a way that has its own creative necessity, but no one dimension is contained in another. It's like a broken line whose various orientations reflect unforeseeable, unexpected events (Foucault was always "surprising" his readers).[97]

NOTES

1. Gilles Deleuze, *Deux régimes de fous et autres textes: textes et entretiens: 1975–1995*, ed. David Lapoujade (Paris: Minuit, 2003), 262, translated as *Two Regimes of Madness: Texts and Interviews 1975–1995*, ed. David Lapoujade, trans. Ames Hodges and Michael Taormina (Cambridge, MA: Semiotext(e), 2006), 281.

2. Gilles Deleuze, "Raymond Roussel ou l'horreur du vide," *Arts*, 933 (23–29 October 1963), 4, reprinted in *L'île Déserte et Autres Textes: Textes et Entretiens, 1953–1974*, Paradoxe (Paris: Editions de Minuit, 2002), translated as *Desert Islands and Other Texts, 1953–1974*, trans. Michael Taormina (Cambridge, MA: Semiotext(e), 2004).

3. Deleuze, *L'île Déserte et Autres Textes*, 285; The Groupe d'information sur les prisons (Prison Information Group), which D. Defert and M. Foucault founded in 1970 and which Deleuze joined in 1971; see Deleuze, *Desert Islands and Other Texts, 1953–1974*, 204.

4. Deleuze, *Deux régimes de fous et autres textes*, 262; Deleuze, *Two Regimes of Madness*, 281.

5. Gilles Deleuze, *Foucault*, Collection "Critique" (Paris: Editions de Minuit, 1986), 105, translated as *Foucault*, trans. Seán Hand (Minneapolis: University of Minnesota Press, 1988), 98 (translation modified).

6. Gilles Deleuze, *Pourparlers, 1972–1990* (Paris: Editions de Minuit, 1990), 123, translated as *Negotiations, 1972–1990*, trans. Martin Joughin (New York: Columbia University Press, 1995), 89.

7. Deleuze, *Foucault*, 1986, 38; Deleuze, *Foucault*, 1988, 30.

8. Deleuze, *Deux régimes de fous et autres textes*, 226; Deleuze, *Two Regimes of Madness*, 241.

9. Deleuze, *Pourparlers, 1972–1990*, 130; Deleuze, *Negotiations, 1972–1990*, 94–5.

10. Deleuze, *Foucault*, 1986, 23; Deleuze, *Foucault*, 1988, 14.

11. Deleuze, *Pourparlers, 1972–1990*, 129; Deleuze, *Negotiations, 1972–1990*, 94.

12. Deleuze, *Pourparlers, 1972–1990*, 116; Deleuze, *Negotiations, 1972–1990*, 84. See also "I take someone's work as a whole; I don't think there's anything bad in a great body of work" with respect to Losey's films (72/50).

13. Gilles Deleuze, *La philosophie critique de Kant* (Paris: Presses Universitaires de France, 1998), translated as *Kant's Critical Philosophy: The Doctrine of the Faculties*, trans. Hugh Tomlinson and Barbara Habberjam (Minneapolis: University of Minnesota Press, 1984).

14. Gilles Deleuze, "Conclusions. Sur La Volonté de Puissance et L'éternel Retour," *Cahiers de Royaumont. Philosophie VII. Nietzsche* (1967), 275.

15. Gilles Deleuze and Michel Foucault, "Introduction Générale Aux Œuvres Complètes de Nietzsche," in *Dits et Écrits*, Quarto, vol. I (Paris: Gallimard, 2001), 590, 591.

16. Deleuze, *Deux régimes de fous et autres textes*, 323; Deleuze, *Two Regimes of Madness*, 346 (translation modified).

17. Deleuze, *Deux régimes de fous et autres textes*, 324; Deleuze, *Two Regimes of Madness*, 347.

18. There are numerous instances in which Deleuze identifies Foucault's current [actuel] and Nietzsche's untimely [intempestif]. For example: "What Foucault saw as the current or the new [l'actuel ou le nouveau] was what Nietzsche called the untimely, the 'non-current,' the becoming that splits away from history." Deleuze, *Deux régimes de fous et autres textes*, 323; Deleuze, *Two Regimes of Madness*, 346; Gilles Deleuze and Félix Guattari, *Qu'est-Ce Que La Philosophie?*, Collection "Critique" (Paris: Editions de Minuit, 1991), 107, translated as *What Is Philosophy?*, trans. Hugh Tomlinson and Graham Burchell (New York: Columbia University Press, 1994), 111–12.

19. Deleuze, *Deux régimes de fous et autres textes*, 322; Deleuze, *Two Regimes of Madness*, 345.

20. Deleuze, *Deux régimes de fous et autres textes*, 323; Deleuze, *Two Regimes of Madness*, 346 (translation modified).

21. In this respect, the letter of Kafka, Nietzsche's posthumous writings, and Foucault's occasional writings occupy the same function.

22. Daniel Defert and François Ewald are the editors of the *Dits et Écrits*, whose publication became unavoidable after Foucault's death thanks to the circulation of pirated copies of the unpublished works, among other difficulties. Nevertheless, the publication was complicated by Foucault's prescription in his will: "no posthumuous publications." Daniel Defert and François Ewald, "Présentation," in *Dits et Écrits*, Quarto, vol. I (Paris: Gallimard, 2001), 9.

23. Deleuze, *Deux régimes de fous et autres textes*, 324–5; Deleuze, *Two Regimes of Madness*, 348 (translation modified).

24. Deleuze borrows this term from the educator Fernand Deligny. I am grateful to Aline Wiane for help with this term (trans.).

25. Deleuze, *Pourparlers, 1972–1990*, 129; Deleuze, *Negotiations, 1972–1990*, 94. "Hours" (heures) designates in Deleuze haecceities, individuations insofar as they are in the process of becoming (40, 50/25–6, 33). The wind that blows upon thought in this way is the problematic in its insistance.

26. Pierre Macherey, "Foucault avec Deleuze. Le retour éternel du vrai," *Revue de synthèse* 108:2 (1987), 277–85 underlines this logical reframing. He rightly notes that the reading Deleuze applies to Foucault has "the objective of laying out Foucault's body of work in terms of the kind of ruptured succession found in an approach that works by successive displacements of its field of investigation, which in turn correspond to the reformulation of his problems. . . . The interpretation proposed by Deleuze tends to show that the movement charged with assuring the passage from one of these problematics to another proceeds through an internal logic of development: it is as though these displacements were interlocking, according to a necessity that belongs to a global signification. Foucault would thus have always been thinking the same thing (*penser la même chose*) to the very extent in which he did not always think about the same things (*penser aux même choses*)" (p. 278). Foucault's thought is placed in a "ruptured" approach that completes his immanent "*topos*" (topique) (p. 284) rather than truly changing it. Macherey, however, insists on the double merit of Deleuze: he restores to Foucault's production its "power and fecundity, or the power it holds to propel itself ceaselessly onto new terrains and to invent new forms of organization" (p. 285).

27. Gilles Deleuze, *Francis Bacon: logique de la sensation* (Paris: Éditions du Seuil, 2002), 35, translated as *Francis Bacon: The Logic of Sensation*, trans. Daniel Smith (Minneapolis: University of Minnesota Press, 2004), 30.

28. Deleuze, *Foucault*, 1986, 79; Deleuze, *Foucault*, 1988, 72.

29. Deleuze, *Francis Bacon*, 2002, 95; Deleuze, *Francis Bacon*, 2004, 102.

30. Deleuze, *Deux régimes de fous et autres textes*, 243; Deleuze, *Two Regimes of Madness*, 260.

31. Gilles Deleuze, *Différence et répétition* (Paris: Presses Universitaires de France, 1968), 223, translated as *Difference and Repetition*, trans. Paul Patton (New York: Columbia University Press, 1994), 172.

32. Gilles Deleuze, *Le Pli: Leibniz et Le Baroque* (Paris: Editions de Minuit, 1988), 88, translated as *The Fold: Leibniz and the Baroque*, trans. Tom Conley (Minneapolis: University of Minnesota Press, 1993), 65.

33. Michel Foucault, *L'usage des plaisirs* (Paris: Gallimard, 1984), 12, translated as *The Use of Pleasure*, trans. Robert Hurley (New York: Pantheon, 1985), 6.

34. Deleuze, *Différence et répétition*, 235; Deleuze, *Difference and Repetition*, 182.

35. Deleuze, *Deux régimes de fous et autres textes*, 227; Deleuze, *Two Regimes of Madness*, 242.

36. Deleuze and Guattari, *Qu'est-Ce Que La Philosophie?*, 108; Deleuze and Guattari, *What Is Philosophy?*, 113.

37. Deleuze, *Deux régimes de fous et autres textes*, 318; Deleuze, *Two Regimes of Madness*, 340.

38. Gilles Deleuze, *L'image-Mouvement* (Paris: Editions de Minuit, 1983), 277, translated as *Cinema 1. The Movement-Image*, trans. Hugh Tomlinson and Barbara Habberjam (Minneapolis: University of Minnesota, 1986), 197; Gilles Deleuze, *L'image-Temps* (Paris: Editions de Minuit, 1985), translated as *Cinema 2. The Time-Image*, trans. Hugh Tomlinson (London: Continuum, 2009).

39. Deleuze, *Le Pli*, 92; Deleuze, *The Fold*, 68.

40. Deleuze, *Deux régimes de fous et autres textes*, 316; Deleuze, *Two Regimes of Madness*, 338. See also Deleuze and Guattari, *Qu'est-Ce Que La Philosophie?*, 191; Deleuze and Guattari, *What Is Philosophy?*, 203.

41. Deleuze, *Pourparlers, 1972–1990*, 129; Deleuze, *Negotiations, 1972–1990*, 94.

42. Deleuze, *Pourparlers, 1972–1990*, 126; Deleuze, *Negotiations, 1972–1990*, 91–2.

43. Deleuze, *Deux régimes de fous et autres textes*, 226; Deleuze, *Two Regimes of Madness*, 241.

44. Deleuze, *Foucault*, 1986, 93; Deleuze, *Foucault*, 1988, 87.

45. Deleuze, *Deux régimes de fous et autres textes*, 226; Deleuze, *Two Regimes of Madness*, 241.

46. Deleuze, *Foucault*, 1986, 56; Deleuze, *Foucault*, 1988, 49.

47. Deleuze, *Foucault*, 1986, 58; Deleuze, *Foucault*, 1988, 51.

48. Deleuze, *Foucault*, 1986, 59; Deleuze, *Foucault*, 1988, 52.

49. Deleuze, *Deux régimes de fous et autres textes*, 227; Deleuze, *Two Regimes of Madness*, 242.

50. Deleuze, *Deux régimes de fous et autres textes*, 228–9; Deleuze, *Two Regimes of Madness*, 244–5.

51. Deleuze, *Foucault*, 1986, 66; Deleuze, *Foucault*, 1988, 59.

52. Deleuze, *Foucault*, 1986, 59; Deleuze, *Foucault*, 1988, 52.

53. Deleuze, *Pourparlers, 1972–1990*, 120; Deleuze, *Negotiations, 1972–1990*, 87 (translation modified.

54. Deleuze, *Deux régimes de fous et autres textes*, 230; Deleuze, *Two Regimes of Madness*, 245.

55. Deleuze, *Deux régimes de fous et autres textes*, 229; Deleuze, *Two Regimes of Madness*, 244.

56. Deleuze, *Deux régimes de fous et autres textes*, 229; Deleuze, *Two Regimes of Madness*, 244.

57. Deleuze, *Foucault*, 1986, 56; Deleuze, *Foucault*, 1988, 48–9.

58. Deleuze, *Deux régimes de fous et autres textes*, 232; Deleuze, *Two Regimes of Madness*, 248.

59. Deleuze, *Deux régimes de fous et autres textes*, 232; Deleuze, *Two Regimes of Madness*, 248.

60. Deleuze, *Foucault*, 1986, 38; Deleuze, *Foucault*, 1988, 31.

61. Deleuze, *Foucault*, 1986, 39; Deleuze, *Foucault*, 1988, 32.

62. Deleuze, *Foucault*, 1986, 40; Deleuze, *Foucault*, 1988, 33 (translation modified: the current translation does not preserve the word "segment," which has an important value in Deleuze's thought).

63. Deleuze, *Foucault*, 1986, 41; Deleuze, *Foucault*, 1988, 33.

64. Deleuze, *Deux régimes de fous et autres textes*, 232–3; Deleuze, *Two Regimes of Madness*, 248–9.

65. Deleuze, *Deux régimes de fous et autres textes*, 232; Deleuze, *Two Regimes of Madness*, 248.

66. Deleuze, *Deux régimes de fous et autres textes*, 233; Deleuze, *Two Regimes of Madness*, 249.

67. Deleuze, *Foucault*, 1986, 80; Deleuze, *Foucault*, 1988, 73.

68. Deleuze, *Foucault*, 1986, 79; Ibid. 72 quoting from Michel Foucault, *Surveiller et punir: naissance de la prison* (Paris: Gallimard, 1975), 207, 229, translated as *Discipline and Punish: The Birth of the Prison*, trans. Alan Sheridan (New York: Vintage Books, 1995), 205, 228.

69. Deleuze, *Foucault*, 1986, 79; Deleuze, *Foucault*, 1988, 72.

70. Deleuze, *Foucault*, 1986, 80; Deleuze, *Foucault*, 1988, 73.

71. Deleuze, *Foucault*, 1986, 80; Deleuze, *Foucault*, 1988, 73.

72. Deleuze, *Foucault*, 1986, 90; Deleuze, *Foucault*, 1988, 84.

73. Deleuze, *Foucault*, 1986, 91; Deleuze, *Foucault*, 1988, 85.

74. Deleuze, *Foucault*, 1986, 62; Deleuze, *Foucault*, 1988, 55.

75. Deleuze, *Foucault*, 1986, 65; Deleuze, *Foucault*, 1988, 58.

76. Deleuze, *Foucault*, 1986, 65, 83; Deleuze, *Foucault*, 1988, 58, 76.

77. Deleuze, *Foucault*, 1988, 90; Ibid. 84.

78. Deleuze, *Foucault*, 1986, 80; Deleuze, *Foucault*, 1988, 73.

79. Deleuze, *Foucault*, 1986, 81; Deleuze, *Foucault*, 1988, 74 (translation modified).

80. Deleuze, *Foucault*, 1986, 89; Deleuze, *Foucault*, 1988, 83.

81. Deleuze, *Foucault*, 1986, 89; Deleuze, *Foucault*, 1988, 82.

82. Deleuze, *Foucault*, 1986, 88–9; Deleuze, *Foucault*, 1988, 82.

83. Deleuze, *Foucault*, 1986, 88; Deleuze, *Foucault*, 1988, 82.

84. Deleuze, *Foucault*, 1986, 88; Deleuze, *Foucault*, 1988, 82 (translation modified – the translator has erroneously put "schematicism" rather than "schematism").

85. Deleuze, *Foucault*, 1986, 88; Deleuze, *Foucault*, 1988, 82 (translation modified).

86. Deleuze, *Foucault*, 1986, 89; Deleuze, *Foucault*, 1988, 83.

87. Deleuze, *Foucault*, 1986, 91; Deleuze, *Foucault*, 1988, 85.

88. Deleuze, *Deux régimes de fous et autres textes*, 238; Deleuze, *Two Regimes of Madness*, 254–5.

89. Deleuze, *Foucault*, 1986; Ibid. 93; Deleuze, *Foucault*, 1988, 88.

90. Deleuze, *Foucault*, 1986, 131; Deleuze, *Foucault*, 1988, 124.

91. Deleuze, *Foucault*, 1986, 138; Deleuze, *Foucault*, 1988, 130.

92. Deleuze, *Foucault*, 1986, 131; Deleuze, *Foucault*, 1988, 124.

93. Deleuze, *Foucault*, 1986, 89; Deleuze, *Foucault*, 1988, 83.

94. Deleuze, *Foucault*, 1986, 49, 51; Deleuze, *Foucault*, 1988, 41, 43.

95. Deleuze, *Pourparlers, 1972–1990*, 144; Deleuze, *Negotiations, 1972–1990*, 106.

96. Deleuze, *Pourparlers, 1972–1990*, 120; Deleuze, *Negotiations, 1972–1990*, 87 (the translator has preserved here the double sense of the French "expérimentez"); cf. Gilles Deleuze and Félix Guattari, *Mille plateaux* (Paris: Éditions de minuit, 1980), translated as *A Thousand Plateaus: Capitalism and Schizophrenia*, trans. Brian Massumi (Minneapolis: University of Minnesota Press, 1987).

97. Deleuze, *Pourparlers, 1972–1990*, 126; Deleuze, *Negotiations, 1972–1990*, 91–2.

CHAPTER 11

Foucault and the "Image Of Thought": Archaeology, Genealogy, and the Impetus of Transcendental Empiricism[1]

KEVIN THOMPSON

In what follows I want to examine Foucault's critical engagement, his *Auseinandersetzung*, with Deleuze's transcendental empiricism.[2] This, of course, is a wide-ranging, complex, multifaceted, and, in many ways, diffuse topic as the encounter lasted over many years and went through significant permutations and shifts in response to developments in the thought and the lives of each of its participants. Accordingly, I want to explore here just one element of this engagement: the decisive role played by Deleuze's critique of the traditional representationalist image of thought and his proposal for a discordant accord of thinking – one that would, as he famously put it, take its bearings from a "fundamental encounter" – in the creation of Foucault's genealogical method.

It is well known that, throughout his early works, Foucault consistently recognized that discursive formations, the objects of archaeological investigation, are nothing other than series of events possessing a variable, though tenuously stable, regularity, that they are a complex of positions (for objects, subjects, and concepts) and sequences (strategies) and nothing more. But he was also clear that because the archaeological method unearths the transcendental historical conditions that govern the positions and strategies within a discursive formation, it was beyond its purview to account for exactly how shifts and ruptures from one epistémè to another were produced, what Foucault called at the time the problem of "epistemological causality" (DE II, 12).

Now my contention is that it was Foucault's engagement during the period from 1970 to 1971 with Deleuze's transcendental empiricism, and especially as this was elaborated in *Différence et répétition*, that enabled him to solve the dilemma of epistemological causality and that the invention of the genealogical method, as a supplement to archaeology, was nothing less than its result.[3] The evidence for this claim lies, I argue, in the first lecture course that Foucault delivered at the Collége de France, from December 1970 through March 1971, a course he entitled, "La volonté de savoir." In particular, as I shall show, it lies in this course's account of the role of "ordeal (*épreuve*)"[4] and that of practices of oath-taking in the genesis of the basic historical forms of the will to know.

The essay is divided into three parts. The first outlines the conceptual space within which the method of archaeological investigation and the problem of "epistemological causality" emerged within Foucault's work. The second turns to the 1971 lecture course and reconstructs its analysis of the relationship between distinct forms of knowledge and their basis in different types of jurisprudence as these develop in Ancient Greece. The essay concludes by arguing that this analysis marks a critical appropriation of Deleuze's concept of the emergence of thought from the shock of the sensible and with it the development of the concept of "power-knowledge" and, thus, the proper invention of Foucault's distinctive method of genealogical investigation.

<h2 style="text-align:center">I</h2>

In order to understand the significance of the critical encounter between Foucault and Deleuze, we must begin by reconstructing some elements of the conceptual space (*Denkraum*) within which Foucault's distinctive method of historical inquiry emerged.

This space was formed by a constellation of thought defined by, among other moments, the unique French tradition of epistemology, a tradition that takes the history of the formal, natural, and social sciences to be a laboratory for the formation and testing of model of knowledge. In particular, this constellation was defined by Jean Cavaillès's – arguably, the source, along with his teacher, Léon Brunschvicg, of this tradition – enigmatic thesis that a truly comprehensive theory of the distinctive form of historicity endemic to scientific rationality, what he famously termed "the continual revision of contents by elaboration (*approfondissement*) and erasure (*rature*)" (SLTS, 78/OC, 560)[5], had to be rooted in a "philosophy of the concept" where discontinuity arises, as he put it, from "the necessity of a dialectic" (SLTS, 78/OC, 560). Foucault can be said to have developed his own unique historical method by thinking the problem of historical discontinuity or rupture within the parameters laid down by, and by that I mean, *with and against*, Cavaillès's dialectic.[6] But what exactly does this really mean?

Cavaillès argued that the history of science is a history of revolution and innovation. One science surpasses another not simply by realizing the axioms of a previous theory, but by posing fundamentally new insights and new concepts that overturn what had preceded them and that move in new, unpredictable directions. Now, what drives this historical process, according to Cavaillès, that is, the necessity paradoxically at work in such a movement, is the necessary failure of any axiomatic system to be able to reach closure, to attain saturation.

Appropriating Gödel's second incompleteness theorem as a model for the historicity of scientific rationality, Cavaillès holds that every theory is inherently fractured – it contains a set of necessarily unresolvable, open problems – and it is thereby necessarily rendered open to its own evolution. It is this inherent structural incompleteness of any axiomatic system that compels each and every theory, from within itself, to surpass itself; one theory breaking out of the prior structure, incorporating its contents, and marking its superiority precisely by means of its discontinuity, its rupture, with the preceding theory. In sum, then, a "dialectic of concepts" renders the historicity of science, "the continual revision of contents by elaboration (*approfondissement*) and erasure (*rature*)", intelligible by uncovering the generative necessity of incompleteness that is immanent in the very nature of scientific theory itself.

Now, for all its promise, Cavaillès's program nonetheless left behind profound problems that came to shape its subsequent legacy and defined the conceptual space it opened. For our purposes here I want to consider just two of these issues, both having to do with the very nature of the historical dialectic that Cavaillès proposed.

The first problem concerns its *content*. The dialectic of the concept articulates historical discontinuities in science in terms of one theory surpassing another by virtue of the subsequent theory incorporating the undecidable propositions, the open problems, in the preceding theory. The dialectic of surpassing preserves a fundamental line of continuity in the substance of such a development. One theory follows upon another by incorporating what exceeded the axiomatic confines of its predecessor's conceptual structure. But this model fails to capture the kind of profound breaks that often occur between theories.

The second problem has to do with the *form* of the historicity of science. Cavaillès's incorporative model clearly rejects any finality of teleological necessity and, in doing so, it opens the movement of historical transformation to a degree of contingency. But by conceiving a theory's need to surpass itself as arising from its own inherent structural incompleteness, and thus as a feature endemic to any theoretical configuration, the model still retains the form of necessity and this renders it incapable of taking sufficient account of the profound arbitrariness and caprice to which the historical record so often testifies.

With the outlines of these questions now in place, I want to turn to a discussion of Foucault's early methodology.

Foucault's archaeological method, building on the work of others – principal among them, of course, Georges Canguilhem – follows Cavaillès in moving from the domain of formal logic, as the normative methodology of science, to the actual practices of knowledge creation, from method to theoretical inquiry itself. This is clearly signaled by archaeology's commitment to the field of positivity,[7] that is, to knowledge, as Foucault puts it, as the "tangled web (*l'écheveau*)" of statements (*énoncés*) (AS, 165). From this commitment came the insight that statements serve specific social roles, what Foucault called their "enunciative function": they define, delimit, and construct the objects *about which* they speak; they signal the subject positions *from which* they are posited; they indicate the broader coexistent network of statements *in which* they operate; and, finally, they betray the institutional settings *by which* they are sustained (cf. AS, Part III, Chapter 2). To describe statements in their positivity is thus to describe their inscription within a specific "discursive formation": a coherent unity defined not by the existent state of affairs in which these statements happen to be caught up, but by the set of rules governing what can count as an object, a subject, a concept, and even a strategy for a network of statements. It is therefore by fulfilling these conditions, Foucault argues, that an ensemble of statements is able to emerge and endure as a cohesive regularity, a body of knowledge comprised of material truth claims, rather than as a mere collection of signs.

Archaeology can, then, to this extent at least, properly be seen as an important elaboration of the kind of immanent analysis of knowledge that Cavaillès's philosophy of the concept had already initiated and that the tradition of historical epistemology in general had sought to develop. But it is also precisely here that Foucault introduces what is clearly a decisive innovation in this tradition: historical discontinuity is not a matter, he contends, of a change simply in the *content* of knowledge; the rupture or break between one system and another is not a matter of a transformation in what is being asserted. The break takes place, rather, on the plane of the *conditions* for the formation of discursive regularity. That is, the historicality of knowledge is endemic to the rules to which a statement must adhere to count as a statement, rather than to the objects about which they make claims.[8] These rules are neither a mere empirical pattern, nor the transcendental logic of constitutive subjectivity; rather, they comprise the anonymous transcendental field, what Foucault famously called the "historical a priori", that conditions what is known and said in a historical epoch (cf. AS, Part III, Chapter 5).

Fidelity to knowledge claims in their positivity, then, entails nothing less than a commitment to their dispersion, just as Cavaillès taught. The history of science is indeed "the continual revision of contents." But such revision is far more radical than any "elaboration (*approfondissement*) and erasure (*rature*)" (SLTS, 78/OC, 560) of one system surpassing another by incorporating its precursor's undecidable propositions could permit. The historical revolutions that define the development of scientific rationality are historical mutations at the level of the a priori conditions under which discursive bodies of knowledge are forged. To remain faithful to the positivity of knowledge thus means that one science or practice cannot be said simply to elaborate and erase the other. Historical discontinuity is a rupture in the very structure of order itself.

Archaeology is thus borne out of a confrontation with the nature of the *content* of Cavaillès's dialectic and a profound embrace of a type of historical inquiry that seeks to remain more faithful to knowledge in all its positivity, a type of inquiry that grasps the very being of knowledge in the unearthing of the shifting historico-transcendental plane that structures it.

And yet, despite the important advances of archaeology, the method still leaves open the other question that it inherits from Cavaillès and that defines the conceptual space within which it operates: the problem of the *form* of discontinuity. Recall that although Cavaillès's incorporative model of historicity, rooted in his appropriation of Gödel's second incompleteness theorem, clearly rejects any kind of simple teleological necessity, it nonetheless still affirms that each and every scientific theory is compelled to surpass itself by virtue of its necessary structural incompleteness. Foucault, along with others working in this same tradition, clearly saw that this model of historical change fundamentally fails to take account of the profound arbitrariness and caprice – in a word, the aleatoriness – of the historical record. But this insight did not, in and of itself, indicate a way out. If archaeology shows that historical change is a matter of wholly arbitrary shifts in the a priori structures of knowledge, that this is where the historicity of science resides, then this still leaves open the question of how a new set of rules of order, a new historical a priori, can emerge? That is to say, if archaeology is a resolutely descriptive discipline, descriptive of historical transformation, it leaves open the question of historical causation: why the reigning historical a priori, the epistémè or archive, of one age gives way to another? This is what Foucault called the problem of "causality in the order of knowledge (*savoir*)" or "epistemological causality" (DE II, 12) and he clearly acknowledged it as an open question left unanswered, even unanswerable, within the methodological strictures of archaeological inquiry. Archaeology, working within the space of Cavaillès' dialectic, thus reformulates the question of the form of discontinuity, but for all that, it still leaves the issue intact.

Now, given this context – namely Foucault's struggle with the problem of epistemological causality within the heritage of the tradition of historical epistemology – I would like to show why Deleuze's transcendental empiricism proved to be, for Foucault, an, perhaps even the, essential catalyst that enabled him to think the aleatoriness of historical change and thus provided him a way beyond the confines of the conceptual space of Cavaillès's dialectic.

II

Two items amongst Foucault's publications in 1970–1 amply testify to the intense engagement with Deleuze's thought that he was pursuing during this pivotal period: the first, the famous review of *Logique du sens* [1969] and *Différence et répétition* [1969], "Theatrum philosophicum"⁹, the second, "L'ordre du discours",

Foucault's inaugural lecture at the Collège de France. Though the latter does not mention Deleuze explicitly, to anyone attentive to the announcement of its central philosophical ambition – that to think the event of discourse demands a "materialism of the incorporeal" (OD, 60), which is a clear reference to the concept of "incorporeal materiality" (DE II, 79) that Foucault had earlier, in the review, invented to denote, albeit hesitantly, Deleuze's liminal philosophy of the phantasm – it clearly indicates that the setting for the investigations he outlines is that of transcendental empiricism.

But as suggestive as these references and allusions may be, they do not, in the end, allow us to get at the core of the engagement of Foucault with Deleuze's thought. More precisely, they fail to indicate the profound role played by the image of thought in this encounter and, as such, in the actual creation of the genealogical method, for although Foucault employs the term 'genealogy' in the inaugural lecture and even assigns it quite specific tasks having to do with the problem of the strange aleatoriness of epistemological causation (what he called there, the "dispersed, discontinuous, and regular" constitution of discursive formations), he did not as yet possess the core methodological concept that defines the distinctive concern of genealogy: power-knowledge.[10] For this, we must turn to the 1970–1 lecture course.

In its opening session, held just a week after the inaugural lecture, Foucault tells us that the fundamental aim of the lecture course is to develop a "morphology of the will to know" (LVS, 3). Now, though Deleuze's work is not treated explicitly in any of the lectures, it is clear that the account of the two forms of the "will to know" that organizes the entire course – the so-called natural desire for knowledge, which Foucault associates principally with Aristotle, and the violent struggle of instinct and desire that invents knowledge, as a surface effect, for its own ends, which Foucault identifies with Nietzsche – is nothing other than an *historicized* version of the representational and differential models of thought around which *Différence et répétition* pivots. On Foucault's reading, the Aristotelian will to know is predicated on a fundamental harmony between natural instinct, desire, and truth such that the attainment of an accord between a statement and the state of affairs that it seeks to depict, apophantic (propositional) truth, results in a feeling of deep and profound satisfaction. While the Nietzschean, or as Foucault also terms it here, the Sophistic form, treats knowledge itself as secondary to the conflict for domination and control between instincts, interests, desires, and fears. Knowledge is thus here the creation of a weapon in service to a more fundamental struggle. Hence, rather than an accord between desire and knowledge, the Nietzschean or Sophistic form posits ongoing war with momentary, ever fragile truces.

Now the core of the lecture course is dedicated to demonstrating that the supposedly natural desire to pursue the satisfaction unique to knowledge (the Aristotelian form) is not, in fact, natural at all, that is to say, that it is not original, but rather that it emerged by virtue of a subtle, but nonetheless, profound trans-formation from the struggle of the instincts (the Nietzschean form). The historical deduction proceeds in two steps: (1) the first establishes that knowledge claims, in general, are rooted in juridical discourse and its associated practices, the techniques for the determination of guilt and innocence (Lecture V: 27 January 1971); (2) the second shows that it was by way of the transformation of these juridical prac-tices that the Aristotelian form was invented out of the Nietzschean form (Lectures VI–VII: 3–10 February 1971).

In the first step, Foucault shows that, in the Archaic Age in Greece (750–500 BCE), decisions about guilt or innocence were not a matter of detached, impartial judgment, but rather the outcome of a violent battle or contest between two adver-saries and their supporters, e.g., Menelaus and Antilochus or Achilles and Hector, a struggle Foucault terms "the ordeal of truth (*l'épreuve de la vérité*)" (LVS, 73). Truth here is thus a force confronted and found *in* the struggle, not outside it or as its reso-lution. By the Classical Age (500–336 BCE) and certainly by the Hellenistic Period (336–146 BCE), rules for establishing truth claims in such disputes had become set-tled and testimony and evidence were taken to be the essential determinants of the case. With this emerged the central formative idea that truth is to be decided based solely upon a complete review of relevant testimony and evidence by those whose sole role in the process is as "bearers (*porteurs*)" or "proclaimers (*énonciateurs*)" of truth (LVS, 70), judges. Foucault concludes that the forms of knowledge that he has isolated, namely the harmonious and discordant models of the will to know, are intertwined with the roles that truth claims play in pre-law and law-governed juris-prudence and that the historical record indicates that the former (the Aristotelian model) arose out of the latter (the Nietzschean model).

Foucault takes this last claim as the point of departure for the second step of his historical analysis and turns to a examination of the techniques involved. His focus is the shifting nature of oaths in juridical practice during these periods. Specifically, he traces the shift from the discordant model to the harmonious model of jurispru-dence and their attendant forms of the will to know to the historical transformation registered in the transition from juridical oaths conceived in terms of δικάζειν (to judge, to ordain, to decide) in the Homeric Age to that of κρίνειν (to decide, to judge) in the Classical Period. δικάζειν, he argues, refers to the oath or pledge that each adversary takes to the battle itself before they enter into it, that is, into the ordeal that they have entrusted to decide their dispute, while κρίνειν denotes the oath or pledge taken by a disinterested party, the judge, whose verdict alone is to decide the outcome of the dispute in question (LVS, 84–94).

Now each of these practices is clearly a specific technique of power whereby the one taking the pledge binds or commits themselves to abide by something other than themselves, whether this be, as in the former, each of the disputant's commit-ment to abide by the results of the battle, their pledge to the battle itself, or, as in the latter, the judge's dedication to the impartiality of the law. And the transformation from one to the other signals a shift, according to Foucault, from knowledge as risk and gamble, even experience though Foucault does not employ the term in this way here,[11] to knowledge derived from careful, detached consideration and deliberation on facts and witnesses. As such, it marks the invention of the Aristotelian will to know out of the prior Nietzschean (Sophistic) form.

III

Now, at this point, we rightly ask: how does this perhaps otherwise highly interesting analysis tell us anything at all about the way in which transcendental empiricism enabled Foucault to address the defining problem of epistemological causality, the problem of the form of historical discontinuity, and what does it have to say about the way in which this led him to create his distinctive genealogical method?

Let me briefly discuss each of these concerns in turn. As I noted above, I believe that Foucault's framing of the lecture course around the two forms of the will to know is an appropriation of Deleuze's distinction between the representationalist (dogmatic) and differential (critical) images of thought. Crucial to this distinction, for Deleuze, is the twofold claim – claims which together constitute the core epistemological doctrines of transcendental empiricism – that (1) the genuinely critical form of thought arises out of and thinks through the shock of the sensible, what Deleuze calls a "fundamental *encounter* (rencrontre *fondamentale*)" (DR, 182), and (2) that the object of this encounter is, as he puts it, "not a quality but a sign" (DR, 182), that is to say, what genuinely critical thought ultimately apprehends, what it grasps, is not some property (quality) of an intuitable object, but rather, the very being of the sensible itself, the virtual differentiation (ideal synthesis)/intensive differenciation (asymmetrical synthesis), whereby all that is, is constituted as "centers of envelopment" (DR, 329 and 359–360).

Now, with respect to the first claim (the relationship of encounter and thought), Foucault's decisive move is to shift the distinction between the images of thought from the domain of abstract systematics, as they are portrayed in *Différence et répétition*, to the dense and unsettling terrain of history. Foucault was thus able to show that the "encounter" that calls forth the discordant accord of thought, the Nietzschean will to know, was, at its inception, a concrete struggle, an ordeal, by virtue of which the claim(s) of one adversary are vindicated over against those of another: as such, *le rencontre est l'épreuve*. And, furthermore, that the transformation that this historical setting undergoes, marked in the shift from the Homeric δικάζειν to the Classical κρίνειν, is the genesis of the harmonious (dogmatic) form of knowledge. This historicized version of transcendental empiricism thus enabled Foucault to conceive of a profoundly *non-reductive* relationship between knowledge and social (in this case, juridical) practices and the wholly capricious, aleatory nature of the historical mutation of these kinds of practices, here, from δικάζειν to κρίνειν, provided him the conceptual model to think "causation in the order of knowledge" beyond the confines of immanent necessitation. Oath-taking in the Homeric Age did not, due to its own structural incompleteness, need to surpass itself and take on a different configuration in the Classical Age. The shift was nothing other than a secondary effect of a random play of relations, a system of regularity thrown off by this game, not its intended result. Transcendental empiricism showed Foucault the necessity of thinking the encounter of thought and practice, the shock of the sensible, and thus, in turn, enabled him to conceive the transformation of discursive formations and the transcendental-historical rules that govern them in terms of the contingency and randomness of this domain. The entanglement of power and knowledge therefore opened the pathway to genealogical analysis. Transcendental empiricism thus allowed Foucault to see epistemological historical causation, the change from one historical a priori to another, as nothing more than the result of an array of divergent series falling into and out of configurations.

Following from this insight, and turning now to the second claim (the object of the encounter), the historicized version of transcendental empiricism enabled Foucault to see, as we have already suggested, that the proper object of historical investigation was not simply knowledge or discourse, but the intertwinement of these with the specific techniques that sanction and enforce them, that is to say, practices of power. The real creation of genealogy as a distinctive method of historical inquiry occurs then precisely at this point. But note that, contrary to many standard readings, the genealogical method is not engendered by the purported inability to render the notion of the historical a priori anything more than an empirical pattern, but rather by the struggle to conceive historical transformation – transformation of the very epochal rules of discursive formations themselves – beyond the confines of Cavaillès' paradigm.[12] Genealogy is therefore not the abandonment of the transcendental for the terrain of the empirical. What Foucault's analyses of the historical genesis of the discordant and harmonious forms of the will to know showed him was that what is to be grasped in the murk and mire of history is not simply empirical facts and patterns, but that these are signs/symptoms that indicate, literally, point to, the shifting sets of rules that govern the space of possibility for what can be said, what can be known, what can be felt, and what can be done: the matrix of power-knowledge. Genealogy, for Foucault, is thus, as Deleuze had said in *Nietzsche et la philosophie* (1962), a kind of "symptomatology and a semeiology": it takes the chance events of the historical record and apprehends in them the transcendental historical structures that envelop them. Genealogy is thus what transcendental empiricism necessarily becomes when the encounter proves to be irremediably historical.

In sum, then, I have argued that Foucault's critical engagement with transcendental empiricism was the catalyst, the impetus, that enabled him to solve the dilemma of epistemological causality and that the invention of the genealogical method, as a supplement to archaeology, was nothing less than its result. But our study of this moment in Foucault's intellectual itinerary allows us to go one step further: it allows us to see that one of the points of convergence in this encounter is a question that lurks behind the work of each figure during this formative period: *Was heißt Denken?* What is it that we call thinking? What has it historically meant to think? What is it to think rightly, critically? and What calls us, commands us even, to think?[13]

And yet, that what compels us to think for Deleuze is the virtual/intensive being of the sensible, while, for Foucault, it is the historical a priori also suggests where they might be said to diverge: the ineluctable historicity of the transcendental.

NOTES

1. I want to thank Kieran Aarons for his comments on an earlier version of this essay.
2. All references to Foucault's works are included in the text according to the following scheme of abbreviation:

   AS   *L'archéologie du savoir* (Paris: Gallimard, 1969)

   OD   *L'ordre du discours* (Paris: Gallimard, 1971)

   DE   *Dits et écrits. 1954–1988*, 4 vols. (Paris: Gallimard, 1994)

   LVS   *Leçons sur la volonté de savoir. Cours au Collège de France, 1970–1971, suivi de Le Savoir d'Œdipe* (Paris: Gallimard/Seuil, 2011)

   All references to Deleuze's works are included in the text according to the following scheme of abbreviation:

   DR   *Différence et répétition* (Paris: Presses Universitaires de France, 1968)

   All references to Cavaillès's works are included in the text according to the following scheme of abbreviation:

   SLTS   *Sur la logique et la théorie de la science* (Paris: Presses Universitaires de France, 1947)

   OC   *Œuvres complètes de philosophie des sciences* (Paris: Hermann, 1994)

3. In pursuing this line of inquiry, I am seeking to develop Daniel Defert's comments about the significance of Deleuze's thought, and specifically that set forth in *Différence et répétition*, for Foucault during this period and in this lecture course, in particular. For Defert's account, see his "Situation du cours" (LVS, 266–75).
4. The term could also be translated as "trial" or "test." I have chosen "ordeal" in order to preserve the sense of an undertaking, a journey even, that is endured, an exploration by which one's abilities are tested and measured.
5. Foucault quotes this passage in his Introduction to the 1978 English translation of Canguilhem's *The Normal and the Pathological* attributing it to Cavaillès, but without specifying an exact reference. See "Introduction par Michel Foucault" (DE III, 435); and the revised version of this text that Foucault submitted for publication in 1984, "La vie: l'expérience et la science" (DE IV, 770).

209

6. I have sought to establish the importance of Cavaillès's work for Foucault in a previous study, "Historicity and Transcendentality: Foucault, Cavaillès, and the Phenomenology of the Concept," *History and Theory* 47 (2008), 1–18.

   For other accounts that seek to examine the relationship between Foucault and Cavaillès, see Stephen Watson, "'Between Tradition and Oblivion': Foucault, the Complications of Form, the Literatures of Reason, and the Esthetics of Existence," in *The Cambridge Companion to Foucault*, ed. Gary Gutting, 1st ed. (Cambridge: Cambridge University Press, 1994), 262–85; David Hyder, "Foucault, Cavaillès, and Husserl on the Historical Epistemology of the Sciences," *Perspectives on Science* 11 (2003), 107–29, reprinted in *Science and the Life-World: Essays on Husserl's Crisis of European Sciences*, ed. David. Hyder and Hans-Jörg Rheinberger (Stanford: Stanford University Press, 2010), 177–98; David Webb, "Cavaillès and the historical *a priori* in Foucault," in Simon Duffy (ed.), *Virtual Mathematics: The Logic of Difference* (Manchester: Clinamen Press, 2006), 100–17; Pierre Cassou-Noguès and Pascale Gillot, "Introduction," and Jean-Michel Salanskis, "Lex deux triades de Canguilhem-Foucault," in Pierre Cassou-Noguès and Pascale Gillot (eds.), *Le concept, le sujet et la science. Cavaillès, Canguilhem, Foucault* (Paris: Vrin, 2009), 7–20 and 237–70; and, finally, David Webb, *Foucault's Archaeology: Science and Transformation* (Edinburgh: Edinburgh University Press, 2012), chapter one.

7. I leave aside here a discussion of the relationship between the "threshold of positivity" and those of "epistemologization," "scienticity," and "formalization" by which Foucault distinguishes various types of discursive formations, a discussion that is essential for comparing the very different kinds of scientific enterprises that Cavaillès and Foucault sought to study (cf. AS, Part IV, Chap 6, Section [d]).

8. The discontinuity between the medical practices of taxonomy in the classical age and clinical therapy in the modern or between the sciences of natural history in the classical period and biology in the modern, to take but two of Foucault's well-known examples, are not results of the varied content of these disciplines, as important as that is. Rather, a tectonic shift from one set of rules for what can count as proper objects, subjects, concepts, and strategies for medical treatment and scientific inquiry occurs here, and this is nothing less than an historical mutation in the categorial structure that governs these practices and the sciences themselves.

9. The review subtly interweaves the problematics and themes of both of Deleuze's early systematic works, demonstrating a profound grasp of just what is at stake in such an enterprise (the danger/promise of acategorical thought), and places the question of the image of thought – the struggle to think free from the tyranny of good will, the obligation to think in common with others, the domination of a certain form of pedagogy, and the exclusion of stupidity (*bêtise*) – at the very center of Deleuze's project of forging a non-representationalist philosophy of difference.

10. More specifically, it is in the inaugural lecture that Foucault, for the first time, sketches a distinctly "genealogical" dimension of his research whose "felicitous positivism" would supplement and elaborate the "applied casualness" of the archaeological or, as he calls it here, its "critical" dimension: "Critique analyzes the processes of rarefaction, but also the regrouping and unification of discourses; genealogy studies their formation, at once,

dispersed, discontinuous, and regular" (OD, 67). In this regard, it is important to recall that Foucault, again in the earlier review, and precisely in terms of his account of the image of thought, had already declared that Deleuze's analysis exhibited the "patience of a Nietzschean genealogist" (DE II, 87).

11. *L'expérience*, cognate here with the German term *Erfahrung*, in the sense of being "experienced" at something; the idea of wisdom or learning gained through exploration, experimentation, or a journey of discovery.

12. For the conventional reading, see Hubert L. Dreyfus and Paul Rabinow, *Michel Foucault: Beyond Structuralism and Hermeneutics*, 2nd ed. (Chicago: University of Chicago Press, 1983) and, more recently, Béatrice Han, *Foucault's Critical Project: Between the Transcendental and the Historical* (Stanford: Stanford University Press, 2002).

13. Martin Heidegger, *Was heisst Denken?* (Tübingen: Max Niemeyer, 1954), 79–80.

CHAPTER 12

The Regularities of the Statement: Deleuze on Foucault's Archaeology of Knowledge

MARY BETH MADER

1. INTRODUCTORY REMARKS ON THE *HISTORICAL FORMATIONS* LECTURE COURSE

Gilles Deleuze wrote over twenty-five books, but only one devoted to a philosopher contemporary to him. This was his 1985 work, *Foucault* (Paris: Les Éditions de Minuit), a collection of six separate pieces on the work of Michel Foucault (1926–84).[1] Although scarcely more than 130 pages long, the slim volume was immediately hailed as an indisputable reference for all interested in Foucault's thought. Roger-Pol Droit held in *Le Monde*, "Whether it be to support or oppose him, it will no longer be possible to read Foucault without referring to [Deleuze's book.]"[2] Together, the compiled studies address nearly the whole sweep of Foucault's lifetime of writings, setting out a comprehensive framework for understanding all of the well-known, major themes of Foucault's philosophical contributions: knowledge, power, subjectivity, historical construction, modernity, penality, and sexuality.

But the book also plainly required a deep grasp of Foucault's corpus, and even to specialist readers was deemed "dense and difficult, at times very difficult."[3] The redoubtable nature of this important book makes supplementary material illuminating it precious. Fortunately, in addition to this published work on his late friend, Deleuze gave two lecture courses on Foucault, *Les Formations historiques*, or *Historical Formations*, in the fall of 1985, and *Le Pouvoir*, or *Power*, in the spring of 1986. Delivered at the University of Paris VIII Vincennes/St Denis, they consist of 25 seminars or roughly 64 hours of lecture. These sources still await full exposition as guides to understanding both Foucault's thought and Deleuze's own philosophy. As an example of their scholarly pertinence, I will discuss an interpretative matter they may help resolve.

"Language, in its appearance and mode of being, is the statement."[4]

Michel Foucault, *The Archaeology of Knowledge*

212

The *Historical Formations* lecture course includes extended treatment of a matter of significant debate in the reception of Foucault's work, and one that continues to vex readers of Foucault's most important publications – including *The Archaeology of Knowledge*, Foucault's only extended effort at presenting a methodological basis for his prior topically focused studies on the history of madness, medical vision and penality, and *The Order of Things*, his magisterial 1966 "archaeology" of the human sciences. One puzzle these works raise is the question of the nature of historical regularity and historical transformation, and of their relations.[5] Numerous objections to Foucault's thought have focused on precisely these issues. Deleuze's reading of *The Archaeology of Knowledge* in the *Historical Formations* lectures takes on these central questions in Foucault scholarship. It does so by following Foucault's startling historiographical prioritization of the regularity of discourses and discursive practices. One of the most perplexing aspects of this discursive account of historical regularity has been Foucault's recourse to the notion of a statement, which assumes the role of an ultimate explanatory unit in the theory advanced in *The Archaeology of Knowledge*. To grasp Foucault's notion of regularity in *The Archaeology of Knowledge*, it is essential to attend to his concept of the statement. Indeed, the only passages that Foucault devotes to an explicit characterization of his sense of the concept of regularity appear in Part IV: Archaeological Description, Chapter 2: "The Original and the Regular," a chapter that treats regularity in the context of the statement.[6] He terms these regularities "enunciative regularities."

It is also critical to note that Foucault proposes his own technical sense of the statement, and takes pains to distinguish the statement from its rivals – the logical proposition, the grammatical sentence, the speech act – as well as to distinguish it from material objects. The most important aspect of the statement, in Foucault's novel sense, is that it is a *function*. Although there are many definitions of a mathematical function, one common definition of it is as a rule for mapping elements of one set onto those of another. Far more than other commentators, Deleuze takes utterly seriously the express Foucauldian assertion that a statement is a 'function.' His entire reading of Foucault's archaeological philosophy rigorously exposes the consequences of this knowing employment of a conceptual armory drawn from specifically mathematical sciences.

It is difficult, though, to know exactly how to understand a statement as a kind of function. Since statements are functions and functions are rules, statements themselves are sorts of rules. But Foucault also specifies that statements are statement-events or statement-things; he wishes to understand statements not in their epistemological roles, as already bearers of a truth value, but as ontological events. Thus, statements are rule-events and rule-things. Moreover, statements both banal and rare are purportedly equally regular, and statements are said to be active, and multiple. Thus, there are multiple, varying kinds of statement regularities.

Deleuze contributes to our understanding of the Foucauldian statement in several ways. He expressly situates Foucault's ontology of discursive regularities in relation to the work of eminent linguists such as Émile Benveniste, William Labov and Noam Chomsky. Deleuze defines Foucault's statement as an intrinsic, heterogeneous rule for passing from one language system to another. He here usefully stresses the notion of an intrinsic variable, as distinct from the notions of intrinsic constant and extrinsic variable. All of scientific linguistics, for Deleuze, conceives of language using these latter two notions, and not the notion of an intrinsic variable. Deleuze describes Foucault's alternative and distinctive conception of a statement in terms of this concept of an intrinsic variable. Of importance here is Deleuze's extended argument that the notion of a statement as intrinsically heterogeneous and generative makes sense, that is, that not all rules are either themselves invariable or are rules for the production of sameness. A statement is an ever-varying rule that governs the possibilities for statements to pass from one language system to another (say, from standard German to Latin, in a given example from Krafft-Ebing). A statement, then, is heterogeneous to itself; groupings of statements are not made on the basis of resemblance. Deleuze completes the demonstration of Foucault's quasi-mathematical account of the statement in terms of two sorts of functions: a "primitive function" that governs the relations of statements to each other, and "derivative functions" that govern the relation of a statement to its subjects, objects and concepts.

Using these developed concepts, Deleuze then produces a fertile analysis of some of the few explicit examples of a statement that Foucault offers in *The Archaeology of Knowledge* – the infamous AZERT as statement, a curve, a line from Proust – to attempt to explain concretely the sense and import of Foucault's complex proposals on historical regularity and transformation. Deleuze treats all of these topics in *Foucault*. By comparison, however, the lectures discuss them in greatly extended fashion, and develop them in light of concrete examples. We hardly possess more vivid traces of the formidable philosophical mind that was Gilles Deleuze than we have in these remarkable lectures.

In the lecture course *Historical Formations*, Deleuze offers a reading of Foucault's theory of the statement. In what follows, I will present two main aspects of this rich account. The first aspect is his account of the statement in relation to the linguistics (Émile Benveniste, William Labov and Noam Chomsky); the second is his reading of the infamous example of a statement, the AZERT order of keys on the French typewriter keyboard.

2. DELEUZE'S READING OF FOUCAULT'S THEORY OF THE STATEMENT

Deleuze painstakingly exposes Foucault's distinctive notion of the statement. It is "so original," he says, "that he could just as well have invented a new word to designate it."[7] The guiding idea for Foucault's innovation, Deleuze thinks, is the notion of an intrinsic variable. Here, Deleuze argues that all scientific enterprises implicitly or explicitly employ a fundamental theoretical tool, namely, the conceptual pair of the intrinsic constant and the extrinsic variable. Foucault's novel concept is that of the intrinsic variable, the notion that variation could be inherent to a system, rule or phenomenon. Further, Foucault does not conceive of this variation as, say, random, but is interested precisely in regular variation, or variation that follows a rule. But with one important difference: the rule itself will admit of variation. Deleuze follows the use of the notion of an intrinsic variable in Foucault's theory of the statement, so I will point out some of those moments.

He stresses the following two characteristics of the statement:

(1) A statement is "astride two languages or two systems."[8]
(2) "the statement is defined by rules for transition between heterogeneous systems."[9]

We'll examine both of these features in order.

(1) First, how is the statement "astride two languages or two systems?"

Deleuze contrasts Foucault's theory of the statement with major schools in linguistics contemporary to Foucault's work. He carries out a comparison of Foucault and Chomsky, for instance, in relation to an example that Deleuze draws from the work of Krafft-Ebing, in particular from his book, *Psychopathia sexualis*. In that study, Krafft-Ebing continuously switches from German to Latin when recounting a case that he considers to be vulgar. The statements of this science of sexuality, then, appear to glide or to transition across languages. Deleuze applies Foucault's thought on the statement to this case. Here, he argues that the distinctive Foucaultian point would be that this ability of the statement to cross languages is misconceived in contemporary linguistics. The misconception would be due to the fact that such linguistics would grant the transitional effect or ability, but it would attribute this effect to forces that are external to the linguistic domain properly speaking. According to Deleuze, Chomsky would hold that the movement from one language to another in this case should be fully explained by an aim or requirement for censorship that is external to the language systems themselves. By contrast, according to Deleuze, Foucault instead locates that ability directly in the statement, on his concept of a statement, of course. The Foucaultian statement is characterized by this *intrinsic* movement across languages or systems of language, where what we mean by a "system of language" is a linguistic system as formalized or established by a linguistic analysis. To explain this switch between languages, then, Foucault does not resort to the influence of social prohibition or of psychological modesty. Deleuze notes that neither is such a switch a move from exposure to hiddenness, since Latin is in fact a known language among even high school students. The Foucaultian idea is that the statement as he conceives of it is something that can move across language systems in virtue of an intrinsic feature, and thus that extrinsic determinants are not needed to explain such movement. It is *in principle* and not *in* fact that a statement moves from one system to another. According to Deleuze, Chomsky would disagree, and would hold that science must be established on the basis of discrete, homogeneous systems. The linguist therefore must distinguish and separate systems, even if in fact people do speak in a way that mixes systems together. Deleuze is skeptical that homogenous systems exist; he instead follows the American linguist William Labov, or Deleuze's reading of Labov, in suggesting that homogeneous systems in fact do not exist. On this view, every statement is an active transition from one system to another, although propositions do indeed belong to a given system.

But such transitions or passages have a regularity to them. There are rules for passage from German to Latin within one and the same sentence, in the Krafft-Ebing example, Deleuze holds. But there are two peculiarities of these rules for the statement's passage. (1) One is that the statements just are the set of rules that govern their transition. (2) The second, and this is perhaps just another way of saying the same thing, is that the rules for transition do not take place at a "more general" level than the statement. Every statement is in fact in transition between heterogeneous systems. It is a matter of transition rules for movement between heterogeneous systems, and not, as it is for propositions, a matter of formation rules for homogenous systems.

(2) Let us now consider Deleuze's claim that "the statement is defined by rules for transition between heterogeneous systems."

He puts it this way:

> the statement *is*, *is* inherent variation, the intrinsic variation by which I pass and continue to pass from one system to another. In other words, there is no homogeneous statement. Heterogeneity is the rule of the statement. Why is it the rule of the statement? All one need do is let oneself be pushed along – that is the rule of the statement. For the statement certainly has a regularity; it has no homogeneity at all. What is the statement's regularity? It is its rule for passage. The statement's rules are the contrary of propositional rules. Propositional rules are the rules according to which a proposition belongs to this or that system, which system is defined by intrinsic constants and defined as homogeneous. The statement, on the other hand, only has rules of passage, rules of variation – that's what defines its regularity. In other words, statement rules are rules of variation, rules that are themselves variable.

Deleuze explains his conception of this internal variability of the statement in relation to the question of the subject or the subject positions of the statement. Here, he opposes Foucault's theory of the statement to the linguistic theory of Emile Benveniste. According to Deleuze, Foucault develops a view of linguistics that is an alternative to Benveniste's. While Benveniste affirmed a strongly 'personalist' linguistics, Foucault's alternative view is decidedly non-personalist and anti-Benvenistian. Benveniste analyzed language from a strongly 'personalist' perspective, holding in fact that the third linguistic person should be considered a false person.

According to Deleuze, Foucault's non-personalist position is indebted to Blanchot's philosophy of language. Blanchot considered the "true subject of the statement" to be the non-person. He held that the indefinite, impersonal pronoun, "one" – as in, "one says," or "they say" – was the expression of the non-person. So, his thought on linguistics valorized the position of the "one." All other linguistic persons, for Blanchot, were "figures" for the "one." This important implication of this view is that the use of these other linguistic persons does not manage to eliminate the fundamentally anonymous character of language. Deleuze holds that Foucault adopts this anti-personalist view, explaining that: "the statement is defined by intrinsic variables, namely, by the set of subject positions to which it refers, each subject position consequently being a figure for the 'one.' " Author, signatory, compiler, are subject *positions* made possible by the fundamentally anonymous *place* created for them by the "one speaks" in language. This means that the anonymous 'one' is a the foundation of all personalist uses of linguistic persons that are not the impersonal, indefinite 'one.'

Deleuze sees this foundational anonymous 'one' as basic to the analysis of the proper noun. He writes: "the proper noun is no more than a figure for this 'one speaks:' Krafft-Ebing, Madame de Sévigné, all subject positions line up as the variables of a 'one speaks.'"[10] As Deleuze explains:

> The subject position of the statement is an intrinsic variable that stems from the statement itself. Whence the examples . . . which are examples from Foucault himself: a literary text relative to an author – that's a subject position! But a letter has no author; it has a signatory. A contract has a signer. An anthology has an editor, etc. All these are subject positions, and you cannot reduce them to the form of an 'I.' They are functions derived from the statement. They are variables intrinsic to the statement.

By contrast, however, "sentences refer to a formal constant, to an 'I' as first person, or as the subject of an enunciation," Deleuze holds. For Deleuze, this means that "the sentence is defined by an intrinsic constant and extrinsic variables. The intrinsic constant is the 'I' as the subject of the enunciation. The extrinsic variables were all of the individuals who could say 'I.'"

3. FOUCAULT'S CHIEF EXAMPLE OF A STATEMENT:
THE FRENCH "AZERT" KEYBOARD LAYOUT

The chief kind of regularity of a Foucaultian statement that is important for Deleuze is the regularity that regularizes or, that in regularizing, actualizes. This takes the statement in a new direction; it is certainly no longer merely comparable to linguistic versions of sentences, propositions, and despite appearances, not even to speech acts. The privileged example of a statement in *Archaeology of Knowledge* is the order of the letters on a French keyboard, once written on a piece of paper, not merely those letters as they appear on a French keyboard. So, that's the main example, (and Deleuze rightly reminds us that it is difficult to choose an example, since it will generally be in words and sentences, that will not be misleading and suggest to us that statements are to be identified with words or sentences!).

We know a statement is a function, a rule for the mapping or passage of statements (of themselves, that is) from one system to another, from German to Latin, or, to use his other example, from William Labov, a passage from Standard American English to African-American Vernacular English. So, how will AZERT fit Deleuze's conception of Foucault's notion of a statement? What does it link in a regular fashion, and how is that regular linking variable?

Deleuze answers this by recourse to the notion of a curve, that is, to a quasi-mathematical notion of a curve. He claims that it is not the difference between statement and referent, or between statement and meaning that interests Foucault, but the difference between statement and what it actualizes or incarnates! The statement

is defined by a regularity, that is, it is the analogue to a curve. A curve regularizes the relations between singular points. AZERT regularizes the relations between singular points, that is, the relations between the letters of the French language and fingers. Between the frequency of letters, the neighborhoods of letters, and the relations of fingers. AZERT is a statement as a curve that passes through the neighborhoods of these singularities. That is, AZERT actualizes relations of forces between letters and fingers in the French language.

Notice how it is a rule that is not more general than itself. One needn't appeal to a rule more general than the disposition of the letters on the keyboard in order to type, after all. Further, AZERT does put finger movements into coordination with keys and with words in a language, and does so as a rule, in a regular way. But it also can vary in a regular way, in that it would prescribe, still, alternate fingerings should one have an injury, and it can determine how it should be linked up with other non-French keyboards. If the curve regularizes singular points both by showing them and by displaying the rule for arriving at them, then AZERT likewise regularizes finger movements both by creating them, and by showing them as required, that is, by being the display of the rule for arriving at those finger movements (including by being based on letter frequency and by the requirements of standardized orthography). In the most interesting moment of Deleuze's account of the Foucaultian statement, then, the statement is always in connection with something outside of itself and other statements, with something that is a non-statement, and beyond its objects, subjects, and concepts. Here, the statement is the heart of the famous Foucaultian effort to retain the distinctiveness of the domains of stating and seeing, while showing their necessary historical connections. For the statement's relation with what is beyond statement, here the movements of typing in French, turn out on this account to be oddly intrinsic features of this element of the being of language.

NOTES

1. Its first two chapters had already seen publication as articles in *Critique*: No. 274, "Un Nouvel archiviste. ('Archéologie du savoir')" (March 1970), 195–209 and No. 343, "Ecrivain non: un nouveau cartographe ('Surveiller et punir')" (December 1975, 1207–27).
2. Roger-Pol Droit, "Foucault, Deleuze et la pensée du dehors," *Le Monde* (September 5, 1986).
3. Didier Éribon, "Foucault vivant. La vie comme une œuvre d'art," *Le Nouvel Observateur* (August 29, 1986).
4. Michel Foucault, *The Archaeology of Knowledge*, 111. (Hereafter abbreviated as *AK*.)
5. About Foucauldian archaeology, Dominique Lecourt correctly observes in *Marxism and Epistemology: Bachelard, Canguilhem, Foucault*, that: "The main determination of the archaeological category of 'practice' is 'rule,' 'regularity.' It is *regularity* that structures discursive practice, it is the rule that orders every discursive 'formation'" (202).
6. His analysis, he suggests, provides openings that "one day perhaps will be explored with greater care" (*AK*, 145).
7. *Les Formations historiques*, 40, my translation. Hereafter abbreviated as *FH*. All translations are my own.
8. *FH*, 74.
9. *FH*, 80.
10. Richard von Krafft-Ebing (1840–1902), Austro-German psychiatrist. Marie de Rabutin-Chantal, Marquise de Sévigné (1626–96), French woman of letters.

BIBLIOGRAPHY

Deleuze, Gilles (1985) Lecture Courses on Foucault, *Les Formations historiques*, or *Historical Formations* (fall 1985).
Deleuze, Gilles (1986a) Lecture Courses on Foucault, *Le Pouvoir*, or *Power* (spring 1986).
Deleuze, Gilles (1986b) *Foucault* (Paris: Les Éditions de Minuit).

Droit, Roger-Pol (1986) "Foucault, Deleuze et la pensée du dehors," *Le Monde* (September 5, 1986).

Éribon, Didier (1986) "Foucault vivant. La vie comme une œuvre d'art," *Le Nouvel Observateur* (August 29, 1986).

Foucault, Michel (1972) *The Archaeology of Knowledge* (London: Tavistock).

Lecourt, Dominique (1975) *Marxism and Epistemology: Bachelard, Canguilhem, Foucault,* (New York: New Left Books).

PART IV

Desire, Power and Resistance

CHAPTER 13

Desire and Pleasure[1]

GILLES DELEUZE

TRANSLATED BY DANIEL W. SMITH

[A] One of the essential theses of *Discipline and Punish*[2] concerned *dispositifs* of power.[3] It seems essential to me in three respects:

1) In itself and in relation to "leftism": the profound political novelty of this conception of power, which is opposed to every theory of the State.

2) In relation to Michel: since it allowed him to go beyond the duality of discursive formations and non-discursive formations, which was still present in *The Archaeology of Knowledge*, and to explain how the two types of formations are distributed or articulated segment by segment (without the one being reduced to the other or their resembling each other ... etc.).[4] It is not a matter of suppressing the distinction but of finding a reason for their relations.

3) For a precise consequence: *dispositifs* of power operate neither through repression nor through ideology. Hence a rupture with an alternative that everyone had more or less accepted. In place of repression or ideology, *D and P* formulated a conception of normalization, and of disciplines.

[B] This thesis concerning *dispositifs* of power seemed to me to move in two directions, in no way contradictory, but distinct. In both cases, these *dispositifs* were irreducible to a State apparatus. But according to one direction, they consisted of a diffuse and heterogeneous multiplicity, "micro-*dispositifs*." According to another direction, they referred to a diagram, a kind of abstract machine immanent to the entire social field (hence panopticism, defined by the general function of seeing without being seen and applicable to any multiplicity). These were, so to speak, the two directions of micro-analysis, both equally important, since the second showed that Michel was not satisfied with a "dissemination."

223

[C] *The History of Sexuality* took a new step forward in relation to *D and P*.[5] The point of view remains, precisely, neither repression nor ideology. But, to move quickly, *dispositifs* of power are no longer content to be normalized; they tend to be constitutive (of sexuality). They are no longer content to form knowledges; they are constitutive of truth (the truth of power). They no longer refer to "categories" that are, despite everything, negative (madness, delinquency as the object of confinement) but to a category that is said to be positive (sexuality). This latter point is confirmed by the interview in *La Quinzaine littéraire*.[6] In this respect, I believe there is a new move forward in the analyses of *HS*. The danger is, is Michel reverting to an analogue of the "constituting subject," and why does he feel the need to resurrect truth, even if he creates a new concept for it? These are not my own questions, but I think these two false questions will be asked as long as Michel has not explained himself further.

[D] For myself, a first question concerns the nature of the micro-analysis that Michel worked out in *D and P*. The difference between micro and macro was obviously not one of size, in the sense that micro-*dispositifs* would concern small groups (the family is no less extended than any other formation). Nor is it a question of an extrinsic dualism, since there are micro-*dispositifs* immanent to the State apparatus, and the segments of the State apparatus also penetrate the micro-*dispositifs* – a complete immanence of the two dimensions. Must we understand the difference, then, to be one of scale? One paragraph of *HS* explicitly refuses this interpretation.[7] But this paragraph seems to make the macro refer to the strategic model, and the micro to the tactical model. This makes me uncomfortable, since micro-*dispositifs* seem to me to have an entirely strategic dimension in Michel's work (especially if one takes into account the diagram from which they are inseparable). Another direction would be that of "relations of force" as determining the micro; see in particular the interview in *La Quinzaine*. But Michel, I believe, has not yet developed this point: his original conception of relations of force, what he calls a *rapport de force*, must be a concept as new as the others.

In any case, there is a difference in kind, a heterogeneity, between the micro and the macro. This in no way excludes the immanence of the two. But in the end, my question would be this: Does this difference in kind still allow us to talk about *dispositifs* of power? The notion of the State is not applicable at the level of a micro-analysis, since, as Michel says, it is not a matter of miniaturizing the State. But is the notion of power still applicable? Is it not itself the miniaturization of a global concept?

Here I come to my first difference with Michel. If I speak, with Félix,[8] of the *agencement* of desire, it is because I am not sure that micro-*dispositifs* can be described in terms of power. For myself, an *agencement* of desire implies that desire is never either a "natural" or a "spontaneous" determination. For example, feudalism is an *agencement* that brings about new relations with the animal (the horse), with the earth, with deterritorialization (the knight's journey, the Crusades), with women (courtly love), . . . etc. Completely mad *agencements*, but always historically attributable. For my part, I would say that desire circulates in this *agencement* of heterogeneous elements, in this type of "symbiosis": desire is one and the same thing as a determined *agencement*, a co-functioning. Of course an *agencement* of desire will include *dispositifs* of power (for example, feudal powers), but they must be situated among the different components of the *agencement*. On a first axis, one can distinguish within *agencements* of desire states of things and enunciations (which would conform to the two types of formations or multiplicities according to Michel). On another axis, one could distinguish the territorialities or reterritorializations and the movements of deterritorialization that an *agencement* entails (for example, all the movements of deterritorialization that the Church brings about, knighthood, peasantry). *Dispositifs* of power would emerge wherever reterritorializations, even abstract ones, are brought about. *Dispositifs* of power would then be a component of *agencements*. But the *agencements* would also be composed of points of deterritorialization. In short, it is not the *dispositifs* of power that assemble [*agenceraient*], nor would they be constitutive; it is rather the *agencements* of desire that would spread throughout the formations of power following one of their dimensions. This is what allows me to respond to the question, necessary for myself, not necessary for Michel: How can power be desired? The first difference, for me, would thus be that power is an affection of desire (it being given that desire is never a "natural reality"). All this is very approximate; there are more complicated relationships between the two movements of deterritorialization and reterritorialization than those I am giving here. But it is in this sense that desire seems to me to be primary and to be the element of a micro-analysis.

[E] I continue to follow Michel on a point that seems to me to be fundamental: neither ideology nor repression (for example, statements, or rather enunciations, have nothing to do with ideology). The *agencements* of desire have nothing to do with repression. But obviously, for *dispositifs* of power, I do not have Michel's firmness; I become rather vague, given the ambiguous status they have for me. In *D and P*, Michel says that they normalize and discipline; I would say that they recode and reterritorialize (I suppose that, here again, there is more than a distinction of words). But given my primacy of desire over power, or the secondary character that *dispositifs* of power have for me, their operations retain a repressive effect, since they crush not desire as a natural given but the cutting edges of *agencements* of desire. I take one of the most beautiful theses of *HS*: the *dispositif* of sexuality reduces sexuality to sex (to the difference between the sexes . . . etc., and psychoanalysis is full of this reductionism). I see there an effect of repression, precisely at the frontier of the micro and the macro: sexuality, as a historically variable and determinable *agencement* of desire, with its cutting edges of deterritorialization, flux, and combinations, will be reduced to a molar instance, "sex," and even if the methods of this reduction are not repressive, the (non-ideological) effect is repressive, insofar as the *agencements* are broken not only in their potentialities but in their micro-reality. Then they can no longer exist except as phantasms, which change and divert them completely, or as shameful things . . . etc. A small problem that greatly interests me: why certain "disturbed" people are more susceptible to shame, and even dependent on shame, than others (the enuretic or the anoretic, for example, are hardly susceptible to shame at all). I thus have need of a certain concept of repression, not in the sense that repression would be brought to bear on a spontaneity, but because collective *agencements* would have many dimensions, and *dispositifs* of power would be only one of these dimensions.

[F] Another fundamental point: I believe that the thesis "neither repression nor ideology" has a correlate, and perhaps itself depends upon this correlate. A social field is not defined by its contradictions. The notion of contradiction is a global and inadequate one that already implies a strong complicity among the "contradictories" in *dispositifs* of power (for example, the two classes, the bourgeoisie and the proletariat). In fact, it seems to me that another great novelty of Michel's conception of power would be: a society does not contradict itself, or rarely. But his response is: it is strategized, it strategizes. I find that very beautiful; I see clearly the immense difference (strategy versus contradiction); I would have to reread Clausewitz in this regard. But I am not completely at ease with this idea.

I would say, for my part, that a society, a social field, does not contradict itself, but what is primary is that it takes flight; it first of all flees in every direction; it is lines of flight that are primary (even if primary is not chronological). Far from lying outside the social field or emerging from it, lines of flight constitute its rhizome or cartography. Lines of flight are the same thing as movements of deterritorialization: they imply no return to nature; they are points of deterritorialization in *agencements* of desire. What is primary in feudalism are the lines of flight it presupposes; the same holds for the tenth through twelfth centuries; the same for capitalism. Lines of flight are not necessarily "revolutionary"; on the contrary, they are what the *dispositifs* of power will seal off, tie up. Around the eleventh century, numerous lines of deterritorialization began to move at the same time: the last invasions; the bands of pillagers; the deterritorialization of the Church; the emigrations of the peasants; the transformation of chivalry; the transformation of cities, which increasingly abandon territorial models; the transformation of money, which is injected into new circuits; the change of the feminine condition with the themes of courtly love, which even deterritorializes chivalrous love, . . . etc. Strategy will only be secondary in relation to lines of flight, to their conjunctions, their orientations, their convergences or divergences. Here again I come back to the primacy of desire, since desire is precisely in the lines of flight, the conjunction and dissociation of flows. It merges with them.

It seems to me, then, that Michel confronts a problem that does not have the same status for me. For if *dispositifs* of power are in some way constitutive, there can only be phenomena of "resistance" against them, and the question bears on the status of these phenomena. In effect, they themselves will neither be ideological nor anti-repressive.

Hence the importance of the two pages in *HS* where Michel says, don't make me say that these phenomena are a struggle . . . . But what status is he going to give to them? Here, several directions: (1) That of *HS*, in which the phenomena of resistance would be like the inverse image of the *dispositifs*; they would have the same characters, diffusion, heterogeneity, . . . etc.; they would be "vis-à-vis."[9] But this direction appears to me to block the exits as much as it opens one up. (2) The direction of the interview in *Politique Hebdo*: if *dispositifs* of power are constitutive of truth, if there is a truth of power, it must have as a counter-strategy a kind of power of truth, against powers.[10] Hence the problem of the role of the intellectual in Michel and his manner of reintroducing the category of truth. Since he rejuvenates it completely by making it depend on power, will he find in this rejuvenation a material that can be turned against power? But here I do not see how. We must wait for Michel to explain this new conception of truth, at the level of his micro-analysis. (3) A third direction would be pleasures, the body and its pleasures. Here again, the same wait for me. How do pleasures animate counter-powers, and how does he conceive of this notion of pleasure?

It seems to me that these are three notions that Michel takes in a completely new direction, but without having yet developed them: relations of force, truths, pleasures.

There are certain problems I face that Michel does not because they are resolved in advance by his own research. Conversely, I tell myself, for some encouragement, that there are other problems I do not face, which of necessity he must confront because of his theses and sentiments. Lines of fight and movements of deterritorialization, as collective historical determinations, do not seem to me to have any equivalent in Michel. For myself, the status of phenomena of resistance is not a problem; since lines of flight are primary determinations, since desire assembles the social field, it is rather the *dispositifs* of power that are both produced by these *agencements* and crushed or sealed off by them. I share Michel's distaste for those who consider themselves marginals; the romanticism of madness, delinquency, perversion, and drugs is less and less bearable for me. But for me, lines of flight, that is, *agencements* of desire, are not created by marginals. On the contrary, they are objective lines that cut across a society, and on which marginals install themselves here and there in order to create a buckle, a whirl, a recoding. I therefore have no need for the status of phenomena of resistance; if the first given of a society is that everything takes flight, then everything in it is deterritorialized. Hence the status of the intellectual, and the political problem will not be the same theoretically for Michel and for myself (I will try to say below how I view this difference).

[G] The last time we saw each other, Michel told me, with much kindness and affection, something like, I cannot bear the word desire; even if you use it differently, I cannot keep myself from thinking or living that desire = lack, or that desire is repressed. Michel added, whereas myself, what I call pleasure is perhaps what you call desire; but in any case I need another word than desire.

227

Obviously, once again, this is more than a question of words. Because for my part I can scarcely tolerate the word pleasure. But why? For me, desire implies no lack; neither is it a natural given. It is an *agencement* of heterogeneous elements that function; it is process as opposed to structure or genesis; it is affect as opposed to sentiment; it is "*haec*-eity" (the individuality of a day, a season, a life) as opposed to subjectivity; it is an event as opposed to a thing or person. And above all, it implies the constitution of a plane of immanence or a "body-without-organs," which is defined solely by zones of intensity, thresholds, gradients, flows. This body is as much biological as it is collective and political; the *agencements* of desire are made and unmade upon it, and it supports the cutting edges of deterritorialization or the lines of flight of the *agencements*. It varies (the body-without-organs of feudalism is not the same as that of capitalism). If I call it the body-without-organs, it is because it is opposed to all the strata of Organization – those of the organism, but also the organization of power. It is the totality of the organizations of the body that will break apart the plane or the field of immanence and impose another type of "plane" on desire, in each case stratifying the body-without-organs.

If I say all this rather confusedly, it is because there are several problems that arise for me in relation to Michel: 1) I cannot give any positive value to pleasure because pleasure seems to me to interrupt the immanent process of desire; pleasure seems to me to be on the side of strata and organization; and it is one and the same movement that desire is subject to the law from within and scanned by pleasures from without; in both cases, there is the negation of the field of immanence proper to desire. I tell myself that it is not by chance that Michel attaches a certain importance to Sade, and myself on the contrary to Masoch. It would not be enough to say that I am masochistic, and Michel sadistic. That would be nice, but it is not true. What interests me in Masoch are not the pains but the idea that pleasure interrupts the positivity of desire and the constitution of its field of immanence (just as, or rather in a different manner, in courtly love there is the constitution of a field of immanence or a body-without-organs in which desire lacks nothing and refrains as long as possible from the pleasures that would interrupt its processes). Pleasure seems to me to be the only means for a person or a subject to "find itself again" in a process that surpasses it. It is a reterritorialization. And from my point of view, desire is related to the law of lack and to the norm of pleasure in the same manner.

2) On the other hand, Michel's idea that *dispositifs* of power have an immediate and direct relationship is essential. But, for me, this is because they impose an organization on the body. Whereas the body-without-organs is the locus or agent of deterritorialization (and hence the plane of immanence or desire), every organization – the entire system of what Michel calls bio-power – brings about reterritorializations of bodies.

3) Could I think of equivalences of this type: what for me is the body-without-organs corresponds to what for Michel is "body-pleasures"? Can I relate the "body–flesh" distinction, of which Michel spoke to me, to the "body-without-organs–organization"

distinction? Very important paragraph in *HS*, on life as giving a possible status to forces of resistance.[11] For me, this life, of which Lawrence spoke, is not at all nature; it is exactly the variable plane of immanence of desire, which passes through every determined *agencement*. Conception of desire in Lawrence, in relationship to positive lines of flight. (Small detail: the way Michel makes use of Lawrence at the end of *HS* is the opposite of the way I make use of him.)

[H] Has Michel advanced the problem that concerned us: to maintain the rights of a micro-analysis (diffusion, heterogeneity, fragmentary character) but at the same time to maintain a kind of principle of unification that is not of the "State," "party," totalization, or representation type?

First of all, on the side of power itself, I return to the two directions of *D and P*: on the one hand, the diffuse and fragmentary character of micro-*dispositifs*, but also, on the other hand, the diagram or abstract machine that covers the whole of the social field. There is a problem that still remains in *D and P*, it seems to me: the relationship between these two instances of micro-analysis. I believe that the question changes slightly in *HS*: here, the two directions of micro-analysis are micro-disciplines on the one hand and bio-political processes on the other.[12] This is what I meant in point C of these notes. Now the point of view in *D and P* suggested that the diagram, which is irreducible to the global instance of the State, perhaps brings about a micro-unification of the small dispositifs. Must we understand now that it is bio-political processes that would assume this function? I confess that the notion of the diagram appears to me to be very rich; will Michel meet up with it again on this new terrain?

But on the side of lines of resistance, or what I call lines of flight: How should we conceive of the relations or conjugations, the conjunctions, the processes of unification? I would say that the collective field of immanence in which *agencements* are made at a given moment, and where they trace their lines of flight, also has a veritable diagram. It is necessary then to find the complex *agencement* capable of actualizing this diagram, by bringing about the conjunction of lines or points of deterritorialization. It is in this sense that I spoke of a war machine, which is completely different from a State apparatus and from military institutions, but also from *dispositifs* of power. We would thus have, on the one hand, a State diagram of power (the State being the molar apparatus that actualizes the micro-elements of the diagram as a plane of organization); on the other hand, the war machine-diagram of lines of flight (the war machine being the *agencement* that actualizes the micro-elements of the diagram as the plane of immanence). I will stop at this point, since this would bring into play two types of very different planes – a kind of transcendent plane of organization over against the immanent plane of *agencements* – and we would fall once again into the preceding problems. And here I do not know how to situate myself in relation to Michel's present research.

[Addition: What interests me in the two opposed states of the plane or diagram is their historical confrontation, and the very diverse forms under which it takes place. In one case, we have a plane of organization and development, which is hidden by nature, but which brings into view everything that is visible; in the other case, we have a plane of immanence, where there is no longer anything but speeds and slownesses, no development, and where everything is seen, heard, . . . etc. The first plane should not be confused with the State, but is linked to it; the second, on the contrary, is linked to a war machine, to a reverie of the war machine. At the level of nature, for example, Cuvier, but also Goethe, conceived of the first type of plane. Hölderlin, in *Hyperion*, but even more so Kleist, conceived of the second type. Suddenly, here are two types of intellectuals, and what Michel says in this respect should be compared with what he says on the position of the intellectual. Or in music, the two conceptions of the sonorous plane confront each other. The power–knowledge link, as Michel has analyzed it, could be explained in this way: powers imply a plane-diagram of the first type (for example, the Greek city and Euclidean geometry). But conversely, on the side of counter-powers and more or less in relation with the war machines, there is the other type of plane, and kinds of "minor" knowledges (Archimedean geometry or the geometry of the cathedrals, which the State will fight against). Is this a form of knowledge characteristic of lines of resistance, which does not have the same form as the other form of knowledge?]

Notes

1. This text was first published as Gilles Deleuze, "Désir et plaisir," ed. François Ewald, *Magazine Littéraire* 325 (October 1994), 57–65. The translation appeared in *Foucault and His Interlocutors*, ed. Arnold I. Davidson (Chicago: University of Chicago Press, 1997), 183–92, and is reproduced with permission. The notes were added by the French editor and, where indicated, by the translator.
2. See Michel Foucault, *Discipline and Punish: The Birth of the Prison*, trans. Alan Sheridan (New York: Pantheon Books, 1977). Hereafter abbreviated as *D and P*.
3. I have left the terms *dispositif* (Foucault) and *agencement* (Deleuze) untranslated in the text, since neither has a suitable English equivalent. Brian Massumi has translated them, respectively, as *apparatus* and *assemblage*; see Gilles Deleuze and Félix Guattari, *A Thousand Plateaus: Capitalism and Schizophrenia*, trans. Brian Massumi (Minneapolis: University of Minnesota Press, 1987). *Agencement*, from the verb *agencer* (to put together, organize, order, lay out, arrange), is used to describe processes as diverse as the ordering of elements, the organization of a novel, the construction of a sentence, the arrangement of a collection, or the layout of an office or apartment. *Dispositif*, from the verb *disposer* (to arrange [flowers], to set [the table], to range [troops], and so on), is generally used to describe a mechanical device or apparatus, such as an alarm or a safety mechanism, and more particularly to describe a military plan of action (for example, *dispositif d'attaque*, "attack force"; *dispositif de défense*, "defense system"; *dispositif de combat*, "fighting plan"). Deleuze here compares his conception of *agencements* of desire to Foucault's conception of *dispositifs* of power, seeing the latter as a stratification of the former. In an important

article written in 1988, Deleuze provides a more complete analysis of Foucault's concept of a *dispositif,* assigning it a greater extension than that allotted to it here; see Gilles Deleuze, "What Is a *Dispositif?*", in *Michel Foucault: Philosopher,* trans. Timothy J. Armstrong (New York: Harvester Wheatsheaf, 1992), 159–68. –TRANS.

4. See Michel Foucault, *The Archaeology of Knowledge,* trans. A. M. Sheridan Smith (New York: Pantheon Books, 1972).

5. See Michel Foucault, *The History of Sexuality: An Introduction,* trans. Robert Hurley (New York: Pantheon Books, 1978). Hereafter abbreviated as *HS.*

6. See Lucette Finas, "Les Rapports de pouvoir passent à l'intérieur des corps," interview with Michel Foucault, *La Quinzaine littéraire* 247 (January 1–15, 1977): 5. Reprinted in Michel Foucault, *Dits et écrits,* ed. Daniel Defert and François Ewald, 4 vols. (Paris: Gallimard, 1994), III: 228–36.

7. See *HS,* 99–100.

8. The reference is obviously to Félix Guattari.

9. See *HS,* 95–7.

10. See Michel Foucault, "La Fonction politique de l'intellectual," *Politique Hebdo* (November 29–December 5, 1976), 31–3. Reprinted in *Dits et écrits,* III: 109–14.

11. See *HS,* 144–5.

12. See ibid. 139–41.

CHAPTER 14

Against the Incompatibility Thesis: A rather *Different Reading of the Desire-Pleasure Problem*

NICOLAE MORAR AND MARJORIE GRACIEUSE

INTRODUCTION

In the introductory chapter of *Dits et Ecrits* (Chronology), Daniel Defert reminds us of a joke between Foucault and Deleuze. In March 1972, soon after the publication of *Anti-Oedipus*, Foucault tells to his friend: "We have to get rid of Freudo-Marxism."[1] To which Deleuze replies, "I'm taking care of Freud, will you deal with Marx?"[2] The revival of the concept of desire in the first volume of *Capitalism and Schizophrenia* represents to a certain extent not simply a radical critique of psycho-analysis and of the 'Oedipus complex', but maybe also Deleuze's part of the bargain with his long-time friend.

To one's surprise, a few years later, in 1976, Foucault seems to demarcate himself from the Deleuze and Guattari's *Anti-Oedipus* since he ends *La Volonté de Savoir* with, by now, a famous dictum: "The rallying point for the counterattack against the deployment of sexuality ought to be not sex-desire, but bodies and pleasures."[3] Given that our desires are coopted as a vehicle in the process of normalization, Foucault sets up an argument whose conclusion amounts to a radical rejection of the concept of desire. He affirms pleasure as the locus of resistance against the mechanisms of control of our conduct. In spite of their earnest friendship, a conceptual chasm seems to appear between these two intellectual friends. And, in a way, how couldn't one see in Deleuze's 1977 letter, *Desire and Pleasure*, the sign of a friend who is reaching out in order to highlight the productive philosophical differences among them?

In that letter, Deleuze tells us that Foucault told him that what he calls desire is what Michel calls pleasure. But, this conceptual difference is not *just a matter of words*. It is a central divergence between them, which, as Jean Rabouin

232

points out, persists long after this early debate took place. In 1983, in his interview "Structuralism and Post-Structuralism," Foucault is asked if the similarities between his thinking and Deleuze's philosophy go as far as endorsing Deleuze's notion of desire. Foucault replies: "No, *precisely not.*"[4]

A numbers of commentators, including Rabouin and Grace[5], have argued that this central difference between Foucault and Deleuze is a *radical* difference that renders their respective philosophies irreconcilable. In this essay, we aim to dismantle this *incompatibility thesis*, which defends the view that in virtue of their differences on the question of desire and pleasure, Deleuze and Foucault's philosophies are profoundly divergent. In order to do so, we reconstruct first Deleuze and Guattari's theory of desire. In the second section, we reiterate Foucault's argument against the notion of desire, and against the ways in which it was (and continues to be) employed in normalizing mechanisms. Once we show that there is no real tension between those notions [in the way that both Deleuze and Foucault construct them], we localize the common discourse that both have targeted: the liberationist perspective. Last, we focus on Deleuze's critique of pleasure as transcendence and on Foucault's pragmatics of desire in order to highlight the core compatibilities between these two thinkers.

1. DELEUZE AND GUATTARI'S NOTION OF DESIRE

It comes as no surprise that Deleuze and Guattari do not propose us just a minor clarification of the notion of desire. As Deleuze says in his interview with Parnet, "we had an enormous ambition, notably when one writes a book, we thought that we would say something new . . . That is, in undertaking our task as philosophers, we were hoping to propose a new concept of desire."[6] We would like to highlight four central features of Deleuze and Guattari's theory of desire[7]. So, what are the characteristics of this new concept of desire?

First, desire is different than interest and it is always a positive assemblage. Desire is a construction of drives, which, from the beginning, is "positively invested in the system that allows you to have this particular interest."[8] In other words, our desires are always prior to our own interests. Moreover, our desires are positive insofar as "what we desire, what we invest our desire in, is a social formation."[9] As Deleuze points out, we are not fundamentally the kind of being that is defined by some lack (perfection, purity, etc.). Rather, desire is essentially constructivist: it constitutes the immanent power of our living materiality, from the perspective of which thinking creatively and acting anew are one and the same process. Thus, we are spending our time constructing concrete arrangements of reality and desiring constellations, which constitute transformative experiences at the occasion of which we articulate our desiring potential to other forces and material singularities ("the real is the artificial and not, as Lacan says, the impossible"[10]). When we say,

I desire *this* or *that*, "we do not extract an object that is presumed to be the object of desire," but we are in the process of constructing that very desire assemblage.[11]

Desires are not our own. They are social from the beginning (the libidinal and political economy are one and the same). This is how we can make sense of our investment in social formations that repress us. It is the interference between desire and social flows that determines the objects of desire. If an individual is intrinsically a "group" or "complex" of intertwined socio-economical dynamisms, the subjective investments of desire are fundamentally unconscious and must therefore be distinguished from the objective interests that appear to consciousness.

The second characteristic of desire is intimately linked to the first one and helps us understand the fundamental problem of political philosophy. If desire is prior to interest or will, we can see how we can reply to Spinoza's question: "why do people fight for their servitude as stubbornly as though it were their salvation?"[12] Dan Smith notes, following Deleuze, "the answer is simple: it is because your desires . . . are not your own, so to speak."[13] They are not just part of one's psychic reality; they are *always already* part of the very social formation one finds oneself in.

Third, desire is an enormous flow that constitutes the delirium of society, along with its historical determinations. The difference between desire and interest maps onto the difference between rational and irrational regimes of desire. In *On Capitalism and Desire*, Deleuze warns us that "once interests have been defined within the confines of a society, the rational way is the way in which people pursue those interests and attempt to realize them."[14] Certainly, rationality is *really* not the defining element here. "Underneath that, you find desires, investments of desire that are not to be confused with investments of interest, and on which interests depend for their determination and very distribution."[15]

This is one of the points that oppose Deleuze and Guattari to psychoanalysis. If reason is not the source of our subjectivity, but it always a region "carved out of the irrational",[16] underneath our rational behavior (our whole investment in our lives, in pensions funds, and so on), there is simply delirium.[17] The psychic and the social, along with an entire political reality, are a historically determined product of desire. Against psychoanalysis,[18] Deleuze claims that "the unconscious functions like a factory, not as a theater."[19] And, if desire produces historically determined social formation, history as such, becomes the history of desire. This point will become particularly important in late Foucault, when in the introduction to the second volume of *The History of Sexuality: The Use of Pleasure*, he claims that his intention is to study "the history of *desiring* man."[20]

Fourth, desire should not be understood as lack but as a productive process – it produces the real. Deleuze conceptualizes the movement of desire in reference to Kant's *Critique of Practical Reason*, where desire is defined in causal terms. "Desire is the faculty which by means of representations is the *cause* of the actuality of the objects of those representations."[21] This new theory of desire emerges, in many ways, as a response to the psychoanalytic tradition, whose conception of desire *as lack* dominated the French intellectual space of the sixties and seventies. For Deleuze, this new theory of desire is equally important in setting up a counterargument for a hedonistic society who would focus only on the fulfillment of its own pleasures.

Famously, in his 1977 letter to Foucault, *Desire and Pleasure*, Deleuze notes that for him the desire – pleasure problem is "more than a question of words." For my part, says Deleuze, "I can scarcely tolerate the word pleasure."[22] What are the reasons that Deleuze raises against Foucault's notion of pleasure?

Deleuze certainly does not deny the value of pleasure in everyday life, but he refuses to erect pleasure as a superior value. He refuses to consider it as a possible criterion for ethics since pleasure is a transcendence that interrupts the process of desire and, thus, imposes on this very process a certain kind of teleology. In writing about Masoch, he insist that "what interests me [in Masoch] is not the pain but the fact that 'pleasure interrupts the positivity of desire' [and the constitution of its field of immanence]."[23] Pleasure interrupts the very immanent process of desire. The importance of this (seemingly radical) difference is further detailed in our next sections.

2. FOUCAULT'S REJECTION OF DESIRE AND THE AFFIRMATION OF PLEASURE

The goal of our second section is to unpack, in a fairly schematic way, the structure of Foucault's argument against the notion of desire as it appears in *La Volonté de Savoir*. There are four important argumentative moves that Foucault makes in order to set up a relation that takes us from desire –> to discourse –> to plurality of discourses and to a system of normalization –> and ultimately, back to the individual through a system of implantation and production of identities.

The first move is from *desire* to *discourse*. The role of the Christian pastoral was to transform one's desires into discourse. "Not only will you confess to acts contravening the law, but you will seek to transform your desire, your every desire, into discourse."[24] Second, once our desires are transformed into discourse, how do we get to the policing of sex? Certainly, "one had to speak of it [sex] as of a thing to be not simply condemned or tolerated but managed."[25] And how do we manage sex?

There are two distinct aspects in Foucault's analysis. One's confession had to be inserted into a system of utility designed by a whole array of public discourses.[26] And, given the normative function of those discourses, certain social formations (the family/the heterosexual monogamy) became the norm (i.e. the legitimate couple). Foucault emphasizes the normative function of those discourses. A medical discourse about health is not just a discourse about a certain organic state. It defines a form of value that society actively promotes. Similarly, biology does not only describe the natural, but it equally sets up normative standards and systems of exclusions by showing what is unnatural or abnormal. A similar process functions for pedagogical or policing discourses. Police had a discourse about the social place where sexuality is considered appropriate behavior. As a consequence, the legitimate couple/the family/the heterosexual monogamy became a norm. What Foucault means by norm is "an internal standard" that would function as a guiding principle for how one ought to mold one's own desires, at the risk of being excluded/rejected if one does conform to it.

Third, thanks to a centrifugal movement, the legitimate couple gained "a right to more discretion."[27] And, what came under scrutiny was the sexuality of all those figures that were not noticed in the past. They had to "step forward and speak", had to "to make the difficult confession of what they were."[28] The common thread here is the question of confessing one's desires. But, how would the order of desire include those forms of sexuality falling outside the norm within its own system of governance?

Fourth, the control of peripheral sexualities "entailed an *incorporation of perversions* and a new *specification of individuals*."[29] Homosexuality is the most emblematic example. The nineteenth-century homosexual became a *personage* at the end of a process of transformation from a case story, from a set of desires, normalized through a complex combination of public and useful discourses (psychological, psychiatric, medical) that implanted perversion into his body as *a raison d'être*.[30]

The strategy here, says Foucault, was not to suppress the alien nature of the homosexual. On the contrary, the goal was to make him visible, to implant in his body a principle of intelligibility, and to make him ultimately an individual whose identity, whose total composition, was entirely saturated by his sexuality. Thus, desire becomes the very vehicle by which a new system of control and management of sexualities is made possible. In order to achieve this, there was a significant shift from the act of transgression itself – "to the stirrings – so difficult to perceive and formulate – of desire."[31] And, confession was the very mechanism that was supposed to reveal the negative, to show our imperfections, our hidden desires, our crimes, our sins, our illnesses, our troubles, all those things that we lack when we are measured up by the norms surrounding us. The "Western man became a confessing animal."[32]

This system does not function through exclusion, but through *specification* and *identification*,[33] and those are the ways in which it penetrates modes of conduct and creates subjectivities. However, this analysis does not preclude the possibility for all those (managed) subjectivities to break loose with the mechanisms of control and to liberate their own desires.

In Part 4 – in the *Objective* section, Foucault considers this objection and he sets up a serious critique against the psychoanalytic theory of desire. He shows that even if psychoanalysts have been claiming that "sex is not repressed",[34] they have still failed to see that "where there is desire, the power relation is already present."[35] Given this power-desire relation, one should not think of desire as lack, nor should one assume that desire is somehow out of the reach of power. The difficulty is that if power is a constitutive element of desire, the only possible outcome is that "we are always already trapped."[36] On the other hand, if power is only external to desire, the promise of liberation becomes our only hope. However, for Foucault, both – the repressive hypothesis and the psychoanalytic explanation – share "the same putative mechanism of power"[37], the juridical one. The idea behind is that the law constitutes desire. This mechanism is restrictive, poor in resources, sparing of its method, monotonous, incapable of invention, doomed to always repeat itself. "It only had the force of the negative on its side."[38] It cannot produce anything and it just posits limits.

Moreover, by being committed to the idea that law constitutes desire, psycho-analysis is committed also to the view that the parent-child relationship is at the root of everyone's sexuality. "It is through them that you gain access to desire."[39] Our desire is thus always somehow constructed around the incestuous desire. Through confession, psychoanalysis "lifts psychical repression"[40] and allows individuals to express it in their discourse. But, at the same time – within the deployment of sexuality – this form of discursive transformation, which was supposed to have an alleviating factor, had also an authoritarian and constraining influence by postulat-ing that one has no sexuality "except by subjecting oneself to this law"[41], to this juridical understanding of desire.

So, what does desire stand for in *La Volonté de Savoir?* Desire definitely stands as a central piece (in the sex-desire doublet) in the deployment of the dispositif of sexuality in order to manage, control, and ultimately produce normalized identities.

3. THE CRITIQUE OF THE LIBERATIONIST PERSPECTIVE

Neither Foucault nor Deleuze and Guattari can accept the *doxa* of sexual rev-olution, for which desire would be a naturally good, pre-discursive energy, and the eternal victim of cultural constraints. The underlying assumption would be that, once the constraints are eliminated, desire would express itself freely and in harmonious ways. This liberationist vision of desire is not simply that of the capitalist merchants of pleasure (for whom people's private interests spontane-ously contribute to the common good and public interest) but it is also that of the 'Freudo-Marxism' tradition (represented especially in the writings of W. Reich and H. Marcuse).

This theoretical position conflates psychical repression and economical exploi-tation. In doing so, it does not break with the system it denounces since it remains prisoner of an old idealist conception of power (the juridico-discursive model, as Foucault identifies it). This model thinks of power according to the old structure of sovereignty, acting primarily as a "law-like", restrictive instance. Here, power is conceived as ideology or repression, whose main formulation is captured by laws and prohibitions. However, this theory of power overlooks the ambivalent nature of the libidinal economy that conditions the economical structures. For Foucault, the liberationist discourse is profoundly self-illusory because it supposes a fundamentally 'good nature' of desire and thus overlooks the fact that liberating our desires is in no way equal to knowing how "to behave ethically in pleasurable relationship with others."[42]

Against the Freudo-Marxist repressive hypothesis, Foucault insists that the problem of struggle is not an economical problem but, above all, a cultural matter that involves a permanent critique of our social formations and desiring investments. As a response, it demands new modes of organization of political power, new ways of relating to our desires and of structuring our practices. In a word, it requires a permanent reassessment of our ways of inhabiting the world and of exercising our power over others and ourselves.

This critical task is precisely the one that Deleuze identified as early as 1974, in his preface to the book of Felix Guattari entitled *Psychoanalysis and Transversality*. If the individual always depends on a collectivity, the analytical activity must conduct a critique of the organizational structures, of the specific theoretical modes of alienation, which determine our beliefs and actions and to which we attach our desires. Introducing coefficients of 'transversality' in the life of desire means opening our social structures and institutional relationships to new modes of connections between different orders (or 'planes').

Transversality, as an epistemological practice, allows us to understand social formations in a new way, as contingent instances of becoming, immanently traversed by connections between inter-affecting bodies. Desire is precisely an existential and transversal power, the material bearer of 'pathic functions', which in turn produce and reproduce (but can also undermine and transform) established hierarchical socio-economical orders. At the very core of social determinism lies therefore desire's coefficient of freedom. Since our desire, through different modes of production, is a productive force that can immanently challenge the economical system as well as make it function.

If desire can indeed take the form of psychic or sexual repression, as internalization of economic exploitation and political domination, the force of desire is nonetheless not reducible to this so-called subjective "interiority" or stasis of desire. The latter are just a reactionary modes of desiring investment. They form a process of subjective self-closure thanks to which dominant socio-economical schema of organization exert and maintain their authority. Moreover, this does not mean that desire could be described as a natural drive that would precede its socio-cultural repression. Rather, desire is coextensive to the social field: socio-economical production is desiring production.

Reich posits a difference of nature between the instinctual and cosmic force of desire and the socio-economical order of repression and Deleuze and Guattari reject his dualism (libidinal vs political economy). They claim that this dualism prevents us from grasping the always already social engineering and thus the radically artificial nature of desire. "We see here the difference with Reich: there is no libidinal economy to impart, by other means, a subjective prolongation to political economy; there is no sexual repression to internalize economic exploitation and political subjection [. . .] this is political economy as such, an economy of flows, which is unconsciously libidinal: *there is only one economy, not two; and desire or libido is just the subjectivity of political economy.*"[43]

This new approach allows us to understand in what sense capitalist economy is precisely grounded on the liberal injunction to liberate and reinvest one's desires in ever-new objects, and thus, allowing for the creation of new markets and the liberation of capitalist consumption itself. The liberal cult of free enjoyment and satisfaction of desires is therefore not a natural expression of desire, but a contingent, cultural organization of our desiring and productive forces which, far from liberating us, binds us to our most reactive tendencies (the living basis of capitalism is affective servitude).

In his preface to *Anti-Oedipus*, Foucault rightly sees a new conception of desire that goes far beyond the Freudo-Marxist doxa. In particular, it goes beyond Reich. As Deleuze and Guattari note in this book, "Reich himself never manages to provide a satisfactory explanation of this phenomenon [why do people desire their own oppression]."[44] The main reason for Reich's failure is that "he reintroduces precisely the line of argument that he was in the process of demolishing, by creating a distinction between rationality as it is or ought to be in the process of social production, and the irrational element in desire, and by regarding only this latter as a suitable subject for psychoanalytic investigation."[45] Deleuze and Guattari do not aim to disclose an ultimate essence of desire, but to show that the unconscious is not the reflection of a so-called human nature, but, rather, the object of a perpetual reinvention of man by man.

This crucial opposition to Reich's blind trust in a desire that would be naturally and spontaneously good shows us why Deleuze and Guattari are not the target of Foucault's critique of desire. The target has always been, as the 1972 joke prompted us to believe, the Freudo-Marxist tradition. While Reich remains caught in a theological vision of desire, preaching orgasmic implosion as a new doctrine of salvation, Deleuze and Guattari radically depart from this view. For them, "desire is never an undifferentiated instinctual energy, but itself the result of a highly developed, engineered setup rich in interactions: a whole supple segmentarity that processes molecular energies and potentially gives desire a fascist determination . . . It's too easy to be antifascist on the molar level, and not even see the fascist inside you, the fascist you yourself sustain and nourish and cherish with molecules both personal and collective."[46]

Thinking of power in a purely immanent and materialist way requires thinking of it as being diffused. Like Foucault's biopower, Deleuze and Guattari's notion of power exerts itself both – at the micro-physical level, by enacting a process of homogenization of conducts, and also – at the macro-physical level, by producing the very conditions of its upheaval. The hypersensitive and nervous subjects of capitalism are radically ambivalent. They can resist power by becoming reactive and increasingly invest in static forms of identity and security (fascism as reactive type of resistance). Or, on the contrary, they can adopt a purely active form of resistance, while realizing that their relative obedience to the system in fact presupposes their intrinsic freedom to obey or to resist.

The entire political problem rests on understanding what Deleuze and Guattari call 'becoming-revolutionary.' One has to become aware of the fact that power always exerts itself on free subjects. Forces of oppression and alienation can also be used *differently* – as a force of self-analysis (schizo-analysis) and self-fashioning. Foucault would certainly endorse this line of argument. The fact that biopower has become a 'power over life' should not prevent us from reclaiming 'a right to desire'[47] in order to reappropriate the forces of our vital and productive bodies. It is certainly our body and all the desire it produces that we wish to liberate from "foreign" domination. It is "on that ground" that we constantly strive to create places of resistance. There is no boundary between these two elements. "I oppress myself inasmuch as that 'I' is the produced of a system of oppression that extends to all aspects of living. The revolutionary consciousness will always be nothing but a mystification unless it is situated within a revolutionary body – within a body that produces its own resistance and liberation."[48]

4. DELEUZE'S CRITIQUE OF PLEASURE AS TRANSCENDENCE *AND* FOUCAULT'S PRAGMATICS OF DESIRE

As we have already mentioned in relation to Deleuze's 1977 letter to Foucault, the desire-pleasure divergence was more than a matter of words.[49] Insofar as pleasure is oriented towards a discharge of energy it can be accomplished only with a sacrifice of desire – with a way of getting rid of desire. In addition, the search for pleasure does not establish any connection with the outside or with others. It remains *ego-logical* through and through. "In its most attractive and indispensable forms, it [pleasure] comes rather as an interruption in the process of desire [. . .] there is a lot of hatred, or fear of desire, in the cult of pleasure. Pleasure is the attribution of the affect [. . .] it is the only means for a person 'to find himself again' in the process of desire which overwhelms him."[50]

This is what Deleuze calls a passive joy. For him, it is merely reaction to an external stimulus. It depends on external causes and, more importantly, it condemns us to seek an impossible object and to produce phantasms. Western thought is nothing but a series of interpretations of desire, which, unfortunately, it all amounts to what Deleuze calls – the two maledictions of desire: "The first malediction of desire, the first malediction that weighs on desire like a Christian curse, and goes back to the Greeks, is that desire is lack. The second malediction is: desire will be satisfied by pleasure, or will be in an enunciable relation with *jouissance*. Of course, there will be those who will tell us that they are not the same things. Nonetheless, there is a peculiar circuit here: desire-pleasure-*jouissance*. And all that, once again, is a way of cursing and liquidating desire."[51]

However, Foucault's concern with the notion of desire does not target Deleuze and Guattari's conception. As he says, in his interview with Jean Le Bitoux, "I'm quite frankly hostile to the pre-Deleuzian or non-Deleuzian notion of desire."[52] Foucault's argument is raised against a negative notion of desire that somehow would *always* play the function of revealing our inner self through the process of confession. He is concerned with the fact that the production of self-discourse – where desire is the primary vehicle – was coopted into a whole of array of standardizing discourses and, made possible a system of (sexual) normalization, which ultimately, produces new identities that can be controlled and managed. In other words, "tell me what your desire is, and I'll tell you who you are [identification] – I'll tell you if you are normal or not, if I can disqualify you and your desires or not [control]."[53]

Deleuze and Guattari's notion of desire *is certainly not negative*. It does not imply lack.[54] It does not produces identities, but only assemblages or multiplicities.[55] And it does so, not by positing new forms of subjectivity that could be controlled. By constructing different assemblages, desire cannot be anymore the vehicle of normalization since normalization demands uniformity, and Deleuze and Guattari's notion of desire produce only heterogeneity.

On the other hand, Foucault was not "fundamentally attached to the notion of pleasure."[56] It was important for him not to think of pleasures as simply what we feel, but also as what we *use* to transform the limits of our sensibility. One should oppose to the techniques of domination (power as action over others' actions) – the pragmatics of self[57] – the active and deliberate cultivation of one's capacity to govern oneself (as action upon one's power to act). Any resistance against established forms of power entails creating new uses of our power for transformation. It means to create new ways of using the very elements (reactive desires and artificial needs) that disempower us and give Power its power. In Deleuze's words, Foucault's pragmatics of desire and pleasure is "a question of "doubling" the play of forces, with a self-relation that allows us to resist, to elude power, [and] to turn life or death against power (*le pouvoir*)."[58] Moreover, it is certainly no longer "a matter of determinate forms, as with knowledge, or of constraining rules, as with power: it's a matter of *optional rules* that make existence a work of art . . . rules at once ethical and aesthetic that constitute ways of existing or styles of life."[59]

An exploration of our potentials for sexuality means first to *desexualize* pleasures and to extract experimentations with our body from the reigns of the norm of sex.[60] It equally implies to compose oneself with other bodies and to become aware of their needs, desires and pleasures. It requires from us to reinvent love and friendship with *and* beyond purely sexual practices. Foucault's move beyond the sexuality principle consists, therefore, in an eroticization of the body in its receptive and active materiality. It is a way to dispossess oneself from one's social identity and to become increasingly susceptible to new types of pleasure.

This is the how these practices of pleasure constitute local strategies of freedom and resistances against *major* politics of sex and the standardization of erotic practices. "It is the *dispositif* of sex that we must break away from, if we aim – through a tactical reversal of the various mechanisms of sexuality – to counter the grips of power with the claims of bodies, pleasures and forms of knowledge, in their multiplicity and their possibility of resistance."[61]

In his interview *Sex, Power and the Politics of Identity*, Foucault makes reference to this positive way of envisioning sexuality, pleasure and desire. Our desiring life and sexuality is something that we ourselves create and, thus, something that we can transform indefinitely. "We have to understand that with our desires, through our desires go new forms of relationships, new forms of love, new forms of creation. Sex is not a fatality: it is a possibility for creative life."[62] Hence, living through one's desires and pleasures (in the most explicit way possible) amounts both to render other possibilities of life visible and to disrupt traditional social codes.

This is certainly what 'care of self' involves in late Foucault. It implies a series of transformative operations one can exert onto oneself in order to become a truly ethical subject. It means the kind of subject that is capable of using knowledge not as a power of social distinction but as a tool for collective and self-transformation. In this context, ethical subjectivity does not preexist the practice of ethics. Rather, it is the product of a constant process of self-experimentation, which not only takes the form of a progressive self-mastery, but can also provide us with a kind of sobriety and joy of self-creation.

CONCLUSION

In short, the desire-pleasure problem is a problem only to the extent that one's analysis focuses primarily on the texts that highlight potential divergences at the expense of numerous philosophical commonalities between these thinkers. It is far from being so significant as to define an incompatibility between Foucault and Deleuze's philosophies. This analysis shows that Deleuze and Guattari were not the target of Foucault's critique of desire in *La Volonté de Savoir*. Equally important, desire comes back and becomes central in *L'usage des plaisirs*, along with a series of sexual practices that are not orgasm driven.

NOTES

1. Daniel Defert, "Chronology," in Christopher Falzon, Timothy O'Leary, and Jana Sawicki (eds.), *A Companion to Foucault* (Chichester: Wiley, 2013), 50.
2. Ibid.
3. Michel Foucault, *History of Sexuality vol. 1, An Introduction* (London: Allen Lane, 1979), 157.
4. Michel Foucault, "Structuralism and Post Structuralism," *Dits et Ecrits* II (Paris: Gallimard, 2001), 1264 (italics added).
5. David Rabouin, "Entre Deleuze et Foucault: Le Jeu du Désir et du Pouvoir," *Critique* 637/638 (June–July 2000): 475–90. Wendy Grace, "Faux Amis: Foucault and Deleuze on Sexuality and Desire," *Critical Inquiry* 36:3 (2009), 53.
6. Gilles Deleuze and Claire Parnet, *From A to Z*, translated/transcribed (into English) by Charles J. Stivale (unpublished manuscript – translation published only as DVD, MIT Press, 2011), 19; from *L'Abécédaire de Gilles Deleuze*, avec Claire Parnet, directed by Pierre-Andre Boutang (1996).
7. We follow here Dan Smith's cartography of the concept of desire as developed in "Deleuze and the Question of Desire: Toward an Immanent Theory of Ethics," *Parrhesia* 2 (2007), 66–78; republished in *Essays on Deleuze* (Edinburgh: Edinburgh University Press, 2012), 175–88.
8. Smith (2007, 74).
9. Smith (2007, 74). The first distinction is between desire and interest. If rational choice theory tells us that we act in such as way as to maximize our interest, for Deleuze and Guattari "our interest exists as a possibility only within the context of a particular social formation, our capitalist formation" (Smith 2007, 73). If I have an interest in becoming an academic, the series of actions that are rationally oriented towards this goal are possible "because my desires, my drives and impulses – are themselves invested in the social formation of what makes that interest possible" (Smith 2007, 74).

10. Felix Guattari, *The Anti-Oedipus Papers*, trans. K. Gotman (New York: Semiotext(e), 2006), 149.
11. Deleuze and Parnet (1996, 20).
12. Gilles Deleuze and Felix Guattari, *Anti-Oedipus, Vol.1 Capitalism and Schizophrenia* (Minneapolis: University of Minnesota Press, 1983), 29.
13. Smith (2007, 74).
14. Deleuze (2004, 262–3).
15. Ibid. 263.
16. Ibid. 262.
17. "All kinds of libidinal-unconscious flows that constitute the delirium of this society." Ibid. 262.
18. Deleuze believes that we cannot reduce a world of delirium to familial determinants. "If you look at delirium whatever it might be about, any delirium whatsoever, it is exactly the contrary of what psychoanalysis has latched onto about it. We don't go into delirium about the father or mother" (Deleuze and Parnet 1996, 20).
19. Deleuze and Parnet (1996, 20).
20. Michel Foucault, *The History of Sexuality: The Use of Pleasure* (New York: Vintage, 1990), 6 (italics added).
21. Deleuze and Guattari (1983, 25).
22. Deleuze, "Desire and Pleasure," trans. Daniel W. Smith, in *Foucault and His Interlocutors*, ed. Arnold I. Davidson (Chicago: University of Chicago Press, 1997), 189.
23. Ibid. 190.
24. Foucault (1979, 23). "The Christian pastoral prescribed as a fundamental duty the task of passing everything having to do with sex through the endless mill of speech" and to transform one's desire into discourse (Foucault 1979, 21 and 23).
25. Foucault (1979, 24).
26. One's confession had to be "inserted into a systems of utility, regulated for the greater good of all, made to function according to an optimum" (Ibid. 24). The optimum for such a utility system is obtain via "useful and public discourses," a whole array of "distinct discursivities which took form in demography, biology, medicine, psychiatry, psychology, ethics, pedagogy, and political criticism" (Ibid. 33).
27. Foucault (1979, 38).
28. "The sexuality of children, mad men and women, and criminals; the sensuality of those who did not like the opposite sex; reveries, obsessions, petty manias, or great transports of rage" (Foucault 1979, 39).
29. Foucault (1979, 43).
30. Ibid. 44.
31. Ibid. 20.
32. Ibid. 59.
33. Foucault (1979, 44 and 48).
34. Ibid. 8 and 81.
35. Ibid. 81.
36. Ibid. 83.
37. Ibid. 85.

38. Ibid. 83.
39. Ibid. 113.
40. Ibid. 128.
41. Ibid.
42. Michel Foucault, "The Ethics of the Care for the Self as a Practice of Freedom," January 20, 1984, in *Philosophy Social Criticism* 12 (1987), 112.
43. Gilles Deleuze, "Three Group-Related Problems," Preface to Félix Guattari, *Psychoanalysis and Transversality: Texts and interviews 1955–1971*, in Deleuze, *Desert Islands and Other Texts 1953–1974* (New York: Semiotext(e), 2004), 195. (italics added)
44. Deleuze and Guattari (1983, 29).
45. Ibid.
46. Gilles Deleuze and Felix Guattari, *A Thousand Plateaus* (Minneapolis: University of Minnesota Press, 1987), 215.
47. Gilles Deleuze and Claire Parnet, *Dialogues*, trans. Hugh Tomlinson and Barbara Habberjam (New York: Columbia University Press, 1977), 147.
48. Felix Guattari, "To Have Done with the Massacre of the Body," in *Chaosophy* (Los Angeles: Semiotext(e), 2009), 207. Translation modified.
49. Gilles Deleuze, "Desire and Pleasure" (1997, 189).
50. Deleuze and Parnet, *Dialogues*, 100.
51. Gilles Deleuze, seminar of 26 March 1973. Available online at www.webdeleuze.com
52. For Foucault's views on Deleuze's notion of desire, see "The Gay Science," *Critical Inquiry* 37 (2011), 389. In the same interview, Foucault raises however a very interesting methodological precaution. "But this is all, let's say on the order of a methodological precaution. The main thing is this notion of an event that is not assigned, and is not assignable, to a subject. Whereas the, let's say, nineteenth-century notion of desire is first and foremost attached to a subject. It's not an event; it's a type of permanent characteristic of the events of a subject, which for this reason leads to an analysis of the subject, a medical analysis of the subject, a judicial analysis of the subject. Tell me what your desire is, and I'll tell you what you are as a subject."
53. Ibid. 389.
54. Deleuze, "Desire and Pleasure," 189.
55. Ibid.
56. Foucault, "Gay Science," 389.
57. Michel Foucault, *The Government of Self and Others* (New York: Palgrave Macmillan, 2010), 5. "I tried to see how and through what concrete forms of the relation to self the individual was called upon to constitute him or herself as moral subject of his or her sexual conduct. In other words, once again this involved bringing about a shift from the question of the subject to the analysis of forms of subjectivation, and to the analysis of these forms of subjectivation through the techniques/technologies of the relation to self, or, if you like, through what could be called *the pragmatics of self*." (italics added)
58. Gilles Deleuze, *Negotiations, 1972–1990* (New York: Columbia University Press, 1995), 98.
59. Ibid.

60. "Sade formulated an eroticism that corresponds to a disciplinarian society (. . .) He bores us, he's a disciplinarian, a sergeant of sex." Michel Foucault, "Sade: Sergent du sexe," *Cinematographe* (1975), 16.
61. Michel Foucault (1997).
62. Michel Foucault, "Sex, Power and the Politics of Identity," an interview conducted by B. Gallagher and A. Wilson in Toronto in June 1982. It appeared in *The Advocate* 400 (August 7, 1984), 26.

CHAPTER 15

Biopower and Control

THOMAS NAIL

INTRODUCTION

What is the relationship between Foucault's concept of biopower and Deleuze's concept of control? Despite the similarities between these two concepts, there is not a single scholarly article that solely thematizes this question, nor a comparative survey of the answers given so far. This essay aims to fill this lacuna. Despite the lack of a full-length interrogation of this question, scholars have taken up several different positions on the relationship between these two concepts. While some distinguish the two concepts based on the content of what they act on (biopower on life vs control on economics), others distinguish them based on the different formal characteristics of how each type of power operates (biopower by management vs control by modulation). These two positions are then subdivided with respect to whether these differences between biopower and control are complementary or oppositional. Finally, a third position argues that biopower and control are both similar and different. The following essay aims to assess and resolve this question with the aide of Deleuze's recently transcribed course lectures on Michel Foucault (1985–6).

But why is there such scholarly division over the relation between these two concepts? At least one explanation for this is that Deleuze only writes about this concept in any length once in 1990, in a short essay entitled, "Postscripts on the Societies of Control." In this essay Deleuze clearly contrasts control with disciplinary power and suggests that Foucault had also moved beyond disciplinary power in his later work. While this suggests some sort of correlation between biopower and control (both coming after disciplinary power), Deleuze makes no mention of their relationship in this text. The other place one would expect to see a direct comparison of these two concepts is in Deleuze's book on Foucault – but with only a couple mentions of biopower in this book, Deleuze offers no satisfactory comparisons with the idea of control. If they were the same, surely Deleuze would have said so, right? Perhaps Deleuze's equivocation in these texts is why the different scholarly positions on biopower and control can all agree on one thing: biopower is not the same as control.

Interestingly, however, Deleuze did compare these two concepts, just not in these texts. One of the more valuable contributions of Deleuze's recently transcribed course lectures on Foucault is that Deleuze offers several hours' worth of direct comparison of biopower and control, that unfortunately never made it into any of his published works. What we find in these lectures from 8 and 15 April 1986 is that Deleuze not only entirely equates biopower and control, but also attributes their shared origin to William Burroughs' essay "The Limits of Control," published in 1975. One year before Foucault introduces the concept of biopower in *La volonté de savoir* (1976), Deleuze claims, based on personal knowledge, that Foucault was "profoundly struck by Burroughs' analysis of social control."[1] In fact, Foucault and Burroughs even presented on the same conference panel on 14 November 1975 at the Semiotext(e) Schizo-Culture colloquium at Columbia University. Burroughs' paper was entitled "The Impasses of Control," and Foucault's was entitled "We are not Repressed." Based on Burroughs' concept of control, Deleuze claims, Foucault develops the idea of biopower.

Can it be that biopower and control are the same? Or is Deleuze making a Foucauldian monster? Do biopower and control define power over the same content? Do they both have all the same formal characteristics? While scholars on this question have laid out three different answers to these questions, the aim of this essay is to argue for a fourth position. The thesis of this essay is thus that biopower and control are the same concept of power in both content and form. In order to defend this thesis, this essay is divided into three main sections. The first section begins by laying out the three scholarly positions adopted thus far on this question and the textual support offered for each position. Once we understand these arguments and their basis in the published works of Deleuze, the second section then compares these positions with the account offered by Deleuze in his 1986 lectures on Foucault. Finally, the third section examines the content and formal characteristics of both biopower and control in this light, ultimately arguing that the two concepts are, and were always, meant to describe the same type of power.

I. Biopower vs Control

The arguments for the difference between biopower and control can be grouped into three distinct types: the argument based on their difference in content, the argument based on their difference in form, and finally, the argument based on their overlap. The aim of this first section is to consider each of these arguments in turn and what textual support is offered in favor of each. Once this is accomplished we can then see, in the next section, if Deleuze's recently transcribed lectures shed any new light on these arguments or not.

Life vs economics

The first argument for the difference between biopower and control is that they refer to different types of content. Biopower, it is argued, is defined by "the political control over life and living beings," while control is defined by explicitly economic and informational content. Steven Shaviro, for example, argues in his essay "The 'Bitter Necessity' of Debt: Neoliberal Finance and the Society of Control" that "far from focusing on biopower or biopolitics, Foucault abandons this direction of his thought"[2] in favor of an economic analysis of neoliberalism in his (1978–9) Collège de France lectures, *The Birth of Biopolitics*. Shaviro quotes Foucault's description of this power as "the image, idea, or theme-program of a society in which there is an optimization of systems of difference, in which the field is left open to fluctuating processes."[3] Thus, for Shaviro, Foucault's abandonment of the concept of biopower marks a theoretical step forward, as well as a step closer to Deleuze's own concept of control societies similarly defined by neoliberal economics. "Both Foucault, in his analysis of neoliberalism, and Deleuze, in his analysis of the control society," Shaviro concludes, "insist upon what I can only call an *economism* at the heart of postmodernity."[4]

I would like to highlight two important points in Shaviro's argument. The first is that Shaviro defines biopower exclusively by its political content: life. For Shaviro, it seems that biopower has no formal characteristics. Or if it does, they are not essential to its definition. This creates an interesting absence of nomenclature for the new concept of non-biopolitical economic power developed in *The Birth of Biopolitics*. The second is that not only are biopower and control different, they are also mutually exclusive. Shaviro argues that

> [Foucault] suggests – contrary to so much of the theorizing that has been done in his name in the years since his death – that we cannot understand contemporary society in terms of the supposed postulation of 'life' as a target and focus of power. We need to follow the proliferation of market logic instead.[5]

Not only are they mutually exclusive, economic power is a clear theoretical advancement over the analysis of biopower. In fact, Shaviro goes as far as to claim that biopolitical analysis cannot understand contemporary society at all.

Shaviro is not the only one to have defined biopower exclusively or even just primarily by the content to which it refers: life. In the *History of Sexuality, Volume 1*, Foucault himself defines biopower as a "political power [that] had assigned itself the task of administering life,"[6] and "brought life and its mechanisms into the realm of explicit calculations."[7] In his (1975–6) lectures, *Society Must be Defended*, Foucault defines biopower as the government of "man in so far as he is a living being."[8] The definition of biopower as the government over living beings has now spread across academic disciplines.

Control, on the other hand, according to Deleuze's published works, is not defined solely by the content of life. Shaviro argues that control is primarily a theory of economic power, and Antonio Negri even describes it as primarily a theory of informational, communicational, or digital power.[9] In both of these cases control is understood as a power over the non-living. Control is defined as non-biopower. Despite their shared agreement on the content-based difference between biopower and control, Shaviro and Hardt and Negri draw opposite conclusions from this difference. For Shaviro, this difference renders biopower outmoded and useless, whereas for Hardt and Negri this is precisely what makes them complementary. "The society of control," they say, "is able to adopt the biopolitical context as its exclusive terrain of reference."[10] Thus, in this first definition biopower and control are different because biopower is the government over the living and control is the government over the non-living.

Management vs modulation

The second argument for the difference between biopower and control is that they have different formal characteristics. Biopower, it is argued, is defined by "the *management* of living beings," while control is defined by "a *modulation*, indifferent to life." Joshua Kurz, for example, argues in his essay "(Dis)locating Control: Transmigration, Precarity and the Governmentality of Control," that "what we are seeing [in contemporary politics] is not a 'population management' paradigm (i.e. bio-politics), but one of 'population modulation' (i.e. control)."[11] "Management," according to Kurz,

> is teleological, outcome-oriented; it is about accomplishing goals set along a predetermined path toward a predetermined end. Modulation, however, is about speed, the amplification or sublimation of turbulence, rhythm; it is about amplifying and redirecting flows whose cause exists outside of the purview of modulation. In short, modulation has no goals, no plan . . . Management and modulation are qualitatively different.[12]

With respect to immigration politics, "biopower," according to Kurz, "is predicated upon a system of enclosures that presume impermeable borders – even if they do not exist in practice."[13] Control, on the other hand, "is no longer about reinforcing the space of enclosure (i.e. US border sanctity), but instead 'thins' the population selectively."[14] This shift in contemporary governance is precisely why, according to Kurz, "Foucault's lectures on *The Birth of Biopolitics* and Deleuze's essay on control largely ignore the term 'biopolitics' and instead, respectively, focus on neoliberalism and the transition from discipline to control."[15]

I would like to flag two important points in Kurz's argument. First, not only is there a qualitative difference in form between biopower and control (management vs modulation), there is also a categorical difference in content (life and populations vs indifference to life and populations).[16] Biopower and control, according to Kurz, are different in every respect and are exclusive: what we are seeing is thus *not* biopower, *but* control. Second, however, only lines later, Kurz claims that control is "primarily *indifferent towards life* . . . except only when it is strategically useful to be otherwise."[17] This raises a couple of questions unanswered by Kurz: does control take life to be the subject of its control or not? When it does, does it then take the formal character of biopower or does it continue the formal process of modulation? Does it change in content or in form? In either case the divisions Kurz has erected are undermined. It seems to me there is an equivocation as to whether these two forms of power are exclusive or complementary, and in what sense they are so.

Matters are only made more complicated when Kurz favorably cites a chart of social power published by John Protevi on his website, which does not seem to allow for the possibility of the overlapping content that Kurz argues for. Protevi's chart shows biopower beginning in 1850 and continuing to the present, and control beginning in 1980 and continuing to the present. In this way Protevi offers an unequivocally complementarist position. According to Protevi's chart, biopower and control are different in form and content and yet complementary and overlapping only *in history*. The only similarity they have in common is that they exist temporally from 1980 onward. Biopower and control thus act on their own respective content according to their own formal characteristics and never merge or overlap with respect to them. Protevi's chart shows biopower's theory of power to be based on governmentality, control's to be based on neoliberalism. Where the primary actor of biopower is the subject, the primary actor of control is the self-entrepreneur.[18] Across eleven categories, Protevi maintains that biopower and control are different.

Just as the argument for the difference between the content of biopower and control had its exclusivist position in Shaviro and complementarist position in Hardt and Negri, so the argument for formal difference has its exclusivist position in Kurz (even if this is not consistently so) and its complementarist position in Protevi (even if this is only historical). But Kurz is not the only one to equivocate on the similarities between biopower and control.

Context and intensification

Thus, the third argument for the difference between biopower and control is that they are both similar and different. This position is equivocal because its proponents are not clear as to what these particular similarities and differences are exactly. The first proponents of this position are Michel Hardt and Antonio Negri. They write together in their book *Empire*, that biopower is the "context," "terrain of reference," or "realm" in which the new paradigm of control societies take place. "The society of control," they say, "is able to adopt the biopolitical context as its exclusive terrain of reference."[19] "In the passage from disciplinary society to the society of control," they say, "a new paradigm of power is realized which is defined by the technologies that reorganize society as a realm of biopower."[20] Finally, they say, "these concepts of the society of control and biopower both describe central aspects of the concept of Empire."[21]

These passages give rise to several questions left unanswered in *Empire*. What exactly are the concrete or formal differences between these clearly different concepts so central to Empire? What does it mean for biopower to be the context or terrain of control? Does this mean that biopower came first and control later? Does this mean that biopower is the content which is acted on by the form of control? If so, does this mean that biopower and control are both defined by the same content of life and populations?

Despite their equivocation about the similarities and differences between biopower and control, Hardt and Negri do offer us a clear account of the invention of the concept of control. While the transition from discipline to control was only implicit in Foucault, they say, Deleuze renders it explicit.[22] Does this suggest that Foucault had not conceived of a form of power after discipline? Surely, that ignores Foucault's creation of the concept of biopower. Or are Hardt and Negri suggesting instead that biopower is the same as control only implicitly, and Deleuze just makes this explicit? This, however, would seem to contradict Hardt and Negri's position that the two concepts are different: one being the terrain of the other. Again, the answers to these sorts of questions are not at all clear.

This same type of equivocation is continued in a slightly different way in Jeffrey Nealon's book, *Foucault Beyond Foucault* (2007). In a section of his book titled, "Through (Foucaultian) Biopower to (Deleuzian) Control," Nealon argues that control is a Foucauldian "intensification" of both discipline and biopower into a whole new form of power. He says,

> following the Foucaultian logic of power we've been developing here, as societies of control extend and intensify the tactics of discipline and biopower (by linking training and surveillance to evermore-minute realms of everyday life), they also give birth to a whole new form.[23]

These passages raises several questions. First, the title of the section seemed to indicate that we were moving from Foucauldian biopower to Deleuzian control, and now the above passage indicates that this move takes place entirely within Foucault's own logic of the intensification of power. The argument here seems to be that the concept of control is Foucault's concept. Nealon then claims that "Deleuze further elaborates on the Foucaultian distinction between discipline and control."[24] So the argument here seems to be that Foucault invents the idea of control (contrasted with discipline and/or biopower?) and Deleuze simply elaborates on it. Thus, my second question, how much does Deleuze elaborate it? Does Deleuze elaborate it so much that it becomes something substantially different from biopower and thus non-Foucauldian? Or are they exactly the same concept just elaborated with different examples? Further, if Foucault had really invited the concept of control, why does Nealon leave this type of power missing in his chart of power on page 45, which shows only biopower from 1850 to the present and no mention of control? In all of these claims Nealon offers no textual support from Foucault saying that biopower was intensified into the concept of control. The only one who talks about control as a type of power is Deleuze.

While Hardt and Negri claim that biopower is the "terrain" of control, and Nealon claims that control is an "intensification" of biopower, in both cases it remains entirely unclear what the exact similarities and differences are between the two forms of power. Again, this scholarly division and equivocation is partly the result of a lack of any explicit comparison between these two concepts in the published works of Deleuze and Foucault. Thus, we turn now to Deleuze's recently transcribed 1985–6 course lectures on Foucault to help shed some light on these questions.

II. THE LIMITS OF CONTROL

Deleuze was so affected by Foucault's death in 1984, that he began writing a book on him immediately. When asked why he wanted to write such a book, Deleuze was quite clear, "it marks an inner need of mine, my admiration for him, how I was moved by his death, and his unfinished work."[25] Deleuze's desire for some kind of reconciliation with Foucault seems to have been a mutual one. According to Didier Eribon, one of Foucault's most heartfelt wishes, knowing that he would not live long, was to reconcile with Deleuze.[26] After speaking at Foucault's funeral, Deleuze's book project on Foucault began as a lecture series given at the Université de Paris VIII between 1985 and 1986. The seminars were recorded by various students on cassettes, which the Bibliothèque Nationale de France converted into digital files. But these lectures were not merely a scholarly commentary on Foucault's work. They were, in the words of Frédéric Gros, "[a] means [of] discovering the founding principles, [and] laying bare the inherent metaphysics of [his] thought."[27] "It is amazing to see," Gros admits in an interview with François Dosse, "how Deleuze, who couldn't have had any knowledge of the Collège de France lectures, was so accurate in his interpretation."[28]

Among many other insights offered by these lectures on Foucault, they are also Deleuze's most sustained description and comparison of the two concepts of bio-power and control. Given the lack of such a comparison in Deleuze's published works and the subsequent division among scholarly interpretations on this topic, these lectures offer us the possibility of further clarifying the relationship between biopower and control.

But before we begin looking at the defining characteristics of biopower and control, according to Deleuze's lectures on Foucault, we should begin with the shared origin of these two concepts. We should begin with William Burroughs. "Control," according to Deleuze "is the name Burroughs gave to modern power,"[29] "and Foucault sees it fast approaching."[30] "A biopolitics of populations," Deleuze says in his 8 April lecture on Foucault,

> what can we call this third [type of power]? We call it, following the American author, Burroughs, a formation of control power. We have therefore: sovereign power, disciplinary power, and control power . . . I am authorized to say this because of Foucault's admiration and familiarity with Burroughs, even though, to my knowledge, he never spoke of him in his writings, his [influence] on him was great, notably the analyses Burroughs made of social control in modern societies after the war [WWII]. After the war this had really struck Foucault.[31]

According to Deleuze, Foucault was inspired by Burroughs' analysis of social control so much that he based the concept of biopower on it. As early as 1961, in *The Soft Machine*, Burroughs was already describing a softer and more flexible system of modern power that worked on the "thought feeling and sensory impressions of the workers."[32] Before the publication of *La Volonté de Savoir* (1976), Burroughs had also published an essay called "The Limits of Control" (1975) that described an idea of control power as a supple and non-totalizing power that works directly on *life*. "All control systems," Burroughs says, "try to make control as tight as possible, but at the same time, if they succeeded completely there would be nothing left to control . . . *Life is will* (motivation) and the workers would no longer be alive, perhaps literally." Thus control, for Burroughs, is always a limited and flexible control of life without totalizing or destroying it. "Control," he says, "needs opposition or acquiescence; otherwise, it ceases to be control." "In fact, the more completely hermetic and seemingly successful a control system is, the more vulnerable it becomes." Such a system, Burroughs continues, "would be completely disoriented and shattered by even one person who tampered with the control [system]." Thus, concession is a crucial part of control, Burroughs writes, because "concession is still the retention of control. Here's a dime, I keep a dollar." Following Burroughs analysis of the flexible social control over life, Deleuze can then make the following claim about Foucault:

> it seems to me that it's truly a misinterpretation to make Foucault into a thinker who privileges confinement. On the contrary: sometimes he subordinates confinement to a more profound function of exteriority, and sometimes he announces the end of confinement in favor of another kind of function of control altogether, defined by open and not closed functions.[33]

"Biopolitics," according to Deleuze, is this new form of power, prefigured by Burroughs, that "manages life in numerous multiplicities and in an open space, controlling life, as a biopolitics of populations."[34]

This brings us to Deleuze's definition of biopower and control. First, how does Deleuze define the type of content that biopower and control take as their object? Biopower, Deleuze says, is defined by the "management of life and populations distributed in an open [i.e. non-totalized, or smooth (*lisse*)] space."[35] But what is a population? A population, Deleuze says, is "a large multiplicity without assignable limits."[36] "We are in the age of the biopolitics of populations," Deleuze says, "where the population can just as easily be the population of grains, sheep, vineyards, as of men; all of them can be taken as populations."[37] While the subject of sovereign power, according to Deleuze is in the end, the sovereign (i.e. God) and the subject of discipline is man, the subject of biopower is the living within man.[38] The civil right of man is thus becoming more and more the social right of living populations. The civil contract, Deleuze says, "is a relation between a person and a person, it is not a relation at the level of a population. You can have conventions between members of a population, but you cannot have contractual relations, it's absolutely impossible."[39] Thus, contemporary illness, workers strikes, genocide, abortion, and political struggles increasingly take place not with respect to a conflict over a contract between persons, but refer to a third: the living population.

So, how does Deleuze define the content and subjects of control? "In the formations of control," Deleuze says, "power and right take for their object, life. But power and right under what form? Under the form of 'the management of life, the management of populations' or under the form of right, the social right to 'assure life in man.'"[40] Deleuze is quite clear, biopower and control are both defined by the management of living populations and their social right in open space. They have exactly the same content.

But how does Deleuze define the form of biopower and control? Both are contrasted with the enclosed spaces of disciplinary confinement and identified with the open spaces of probability. According to Deleuze, the process of rendering probable the unpredictable is the key formal aspect that defines both biopower and control. In his 8 April lectures on Foucault, Deleuze says:

> it goes without saying that confinement is absolutely useless. What is more, it is becoming expensive, it's becoming stupid, and socially irrational. The calculus of probabilities is much better than the walls of a prison. It is a control power and no longer a disciplinary power. I think this must be said, and said equally for all the elements in Foucault.[41]

Control power, according to Deleuze, is what comes after disciplinary power and is defined by the calculus of probabilities in Foucault's work. Deleuze defines biopower in exactly the same way. "Biopolitics," Deleuze says, "never stops rendering probable, it aims to render probable the rise in birth rates, for example; it aims to oversee [*surveiller*], it is a management . . . implies a management of probable phenomena, births, deaths, marriages, etc."[42] "We see here," Deleuze continues,

> the importance of the difference between discipline and biopolitics. Biopolitics takes place in an open space of great multiplicities whose limits cannot be assigned. They are only manageable according to the calculus of probabilities, by the development of a calculus of probabilities in the sense of the social control of probabilities, probabilities of marriage in a nation, probabilities of death, probabilities of birth, etc.[43]

The age of confinement is quite different than the age of biopolitics. "The age of the biopolitics of populations," Deleuze says, is defined by

> probability scales, that replaces the assignable limits of confinement. That is to say, zones of probability. You have zones of probability for French people going on vacation to Spain, etc. There are no more limits: you have no need for limits. Do you understand why this is not confinement? The third age is no longer that of confinement. With confinement, there is no longer anything to be done, because the assignable limits are replaced by zones of frequency. It is the zones of frequency that count. Why do you need to lock people up when you know you can find them all on the highway at a given day and hour?[44]

Thus, biopolitics and control, according to Deleuze, are both defined by the management and control of probabilities: probabilities of people on vacation, of cars on the highway, as well their control through the use of a unified system of magnetic cards. With the advent of home nursing teams, the institution is no longer one of confinement but of home monitoring and management.

In conclusion, we can locate for the first time, in Deleuze's lectures on Foucault, a clear equivalence between biopower and control in both content and form. Both take the life of populations as their object and the management of probabilities as their defining formal characteristic. These lectures thus pose interesting implications for the previous scholarly arguments for the relative or absolute differences between biopower and control. In the third and final section of this paper, I will thus examine the implications of these lectures on the three types of scholarly arguments from the first section. In this final evaluation I conclude that there is no meaningful difference between biopower and control.

III. BIOPOWER | CONTROL

Before looking at the implications of these lectures for the previous three scholarly arguments, it is important to note their speculative character. It must be admitted that nowhere in Deleuze or Foucault's previously published writings do we find any direct contrast between biopower and control. The scholarly arguments for the various differences between biopower and control have largely hinged on interpretive comparisons based on what Deleuze or Foucault did *not* say. For example, why does Foucault *not* talk about biopower very much in his lectures on *The Birth of Biopower*? Why does Deleuze *not* directly equate biopower and control in his essay on control societies? The arguments for the difference between biopower and control have all hinged on the absence, rather than the presence, of a direct comparison between them. Deleuze's lectures on Foucault, on the other hand, offer us the first positive comparison between these two concepts. So what can we conclude about the implication of these lectures for these three arguments for the difference between biopower and control?

The first argument we looked at was the argument that biopower and control responded to different content. Biopower, it is argued, is defined by "the political control over life and living beings," while control is defined by explicitly economic and informational content. The textual support Steven Shaviro offers for this argument is that "Foucault abandons this direction of his thought" in favor of an economic analysis of neoliberalism in his (1978–9) College de France lectures, *The Birth of Biopolitics*. Joshua Kurz uses this same argument. Not only does Foucault abandon the theory of the management of life, these authors argue, but this theory also became useless for understanding contemporary economic phenomena. The fact that Foucault says nothing about biopower in his lectures on biopolitics means that he has abandoned it.

There are three problems with this argument. First, Foucault does not abandon biopower in his lectures on neoliberalism. In fact, Foucault says precisely the opposite:

> it seems to me that the analysis of biopolitics can only get under way when we have understood this general regime that we can call the question of truth, of economic truth in the first place, within governmental reason . . . only when we know what this governmental regime called liberalism was, will we be able to grasp what biopolitics is.[45]

Not only does Foucault not abandon the concept of biopower, the entire lecture series is devoted to providing a genealogy of its emergence in liberalism. Accordingly, the second problem with this argument is that in these lectures Foucault argues that economic rationality is fundamental to biopolitics. In fact, we cannot understand one without the other. Foucault defines both economic rationality and biopolitics as the management of unpredictable populations. Populations, as Deleuze rightly notes, include both biological and non-biological populations. Economic phenomena are thus not the opposite of living phenomena. The third problem with this argument is that it lacks any direct textual support in Deleuze's work. We find exactly the opposite claim in Deleuze's lectures on Foucault, when Deleuze says that "in the formations of control power, power and right take for their object, life . . . 'the management of life, the management of populations.'"[46] Accordingly, biopower is not a useless theory of contemporary power and control is not a theoretical advancement over it: they respond to the same content. There is clear textual support from both Deleuze and Foucault that biopower and control both take living populations as their object.

The second argument we looked at was the argument that biopower and control are defined by different formal characteristics. Biopower, it is argued, is defined by management, while control is defined by modulation. Management, according to Kurz, is teleological and defined by a system of enclosures that presume impermeable borders. Modulation, on the other hand, according to Kurz, is non-teleological and defined by the amplification and redirection of flows in open spaces.[47] Management and modulation are thus formally different.

Here again, there are three problems with this argument. First, Foucault does not define biopolitical management by enclosed spaces. In both *Security, Territory, Population* and *The Birth of Biopolitics*, Foucault says exactly the opposite.

> This analysis is not at all the ideal or project of an exhaustively disciplinary society in which the legal network hemming in individuals is taken over and extended internally by, let's say, normative mechanisms. Nor is it a society in

which a mechanism of general normalization and the exclusion of those who cannot be normalized is needed. On the horizon of this analysis we see instead the image, idea, or theme-program of a society in which there is an optimization of systems of difference, in which the field is left open to fluctuating processes, in which minority individuals and practices are tolerated, in which action is brought to bear on the rules of the game rather than on the players, and finally in which there is an environmental type of intervention instead of the internal subjugation of individuals.[48]

Biopolitics is not defined by enclosures or confinement, but by the management of fluctuating processes in an open field. Even with respect to "so-called" town planning in the eighteenth century, Foucault points out how this was not a matter of enclosure but of "the spatial, juridical, administrative, and economic opening up of the town: resituating the town in a space of circulation."[49] The opening up of economic circulation between towns is precisely how Foucault characterizes economic liberalism: as the "the form of competition between states in an open economic and political field."[50]

The second problem with this argument is that Foucault also does not define biopolitical management as teleological. Again, he says the opposite. According to Foucault, "the first great theorist of what we could call bio-politics, bio-power," Jean-Baptiste Moheau, describes how government cannot plan society with absolute certainty in advance, but instead must respond to the fluctuation of natural givens: the milieu. "The town," Foucault says, "will not be conceived or planned according to a static perception that would ensure the perfection of the function there and then, but will open onto a future that is not exactly controllable, not precisely measured or measurable, and a good town plan takes into account precisely what might happen."[51] Biopolitical management thus is not a certain plan for the present, it is a potential plan for an uncertain future.

The third problem with this argument is that there is no textual support for it. In fact, this argument is directly contradicted by Deleuze, in his lectures on Foucault, as well as by Foucault himself. In his clearest articulation of this, Deleuze says: "In the formations of control, power and right take for their object, life . . . under the form of 'the management of life, the management of populations.'"[52] Control is management. Bringing the three concepts of control, biopower, and management together, Deleuze says:

We see here the importance of the difference between discipline and biopolitics. Biopolitics takes place in an open space of great multiplicities whose limits cannot be assigned. They are only manageable according to the calculus of probabilities . . . in the sense of the social control of probabilities.

Discipline normalizes closed spaces, whereas biopower and control both manage open spaces according to a calculus of probabilities. Kurz's argument is also contradicted by Foucault in his description of pastoral power, which is not a disciplinary mechanism based on the teaching of general normative principles, "but rather," a teaching "by a daily modulation, and this teaching must also pass through an observation, a supervision, a direction exercised at every moment and with the least discontinuity possible over the sheep's whole, total conduct."[53] With respect to crime, drugs, and taxes, Foucault similarly argues that instead of trying to control them absolutely through normalization, biopolitics actively controls them through a continual modulation of incentives and within probabilistic limits.

The third argument for the difference between biopower and control we looked at was the argument that there are both similarities and differences between biopower and control. In particular, biopower is said to be the "context" or "terrain" of control, according to Hardt and Negri, or that control is an "intensification" of biopower, according to Nealon. Again, there are three problems with these arguments. First, neither of these arguments state exactly what characteristics of biopower and control are shared and which are not. If biopower is the context of control or control is an intensification of biopower, this does not tell us much of anything about the difference between them. It only tells us that "there are some differences."

Second, these arguments lack textual support in Foucault's work. While Foucault does speak of biopower as an intensification of discipline, as is argued by Hardt and Negri, Foucault does not, however, speak of control as an intensification of biopower. Nealon's argument is thus a creative attempt to reconcile biopower and control in the absence of any published text from either of the authors on the subject. Hardt and Negri go even further in their speculation by suggesting that the idea was already implicit in Foucault and Deleuze just made it explicit. This is an interesting idea, but one which Hardt and Negri provide no textual support for in Foucault's work.

The third problem with both of these arguments is that their interpretations are contradicted by Deleuze's lectures on Foucault. In these lectures, as I have shown in the sections above, Deleuze identifies biopower and control in both form and content. Further, there is no place in his lectures where he contrasts them at any point. The argument that control was already implicit in Foucault's work and Deleuze just made it explicit, however, does have some merit. Although this would require some extensive textual support in Foucault, one could argue that this is precisely what Deleuze's lectures on Foucault do. But this argument is true only on the condition that the two ideas remain the same and not, as Hardt and Negri, argue, different (insofar as they argue biopower is the terrain of control). This is another point of equivocation in Hardt and Negri's argument. Is control up to and nothing more than the explication of the idea of biopower, already at work in Foucault, or does control at some point become different enough to make biopower its terrain of action?

CONCLUSION

Whether Deleuze makes explicit the idea of control implicit in Foucault's concept of biopower, or Foucault makes explicit the idea of biopower in Burroughs' concept of control, the best supported textual conclusion we can make at this point in the debate is that biopower and control are synonymous in both content and form. Both take the life of populations as their content and the management of probability as their form. But the statistical control over the life of populations should not be understood in the limited sense of biological beings alone. There is also a life of the city, a life of crime, political life, economic life, etc. Foucault and Deleuze are both quite clear in their examples of biopolitics that it includes the management of city-planning, money, transportation, crime, information, communication, water, sheep, grain and the climate, just as much as it is the statistical management of human births, deaths, marriages and illness. These are all living forces insofar as they are ultimately uncertain and non-totalizable phenomena. Accordingly, they cannot be managed as individuals, but only as populations with non-assignable limits: as multiplicities, as zones of frequency.

NOTES

1. Gilles Deleuze, *Lectures de Cours sur Michel Foucault (1985–1986)*, 8 April 1986. Transcribed lectures and original audio files are available at http://www.cla.purdue.edu/research/deleuze/Course%20Transcriptions.html
2. Steven Shaviro, "The 'Bitter Necessity' of Debt: Neoliberal Finance and the Society of Control," *Concentric: Literary and Cultural Studies* 37:1 (2011), 7.
3. Michel Foucault, *The Birth of Biopolitics: Lectures at the Collège de France, 1978–79*, trans. Michel Senellart (Basingstoke: Palgrave Macmillan, 2008), 259–60.
4. Shaviro, "The 'Bitter Necessity' of Debt," 7.
5. Ibid.
6. Michel Foucault, *The History of Sexuality: Volume 1, An Introduction* (New York: Vintage, 1990), 139.
7. Foucault, *The History of Sexuality: Volume 1*, 143.
8. Michel Foucault, *Society Must be Defended: Lectures at the Collège de France, 1975–76*, ed. Mauro Bertani and Alessandro Fontana, trans. David Macey (New York: Picador, 2003), 240.
9. Gilles Deleuze, *Negotiations, 1972–1990* (New York: Columbia University Press, 1995), 174.

10. Michael Hardt and Antonio Negri, *Empire* (Cambridge, MA: Harvard University Press, 2000), 24.
11. Joshua Kurz, "(Dis)locating Control: Transmigration, Precarity and the Governmentality of Control," *Behemoth: a Journal on Civilization* 5:1 (2012), 32.
12. Kurz, "(Dis)locating Control," 32.
13. Ibid. 42.
14. Ibid. 34.
15. Ibid. 33.
16. ". . . contemporary governance is no longer territorial (although it retains territorial elements), [7] nor is it directed at a bounded population (although it does not supersede population-level projects entirely), nor is it about the preservation and promotion of life (although it sometimes does this). To be more precise, there is a new diagram of power at work that is primarily indifferent towards life . . . except only when it is strategically useful to be otherwise." Ibid. 32–3.
17. Ibid. 33.
18. http://www.protevi.com/john/Foucault/powerchart.pdf
19. Hardt and Negri, *Empire*, 24.
20. Ibid.
21. Ibid. 25.
22. Ibid. 25, and Michel Hardt, "La société mondiale de contrôle," in Éric Alliez (ed.), *Gilles Deleuze une vie philosophique* (Paris: Les Empêcheurs de penser en rond, 1998), 359.
23. Jeffrey Nealon, *Foucault beyond Foucault: Power and its Intensifications since 1984.* (Stanford: Stanford University Press, 2008), 68.
24. Nealon, *Foucault beyond Foucault*, 68.
25. Gilles Deleuze, *Negotiations*, 94.
26. François Dosse, *Gilles Deleuze & Félix Guattari: Intersecting Lives*, trans. Deborah Glassman (New York: Columbia University Press, 2010), 328.
27. Frédéric Gros, "Le Foucault de Deleuze: une fiction métaphysique," *Philosophie* 47 (September 1995), 54.
28. Dosse, *Gilles Deleuze & Félix Guattari*, 327. Frédéric Gros, interview with the author.
29. Gilles Deleuze, *Negotiations*, 71.
30. Gilles Deleuze, *Negotiations*, 178.
31. Deleuze, *Lectures de Cours sur Michel Foucault*, April 8, 1986.
32. William Burroughs, *The Soft Machine* (New York: Grove/Atlantic Inc., 2011), 93.
33. Deleuze, *Lectures de Cours sur Michel Foucault*, April 8, 1986.
34. Ibid.
35. Ibid.
36. Ibid.
37. Ibid.
38. Ibid.
39. Ibid.
40. Ibid. April 15, 1986.
41. Ibid. April 8, 1986.
42. Ibid. January 14, 1986.

43. Ibid. April 8, 1986.
44. Ibid. April 8, 1996.
45. Foucault, *The Birth of Biopolitics*, 21–2.
46. Deleuze, *Lectures de Cours sur Michel Foucault*, April 15, 1986.
47. Kurz, "(Dis)locating Control," 32.
48. Foucault, *The Birth of Biopolitics*, 259–60.
49. Michel Foucault, *Security, Territory, Population: Lectures at the Collège De France, 1977–78*, ed. and trans. Michel Senellart, François Ewald and Alessandro Fontana (Basingstoke: Palgrave Macmillan, 2007), 13.
50. Foucault, *Security, Territory, Population*, 293.
51. Foucault, *Security, Territory, Population*, 20.
52. Deleuze, *Lectures de Cours sur Michel Foucault*, April 15, 1986.
53. Foucault, *Security, Territory, Population*, 181.

CHAPTER 16

Two Concepts of Resistance: Foucault and Deleuze

DANIEL W. SMITH

In a letter Deleuze addressed to Foucault in 1977, shortly after the publication of the first volume on *The History of Sexuality* (and which has since been published under the title "Desire and Pleasure"), Deleuze laid out several distinctions between his own philosophical trajectory and Foucault's, one of which concerns, precisely, the status of Foucault's concept of *resistance*. "It seems to me that Michel confronts a problem that does not have the same status for me," Deleuze wrote.

> If *dispositifs* of power are in some way constitutive [for Foucault], there can only be phenomena of "resistance" against them, and the question bears on the status of these phenomena . . . For myself, the status of phenomena of resistance is not a problem; since lines of flight are primary determinations, since [it is] desire [– and not power – that] assembles the social field . . . if the first given of a society is that everything takes flight, then everything in it is deterritorialized.[1]

A Thousand Plateaus (which was published in 1981, four years after Deleuze penned his letter) contains a now well-known footnote where Deleuze and Guattari elaborate these claims:

> Our only points of disagreement with Foucault are the following: (1) to us the [social] assemblages seem fundamentally to be assemblages not of power, but of desire (desire is always assembled), and power seems to be a strati-fied dimension of the assemblage; (2) the diagram and abstract machine have lines of flight that are primary, which are not phenomena of resis-tance of counterattack in an assemblage, but cutting edges of creation and deterritorialization.[2]

What I would like to do in this chapter is examine Deleuze's critique of the concept of resistance. The point is not to choose one thinker over another, but to provide a kind of necessary *conceptual* analysis. If the task of philosophy is to create concepts, as Deleuze says; and if concepts divide up and distribute our world in different ways, then the differences in concepts can have certain ramifications – even if, as in the case of Deleuze and Foucault, they are dealing with similar problems. But in the end, I would, nonetheless, like to revive an aspect of Deleuze's thought that has not been, unfortunately, one of his lingering legacies – even though, for a certain period of time, it is the aspect of his thought that was most well-known: namely, the theory of desire.

THE PLACE OF "RESISTANCE" IN FOUCAULT'S TRAJECTORY

The first thing I would like to do is to follow the trajectory of Foucault's thought to see why he was led to develop a concept of "resistance" in the first place. Foucault's thought is often divided into three periods, or three axes: (1) his early work on discourse and the conditions of knowledge (*Madness and Civilization, The Birth of the Clinic, The Order of Things, The Archaeology of Knowledge*); (2) a middle period, in the 1970s, on the mechanisms of power (*Discipline and Punish, History of Sexuality, Volume 1*); and (3) his final work on ethics or modes of "subjectivation" (*History of Sexuality, Volumes 2 and 3*). The concept of resistance arises at a specific moment in this trajectory – at the end of the period on power – and there is a precise reason why Foucault was led to develop a concept of resistance at this point. Indeed, Foucault was precipitated from one period to another by certain problems that arose in the domain he was then considering – they are, as it were, fault lines or cracks in his thought, sending it off in new and different directions.

Foucault's first period concerned, in part, the role of discourse in knowledge, and the relation of discursive formations to what Deleuze would call "fields of visibility." We find in Foucault's work, for instance, an analysis of the discourse of madness or mental illness (in *Madness and Civilization*), which finds its "field of visibility" (at a historically determinate moment) in the asylum, as a place where the mad are "made visible." Similarly, we find in *Discipline and Punish* an analysis of the discourse of delinquency and criminality, as well as an analysis of the prison as its field of visibility. These two fields – the field of discourse and the field of visibility – are not the same, and have complex relations. The discourse of penal law, for instance, which defines which actions are criminal or illegal, is not the same as the discourse surrounding the prison, which deals with the question of how to manage the prisoners incarcerated there. Hence the first problem (or set of problems) that arose in Foucault's work: how, Foucault was asked, did he account for the relation between discourses and their corresponding fields of visibility – and even more to the point, how could he account for the discontinuity between historical *epis-*

temes? (One of Foucault's aims – notably in *The Order of Things* – was to show that "knowledge" has had various epistemic formations: from the Renaissance (sixteenth century) through the Classical Age (mid-seventeenth century through the end of the eighteenth century) to the Modern Age (nineteenth century through at least the mid-twentieth century).)

Foucault found an answer to these problems in the concept of power relations: every form of knowledge (as both a field of discourse and a field of visibility) is itself an integration of power relations, which Foucault defined as a capacity to affect and to be affected – or what he elsewhere termed "governmentality," which precedes the formation of any given government. In his middle works, Foucault wound up isolating and analyzing two primary forms of governmentality: "disciplinary power" or "anatomo-politics," which is exerted on individual bodies, and "bio-power," which is exerted on large populations. Power relations themselves are never given or known – knowledge is still presented in terms of the two fields of discourse and visibility – but it is the exercise of power relations that makes knowledge possible, and it is their shifting relations that accounts for the discontinuities between formations of knowledge.

It was at the end of his considerations of the question of power that the problem of *resistance* arose – this is the second profound fault line in Foucault's thought. If power is ubiquitous, if it covers the entire social field, if it is these power relations that provoke and condition our forms of knowledge, then is it possible to alter these power relations themselves, to change them, to combat them – in short, to *resist* them? In a sense, this is the question that obsessed Foucault in his final works, and that provoked his shift – which occurred between the first and second volumes of the *History of Sexuality* – away from questions of power to questions of ethics and processes of subjectivation.

This then, is our initial question: what exactly is the status of *resistance* in these later works of Foucault? It is true that Foucault will say that resistance is "primary" in relation to power relations, since it entails a relation with the outside.[3] In this sense, one could perhaps speak of a progressive "deepening" in Foucault's work as it develops: power relations condition the forms of knowledge, but resistance is primary in relation to power. Yet the idea that "resistance is primary in relation to power" is easier to say than to conceptualize, and no one was more aware of this than Foucault himself. The eight years that separate the first two volumes of the *History of Sexuality* (1976–84) testify to this, and to the profundity of the problem that Foucault was grappling with.

In his great essay "The Lives of Infamous Men," Foucault had written that "the most intense point of a life, the point where its energy is concentrated, is where it comes up against power, struggles with it, attempts to use its forces and to evade its traps."[4] Indeed, the book for which this essay was intended to serve as an introduction was to be what Foucault called an "anthology of existences," that is, a documentation of the existence of people, in the past, whose lives would have disappeared into total obscurity had they not had a single run-in with the mechanisms of power, and left a tiny trace in an archive somewhere: petty criminals, inconsequential usurers, scandalous monks. For instance, in the archives of the hospital in Charenton, France, Foucault finds a short entry concerning one Mathurin Milan, admitted to the hospital on 31 August 1707, accused of madness. The entry reads:

> His madness was always to hide from his family, to lead an obscure life in the country, to have actions at law, to lend usuriously and without security, to lead his feeble mind down unknown paths, and to believe himself capable of the greatest employments.[5]

One can see why Foucault's eye would have been attracted to this entry, which he found in the archives of the Bibliothèque Nationale in Paris (where Foucault spent a good percentage of his adult life). Mr. Milan seems to have led a not unordinary life: he lived alone and avoided his family, though he also engaged in suspicious money-lending and legal practices. Yet Mr. Milan was admitted to the Charenton hospital as "mad" for these very reasons – one of many obscure and "infamous" lives that was "reduced to ashes in the few sentences that struck them down." Indeed, as Foucault comments, one of the questions provoked by reading Milan's entry in the Charenton hospital archives concerned "the reason why people were so zealous to prevent the feebleminded from walking down unknown paths."[6]

"The Lives of Infamous Men" was published in January 1977, not long after the publication of the first volume of the *History of Sexuality*, and the intended anthology was to have included the cases of Pierre Rivière ("having slaughtered my mother, my sister, and my brother . . .") and Herculine Barbin ("being the recently discovered memoirs of a nineteenth-century French Hermaphrodite"). One can see how cases like those of Mathurin Milan pose the problem of resistance in an acute manner. As subjects, we are determined as much by forms of knowledge – for instance, by the categories and roles by which we are classified and identified (you are a man, or a woman, or a homosexual, or a teacher, or a student . . .) – as by the strategies of power that are constantly exerted upon us – ordering our time, distributing our space, making us develop our powers and capacities (such as our labor power) in determinate ways (such as the maximization of labor capacity in Fordism). How does someone like Milan resist these exercises of power? Foucault early on gave up on the idea that our "experience" had an independent existence prior to the exertion of power upon it. Power relations are ubiquitous, and are immanent to experience itself. The idea that power is imposed upon our experience from without is precisely the old conception of power that Foucault strove to contest throughout his writings.

It is thus from *within* the context of power relations that resistance must arise. But here is where we can see two conceptions of resistance in Foucault: a *reactive* and an *active* type of resistance (borrowing these terms from Deleuze's reading of Nietzsche). The very concept seems to imply a reactive conception: resistance would seem to be defined as a reaction or as a response to a given exercise of power. We all know the paradigmatic case: the person in grade school who reacts to every command to sit down and sit up, to form a straight line, to stop talking in class, to raise your hand when you need to go to the toilet. Such a person resists power, everywhere and always, constantly testing its limits. And such a conception is repeated on a larger scale, socially and politically. As a mere reaction to power, however, resistance is quickly reappropriated and restratified, and the "knots of power" quickly reform around it.[7] Foucault's question then became: what is an *active* conception of resistance (which is simply another way of answering the question of how resistance is primary in relation to power)?

The answer to this question came in Foucault's final works: power becomes active when it is directed, not against another exercise of power, but against itself. Resistance becomes active in the relation to oneself, the ability each of us has to affect oneself, the affect of the self by itself. In affecting myself, I open up the possibility of creating myself in a way that differs from the present forms of knowledge, and the present constraints of power. In reading Foucault's biographies, and his last interviews, it seems clear that this active conception of resistance was developed, or at least confirmed, by Foucault's experiences in California, where he went to teach at Berkeley. In San Francisco, he discovered a gay community that had little parallel in Paris, and which had been created, not by a wholesale frontal reaction against a homophobic culture, but rather step by step, on the basis of individuals exerting power on themselves, affecting themselves, constituting themselves as gay, and then linking up, slowly but surely, into a group or community that, by the time Foucault arrived, had a significant political presence and political power. In this sense, Foucault's philosophy recapitulated the three questions of Kant's philosophy: (1) What can I *know?* (What can I see and articulate within any given historical *episteme?*); (2) What can I *do?* (What power may I claim and what resistances may I counter?); and most importantly (3) What can I *be?* (How can I produce myself as a subject? How can I *be* otherwise? How can I '*think* otherwise'?) The answer to the latter question is given, in part, by the capacity of power or force to affect itself.

FROM FOUCAULT TO DELEUZE

The ambiguities of Foucault's position here, however, have often been noted. Most often, Foucault's later turn toward ethics, or modes of subjectivation (ways I can affect myself, ways I can produce myself as a subject) has been interpreted in merely aesthetic and private terms: I can treat myself or my life as a work of art, something to be fashioned creatively, but that creation is ultimately a kind of private endeavor, far removed from political realities. This is how Richard Rorty tended to read Foucault's later work, though the example of the gay community in San Francisco shows that "affecting oneself" is far more than an aesthetic enterprise. More importantly, Foucault's work on ethics or "modes of subjectivation" touches on a profound point that allows us to link up Foucault's work with Deleuze's. In *The Use of Pleasure*, Foucault says that the affect of the self by itself presumes a determination of an "ethical substance" that is to be affected – whether it is pleasure, desire, the flesh, one's feelings, and so forth. He summarized the ethical conduct of various periods in some familiar slogans. For the Greeks, it was "Know yourself!" following the Socratic dictum. For the Romans, it was "Master yourself!" where the ethical substance to be affected was the passions, which needed to be mastered and harmonized. For the Christians, it was "Deny yourself!" and what needed to be denied were the cravings of the flesh, and their concupiscence. For us moderns, the slogan has become "Express yourself!", that is, express the feelings and desire that constitute you – that constitute what you really *are*. Foucault's whole conception of ethics implies a determination of the ethical substance that is to be affected.

In his book on Foucault, Deleuze himself poses a question that, in retrospect, has an enormous resonance. "Is the affect of self by self pleasure," he asks, "or desire?"[8] This question refers to a minor dispute between Foucault and Deleuze that nonetheless has important implications for the question at hand, namely, the status of "resistance" in the two thinkers. In Deleuze's 1977 open letter to Foucault, "Desire and Pleasure," with which we began, Deleuze recounts that Foucault once said to him:

> I cannot bear the word desire; even if you use it differently, I cannot keep myself from thinking or living that desire = lack, or that desire is repressed. Michel added, whereas myself, what I call pleasure is perhaps what you call desire; but in any case, I need another word than *desire*.
>
> Obviously, once again, this is more than a question of words. Because for my part, I can scarcely tolerate the word *pleasure*. But why? For me, desire implies no lack; neither is it a natural given. It is an *agencement* [*assemblage*] of heterogeneous elements that function . . . I cannot give any positive value to pleasure because pleasure seems to me to interrupt the immanent process of desire; pleasure seems to me to be on the side of strata and organization . . . Pleasure seems to me to be the only means for a person or a subject to "find itself again" in a process that surpasses it.[9]

These comments seem to reveal that, at the end of his career, in the midst of his reflections on resistance, Foucault was led to a point that suddenly seemed to find itself linked up, in complicated and sometimes obscure ways, with Deleuze's earlier work on desire. Deleuze seemed to have a premonition of these linkages: "Could I think of equivalences of this type," he asked himself, "what for me is the body without organs corresponds to what for Michel is body-pleasures? Can I relate the 'body–flesh' distinction, of which Michel spoke to me, to the 'body without organs–organization distinction?'"[10] Yet although Deleuze raises these questions, he admits that he does not know how to answer them. "I do not know how to situate myself," he confesses, "in relation to Michel's present research."[11]

If Deleuze was unable to situate his own work in relation to Foucault in 1977, the intervening years have perhaps given us a more perspicacious perspective. Why does the concept of resistance, which arises in Foucault's work for determinable reasons, find no precise equivalent in Deleuze? Why does Deleuze appeal to a concept of desire rather than power/resistance (or even pleasure)? To attempt to answer these questions, we must look at *Anti-Oedipus*, which Deleuze co-authored with Félix Guattari and published in 1972. *Anti-Oedipus*, I would argue, goes back to two fundamental thinkers as its precursors. On the manifest surface, these two thinkers would seem to be Freud and Marx. Both Freud and Marx insisted, in their own ways, that our conscious thought is determined by forces that go beyond consciousness – forces that are, as we say, "unconscious" (though we are far too used to this word; it would be better to formulate a new one). Put crudely, in Marx, our thought is determined by our class ("class consciousness"); in Freud, we are determined by our unconscious desires (stemming, usually, from familial conflicts). The nature of the relationship between these two unconsciousnesses – the "political economy" of Marx and the "libidinal economy" of Freud – was a question that numerous thinkers tried to answer. For a long time, the relation between the two economies had been formulated in terms of the mechanisms of "introjection" and "projection": as an individual, I introject the interests of my class, my culture, my social milieu, which eventually come to determine my consciousness (my "false" consciousness); at the same time, the political economy was seen as a projection of the individual desires of the population that produced it. In *Anti-Oedipus*, Deleuze and Guattari famously reject these mechanisms: they argue that political economy (Marx) and libidinal economy (Freud) are *one and the same thing*. We have perhaps heard this thesis too many times to comprehend its truly revolutionary nature, and this is perhaps because the two fundamental precursors of *Anti-Oedipus* are not Freud and Marx, despite appearances, but rather Nietzsche and Kant. Understanding their role as precursors will help us see more clearly the relation between Foucault and Deleuze on the question of resistance.

NIETZSCHE ON LIBIDINAL AND POLITICAL ECONOMY

Let me turn first to Nietzsche. There are two aspects of his thought that are relevant here: his theory of the drives (a libidinal economy), and his theory concerning the genealogy of morality (a political economy). As an example of what

Nietzsche means by a drive, consider this brief discussion of the drives from Nietzsche's early book, *Daybreak*:

> Suppose we were in the market place one day and we noticed someone laughing at us as we went by: this event will signify this or that to us according to whether this or that drive happens at that moment to be at its height in us – and it will be a quite different event according to the kind of person we are. One person will absorb it like a drop of rain, another will shake it from him like an insect, another will try to pick a quarrel, another will examine his clothing to see if there is anything about it that might give rise to laughter, another will be led to reflect on the nature of laughter as such, another will be glad to have involuntarily augmented the amount of cheerfulness and sunshine in the world – and in each case, a drive has gratified itself, whether it be the drive to annoyance, or to combativeness or to reflection or to benevolence. This drive seized the event as its prey. Why precisely this one? Because, thirsty and hungry, it was lying in wait.[12]

This is the source of Nietzsche's doctrine of *perspectivism* ("there are no facts, only interpretations"), but what is often overlooked is that, for Nietzsche, it is our *drives* that interpret the world, that are perspectival – and not our egos or our conscious opinions. All of us, as individuals, contain within ourselves such a vast confusion of conflicting drives that we are, as Nietzsche liked to say, multiplicities, and not unities. It is not so much that I have a different perspective on the world than you; it is rather that each of us has multiple perspectives on the world because of the multiplicity of our drives – drives that are often contradictory among themselves. *Within ourselves*, Nietzsche insists, we can at the same time be egoistic or altruistic, hard-hearted or magnanimous, just or unfair, can cause pain or give pleasure. Moreover, our drives are in a constant struggle or combat with each other: my drive to smoke and get my nicotine rush is in combat with (but also coexistent with) my drive to quit. This is also where Nietzsche first developed his concept of the *will to power* – at the level of the drives. "Every drive is a kind of lust to rule," he writes, "each one has its perspective that it would like to compel all the other drives to accept as a norm."[13]

We can try to combat the drives, of course, and struggle against them – indeed, this is one of the most common themes in philosophy: the fight against the passions. In another passage from *Daybreak*, Nietzsche says that he can see only about six fundamental methods we have at our disposal for combating a drive. For instance, we can avoid opportunities for its gratification (no longer hiding packs of cigarettes at home); or we can implant regularity into the drive (having one cigarette every four hours so as to at least avoid smoking in between); or we can engender disgust with the drive, giving ourselves over to its wild and unrestrained gratification (smoking non-stop for a week) to the point where we become disgusted with it. But then Nietzsche asks: *who* exactly is combating the drives in these various ways? His answer:

> [The fact] *that* one *desires* to combat the vehemence of a drive at all, however, does not stand within our own power; nor does the choice of any particular method; nor does the success or failure of this method. What is clearly the case is that in this entire procedure our intellect is only the blind instrument of *another* drive which is a *rival* of the drive whose vehemence is tormenting us . . . While "we" believe we are complaining about the vehemence of a drive, at bottom it is one drive *which is complaining about the other*, that is to say: for us to become aware that we are suffering from the *vehemence* [or *violence*] of a drive presupposes the existence of another equally vehement or even more vehement drive, and that a *struggle* is in prospect in which our intellect is going to have to take sides.[14]

Instinctively, Nietzsche says, we take our *predominant* drive and for the moment turn it into the *whole* ego, placing all our weaker drives perspectively *farther away*, as if those other drives weren't *me* but rather an *it* (this is the origin of Freud's idea of the *id*, which simply means the "it"). When smokers continually say they are trying to stop smoking, it simply means that their conscious intellect is taking sides with a particular drive: the drive to quit, rather than the drive to light up, which nonetheless remains stronger than the former. When we talk about the "I," we are simply indicating which drive, at the moment, is strongest and sovereign: the feeling of the "I" is the strongest wherever the preponderance lies, even though it can flicker from drive to drive. What we call thinking, willing, and feeling are all "merely a relation of the drives to each other."[15] But the drives remain largely unknown to the conscious intellect. Nietzsche concludes:

> However far a man may go in self-knowledge, nothing can be more incomplete than his image of the totality of *drives* which constitute his being. He can scarcely name the cruder ones: their number and strength, their ebb and flood, their play and counterplay among one another – and above all the laws of their *nutriment* – remain unknown to him.[16]

In other words, there is no struggle of reason against the drives; what we call "reason" is nothing more than a certain "system of relations between various passions," a certain ordering of the drives.[17] In the *Gay Science*, Nietzsche considers the familiar example we have of becoming more reasonable as we grow older. "Something that you formerly loved as a truth or probability strikes you as an error," Nietzsche surmises, so you cast it off "and fancy that it represents a victory for your reason." But it is less a victory for reason than a shift in the relations among the drives. He continues:

> Perhaps this error was as necessary for you then, when you were a different person – you are always a different person – as are all your present "truths" . . . What killed that opinion for you was your new life [that is, a new drive] and not your reason: *you no longer need it*, and now it collapses and unreason crawls out of it into the light like a worm. When we criticize something, this is no arbitrary and impersonal event; it is, at least very often, evidence of vital energies in us that are growing and shedding a skin. We negate and must negate because something in us wants to live and affirm – something that we perhaps do not know or see as yet.[18]

Nietzsche's entire critique of traditional metaphysics – his critique of logic, of the categories, of the ego, of religion – is undertaken from the perspective of the libidinal economy of drives.

But this is where the question of morality (political economy) comes in for Nietzsche. Drives differ from instincts – instincts are predetermined (hawks fly, lions hunt, beavers build dams), whereas drives are not. Humans, says Nietzsche, are undifferentiated animals. Since the drives are not completely determined, one of the functions of morality is to establish an "order of rank" among the drives or impulses. "Wherever we encounter a morality, we also encounter valuations and an order of rank of human impulses . . . Now one and now another human impulse and state held first place and was ennobled because it was esteemed so highly."[19] Consider any list of impulses – they are almost immediately categorized as virtues and vices: industriousness is a virtue, sloth is a vice; obedience is a virtue, defiance and insubordination are vices; chastity is virtuous, promiscuity a vice; these days, not smoking is a virtue, smoking is a vice. When Nietzsche inquires into the *genealogy* of morality, he is inquiring into the *conditions* of any particular moral ranking of the impulses: why certain impulses are selected *for* and certain impulses are selected *against*.

Nietzsche argues that the *value* inherent in most moral rankings is what he calls the "herd instinct." The drives that were selected *for* were those that served the needs of the community, the furtherance of the "species": impulses that were "unegoistic," drives toward self-abnegation, self-sacrifice, etc. Selflessness is a virtue, selfishness a vice. More generally, Nietzsche would argue that herd morality is an instinct *against Life*. But there is no distinction between nature and artifice here: it is not as if we could simply remove the mechanisms of morality and culture and allow the drives to exist in a "free" and "unbound" state. There is no "natural" or "spontaneous" state of the drives, except as an Idea. The impulse toward the herd, toward the community, is itself a drive, in competition with the other drives: we never leave the domain of the drives. Kant liked to say that we can never get beyond our representations; Nietzsche surmises that what we can never get beyond is the reality of the drives.[20] But in fact, the drives and impulses are always *assembled* or *arranged* in different ways, in different individuals, in different cultures, in different eras, in different moralities – which is why Nietzsche always insisted that there is a plurality of moralities, and what he found lacking in his time was an adequate *comparative* study of moralities.

Now Deleuze, it seems to me, takes up this Nietzschean schema, *mutatis mutandis*. On the one hand, what he calls "desire" is nothing other than the state of the impulses and drives: "Drives are simply the desiring-machines themselves."[21] On the other hand, like Nietzsche, Deleuze insists that the drives never exist in a free and unbound state, nor are they ever merely individual; they are always arranged and assembled, not only by moral systems, but more generally by every social formation. The social formations analyzed in *Capitalism and Schizophrenia* – "primitives," States, capitalism, war machines – are a typology of different ways in which the drives and affects can be assembled. Deleuze and Guattari note that the schema of *Anti-Oedipus* was partly inspired by Pierre Klossowski's books *Nietzsche and the Vicious Circle* and *Living Currency*. "In his recent works, Klossowski indicates to us the only means of bypassing the sterile parallelism where we flounder between Freud and Marx by discovering . . . *how affects or drives form part of the infrastructure itself*."[22] Although the claim that there is no difference in nature between libidinal and political economy has complex practical consequences, it is fairly straightforward theoretically, and two distinctions may help clarify Deleuze and Guattari's thesis.

The first is the distinction between desire and interest. A well-known school of economics sees human beings as rational agents who seek to maximize their interest. Someone who wants to become a professor, for instance, could pursue that interest by applying to a university, taking courses, writing a thesis and attending conferences, in the hope of ultimately securing an academic position. Such an interest can be pursued in a highly rational manner. But that interest, and the means to pursue it, only exists within the context of a particular social formation. If someone decides to pursue that interest in a concerted and rational manner, it is because their desire – their drives and affects – is already invested in the social formation that makes that interest possible. For this reason, Deleuze insists that desire is always *positive*. Normally, we tend to think of desire in terms of *lack*: if we desire something, it is because we lack it. But Deleuze reconfigures the concept of desire: what we desire – what our drives and affects are invested in – is a social formation. Lack appears only at the level of interest, and in multiple ways: one may have an interest in obtaining an academic position one does not have (a first lack), only to discover that a competitive job market makes it impossible to obtain that position (a second lack). Marketing and advertising are aimed at the manipulation of interest: I reach for a favored brand of toothpaste because I have now an interest in white teeth and fresh breath. This is why Deleuze and Guattari argue that the fundamental problem of political philosophy is one that was formulated most clearly by Spinoza: "Why do people fight for their servitude as stubbornly as though it were their salvation?"[23] The answer: because your desire is never your own. Desire is not a psychic reality, nor is it strictly individual; rather, your drives and affects are from the start part of the social infrastructure.

The distinction between interest and desire, in turn, parallels the distinction between the rational and the irrational, though Deleuze rarely uses these terms. "Once interests have been defined within the confines of a society, what is rational is the way in which people pursue those interests and attempt to realize them," such as the interest for a job or white teeth. "But underneath that," Deleuze explains:

> you find desires, investments of desire that are not to be confused with investments of interest, and on which interests depend for their determination and very distribution: an enormous flow, all kinds of libidinal-unconscious flows that constitute the delirium of the society.[24]

Every society is thus a distribution of the rational and the irrational, but the rational is always the rationality of something irrational:

> Reason is always a region carved out of the irrational. It is not sheltered from the rational, but is a region traversed by the irrational and is simply defined by a certain relationship between irrational factors. Beneath all reason there is delirium and drift. Everything about capitalism is rational, except capital . . . A stock market is a perfectly rational mechanism, you can understand it and learn how it works; capitalists certainly know how to use it; yet it's completely delirious, it's crazy . . . It's just like theology: everything about it is perfectly rational if you accept sin, the immaculate conception, and the incarnation . . .[25]

Deleuze's Inversion of Kant's Theory of Desire

Why then do Deleuze and Guattari present *Anti-Oedipus* as a theory of desire rather than a theory of drives? Here again, on the manifest surface, the obvious response is that *Anti-Oedipus* constitutes a critique of psychoanalysis, and thus is necessarily indexed on the theory of "unconscious" desire found in both Freud and Lacan. At a certain level, *Anti-Oedipus* presents itself as a theory of the "real," in Lacanian terms, but the real is analyzed in purely positive terms, and not as a lack, an impossibility, or a gap in the symbolic, as in Lacan.[26] It is no doubt not by chance that, after the appearance of *Anti-Oedipus*, Lacan's own work turned increasingly toward the theory of the drives.[27] Yet in the end, the theory of desire found in *Anti-Oedipus* is indexed less on Freud or Lacan than on Kant, and particularly Kant's second critique, the *Critique of Practical Reason*. One might surmise (correctly) that Deleuze has little sympathy with the second critique, with its appeal to a transcendent moral law and the categorical imperative (which Deleuze will replace with immanence and a "problematic" imperative). But if Deleuze and Guattari explicitly model *Anti-Oedipus* on the *Critique of Pure Reason*, it is because Kant presents the second critique in its entirety as a theory of desire. We must therefore analyze the way in which Deleuze and Guattari take up and modify Kant's concept of desire in *Anti-Oedipus*.

Kant argued that there are three fundamental faculties of the mind: the faculty of *knowledge*, the faculty of *desire*, and the *feeling of pleasure and displeasure* (third critique).[28] These definitions are derived from the nature of our representations: every representation we have can be related to something other than itself – that is, both to an *object* and to the *subject*. In the faculty of knowledge (first critique), a representation is related to an *object*, from the viewpoint of its *agreement* or *conformity* with it (theory of reference, or denotation). In the faculty of the feeling of pleasure and pain (third critique), the representation is related to the *subject*, insofar as the representation affects the subject by intensifying or weakening its vital force (Deleuze will develop this idea in his concepts of affectivity and intensity). Finally, in the faculty of desire (second critique), the representation is likewise related to an object, but in this case it enters into a *causal* relationship with its object. Kant's definition of the faculty of desire is extraordinary: it is "a faculty which by means of its representations is the cause of the actuality of the objects of those representations."[29] On the surface, the definition sounds like magic: if I have a representation in my mind, the faculty of desire is capable of producing the object that corresponds to it.

Readers of Kant, however, know why he defines the faculty of desire in causal terms: the problem of *freedom* concerns the operation by which a free being can be said to be the cause of an action. I have a representation in my mind of the killing of my enemy, and the faculty of desire carries out that action in the world. In acting freely, the agent produces something that is not reducible to the causal determinism of mechanism. "Practical reason," Kant writes, "does not have to do with objects for the sake of *knowing* them but with its own ability to *make them real*."[30] Kant was aware, of course, that real *objects* can be produced only by an external causality and external mechanisms; yet this knowledge does not prevent us from believing in the intrinsic power of desire to create its own object, if only in an unreal, hallucinatory, or delirious form. In what Kant calls the "pathological" productions of desire, what is produced by desire is merely a *psychic reality*.[31] Nonetheless, Kant brought about a Copernican Revolution in practical philosophy to which Deleuze is strongly indebted, and explicitly so: desire is no longer defined in terms of *lack* (I desire something because I do not have it), but rather in terms of *production* (I produce the object because I desire it). The fundamental thesis of *Anti-Oedipus* is a stronger variant of Kant's claim. "If desire produces," Deleuze and Guattari write, "its product is real. If desire is productive, it can be productive only in the real world and can produce only reality."[32] How does Deleuze come to justify this extraordinary claim, which seems even more extraordinary than Kant's?

For Kant, the essential question concerns the *higher form* that each faculty is capable of (a form which is no longer merely "pathological"). A faculty has a higher form when it finds *within itself* the law of its own exercise, and thus is said to function *autonomously*. The higher form of desire, for Kant, is what he calls the "will." *The will is the same thing as desire*, but raised to its higher form. Desire becomes will when it is determined by the representation of a pure form – namely, the moral law, which is the pure form of a universal legislation (the categorical imperative). Practical reason "has to do with a will which is a causality inasmuch as *reason* contains its determining ground."[33] For Kant, it is only under such conditions that we can be said to be acting freely. For Deleuze, however, it is significant that, in Kant, the moral law requires the intervention of the three great transcendent Ideas as its postulates. "Freedom," as the "fact" of morality, implies the cosmological Idea of a supra-sensible world, independent of any sensible condition. In turn, the abyss that separates the noumenal Law and the phenomenal world requires the intermediary of an intelligible author of sensible Nature or a "moral cause of the world," that is, the theological Idea of a supreme being, or God. This abyss, finally, can only be bridged through the "postulate" of an infinite progress, which requires the psychological Idea of the immortality of the soul. In other words, having denounced the transcendent Ideas of Soul, World, and God in the first Critique, Kant resurrects each of them, one by one, in the second Critique, and gives them a practical determination.

Deleuze, of course, rejects this appeal to transcendence on Kant's part, and in effect he asks: would it be possible to develop a theory of desire that did not appeal to the moral law and the transcendent Ideas that serve as its postulate (which turn desire into a "will"), but instead synthesized desire with a conception of Ideas that are purely immanent? This is precisely what takes place in the opening two chapters of *Anti-Oedipus*: the three syntheses by which Deleuze and Guattari define "desiring-machines" (conjunction, connection, disjunction) are in fact the three same Ideas that Kant defines as the postulates of practical reason – Self, World, and God – but now stripped entirely of their transcendent status, to the point where neither God, World, nor Self subsists. *Anti-Oedipus* is thus an attempt to rewrite the transcendent theory of desire developed in the *Critique of Practical Reason* from a purely immanent viewpoint. But what does it mean to speak of a purely *immanent* theory of desire?

In Kant, God is the master of the disjunctive syllogism: he creates the world by parceling out predicates according to the either/or disjunction: you can be man *or* woman, black *or* white, but not both. Deleuze turns this into a diabolical "disjunctive synthesis," in which both sides of every disjunctive are affirmed at once: man *and* woman, black *and* white. In Kant, the Idea of the World is derived from the hypothetical syllogism "if . . . then," a causal chain which, when extended to infinity, gives the Idea of the World, the Universe, the totality of all that is. Deleuze turns this into a connective synthesis, an "and . . . and" that is open-ended, rhizomatic, never totalizable, and produces a *chaosmos* rather than a World. In Kant, finally, the Self is derived from the categorical syllogism, a substance that lies behind all our representations. Deleuze turns this into an immanent conjunctive synthesis, which produces a kind of counter-self, a schizophrenic self, defined merely by a series of intensive states. In sum: "The Grand Canyon of the world, the 'crack' of the self, and the dismembering of God."[34] Deleuze gives a purely *immanent* characterization of the three syntheses that Kant defines in transcendent terms: connection (the dissolution of the Self), conjunction (the destruction of the World), and disjunction (the death of God). Desire (the relations between the drives and affects) is constituted by tracing out series and trajectories following these immanent syntheses within a given social assemblage. *Anti-Oedipus* is the *Critique of Practical Reason* turned on its head: an immanent theory of desire that refuses to synthesize desire with the transcendent Ideas that would turn it into the "will" (in the Kantian sense).

FROM RESISTANCE TO CAPTURE

Anti-Oedipus, then, is a kind of amalgam of Nietzsche and Kant: Kant's theory of desire rendered immanent under a Nietzschean inspiration. Deleuze does not flag these links; indeed, Deleuze was so imbued with the history of philosophy that he naturally seemed to be following the thought of the great philosophers, always pushing them to their differential and immanent limit, freeing them from the great terminal points of traditional metaphysics, God, the World, and the Self. But this sketch of Deleuze's theory of desire is enough to make clear why the question of resistance does not arise in Deleuze's philosophy. If resistance becomes a question in Foucault, it is because he begins with the question of knowledge (what is articulable and what is visible), finds the conditions of knowledge in power, but then has to ask about the ways one can resist power, even if resistance is primary in relation to power. It is Foucault's starting point in constituted knowledges that leads him to pose the problem of resistance. One finds a comparable trajectory, to a certain extent, in Lacan, or at least certain Lacanians: if one begins with the Symbolic, one is led to seek the gaps or ruptures in the Symbolic that are produced by the Real. One could say that the status of the Real in Lacan is analogous to the status of resistance in Lacan.

Deleuze's ontology, by contrast, operates in an almost exactly inverse manner. Put crudely, if one begins with a status quo – knowledge or the symbolic – one must look for a break or rupture in the status quo to account for change. Deleuze instead *begins* with change, with becoming, with events. For Deleuze, what is primary in any social formation are its lines of flight, its movements of deterritorialization, which are *already* movements of resistance. "Far from lying outside the social field or emerging from it," Deleuze writes, "lines of flight constitute its rhizome or cartography."[35] Resistance, in a sense, is built into Deleuze's ontology, and for this reason, the conceptual problem he faces wound up being quite different from Foucault's. If a social field "flees" or "leaks" in every direction, the primary question is how any social formation manages to *capture* these movements, to integrate, to stratify them – and it is precisely "organizations of power" that effect this integration and capture. This explains the statement in Deleuze's 1977 letter with which we began: "If *dispositifs* of power are in some way constitutive [for Foucault], there can only be phenomena of 'resistance' against them . . . For myself, the status of phenomena of resistance is not a problem, since lines of flight are primary determinations."[36] This claim reaches its culmination in the analysis of capitalism found in *Anti-Oedipus*: capitalism is a vast enterprise of deterritorialization and decoding, pushed to an almost schizophrenic limit, which nonetheless reterritorializes and recodes with one hand what it decodes and deterritorializes on the other.

But this leads to a final problem. If resistance is not a conceptual problem in Deleuze, it is because it is, in effect, built into his ontology. But a different problem comes to the fore in Deleuze, which gets at the same issue Foucault was confronting with the problem of resistance, but from an inverted position. It is a problem that remained unaddressed in *Anti-Oedipus*, and would only receive a solution in *A Thousand Plateaus*, and it is precisely the problem of *the organization of power*. "Our problem is as follows," Deleuze said in a 1973 interview, shortly after the publication of *Anti-Oedipus*:

> Given a system [capitalism] that escapes in every direction and that, at the same time, continually prevents, represses, or blocks escape routes by every available means, what can we do so that the escapes may no longer be individual attempts or small communities, but instead truly constitute a revolutionary machine?[37]

In other words, it is our own desire that organizes power and its system of repression, such that we all invest our desire in the very social machine that represses us and defines our interests. But this forces upon Deleuze a manner of posing the problem of resistance in a new way: can desire organize power in such a way that the social machine it constitutes is truly a revolutionary machine? "The real problems," as Guattari says, "are problems of organization."[38]

It is precisely this issue that Deleuze and Guattari address in the "Treatise on Nomadology" in *A Thousand Plateaus* with their concept of the "war-machine." It is, in my opinion, one of the most original and important texts in Deleuze's corpus, and lies at the core of his political philosophy. Why have revolutions gone badly? Because, until now, there has not existed within the revolutionary field a social machine that did not produce an embryonic State apparatus, or a party apparatus, which is the very institution of repression. Until now, revolutionary parties have constituted themselves as synthesizers of interests, rather than functioning as analyzers of desires. The question of revolution must be pushed to the level of desire: if it is desire that organizes power, is desire capable of organizing a social machine that does not reproduce a State apparatus? It is not enough simply to say that escape, resistance, and deterritorialization are primary in any social system. What is necessary is an organization of power that is capable of organizing and uniting these modes of escape *without reproducing a State apparatus*. This is why, for Deleuze, it is the concept of the war-machine that poses the true problem of revolution: "How can a war machine account for all the escapes that happen in the present system without crushing them, dismantling them, and without reproducing a state apparatus?"[39]

In this sense, the war machine is a social assemblage that is constructed directly on a line of flight: it is itself a movement of decoding, of deterritorialization – which is why it tends to disappear and abolish itself, or be appropriated by the State. Indeed, it seems likely to me that Deleuze and Guattari were attempting to identify the kind of social formation that would correspond to the mode of existence of "activity" and "affirmation," in the Nietzschean sense.[40] If the State is a *reactive* formation, the nomadic war-machine must be seen as an *active* formation, one that follows the movement of a line of flight. It is here that the problem of resistance appears in Deleuze's work at its most acute point: the analysis of the war-machine as a collective organization of power. The true confrontation concerns the relation between Foucault's problem of resistance and Deleuze's problem of capture.

NOTES

1. Gilles Deleuze, "Desire and Pleasure," in this volume, pp. 226–7. This text was first published as Gilles Deleuze, "Désir et plaisir," ed. François Ewald, *Magazine Littéraire* 325 (October 1994), 57–65. The translation appeared in *Foucault and His Interlocutors*, ed. Arnold I. Davidson (Chicago: University of Chicago Press, 1997), 183–92.
2. Gilles Deleuze and Félix Guattari, *A Thousand Plateaus*, trans. Brian Massumi (Minneapolis: University of Minnesota Press, 1987), 531n39.
3. Gilles Deleuze, *Foucault*, trans. Seán Hand (Minneapolis: University of Minnesota Press, 1988), 89.
4. Michel Foucault, "The Lives of Infamous Men," in *The Essential Works of Foucault, 1954–1984, Volume 3: Power*, ed. James D. Faubion, trans. Robert Hurley (New York: New Press, 2001), 157–75: 158.
5. Ibid. 158.
6. Ibid. 158.
7. Deleuze, *Foucault*, 89.
8. Ibid. 106.
9. Deleuze, "Desire and Pleasure," in this volume, pp. 227–8.

10. Ibid. 228.
11. Ibid. 229.
12. Friedrich Nietzsche, *Daybreak: Thoughts on the Prejudices of Morality*, trans. R. J. Hollingdale (Cambridge: Cambridge University Press, 1982), §119, 76.
13. Friedrich Nietzsche, *Will to Power*, trans. Walter Kaufmann and R. J. Hollingdale (New York: Random House, 1967), §481, 267.
14. Nietzsche, *Daybreak*, §109, 64–5.
15. Friedrich Nietzsche, *Beyond Good and Evil*, in *Basic Writings of Nietzsche*, ed. and trans. Walter Kaufmann (New York: Modern Library, 1968), §36, 237.
16. Nietzsche, *Daybreak*, §119, 74.
17. Nietzsche, *Will to Power*, §387, 208.
18. Friedrich Nietzsche, *The Gay Science*, trans. Walter Kaufman (New York: Vintage, 1974), §307, 245–6.
19. Nietzsche, *The Gay Science*, §116 and §115, 174.
20. Nietzsche, *Beyond Good and Evil*, §36, 237: "Suppose nothing else were 'given' as real except our world of desires and passions, and we could not get down, or up, to any other 'reality' besides the reality of our drives . . . In the end, it is not only permitted to make this experience; the method of conscience demands it."
21. Gilles Deleuze and Félix Guattari, *Anti-Oedipus: Capitalism and Schizophrenia*, trans. Robert Hurley, Mark Seem, and Helen R. Lane (New York: Viking Penguin, 1977), 35.
22. Deleuze and Guattari, *Anti-Oedipus*, 63. See Pierre Klossowski, *Nietzsche and the Vicious Circle*, trans. Daniel W. Smith (Chicago: University of Chicago Press, 1997); Pierre Klossowski, *Living Currency*, ed. Vernon W. Cisney, Nicolae Morar, and Daniel W. Smith (London: Bloomsbury, 2017).
23. Deleuze and Guattari, *Anti-Oedipus*, 29.
24. Gilles Deleuze, "On Capitalism and Desire," in *Desert Islands and Other Texts, 1953–1974*, ed. David Lapoujade, trans. Michael Taormina (New York: Semiotext(e), 2004), 262–3.
25. Ibid. 262.
26. For a reading of Deleuze's relation to Lacan, see Daniel W. Smith, "The Inverse Side of the Structure: Žižek on Deleuze on Lacan," in *Essays on Deleuze* (Edinburgh: Edinburgh University Press, 2012), 312–24.
27. See Slavoj Žižek, *Organs without Bodies: Deleuze and Consequences* (London: Routledge, 2003), who analyzes "Lacan's path from desire to drive" (102).
28. Immanuel Kant, *Critique of Judgment*, trans. James Creed Meredith (Oxford: Oxford University Press, 1952), Introduction §3, 15–16: "The faculties of the soul are reducible to three, which do not admit of any further derivation from a common ground: the *faculty of knowledge*, the *feeling of pleasure and displeasure*, and the *faculty of desire*."
29. Kant, *Critique of Judgment*, Introduction, §3, 16n1.
30. Immanuel Kant, *Critique of Practical Reason*, in *Practical Philosophy*, ed. Mary J. McGregor (Cambridge: Cambridge University Press, 1996), "Critical Elucidation of the Analytic of Pure Practical Reason," 5:89, 212.
31. Deleuze and Guattari, *Anti-Oedipus*, 25.
32. Ibid. 26.

33. Kant, *Critique of Practical Reason*, "Critical Elucidation of the Analytic of Pure Practical Reason," 5:89, 212.
34. Gilles Deleuze, *Logic of Sense*, trans. Mark Lester with Charles Stivale, ed. Constantin V. Boundas (New York: Columbia University Press, 1990), 176.
35. Deleuze, "Desire and Pleasure," 187.
36. Ibid. 188–9.
37. Deleuze, *Desert Islands*, 279–80.
38. Ibid. 264.
39. Ibid. 279–80. See also 280: "Today, we're looking for the new mode of unification in which, for example, the schizophrenic discourse, the intoxicated discourse, the perverted discourse, the homosexual discourse, all the marginal discourses can subsist, so that all these escapes and discourses can graft themselves onto a war-machine that won't reproduce a State or Party apparatus."
40. Nietzsche pointed to the problem of the war machine in *Thus Spoke Zarathustra*: "Where the state *ends* – look there, my brothers! Do you not see it, the rainbow and bridges of the overman?" Friedrich Nietzsche, *Thus Spoke Zarathustra*, First Part, § 11, "In the New Idol," in *The Portable Nietzsche*, trans. Walter Kaufman (New York: Viking, 1977), 163.

Appendix

CHAPTER 17

Meeting Deleuze

PAUL RABINOW

I must have sent him a letter; Deleuze's response was rapid and welcoming. Can one imagine Deleuze and Foucault in the age of e-mail? This was not long after the death of Foucault and Deleuze's loss and remorse were already clear. Finding his apartment not far from Clichy was easy although this section of Montmartre was not one that one thought of as being inhabited by painters and intellectuals in the late twentieth century. He greeted us warmly with his gravelly voice. I can't remember if we shook hands as Deleuze had these long finger nails and such a gesture might have been awkward. Regardless, the reception and exchange was anything but stilted and we plunged right in without much ado. Deleuze knew I had been close to Foucault and apparently that Foucault had displayed some trust in me. That was enough to open the door.

The interview that resulted and was published in our fledgling and short-lived attempt at a newsletter (and subsequently in French from the tape and then once again back into English) was fluid and comfortable. Deleuze wanted to talk. What he said was crisp; it highlighted Foucault and his different entries into things of the world, which he interpreted as stemming from their fundamentally different temperaments. As this was a time of clarification of his relations with a friend and a friendship, neglected and now gone, Deleuze was accommodating but more importantly was making sense of how they differed. For a philosophy of multiplicities such cartographic work came gracefully.

I can't remember having any extensive discussions with Foucault about Deleuze. This was partially because my co-author Hubert Dreyfus was constantly asking Foucault about Heidegger and Foucault was adroit and polite in not giving an answer. Further, as Habermas was a frequent visitor to Berkeley during the early 1980s there were also questions about Foucault's relation to the Frankfurt School with whom Foucault claimed to have little previous familiarity. Personally, I was interested in his views on Max Weber who at that point was not a prominent figure in France having been associated with Raymond Aron. Finally, Dreyfus and

I tended to stay away from discussing other French thinkers such as Derrida as we were not interested in the polemics and passions that many American scholars were engaged in at the time. Foucault did not bring them up.

It was only after Foucault's death that the topic of his relations with Deleuze came into view, especially given Deleuze's prominence at the funeral. I garnered intimations about the history of their relations from conversation with those in Foucault's inner circle. That Foucault was somehow a defensive rival of Deleuze is not very believable to me. He had been clear for years that the concept of desire and its psychoanalytic apparatus was not something he shared: it was exterior and foreign to him. Leaving aside the intricacies of Parisian innuendo and any strategically reconstructed memories, I know that Foucault was friendly with Leo Bersani at Berkeley. Although Foucault never shared Bersani's psychoanalytic views on sexuality, that conceptual distance did not hinder them from being amicable.

Finally, the famous pronouncement "*le siècle sera Deleuzian*" has been massively misinterpreted in the so-called Anglo-Saxon world (what the French mean is Anglophone). It is actually quite cutting: "*le siècle*" refers to eighteenth-century courtiers steeped in flattery and rhetoric. Although hardly immune to the rewards of *le siècle* that had grown steadily around him, Foucault had become increasingly encircled and felt stifled by it. For example, he changed his lectures from the late afternoon to the early morning hoping students would not be up at nine in the morning; he fantasized about retreating to the countryside. He knew what a mixed blessing fame could be.

The idea that Foucault stopped writing for seven years because of Deleuze is patent nonsense. First of all, Foucault was not silent. He was giving lectures at Berkeley and elsewhere in the United States. More importantly, the four years of his lectures at the *Collège de France*, especially the last three, are unquestionably among the richest and most challenging of his entire work. They had nothing to do with his relations or non-relations with Deleuze.

The dynamics of the Klaus Croissant affair has been described by Dosse. We should remember that these years of German terrorism represent roughly the same period of time when Foucault was analyzing the German neo-liberal school of economics, and while not endorsing this form of terrorism, he certainly did not equate it with fascism. His involvement in the affair concerned the actions of the French state whose legitimacy he questioned.

As to Deleuze's openness to the election of Mitterrand, Foucault could not have differed more; although, once again, Foucault's reactions had nothing to do with Deleuze. Election results are officially announced at 8pm of the voting day. There are no exit polls. I was at Foucault's apartment just before eight and he already knew that Mitterrand had been elected. He was in a dark and foul mood. We went later that night during a wondrous thunderstorm to the Bastille crowded with joyous celebrants; Foucault's mood only darkened.

His prognosis was born out. The Socialist government, even after its rapid turn to the center one year into Mitterrand's term, did not broach criticism or even hesitation. That the Minister of Culture in the Mitterrand Government, Jack Lang, could refer to Foucault and Bourdieu as "clowns" indicates that their analysis of the possibilities for working with that government in a serious way were more on the mark than that of Deleuze and others whose hope for change clouded their vision.

Why had Foucault and Deleuze let their friendship, even at the conceptual level, wither? We will never really know. However, there were profound divergences between them especially concerning Communism and Israel. Their deep and to a degree tacit allegiance, on one side or the other, constituted force lines that drew them away from each other rather than toward an agonistic confrontation of clarification as had been the case concerning the status of desire and psychoanalysis. Again entering this subterranean force field that apparently made them each deeply uncomfortable given their former proximities at Vincennes and elsewhere would have forced them into formulating positions which would have made their wrenching divergences visible and exploitable. As both Foucault and Deleuze lived in an atmosphere of the waning days of the engaged intellectual – Sartre after all had only died in 1980 – and were both under constant pressure to sign petitions, align themselves with groups, think for others, it is completely comprehensible that they would drift apart. Yet, ultimately Deleuze's remorse was wrenching.

Finally, there is the question of Israel and the Palestinians. Foucault certainly did not embrace the radical positions of Jean Genet or, for that matter, of Deleuze and many others in France. It is worth remembering that these were the years after the 1976 war – not today. In any case, the in many cases only slightly buried anti-Semitism had a long lineage on parts of the revolutionary French left; it was total anathema to Foucault. The fact that he risked his life by secretly hosting meetings between Israelis and Palestinians in his apartment is well known. In the casual and irresponsible accounts of these meetings, it is not always mentioned that there had been bombings of other apartments where such meetings were scheduled to take place. There was a machine gun carrying policeman not far from Foucault's apartment protecting another participant in these sporadic negotiations. Despite the insidious innuendo of Edward Said that Foucault was not sufficiently anti-Israeli, it is true that Foucault had made a gesture but had not "taken sides," although any form of anti-Semitism was, as the expression goes, intolerable.

CHAPTER 18

Foucault and Prison

GILLES DELEUZE AND PAUL RABINOW

Before moving to more general questions on intellectual and the political arena, could you explain your relationship to Foucault and the GIP?

Gilles Deleuze: So you want to begin with the GIP. You will have to double-check what I tell you. I have no memory; it is like trying to describe a dream; it's rather vague. After '68, there were many groups, very different groups, but necessarily compact ones. It was post-68. They survived; they all had a past. Foucault insisted on the fact that '68 had no importance for him. He already had a history as an important philosopher, but he was not burdened with a history from '68. That is probably what allowed him to form such a new type of group. And this group gave him a kind of equality with other groups. He would never have let himself be taken in. The GIP allowed him to maintain his independence from other groups like the Proletarian Left. There were constant meetings, exchanges, but he always preserved the complete independence of the GIP. In my opinion, Foucault was not the only one to outlive a past, but he was the only one to invent something new, at every level. It was very precise, like Foucault himself. The GIP was a reflection of Foucault, a Foucault–Defer invention. It was one case where their collaboration was close and fantastic. In France, it was the first rime this type of group had been formed, one that had nothing to do with a party (there were some scary parties, like the Proletarian Left) nor with an enterprise (like the attempts to revamp psychiatry).

The idea was to make a "Prison Information Group." It was obviously more than just information. It was a kind of thought experiment. There is a part of Foucault that always considered the process of thinking to be an experiment. It's his Nietzschean heritage. The idea was not to experiment on prisons but to take prison as a place where prisoners have a certain experience and that intellectuals, as Foucault saw them, should also think about. The GIP almost had the beauty of one of Foucault's books. I joined wholeheartedly because I was fascinated. When the two of them started, it

288

was like stepping out into the darkness. They had seen something, but what you see is always in darkness. What do you do? I think that is how it started: Defert began distributing tracts among the families waiting in lines during visiting hours. Several people would go, and Foucault was sometimes with them. They were quickly singled out as "agitators." What they wanted was not at all to agitate, but to establish a questionnaire that families and prisoners could complete. I remember that in the first questionnaires there were questions about food and medical care. Foucault must have been very reassured, very motivated, and very shocked by the results. We found something much worse – notably the constant humiliation. Foucault the observer then passed the mantle to Foucault the thinker.

The GIP was, I think, a forum for experimentation until *Discipline and Punish*. He was immediately sensible to the great difference between the theoretical and the legal status of prisons, between prison as a loss of freedom and the social uses of prison, which is something else altogether, since not only do they deprive an individual of his or her freedom, which is already huge, but there is systemic humiliation – the system is used to break people, and that is separate from taking away one's freedom. We discovered, as everyone knew, that there was a form of justice with no supervision that had taken shape in prison ever since the creation of a prison within the prison, a prison behind the prison, known as the "*mitard*" [solitary confinement]. The QHS[2] did not yet exist. Prisoners could be sentenced to solitary without any possibility of defending themselves. We learned a great deal. The GIP worked alongside the prisoners' families and former inmates. Like everything special, there were some very funny moments, like the time we first met with former inmates and each one wanted to be more of a prisoner than the others. Each one had always experienced something worse than the others.

What was the group relationship to politics?

Foucault had a keen political intuition, which was something very important for me. Political intuition, for me, is the feeling that something is going to happen and happen *here*, not somewhere else. A political intuition is a very rare occurrence. Foucault sensed that there were little movements, small disturbances in the prisons. He was not trying to take advantage of them or cause them. He saw something. For him, thinking was always an experimental process up until death. In a way, he was a kind of *seer*. And what he saw was actually intolerable. He was a fantastic seer. It was the way he saw people, the way he saw everything, in its comedy and misery. His power of sight was equivalent to his power to write. When you see something and see it very profoundly, what you see is intolerable. These are not the words he used in conversation, but it is in his thinking. For Foucault, to think was to react to the intolerable, the intolerable things one experienced. It was never something visible. That was also part of his genius. The two parts complement each other: thinking as experimentation and thinking as vision, as capturing the intolerable.

A kind of ethics?

I think it served as an ethics for him. The intolerable was not part of his ethics. His ethics was to see or grasp something as intolerable. He did not do it in the name of morality. It was his way of thinking. If thinking did not reach the intolerable, there was no need for thinking. Thinking was always thinking at something's limit.

People say it is intolerable because it is unjust.

Foucault did not say that. It was intolerable, not because it was unjust, but because no one saw it, because it was imperceptible. But everyone knew it. It was not a secret. Everyone knew about this prison in the prison, but no one saw it. Foucault saw it. That never stopped him from turning the intolerable into humor. Once again, we laughed a lot. It was not indignation. We were not indignant. It was two things: seeing something unseen and thinking something that was almost at a limit.

How did you become a part of the GIP?

I was completely convinced from the start that he was right and that he had found the only new type of group. It was new because it was so specific. And like everything Foucault did, the more specific it was, the more influence it had. It was like an opportunity that he knew not to miss. There were completely unexpected people involved who had nothing to do with prisons. I am thinking, for example, of Paul Eluard's widow who helped us a great deal at one point for no special reason. There were very consistent people like Claude Mauriac, who was very close to Foucault. When we made connections at the time of the Jackson affair and problems in American prisons, Genet stepped forward. He was great. It was very lively. A movement inside the prisons was formed. Revolts took shape. Outside, things were going in every direction, with prison psychiatrists, prison doctors, the families of inmates. We had to make pamphlets. Foucault and Defert took on endless tasks. They were the ones with the ideas. We followed them. We followed them with a passion. I remember a crazy day, typical for the GIP, where the good and tragic moments came one after the other. We had gone to Nancy, I think. We were busy from morning to night. The morning started with a delegation to the prefecture, then we had to go to the prison, then we had to hold a press conference. Some things took place at the prison, and then we ended the day with a demonstration. At the start of the day, I told myself I would never make it. I never had Foucault's energy or his strength. Foucault had an enormous life force.

How did the GIP disband?

Foucault did what everyone else was contemplating: after a while, he disbanded the GIP. I remember Foucault was seeing the Livrozets frequently. Livrozet was a former inmate. He wrote a book for which Foucault did a beautiful preface. Mrs Livrozet was also very active. When the GIP disbanded, they continued its work with the CAP the "Comité d'Action des Prisonniers" [Prisoners' Action Committee] that was going to be run by former inmates. I think Foucault only remembered the fact that he had lost; he did not see in what way he had won. He was always very modest from a certain point of view. He thought he had lost because everything closed down again. He had the impression that it had been useless. Foucault said it was not repression but worse: someone speaks but it is as if nothing was said. Three or four years later, things returned to exactly the way they were.

At the same time, he must have known what an impact he had made. The GIP accomplished many things; the prisoners' movements were formed. Foucault had the right to think that something had changed, even if it was not fundamental. It's an oversimplification, but the goal of the GIP was for the inmates themselves and their families to be able to speak, to speak for themselves. That was not the case before. Whenever there was a show on prisons, you had representatives of all those who dealt closely with prisons: judges, lawyers, prison guards, volunteers, philanthropists, anyone except inmates themselves or even former inmates. Like when you do a conference on elementary school and everyone is there except the children, even though they have something to say. The goal of the GIP was less to make them talk than to design a place where people would be forced to listen to them, a place that was not reduced to a riot on the prison roof, but would ensure that what they had to say came through. What needed to be said is exactly what Foucault brought out: namely, we are deprived of freedom, which is one thing, but the things happening to us are something else altogether. They own us. Everyone knows it, but everyone lets it happen.

Wasn't one of the functions of the intellectual for Foucault to open a space where others could speak?

In France, it was something very new. That was the main difference between Sartre and Foucault. Foucault had a notion, a way of living the political position of the intellectual that was very different from Sartre's, one that was not theoretical. Sartre, no matter what his force and brilliance, had a classical conception of the intellectual. He took action in the name of superior values: the Good, the Just and the True. I see a common thread that runs from Voltaire to Zola to Sartre. It ended with Sartre. The intellectual taking action in the name of the values of truth and justice. Foucault was much more functional; he always was a functionalist. But he invented his own functionalism. His functionalism was seeing and speaking. What is there to see here? What is there to say or think? It was not the intellectual as a guarantor of certain values.

I know that he later discussed his conception of truth, but that was different. "Information" was not the right word finally. It was not about finding the truth about prison, but to produce statements about prison, once it was said that

291

neither the prisoners nor the people outside prison had been able to produce any themselves. They knew how to make speeches about prison, etc. but not produce them. Here as well, if there was any communication between his actions and his philosophical work, it was that he lived like that. What was so exceptional about Foucault's sentences when he spoke? There is only one man in the world I have ever heard speak like that. Everything he said was decisive, but not in the authoritarian sense. When he entered a room, it was already decisive; it changed the atmosphere. When he spoke, his words were *decisive*. Foucault considered a statement to be something very particular. Not just any discourse or sentence makes a statement. Two dimensions are necessary: seeing and speaking. It is more or less words and things. Words are the production of statements; things are the seeing, the visible formations. The idea is to see something imperceptible in the visible.

Does producing statements mean letting someone speak?

In part, but that is not all. We said – it was the theme – like the others, we said: others must be allowed to speak, but that was not the question. Here is a political example. For me, one of the most fundamentally important things about Lenin was that he produced new statements before and after the Russian Revolution. They were like signed statements; they were Leninist statements. Can we talk about a new type of statement or one that emerges in a certain space or under certain circumstances that are Leninist statements? It was a new type of statement. The question is nor to seek the truth like Sartre, but to produce new conditions for statements. 1968 produced new statements. They were a type of statement that no one had used before. New statements can be diabolical and very annoying and everyone is drawn to fight them. Hitler was a great producer of new statements.

Did you find that political sufficient at the time?

Was it enough to keep us occupied? Certainly. Our days were completely full. Foucault brought with him a type of practice that had two fundamentally new aspects. How could that not have been sufficient? Your question is too harsh in a way. Foucault would have said that it was not sufficient because in one sense, it failed. It did not change the status of the prisons. I would say the opposite. It was doubly sufficient. It had a lot of resonance. The main echoes were the movement in the prisons. The movement in the prisons was not inspired by either Foucault or Defert. The GIP amplified the movement because we also wrote articles and spent our time hassling the people in the Ministry of Justice and the Interior Ministry. Now there is a type of utterance on prisons that is regularly made by inmates and non-inmates that would not have been imaginable before. It was successful in this way.

You have a much more fluid view of the social world than Foucault. I am thinking of A Thousand Plateaus. *Foucault uses more architectural metaphors. Do you agree with this description?*

Completely. Unfortunately, in the final years of his life, I did not see him much, and of course I now regret it deeply, because he was one of the men I liked and admired the most. I remember we talked about it when he published *The Will to Knowledge*. We did not have the same conception of society. For me, a society is something that is constantly escaping in every direction. When you say I am more fluid, you are completely right. It flows monetarily; it flows ideologically. It is really made up of lines of flight. So much so that the problem for a society is how to stop it from owing. For me, the powers come later. What surprised Foucault was that faced with all of these powers, all of their deviousness and hypocrisy, we can still resist. My surprise is the opposite. It is owing everywhere and governments are able to block it. We approached the problem from opposite directions. You are right to say that society is a fluid, or even worse, a gas. For Foucault, it is an architecture.

You spoke with him about this?

I remember that at the time of *The Will to Knowledge*, which was, I think, the start of a kind of intellectual crisis, he was asking himself many questions. He was in a kind of melancholy and, at the time, we spoke a great while about his way of viewing society.

What were your conclusions? Did you grow apart?

I always had enormous admiration and affection for Foucault. Not only did I admire him, but he made me laugh. He was very funny. I only resemble him in one way: either I am working, or I am saying insignificant things. There are very few people in the world with whom one can say insignificant things. Spending two hours with someone without saying a thing is the height of friendship. You can only speak of trifles with very good friends. With Foucault, it was more like a sentence here or there. One day during a conversation, he said: "I really like Péguy because he is a madman." I asked: "Why do think he is a madman?" He replied: "Just look at the way he writes." That was also very interesting about Foucault. It meant that someone who could invent a new style, produce new statements, was a madman. We worked separately, on our own. I am sure he read what I wrote. I read what he wrote with a passion. But we did not talk very often. I had the feeling, with no sadness, that in the end I needed him and he did not need me. Foucault was a very, very mysterious man.

Notes on Contributors

Samantha Bankston is Associate Professor in the Department of Humanities and Social Sciences at Sierra Nevada College, where she is also the Honors Program Director. Her research is focused in the areas of continental philosophy, feminist philosophy, literature and modern art. She has published numerous articles on contemporary continental philosophy, and two books: *Deleuze and Becoming(s)* (Bloomsbury/Continuum, 2015) and *Deleuze and Žižek* (Palgrave Macmillan, 2016). She is also the translator of Anne Sauvagnargues' *Deleuze and Art* (Bloomsbury/Continuum, 2014).

Gilles Deleuze (1925–95) was Professor of Philosophy at the University of Paris, Vincennes - St. Denis. He published numerous books, including *Nietzsche and Philosophy* (1962), *Kant's Critical Philosophy* (1963), *Difference and Repetition* (1968), *The Logic of Sense* (1969) and *Foucault* (1986). He also coauthored with Félix Guattari *Anti-Oedipus* (1972), *A Thousand Plateaus* (1980) and *What is Philosophy?* (1991).

François Dosse is Professor at the IUFM Créteil, the Paris Institute for Political Studies, and the Center for Cultural History, University of Versailles/Saint-Quentin-en-Yvelines. He has published several important books on intellectual history, including *History of Structuralism: The Rising Sign, 1945–1966*, *History of Structuralism: The Sign Sets, 1967–Present* and *Gilles Deleuze and Félix Guattari: Intersecting Lives* with Columbia University Press.

Alex Feldman is a PhD candidate in philosophy at Pennsylvania State University. He is currently writing a dissertation on Foucault and Canguilhem. Research interests include twentieth-century French and German continental philosophy, historical epistemology and social philosophy.

Michel Foucault (1926–84) held the chair in the History of Systems of Thought at the Collège de France from 1969 until his death. He was heavily involved in political activist movements throughout his life, advocating on behalf of students, workers, prisoners, homosexuals and others. His vast body of research operates at the intersections of systems of knowledge, power and ethics. He is the author of *History of Madness* (1961), *The Birth of the Clinic* (1963), *The Order of Things* (1966), *The Archaeology of Knowledge* (1969), *Discipline and Punish* (1975), *The History of Sexuality*, 3 volumes: *Introduction* (1976), *The Use of Pleasure* (1984) and *The Care of the Self* (1984).

Marjorie Gracieuse was research assistant of the Leverhulme Research Project in Bioethics and Biopolitics at the University of Warwick. She is currently an affiliate member of the ERRAPHIS research laboratory (Toulouse, France) and teaches philosophy and French literature at the *Institut Florimont* in Geneva, Switzerland. Her current work focuses on the pragmatist philosophy of education and on developing the practice of philosophy for children and teenagers in schools.

Frédéric Gros is Professor of Political Philosophy at the Institut d'Etudes Politiques in Paris. He has published extensively on Michel Foucault's writings. His books include *Michel Foucault* (1996) and *Foucault et la folie* (1997, both Presses Universitaires de France).

Kris Klotz is a PhD candidate in philosophy at Pennsylvania State University. His research interests include nineteenth- and twentieth-century continental philosophy and social and political philosophy.

Colin Koopman is Associate Professor of Philosophy and 2011–12 Wulf Professor of Humanities at the University of Oregon. He has published articles on Foucault in *Philosophy & Social Criticism, Foucault Studies* and *Journal of the Philosophy of History*. He is the author of *Pragmatism as Transition: Historicity and Hope in James, Dewey, and Rorty* (Columbia University Press, 2009) and *Genealogy as Critique: Problematization and Transformation in Foucault and Others* (Indiana University Press, 2012).

Leonard Lawlor received his PhD in philosophy from Stony Brook University in 1988. He taught at the University of Memphis from 1989 to 2008 where he became Faudree-Hardin Professor of Philosophy. In 2008, he became Edwin Erle Sparks Professor of Philosophy at Pennsylvania State University, where he continues to teach and serve as Director of Graduate Studies in Philosophy. He is the author of eight books, including: *This is not Sufficient: An Essay on Animality in Derrida* and *Derrida and Husserl: The Basic Problem of Phenomenology*. His most recent book is

From Violence to Speaking out: Apocalypse and Expression in Foucault, Derrida and Deleuze (Edinburgh University Press, 2016).

Mary-Beth Mader is Professor of Philosophy at the University of Memphis. Her work on Deleuze can be found in *Sleights of Reason: Norm, Bisexuality, Development* and "Whence Intensity?: Deleuze and the Revival of a Concept." Her essays on Foucault include "Foucault and Social Measure," "Foucault's Metabody" and "Modern Living and Vital Race: Foucault and the Science of Life." She is currently translating Deleuze's 1985–1986 lecture courses on Foucault.

Nicolae Morar is Assistant Professor in Philosophy and Environmental Studies and an Associate Member with the Institute of Ecology and Evolution at University of Oregon. Morar is the co-editor of *Perspectives in Bioethics, Science, and Public Policy* (Purdue University Press, 2013) and of a *Foucault Studies* Special Issue on Foucault and Deleuze (2014). He is currently completing a monograph titled *Biology, BioEthics, and BioPolitics: How To Think Differently About Human Nature*.

Thomas Nail is Associate Professor of Philosophy at the University of Denver. He is the author of *Returning to Revolution: Deleuze, Guattari and Zapatismo* (Edinburgh University Press, 2012), *The Figure of the Migrant* (Stanford University Press, 2015) and *Theory of the Border* (Oxford University Press, 2016). His work has appeared in *Angelaki, Theory & Event, Philosophy Today, Parrhesia, Deleuze Studies, Foucault Studies* and elsewhere. His publications can be downloaded at http://du.academia.edu/thomasnail

Antonio Negri is an ex-Professor in Padua and an independent researcher. His areas of research include globalization, Marxism and anticapitalism. He has published many books, including *Time for Revolution* (Continuum, 2003), *Subversive Spinoza: (Un)Contemporary Variations* (Manchester University Press, 2004) and *Political Descartes: Reason, Ideology, and the Bourgeois Project* (Verso, 2007). He has also coauthored four books with Michael Hardt: *Labor of Dionysus: A Critique of the State- Form* (University of Minnesota Press, 1994), *Empire* (Harvard University Press, 2000), *Multitude: War and Democracy in the Age of Empire* (Penguin, 2004), and *Commonwealth* (Belknap Press of Harvard University Press, 2009).

Paul Patton is Scientia Professor of Philosophy at the University of New South Wales in Sydney, Australia. He is the author of *Deleuze and the Political* (Routledge, 2000) and *Deleuzian Concepts: Philosophy, Colonization, Politics* (Stanford University Press, 2010). He is editor of *Nietzsche, Feminism and Political Theory* (Routledge, 1993) and *Deleuze: A Critical Reader* (Blackwell, 1996). He is co-editor (with Duncan Ivison and Will Sanders) of *Political Theory and the Rights of*

Indigenous Peoples (Cambridge University Press, 2000), (with John Protevi) of *Between Deleuze and Derrida* (Continuum, 2003) and (with Simone Bignall) *Deleuze and the Postcolonial* (Edinburgh University Press, 2010).

John Protevi is the Phyllis M. Taylor Professor of French Studies and Professor of Philosophy at Louisiana State University in Baton Rouge, Louisiana. His latest books are *Political Affect: Connecting the Social and the Somatic* (2009) and *Life, War, Earth: Deleuze and the Sciences* (2013, both Minnesota University Press).

Paul Rabinow is Professor of Anthropology at the University of California at Berkeley. His works include *Essays on the Anthropology of Reason* (Princeton University Press, 1996), *Marking Time: On the Anthropology of the Contemporary* (Princeton University Press, 2007), *Designs for an Anthropology of the Contemporary* (Duke University Press, 2008), (with Hubert Dreyfus) *Foucault: Beyond Structuralism and Hermeneutics* (Chicago University Press, 1983), (with Talia Dan- Cohen) *A Machine to Make a Future: Biotech Chronicles* (Princeton University Press, 2006), *Anthropos Today: Reflections on Modern Equipment* (Princeton University Press, 2003). In addition, he has edited many books, such as *The Essential Works of Michel Foucault, 1954–1984*, vol. 1, *Ethics, Subjectivity and Truth* (New Press, 1997), (with Nikolas Rose) *The Foucault Reader* (Vintage, 1984) and *The Essential Foucault* (New Press, 2003).

Anne Sauvagnargues is Professor of Philosophy at the University of Paris-Nanterre, France, and specializes in the philosophy of Gilles Deleuze. She co-directs the collection 'Lignes d'art' with Fabienne Brugère for Presses Universitaires de France, and has published *Deleuze, Transcendental Empiricism* (Presses Universitaires de France, 2008), *Deleuze and Art* (Bloomsbury Press, 2013) and *Artmachines: Deleuze, Guattari, Simondon* (Edinburgh University Press, 2015).

Janae Sholtz is Associate Professor of Philosophy at Alvernia University, Coordinator of Women's and Gender Studies, and an Alvernia Neag Professor. She is the author of *The Invention of a People, Heidegger and Deleuze on Art and the Political* (Edinburgh University Press, 2015). Her research focus is continental philosophy, aesthetics, social and political philosophy, and feminist theory, and current research interests include applications of schizoanalysis (especially to feminism), dramatization and limit-experiences, immanence and the ethics of the event, political ontology, affect theory, and art as a form of resistance.

Daniel W. Smith is Professor of Philosophy at Purdue University. He is the author of *Essays on Deleuze* (Edinburgh University Press, 2012) and the editor, with Henry Somers-Hall, of the *Cambridge Companion to Deleuze* (Cambridge University Press,

2012). He has translated numerous books from the French, including works by Gilles Deleuze, Pierre Klossowski, Isabelle Stengers and Michel Serres.

Kevin Thompson is Associate Professor in the Department of Philosophy at DePaul University. Kevin was educated at the University of Memphis. His areas of specialization are German Idealism, Contemporary French Philosophy, and the history of political theory. He co-edited and contributed to *Phenomenology of the Political* (Kluwer, 2000) and has published articles on Kant, Hegel and Foucault.

Index

abstract machine, 191, 223, 229, 264
acategorical thought, 13, 51–3, 57, 161, 210
accident, 16, 26, 42, 45, 52–3, 122, 181
action, the philosophy of, 73–4, 78–9
active/reactive, 161, 183, 240–1, 268, 280
actual, 165–8, 175, 179, 193–4, 196, 202
   actualization, 65–6, 68, 125, 132, 133,
      176, 180–1, 183–5, 190, 192, 218, 229
   and virtual, 125, 132, 175–6, 180–2,
      184–5, 187, 191, 193, 194
affect, 65, 69, 146, 228, 239, 274–5, 278
affirmation, 13, 22, 43, 45–7, 50–1, 56, 73,
   75, 104, 110, 277, 280
affirmative thought, 13, 105
affirmativism, 100–1
Althusser, Louis, 73
analytic/diagnostic, 178–80, 185, 194
anarchic difference, 48, 51, 57
animal, 146–7
apparatus [*dispositif*], 4, 74–6, 80, 121, 124,
   126, 132, 139, 168, 179, 183, 186, 190,
   192, 194, 223–31, 237, 242, 264, 279
   of capture, 170
   see also assemblage; State apparatus
appearance, 39–40
archaeology, 59–61, 65, 157, 179, 183,
   187–9, 200, 202–4, 209, 219
archive, 61, 65, 129–30, 167–8, 174,
   179–80, 185, 187, 189–92, 194
Artaud, Antonin, 30, 134
assemblage [*agencement*], 4, 99, 131, 139,
   163, 165, 175–6, 186, 190, 194,

224–30, 233, 234, 241, 264, 269, 278,
   280; *see also* apparatus
auto-affectation, 69, 135, 268–9
AZERT, 133, 136, 214, 218

battle, 42–3, 45, 51, 120, 206; *see also* event
becoming, 26, 55–6, 59, 66, 68, 105, 108,
   140, 143, 146–7, 152–3, 165–8, 170,
   174–95, 278
biopolitics, 74, 75, 79, 229, 249–51,
   255–61
biopower, 2, 20, 31, 74–5, 79, 228, 240,
   247–62, 266
Blanchot, Maurice, 30, 62, 66–7, 131,
   133–4, 217
bodies, 40–4, 46–7, 65, 69, 75–6, 132, 161,
   228, 238, 140, 242
body of knowledge, 192, 203
body of work, 179–81
body-without-organs, 176, 228, 270
Burroughs, William, 248, 254–5, 261

capitalism, 4, 80, 113, 139, 170, 226, 228,
   239–40, 274–5, 279
capture, 176, 186, 188–90, 192–3,
   279–80
categorical imperative, 276–7
categories, 51–4, 189, 191
Cavaillès, Jean, 201–4
chance, 26, 54, 56, 66–7
Chomsky, Noam, 215–16
Christianity, 69–70, 235, 241, 269

class, 64, 162, 270
  struggle, 76
common sense, 44, 48
concepts, creation of, 26, 31, 100, 163, 265
confession, 236–7, 241, 244
content/expression, 60, 63, 70, 79–80
contingency, 51, 98, 183–5, 208, 239
  and history, 139–10, 202
contradiction, 49–50, 90, 94–108, 112–13,
  115, 226
control, 65, 122, 191, 236, 241, 244, 247–61
  society of, 2, 4, 31, 249–50, 252, 257
creative repetition, 140–1, 143, 145, 153, 156
crisis, 26, 180, 182–5, 194–5
  and creation, 182–4, 195
critical philosophy, 88–92, 107–9, 110–11,
  113, 210
Croissant Affair, 5, 17–18, 164
curve, 65–6, 68, 218

death, 134, 153, 241
  and event, 30, 42–3, 45, 51, 53
  of God, 41, 67, 278
  of Man, 13, 67
Deleuze, Gilles, works
  "Desire and Pleasure," 163, 232, 235,
    264, 269
  Difference and Repetition, 47, 103–4, 115,
    120, 141, 145, 156, 175, 182–3, 187–8
  The Fold, 26
  Historical Formations, 212–14
  The Logic of Sense, 22, 26–7, 30, 41,
    45–7, 104–6
  Nietzsche and Philosophy, 101, 155, 160, 162
  "On Capitalism and Desire," 234
Deleuze, Gilles and Félix Guattari, works
  Anti-Oedipus, 19, 24, 112, 174–6, 232,
    270, 275–9
  Capitalism and Schizophrenia see Anti-
    Oedipus and Thousand Plateaus
  Thousand Plateaus, 25, 163, 176, 185, 192,
    264, 279, 293
  What is Philosophy?, 25, 100, 139–41, 146,
    154, 165–6
Deleuzian century, 4, 6, 38, 79, 161, 286
delinquency, 60, 63
desire, 3, 20–1, 70, 74–5, 108, 224–9,
  232–52, 244–5, 264, 270, 274–80
  and discourse, 235
  and drives, 233, 274

and interest, 233–4, 243, 274–5
and knowledge, 205
and lack, 3, 228, 231, 233–5, 237, 241,
  269, 274–6
and pleasure, 3, 20–1, 139, 228, 232–3,
  235, 240–2, 269, 271, 276
and power, 163, 225, 237
deterritorialization, 163, 224–9, 264, 278–80;
  see also reterritorialization; territorialities
diagnosis, 99, 168–9
diagnostic/analytic, 178–80, 185, 194
diagram, 45, 66–8, 132–3, 135, 176, 181–2,
  184, 190–4, 223–4, 229–30, 264
dialectic of concepts, 201–2, 204
dialectic of contradiction, or negative
  dialectics, 50, 78, 80, 87, 89–90, 94–8,
  100–6, 108–9, 112–13, 115
dice throw, 46, 54, 56, 66, 129
difference, 45, 48–54, 56–7, 73, 94, 96–97,
  101–5, 112, 141–3, 161, 168, 175
  and recurrence, 51, 54–7
differenciation, 125, 133, 135, 142, 207
differentiation, 38, 48, 98, 120–5, 207
disciplinary diagram, 65, 132, 191
discipline, 31–2, 122, 126, 132, 149, 168,
  170, 191, 193, 225, 247, 252, 255–6,
  259–60, 266
discourse, 75, 120, 124, 162–3, 167, 186–7,
  208, 210, 213, 235–8, 241, 265–6
  and desire, 235
  and event, 26, 43, 77, 169
  philosophical, 38–9, 42
  unity of, 187, 203
disjunctive synthesis, 47, 277
divergent series, 38, 40, 42, 47
double, 28–30, 67–9, 144, 181–2,
  184–6, 191, 194
drama, 27, 98, 125
drives, 270–5
  and desire, 233, 274
  and instincts, 273
drugs, 54–5
dualism, 194
Duns Scotus, 26, 51, 56–7

economic rationality, 258, 274
economy, 25, 69, 123–6, 170, 238–9,
  247, 249–50, 257–9, 270, 274
  libidinal, 238–9, 270, 273–4
  political, 72, 77, 80, 234, 239, 270, 273–4

emergence, 66, 167, 201
of the new, 107, 165–6
empirical, 93, 208
empiricism, 93–4
transcendental, 188, 200, 204–5, 207–9
encounter, 63, 77–8, 146, 181, 183, 207–9
Epicurus, 40–2
episteme, 74, 78–9, 124, 265, 268
epistemological causality, 200–1, 204–5, 207
epistemology, 60–1, 185–8, 192
essence, 39, 44–5, 122
eternal return, 55–6, 140, 143, 145, 158, 161
eternity, 23, 27, 39, 42, 44, 54, 56
ethics, 79, 235, 242, 265–6, 268–9, 290
event, 13, 22, 25–7, 39, 42–7, 51–5, 78,
104–6, 143, 149, 156, 165–7, 169, 195,
200, 205, 208, 213, 245, 271, 278
excess, 26, 57
and absence, 38–9, 45
experience, 32, 47, 91, 125–6, 188, 192, 267
experiment, 89–90, 94–9, 103–8, 111,
113–15, 195, 211, 242, 288–9
expression, 51, 54, 60, 63, 185
exteriority, 66, 75, 131, 133–4, 186, 192, 255
extrabeing, 49

fold, 67–70, 129–30, 133–5, 139, 142, 183,
187, 189, 193–4
force, 64–9, 75–6, 120–2, 124, 131–3, 135,
161, 176, 180–6, 189–94, 224, 238–41
as affectivity, 67–8, 132–3, 190, 266
Foucault, Michel, works
Archaeology of Knowledge, 60–2, 65,
70, 167–8, 185–6, 189–90, 212–14,
218, 223
The Birth of Biopolitics, 249, 251, 257
The Birth of the Clinic, 63, 134
Discipline and Punish, 60, 63, 65, 72, 74–6,
82, 106, 120, 165, 168, 182, 190–1,
223
Dits et Écrits, 178–80
The History of Madness, 63, 68, 106
The History of Sexuality, 19–20, 120, 161,
163, 169, 175, 183, 186, 224, 249
"The Lives of Infamous Men," 266–7
The Order of Things, 30, 61–2, 67–8, 134,
144, 146, 266
Raymond Roussel, 60–1, 63
The Use of Pleasure, 22, 68, 70, 269
The Will to Knowledge, 21, 69, 105–6, 293

freedom, 29, 238, 240, 242, 276–7, 289, 291
Freud, Sigmund, 19–20, 42, 46–7, 112, 232,
237–9, 270, 272, 274–5
future, 44–5, 55–7, 67, 70, 140, 144–5, 259

genealogy, 63, 65, 121–3, 126–7, 205,
208, 210
God, 44, 67, 255, 277–8
good sense, 44, 47, 49
government, 121–4, 169–70, 251,
258–9, 266
governmental reason, 123, 258
of others, 69, 79
of self, 22, 69
Greeks, 22–3, 69–70, 134–5
grid of intelligibility, 120–5; *see also* power
Gros, Frédéric, 29

Hardt, Michael, 250–3, 260–1
Hegel, G. W. F., 50, 92–7, 100–6, 109,
112–14
Hegelianism, 95–7, 101, 106–7, 112
Heidegger, Martin, 68, 133–4, 140–7, 152–7
historical a priori, 167, 191–2, 203–4, 208–9
historical formations, 59–63, 68, 70, 130–1,
133, 177, 182–3, 187–9, 191, 194
history, 25–6, 35, 44, 47, 59, 66–7, 74, 99–100,
130, 165–6, 168, 174–95, 207–8
and discontinuity, 23, 25–6, 67, 74, 167,
201–4, 207, 210, 265–6
and novelty, 125
history of philosophy, 22, 39, 51, 56, 78,
93–4, 100, 177, 195
homosexuality, 69, 236, 249
Hume, David, 93–4, 112
humor, 40, 290
Hyppolite, Jean, 112

Idea, 50, 122, 182, 273, 277–8
ill humor, 53–4
ill will, 48, 53–4
illusion, 41
image of thought, 135, 176, 200, 205,
207, 210
immanence, 22, 24, 92–4, 96, 131–2, 187–8,
191, 194, 224, 228–30, 235, 276–8
immanent critique, 90, 92–4, 99, 108
inactuell intempestif, 26, 166, 178–9, 196;
see also untimely
indeterminacy, 96–9, 101–3, 108

individuation, 120, 122–3, 125, 175–6
inside, 67, 134–235
   and outside, 40, 44, 67–70, 134–5
instinct/drive, 273
intellectuals, 5, 16–17, 89
"Intellectuals and Power," 87, 89, 141,
   157, 159
intensity, 26–7, 49, 156, 176, 228
irony, 40
irrational/rational, 234, 239, 275
Israel/Palestine, 18, 164, 287

judgment, 89–92, 103, 108–11, 206

Kant, Immanuel, 23, 35, 62, 64–5, 90–3,
   111, 187–9, 268, 274–8
   The Critique of Judgment, 276
   The Critique of Practical Reason, 234,
     276–8
   The Critique of Pure Reason, 111,
     276–7
Kantianism, 23, 62, 90–2, 131, 187–8
Klossowski, Pierre, 5, 12–13, 161, 274
knowledge, 23–5, 28, 35, 52, 54, 60–1, 65,
   74, 130–2, 135, 183, 186–7, 190–3,
   201, 206–7, 242, 266–7
   conditions of, 93, 156, 265, 278
   content of, 202–3
   and discourse, 162, 186, 265
   and history, 186–7, 201–4
   and power, 28, 64, 70, 121, 132–3,
     135, 163, 189–94, 201, 205,
     208, 230
Krafft-Ebing, Richard von, 214–17

Labov, William, 216, 218
Lacan, Jacques, 19–20, 233, 275,
   278, 281
language, 61–3, 130–1, 133, 146, 191–2
Leibniz, G. W., 50, 57, 184
liberalism, 4, 124, 170, 258–9
lines of flight, 163, 166, 176, 226–9, 264,
   278–80, 293
linguistics, 214–17
literature, 30–1

macro and micro, 224–5
Marx, Karl, 72, 77, 80, 176, 270
Marxism, 162, 170

materiality, 25, 41, 44, 73, 130, 133, 163,
   233, 240, 242
   incorporeal, 22, 40, 41, 205
metaphysics, 41–5, 90–2, 121, 140, 142
micro and macro, 224–5
micro-analysis, 223–5, 227, 229
micro-*dispositifs*, 223–4, 229
milieu, 189, 259
mimesis, 41–2, 45–6, 52–4, 57
Mitterrand, François, 5, 19, 286–7
molar, 21, 132, 176, 225, 229, 240
molecular, 21, 132, 176, 240
mouth, 46–7
multiplicity, 120–4, 161, 175–7, 225, 241–2,
   255–6, 261

negative, 23, 49–51, 89–90, 95–108, 112–13,
   142, 236–7, 241
negative dialectics, or dialectic of
   contradiction, 50, 78, 80, 87, 89–90,
   94–8, 100–6, 108–9, 112–13, 115
neoliberalism, 73, 121, 124, 126, 170, 249,
   251
new, 165–6, 168
   and creation, 26, 184
   and history, 125
New Philosophers, 5, 18, 164
Nietzsche, Friedrich, 11–12, 21–2, 25, 56,
   59, 64, 66–7, 100–1, 104, 114, 133,
   140, 143, 158, 161, 166, 178–81, 196,
   205–7, 270–4, 278, 280
   Daybreak, 281
   The Gay Science, 272
nonbeing, (non)being, ?-being, 105, 132

Other, 50, 167–8
Outside, 59, 65–6, 133, 193–4, 240, 266
   and inside, 40, 44, 67–70, 134–5

panopticism, 223
Panopticon, 31, 66, 74–6
panoptics, 60
parrēsia 139–41, 147, 152, 154, 157
Péguy, Charles, 25, 165
perception, 41, 48
phantasm, 28, 39–42, 45–7, 51, 53,
   205, 241
phenomenology, 44–5, 130, 186, 188, 192
Phenomenology of Perception, 41

physics, 41, 43, 45
plane of immanence, 24, 228–30
plane of organization, 229–30
Plato, 38–40, 154, 156
Platonism, 22, 25–6, 38–40, 161
pleasure, 69, 227
    and desire, 3, 20–1, 139, 228, 232–3, 235,
        240–2, 269, 271, 276
poststructuralism, 109
potency [*puissance*], 75, 77–80
power, 17, 21–2, 24, 28, 31, 64–5, 67–70,
        73, 75, 77–80, 121–2, 133, 139–40,
        161, 163, 170, 175, 183, 186, 189–93,
        223–8, 237–42, 247–56, 264–6, 268,
        279–80
    as action on action, 121–2, 241
    relations, 28, 64–5, 75, 79, 132, 192–3,
        266–8
    see also grid of intelligibility
pragmatics, 175, 181, 186, 192,
        240–1, 245
pragmatism, 113
Prison Information Group (GIP), 5,
        13–17, 141, 147–52, 157–9,
        288–92
    as non-representational, 5, 151–2
problem, 38, 46, 50, 98, 102–5, 182,
        184–5, 192
    creation of, 102
problematization, 89–90, 94, 97–100,
        102–7
Protevi, John, 251
Proust, Marcel, 21, 132, 214
psychoanalysis, 19, 42, 225, 232, 234,
        272–3, 275, 277

rational/irrational, 234, 239, 275
Reason, 73, 92, 94, 102, 131, 179, 234,
        272–3, 275, 277
receptivity/spontaneity, 62, 64–6, 131,
        133, 186, 189, 193
refrain, 153
Reich, Wilhelm, 237, 239
repetition, 45–6, 48–51, 56, 142–6, 152–3
representation, 42–3, 49–50, 141–2, 159,
        229, 234, 276–8
resistance, 67–8, 75, 77, 133, 135, 142,
        193, 226–7, 229–30, 240–2, 264–71,
        278–80

reterritorialization, 225, 228, 279
Revel, Judith, 23–4
revolution, 72, 78, 80, 240, 279–80
Roussel, Raymond, 30–1, 37, 60–1, 68, 134

Sacher-Masoch, 102–3, 115, 228, 235
sadism, 103
Sartre, Jean-Paul, 15–16, 44, 88, 95, 291–2
schematism, 64–5, 73, 189, 193
schizoanalysis, 109–10, 240
schizophrenia, 24, 278–9, 282
scientific rationality, 201–3
seeing and saying, 22–3, 25, 28–30, 60–3,
        65–6, 70, 130–2, 135, 186–9, 192–3,
        219, 278, 291–2
seen and spoken *see* seeing and saying
self, 44, 57, 68–70, 135, 194, 240–2, 245,
        268–9, 278
self-creation, 241–2, 268
shame, 140–1, 143, 145–7, 152–3, 226
Shaviro, Stephen, 249–51, 257
simulacrum, 12–13, 39–42, 45–6
Smith, Dan, 103, 115
Sophists, 38, 40, 57
speaking *before* others [*devant*], 146–7, 152
    for others [*pour*], 89, 139–41, 146–8,
        154, 159
Spinoza, 20–1, 23, 27, 51, 56–7, 75, 234,
        275
Spivak, Gayatri Chakravorty, 159
spontaneity/receptivity, 62, 64–6, 131, 133,
        186, 189, 193
Sraffa, Piero, 77, 83
State apparatus, 123, 162–3, 223–4, 229,
        279–80
statements, 65, 151, 157, 167, 186–92, 203,
        213–19, 291–3
statification, 122–3
Stoics, 22–3, 27, 40, 42, 46
strategy, 59, 64–5, 73, 75–8, 120–1, 178–9,
        226–7
structuralism, 4, 24, 74, 130
stupidity, 48, 52–4
subjectivity, 223, 234, 239, 241–2
    production of, 79–80, 134

temporality, 23, 25, 29, 102, 180
    and unity, 55
territorialities, 225

truth, 4, 16, 21–2, 25, 39–41, 52–5, 73–4,
    77–8, 121, 124–5, 206, 224, 227,
    272–3, 291–2

unconscious, 108, 234, 239, 270, 275
unity of being, of substance, 51, 55
univocity, 51, 53–4, 56, 161
untimely, 26, 59, 166–7, 178–80, 196;
    see also inactual

verb, 43–4
violence, 23, 64, 69, 77, 132, 134, 272

virtual/actual, 125, 132, 175–6,
    180–2, 184–5, 187, 191,
    193, 194
visible and utterable see seeing and saying

war, 120–1
war-machines, 229–30, 279–80, 282
will to know, 73, 201, 205–8
will to power, 22, 271
Wittgenstein, Ludwig, 77

Zarathustra, 55–6, 161